Erin -
Thank you so much for your the Rob

ENTREPRENEURSHIP
THE DISNEY WAY

This book focuses on the business story of Walt Disney and the company he built. Combining a unique blend of entrepreneurship, creativity, innovation, and a relentless drive to bring out the best in his teams, Walt Disney created one of the most successful ventures in business history. Outlining the specific processes of the company, Goldsby and Mathews provide the reader with the tools they need to embrace their own entrepreneurial leadership style, to lead effectively, to be more innovative, and to build a successful organization.

Through the lens of Disney, the reader learns the fundamentals of entrepreneurship, innovation, and leadership. Beginning with a general introduction to the concepts relevant to the entrepreneurial organization today, the book examines how Disney built his empire and how the company remains an industry leader. The book also provides the opportunity to take the Entrepreneurial Leadership Instrument, which measures one's style in leading entrepreneurial ventures. The book is divided into two parts:

- Part I provides an overview of Disney's entrepreneurial journey, including the topics of vision, risk-taking, financing, and human resource management;
- Part II examines the company's transition from a family business into a global operation, including topics such as succession planning and strategy. Part II also explores Disney Parks and Resorts, the part of the company that interacts directly with customers, including topics such as culture, employee engagement, customer service, and customer experience.

Entrepreneurship the Disney Way brings entrepreneurship, innovation, and leadership to life through the compelling story of one of the most recognizable businessmen and companies of our time. The authors' interviews with high-level executives provide the reader with a rare inside look into the way his company functions. Disney fans, executives, and students of entrepreneurship, innovation, and leadership will find it a delightful and informing read.

Michael G. Goldsby is the Chief Entrepreneurship Officer and Stoops Distinguished Professor of Entrepreneurship at Ball State University, USA.

Rob Mathews is the Director of the Institute for Entrepreneurship and Free Enterprise at Ball State University, USA.

ENTREPRENEURSHIP THE DISNEY WAY

Michael G. Goldsby and Rob Mathews

Routledge
Taylor & Francis Group

NEW YORK AND LONDON

First published 2019
by Routledge
52 Vanderbilt Avenue, New York, NY 10017

and by Routledge
2 Park Square, Milton Park, Abingdon, Oxon, OX14 4RN

Routledge is an imprint of the Taylor & Francis Group, an informa business

© 2019 Taylor & Francis

Library of Congress Cataloging-in-Publication Data
A catalog record for this book has been requested

ISBN: 978-1-138-73754-9 (hbk)
ISBN: 978-1-138-73755-6 (pbk)
ISBN: 978-1-315-18528-6 (ebk)

Typeset in Bembo
by Apex CoVantage, LLC

To Dr. Donald F. Kuratko (Dr. K), mentor and friend,
and
Dr. Thomas J. Goldsby, brother and friend
—Mike

To my wife, my partner, my confidant, Julie, the only one who truly knows the faith, sacrifice, battle, grit, and determination it took to seize this opportunity.

Julie, Nate, and Lindsey—my inspiration. You have sacrificed so much for my entrepreneurial dreams. I love you.
—Rob/Dad

CONTENTS

ACKNOWLEDGMENTS

The content of this book was developed over a ten-year period of studying the Walt Disney Company. First, I want to thank my co-author, Dr. Rob Mathews, for taking this professional journey with me over the years. I also want to thank Margo Allen for everything she makes possible for Rob and me at Ball State. I also appreciate the support of President Geoff Mearns, Provost Dr. Susana Rivera-Mills, and Dr. Mark Myring, Dean of the Miller College of Business. My good friends Dr. Chris Neck and Dr. Jim Bishop have been instrumental in the attainment of my doctorate and my scholarly record. Dr. Min Basadur has also been an incredible teacher to me over the last twenty years, and his generosity with his knowledge, encouragement, and advice is always appreciated.

I have also had incredible support and encouragement from the business world. Several friends from world-class companies have had a tremendous impact on my thinking about innovation and business. In particular, Dan Cockerell and Lee Cockerell have been very generous with their time and support in teaching me how a legendary company stays impactful and relevant. Richard Perez and Shannon Wagers at Procter & Gamble have taught me about the creative process of inventing new products for large markets. Wil Davis, Scott Wright, and Roy West have been great partners in our work with the North American Retail Hardware Association.

There have been many good people who have given me great advice and direction over the years. Dr. Jon Shepard, Dr. Brian Burton, Dr. Rich Wokutch, and Dr. John Christman made my career opportunities possible. Several education colleagues have been helpful in shaping my thinking over the years, such as Dr. Alex Bruton and Stephen Kenny of Calgary, Alberta; Dr. Ed Leach, Dr. Mary Kilfoil, and Dr. Aaron Newman at Dalhousie University in Halifax, Nova Scotia; Dr. Jeff Hornsby of the University of Missouri-Kansas City; and Dr. Tom

Nelson of the University of South Alabama. I always enjoy the company of these scholars and teachers.

I also appreciate the literary expertise and guidance of Alston Slatton, Sharon Golan, and Erin Arata in making this book possible. They run a first-class operation, and it was a pleasure to work with them during the writing process.

Finally, I would like to thank my friends and family who have always supported me in my life. I am blessed to have great friends like Karl Mesarosh, Jamie and J.J. Eubanks, Seth Burris, Rich Chumley, James Briscoe, Martin and Meribe Nyberg, Stephen Gregory, Bob Helfst, and Carol Dean. And my amazing family has always made life fun and exciting, so special thanks to my wife Beth, and Will, Andy, and Sarah; parents Joe and Sujane Goldsby; brother Tom Goldsby and Kathie, Emma, and Aiden; Uncle Hugh McNeely; Ivis and Mary McNeely; Nora Goldsby; in-laws Bill and Jan Swinney; and Tim, Steve, and Michelle Swinney. Thank you for your encouragement of me to pursue my dreams.

—Mike

There are so many people who have so heavily invested in me over the years. First, to my wife Julie and my kids Nate (eleven) and Lindsey (nine), you have sacrificed so much for my entrepreneurial dreams, including this book. You are a true inspiration to me every day. Our many *research* trips to Disney make this book that much more special. To my friend, colleague, and co-author, Dr. Mike Goldsby, thank you for the opportunity to work on this book and the Entrepreneurial Leadership Instrument—among so many other things over the years. I am eternally grateful. This book has been a fun ride! To my dad, Doug, who instilled a very strong work ethic in me, and my mom, Jean, who would have been so proud of this book if she were still with us today. To my sister, Suzi, who always makes me smile, and believes in me and encourages me.

To my colleagues and friends at Ball State University, Rich Maloney, Stephanie Wilson, Wil Davis, Dr. Ronda Smith, Rhonda Wilson, Ted Ward, Shawn Sullivan, Kamille Webb, Gloria Pavlik, Brandon Smith, Charity Coffman, Neal Coil, and all of our EntreLeaders participants, among others, your commitment to excellence, inspiration, and encouragement have meant so much to me. To our administrators, particularly President Geoff Mearns, Provost Dr. Susana Rivera-Mills, and Dean Dr. Mark Myring. To Margo Allen, your support during this time was instrumental in getting the necessary work done to put this high-quality book together.

To my partners at the North American Retail Hardware Association (NRHA), especially my friend, Scott Wright, thank you for your support, encouragement, and belief in me—it means so much. To my many former employees, I know I let you down at times, but I learned a great deal from you, and for that I am grateful. To my business partner, Chad Weyenberg, thank you for your support and the complement your strengths are to mine. To Alston Slatton, Sharon Golan, and Erin Arata for making this book possible, thank you. To our graphic designer, who wishes to remain nameless, your work was spectacular—thank you so much.

To Dan Cockerell, your insights and friendship over the years are much appreciated. And Lee Cockerell, your book and social media posts are so full of wisdom and inspiration. Jamie and J. J. Eubanks, your Disney-related business success and encouragement have been inspirational. To our Disney friends, acquaintances, and countless frontline cast members, thank you for your time and investment in us.

To my longtime entrepreneurship mentor, Dr. Donald F. Kuratko (Dr. K), you inspired me to get into this field, and to pursue my doctorate and writing with passion. To my friend and former colleague, Dr. Jeff Horsnby, your support has been instrumental in my success over the years. To my former and current students and graduate assistants, I learn as much or more from you as you learn from me. To my dissertation committee members, Dr. Roger Wessel (Chair), Dr. Amanda Latz, Dr. Mike Goldsby, and Dr. Tom Harris, you taught me how to be taken seriously as a researcher and writer. Dr. Wessel, your profound impact on me has a lot to do with the quality of this book—thank you.

Thank you to Min Basadur, whose innovation systems have taught me to think and behave differently, and whose wise mentorship over the years has greatly elevated my innovation, problem-solving, facilitation, and research skills. To our friends and colleagues at P & G, Shannon Wagers and Richard Perez, thank you for your support and wisdom. To Roy West, my friend and mentor, your investment in me is immeasurable, and I can't thank you enough. Thank you to my pastoral leaders and brothers in the faith, Gregg Parris, Sam Wrisley, Rich Maloney, Wil Davis, Randy Tempest, Jeff Hughes, and Rick Rowray, among others, who have been instrumental in keeping me on track spiritually. To my wife, Julie, of twenty years, I cannot thank you enough for your love, support, and unwavering belief in me—even when I did not believe in myself (which was most of time). Finally, and most importantly, thank you to Jesus, my lord and savior, for loving me unconditionally despite my many flaws.

—Rob

INTRODUCTION

Mike's Disney Story

In 2008, I was attending the Academy of Management Conference in Anaheim, California, and due to an unexpected delay in my flight back to Indiana I had to stay an extra night in town. With nothing planned on my schedule, I decided to walk down the street to Disneyland. After a hectic international conference where I was giving research presentations and interviewing a string of job candidates, I was ready for a break. Little did I expect how much fun I would actually have on this excursion. After all, I was just looking for something to do before catching a red-eye flight back to the Midwest.

With a travel bag slung over my shoulder, I stepped out of the Anaheim Hilton into a beautiful, sunny Southern California morning. I have to admit I was a little excited to see what the day had in store for me, which put a little more pep in my stride walking to the park. Anyone who visits theme parks knows the exhilarating feeling of anticipation you get when you're on your way to a day of fun. Once I arrived at the park, it was time to drop down sixty-nine dollars for my ticket, go through security, and pass through a busy turnstile. It was worth the wait. After finally entering the front gates of the park, I took in the welcoming sight of Main Street, U.S.A., the thoroughfare that takes you by the many shops and galleries in Disneyland. Sleeping Beauty Castle could be seen at the end of the street, and it drew me into the heart of the park, which is situated between Tomorrowland, Fantasyland, Adventureland, and Frontierland. I rode as many rides as I could and enjoyed dining in a couple of the themed restaurants. Experiencing this much fun seemed like rare moments from long ago.

Around 3 p.m. my legs began to tire, so I stopped to take a break and catch my breath. Sitting on a bench in the circle hub in front of Sleeping Beauty

Castle, I looked around and took in the scene going on around me. Families were walking and skipping hand in hand around the hub, adults wearing Mickey Mouse ears were having their pictures taken in front of a Walt Disney statue, and people of all backgrounds passed by the beautiful landscaping, stores, and attractions of the park. I heard children laughing, upbeat big band music, and the sound of excited screams coming from the direction of the thrill rides in the surrounding lands. Sitting on that bench I felt a relaxed childlike joy I had not experienced in a long time. At that moment, I made a decision that I must learn more about the company that created this powerful customer experience. Experiencing transcendental moments running in Death Valley, sitting on the edge of the Grand Canyon, and hiking in the Grand Teton mountains have provided exhilarating moments in my life, but this was different. This experience was man-made. Questions requiring answers started flying into my mind: How did Walt Disney build this? Who was this Walt Disney guy anyway? What was he all about? Why was Disneyland still successful many years after his death? How did the Walt Disney Company remain relevant while other iconic American companies and experiences vanished during the same period? How was the company able to put a big smile on my face even as I opened up my wallet all day long on souvenirs, food, and drinks? And perhaps the questions that called to me the most were, why did I feel a sense of sadness at the thought of leaving the park later that day, and why did I have a longing to come back as soon as I could? I had to get answers to these questions.

As an entrepreneurship professor who teaches complex problem-solving and design, I thought if I could get answers to these questions I would have insight into a set of best practices for helping others infuse creativity into their business enterprises. I began to think about how Disneyland and the other Disney businesses might encompass the themes and topics I try to pass on to my students. Disney could be a great vehicle to anchor the subjects I teach. After arriving back in Indiana, I began my immersion in all the literature I could find on Disney. I read every book and watched every video I could acquire on Disney the man and Disney the company. After finishing Bob Thomas's popular book *Walt Disney: An American Original* and Neil Gabler's masterful biography *Walt Disney: The Triumph of the American Imagination*, I came to the conclusion that if you understood what made Disney successful you would have the key knowledge needed to achieve the dreams in your own life. I continued to read books on the history of the Walt Disney Studios and theme parks. The more I read, the more I found confirmation that Disney would be perfect for my teaching purposes.

There's perhaps no better company for teaching entrepreneurial principles. Once you begin to study Disney, you discover that it's much like peeling an onion, as one story about Walt Disney might lead to another story about Henry Ford or to another story about Ray Kroc or to another about Robert Moses. Even more so, stories about today's Walt Disney Company might bring in iconic characters like Steve Jobs or George Lucas. It seemed that where goes Walt Disney, so goes American history in the twentieth and twenty-first centuries. I began to work these stories about Disney into my classroom lectures and corporate talks and found that audiences enthusiastically responded to the messages. Students, managers, and entrepreneurs would stay long after my presentations to share their own thoughts about Disney with me. Finding people so excited about a subject matter did not happen before. But more importantly, it seemed my audiences better understood the principles I was trying to teach when I wrapped them around Disney stories. It became clear to me that I had discovered a gold mine of inspiration and lessons which needed more mining. Now it was time to go a step further than books and videos and immerse myself more fully in the Disney universe.

Over the next year, I took four trips to Disneyland and Walt Disney World to better understand firsthand how Disney provides memorable and satisfying experiences for its customers. On each trip, I took notes on how Disney delivered its services and products to me, and I placed special attention on the elements that separated it from other businesses. I visited rival theme parks for comparison, and each time I found ingredients of the Disney magic missing from the competition. Interestingly, this Disney lens wasn't limited to theme parks. It soon extended to the rest of my life. It became my reference point for deciding whether I was receiving good service on an airline, for example, or whether a restaurant's theming was coherent and interesting. Whenever I found something missing or poorly done, I would immediately ask myself, how would Disney have done this instead? It then influenced the way I interacted with others in my job. Instead of telling a visitor on campus where they needed to go for help, I walked them to the office they needed. I picked up litter when I saw it on a pathway just as I saw managers at the park doing during their rounds. I thought about how I could improve the student experience in my classes. How could I remove any frustrations from students taking my courses? How could I make the material flow in a smoother and more continuous fashion so they gradually absorbed what I was trying to teach them at a deeper level? How could I make the classes more memorable? Applying the Disney methodology worked in my classes. I redesigned my classes around the idea of what I would like if I were taking it. What would I appreciate? What outcomes would demonstrate that the class was providing the value I sought? I even ran focus groups with professionals, asking them what outcomes they would want from a graduate program in entrepreneurship. I then designed my classes with those keys in mind. As a result, the classes have become a better experience for both the students and me. Enrollment increased in my class sections, and I consistently score near perfect on student evaluations; but more importantly, more of my graduate students are starting businesses than ever before.

After my immersion in the Disney literature and my anthropological trips to the parks, I was fortunate to make some friendships with executives from the company. These corporate entrepreneurs were very helpful in explaining to me why the company was so successful. In particular, I noticed how genuinely nice and considerate the executives at the Walt Disney Company are. They are very deliberate and disciplined in how they work with others, holding to values of mutual respect and civility. In turn, all the ranks of the company work together to ensure each customer experiences the Disney magic. I learned a lot from them about how creativity can be expressed in a big business by bringing vision and the human spirit together with the realities of economics. Simply put, when the bottom line is healthy, there are more resources for visionary projects. Business has to be good for the dreamer to have access to capital for more fun projects.

My immersion in the company went beyond the executive ranks as well. Further interactions with the company's legal, finance, supply chain, and marketing experts helped me round out my understanding of Disney's success. As former director of our Entrepreneurship Program, I also created a unique learning opportunity for our students at Ball State, called the Disney Entrepreneurial Experience, with my colleague and co-author Rob Mathews. We took a group of students each year to Walt Disney World to visit Team Disney headquarters for an afternoon with the Parks and Resorts Division, followed by behind-the-scenes guided tours of the parks. Our students learned how the business and operations work backstage to make the magic happen onstage. In my current role as Ball State University's Chief Entrepreneurship Officer and Executive Director of the Institute for Entrepreneurship and Free Enterprise, Rob and I created a similar program for up-and-coming leaders at Ball State called EntreLeaders, which included an immersive experience at Walt Disney World hosted by retired Magic Kingdom Vice President, Dan Cockerell. I'm extremely fortunate that Rob is as much a Disney fan as I am. Besides the training programs we've created around Disney, Rob and I have attended the Disney Institute and Disney Customer Experience Summit together as well. He and I share something we've learned or thought about Disney almost every day. Also, coinciding with work I did overseas for the U.S. State Department, I have been able to take side trips to Hong Kong Disneyland to see how the company operates in international markets. This book is the culmination of the insights gained from these friendships, trips, and literature reviews.

The timing of my interest in Disney was superb. I watched my Disney friends move up the organization and along the way vicariously learned how the company operates at the different levels. But just as important, this ten-year stretch has occurred during the second Golden Age of the Walt Disney Company. In 2005, Bob Iger took the reins of the company as its sixth Chief Executive Officer. During this time, Disney has acquired Marvel Entertainment, Pixar, and Lucasfilm. Creating new content for these properties provided the company with a wealth of characters and story content with which to work. Propelled by such successes as *Star Wars: The Force Awakens* and *Marvel's The Avengers*, the company's market capitalization is over $150 billion, with 2017 revenue topping $55 billion and net profits totaling nearly $9 billion under Iger's leadership. The theme parks continue to be just as active. Existing properties like Disney California Adventure Park and Walt Disney World expanded. New properties like Shanghai Disneyland were developed, and new ships were added to their cruise fleet. Iger has the company firing on all cylinders.

The more I learned about Disney and the deeper I dove into the company's operations, the more impressed I became with it. As I saw the positive impact that thinking like Disney was having in my job and life, I began to believe that there might be a large audience for a book that shared the lessons I was collecting from my research and interactions with the company. It's my belief that Walt Disney and the company he created serve as the perfect vehicles for learning about all expressions of entrepreneurship in our economy. Thus, Alston Slatton, our editor at Routledge, suggested that the title of this book should be *Entrepreneurship the Disney Way*. As you'll see as you read this book, the Walt Disney Company's story embodies the themes of startup, family business, succession, and corporate entrepreneurship. No company better illustrates these different areas of entrepreneurship than Disney.

Rob's Disney Story

My Disney story started at the age of seven when I first visited Walt Disney World with my family. We had just spent some time with my grandparents in Sarasota, Florida, and next headed to the iconic Orlando resort. My cousins traveled with my grandparents, and we met them at Fort Wilderness Campground on Disney property. I was instantly hooked on the incredible atmosphere, but I had no idea what the resort would become and just how much I would fall in love with it and all things Disney in my adulthood. We visited Walt Disney World twice more in my teen years, and the growth of the resort was evident. Little did I know Michael Eisner was in the middle of radically transforming Disney Parks and Resorts into a global powerhouse at that time. After college, my wife Julie and I moved to Naples, Florida, to work in my father's business on Marco Island. We visited Walt Disney World several times during the nearly three years we lived there, and the fascination with the sprawling campus was starting to grow in us. I was particularly fascinated with the business model at that point. I observed people from all kinds of backgrounds having phenomenal experiences and spending so freely. What entrepreneur wouldn't want to learn more about such a successful venture? Through the stresses of family business and moving to a vastly different environment that catered heavily to retired demographics, Walt Disney World became our happy place.

We moved back to Indiana, and the opportunities to go to Orlando disappeared for several years. We talked about going back, but it just never worked out, yet Disney World still held a special place in our hearts. After many years, the opportunity had finally come to revisit Walt Disney World. As Mike mentioned, he became fascinated with Disney Parks and Resorts after attending a conference in Anaheim. The following year, we dreamed up the concept of taking our senior entrepreneurship majors at Ball State University to Walt Disney World. Julie ended up going on that first trip almost eleven years ago, and on that adventure we developed the Disney fever more than ever. I remember eating at Captain's Grille at the Yacht and Beach Club resorts. We instantly connected with the impressive facilities at the Yacht and Beach clubs (especially the pool!) and the ambience of the hotels, and started planning our next visit with our son Nate, who was a little over two years old at that time. We had a convention coming up the following spring in Orlando, and it would be the perfect time to take Nate. The five days we had planned got off to a great start, as we got a free upgrade to a club level room, but between Julie not feeling well and Nate deciding that was the time to be a difficult toddler, the visit didn't go as expected. At the end of the trip, a major ice storm in Indiana forever changed the course of our Disney fandom. All flights to Indianapolis were canceled for days, and we ended up at the Beach Club for four more days. The staff was extremely accommodating under the circumstances, which impressed us a great deal. Julie started feeling better, and Nate had a great time. From that point on, our family has taken at least two visits to Walt Disney World each year, and we have also managed to visit Disneyland several times over the last five years. We are a Disney family, as evidenced by our knowledge of the company, apparel, social media posts, and hordes of trading pins.

I've also planned the university trips to Orlando the last eleven years. We have met some truly amazing people and made some great friends there. The annual journey has also heavily impacted a great number of students and professionals over the years, many of whom call it their best experience during their time at the university. The last three years I've had the privilege of planning the trip for our EntreLeaders staff entrepreneurial leadership development group, and I've been fortunate to witness my peers—inspired by Disney principles—go back and make positive changes in the university.

One of my family's most memorable trips to Walt Disney World came six years ago. We stayed at the Beach Club resort for a week just after Christmas. I had drawn up a detailed plan for the entire trip, and it went off without a hitch. My parents joined us, and my mom, who came down with pulmonary fibrosis soon after that trip, said before her death four years later that it was one of the best memories of her life. Disney parks and resorts have that kind of power, and the secret sauce of how that happens is what this book is all about.

The more I experienced Disney parks and resorts over the years, the more I wanted to learn about what made the Walt Disney Company so different. As I began to study the history of the company, I became fascinated with Walt's creativity, persistence, and futuristic approach to business. I also became thoroughly impressed with the incredible growth of the company during the Eisner and Iger years.

While I love Disney parks and resorts for the happy places they are, the magic that is created within their boundaries, and the escape from reality they provide, we have always been captivated by just walking around and experiencing the brilliance of the business model behind them. The human, personal, and physical details of Disney parks and resorts are impeccable, and the emotions they create are amazing and carefully orchestrated. For me, they are my home away from home, and they feed my desire to be entertained in an immersive environment and to explore my imagination, make lasting memories with my family, quench my thirst for learning and understanding, and flex my strategic mind. This book is the culmination of years of visiting and studying Disney parks and resorts, asking cast members literally hundreds of business-related questions, talking to and developing friendships with executives, reading countless books on all things Disney, visiting the Disney Family Museum, and attending various training sessions. I'm excited to share with you my insights on what makes Disney Parks and Resorts such an impressive entrepreneurial success story.

On a lighter note, my favorite Disney park attractions are—it's so hard to pick just one (so I won't!)—Expedition Everest, Incredicoaster, Avatar Flight of Passage, and Radiator Springs Racers (I'm thinking it's a pretty safe bet that a *Star Wars* attraction will be added to this list in the near future). I also have a great appreciation for the clever Imagineering behind the Seven Dwarfs Mine Train and Slinky Dog Dash roller coasters. My favorite Disney resort hotels are Beach Club, Wilderness Lodge, and the Grand Californian. Le Cellier, Yachtsman Steakhouse, and California Grill (watching the Magic Kingdom fireworks show from atop the Contemporary Resort at California Grill just cannot be topped!) top the charts for me in terms of Disney restaurant experiences. The cronut and Yachtsman freshly made fruit sorbet are my frontrunners for best desserts at Disney parks and resorts. My family and I thoroughly enjoy pin collecting—particularly limited edition pins (too much, in fact!). Our family also loves the Fairways miniature golf course in the Epcot resort area, as there is nothing else like it out there. We've experienced just about everything imaginable at Disney's domestic parks, and I would like to add more international experiences next.

Book Outline

We will tell the Disney story by examining the different eras of the company's history, with the first four chapters covering Walt Disney's reign and chapters five through seven examining the post-Walt Disney years. Two frameworks will be utilized to study these eras. In Part 1, we contend that entrepreneurial leaders tend to operate businesses around one of four styles, in which the characteristics of an artist, scientist, builder, or evangelist are embodied. Some leaders excel in one or two areas, but there are some legendary ones who embody all four during their careers. We maintain that Walt Disney's entrepreneurial journey consisted of developing all four styles as the company evolved into a media giant. If you understand how Walt Disney built his company and why it's successful today, you'll understand how any company can remain relevant and impactful by operating with these different entrepreneurial characteristics. Thus, the Disney story serves not just to inspire us to pursue our dreams but also helps us gain insights into different approaches for maximizing a company's growth.

Therefore, Chapter 1 covers Walt as a young man learning his craft, creating his first products, and embodying the sensibilities of an artist. Chapter 2 covers his experimental years, when he tinkered like a scientist. His focus on empowering his team of artists with cutting edge technologies and practices led to some of his greatest achievements in filmmaking. Chapter 3 covers the next stage of his career as a builder. During these years, he scaled his productions by making a feature-length animated movie and building a state-of-the-art studio. Chapter 4 covers the final stage of his life, when he became more of an evangelist. Walt brings his mission directly to his audience by inventing the modern theme park, testing his popularity in the eastern United States, and even reimagining how a community could operate if it lived by the Disney way.

Part 2 deals with the challenges and successes of the company after Walt's death. Walt Disney built his company into an entertainment powerhouse, but his life was a tough act to follow. This part of the book focuses on three topical areas: post-Walt leadership, the entrepreneurial spirit of today's Disney Parks and Resorts, and how Disney provides lasting memories for Parks and Resorts guests through cast member engagement and unforgettable experiences. Chapter 5 examines each of the company's chief executive officers and other key players after Walt's death in 1966 through today. In this chapter, we outline each leader's entrepreneurial leadership style based on their unique focus and talents. With little attention spent on genuinely new lines of business the twelve years after Walt's death—and later his brother Roy's in 1971, right after the opening of Walt Disney World—the company stagnated and became a takeover target for the corporate raiders coming on the scene in the early 1980s. However, the over thirty years that followed with Michael Eisner and then Bob Iger at the helm became periods of massive growth for the Walt Disney Company. Eisner was the artistic idea man that the company needed at that pivotal time. As a previous movie executive, Eisner provided great experience in looking at creative concepts and greenlighting ones with the most potential for the big screen. However, a big reason for the company's success during Eisner's revival of Disney was the co-leadership of Frank Wells, the company's President. Wells was a very savvy, levelheaded executive who built up the success of Eisner's big ideas. The transformation of the Walt Disney Company from more of a family business to a global media empire happened under this team's guidance. Iger built on the success of Eisner and Wells and expanded the company's potential through mergers and acquisitions, innovation, and brand integration. The growth of the company during this era is due to Iger being a master builder and part scientist. Iger may very well retire within a year or two of the publication of this book; it will be interesting to see what type of leader the company deems is needed for its next stage. The most poignant lesson for this chapter is that it takes all kinds of styles to lead organizations, and leaders with different styles can all be successful and leave their mark on an organization. In other words, there is more than one way to lead a company. Chapter 6 examines the Disney Parks, Experiences, and Consumer Products Division—particularly Parks and Resorts—of the company in more detail. While Disney is still a powerhouse in all forms of media entertainment and merchandising, it's in the theme parks where the reader has the best opportunity to see up close and personal how the company runs. After all, most people will not get a chance to interact with the company's studios other than from a theater seat or couch in their living room. However, over 100 million people visit Disney theme parks and resorts every year and are treated to the company's storytelling prowess, design excellence, hands-on management, and world-class guest service. This chapter primarily focuses on the people and operational side of the Disney Parks and Resorts business model. We examine the key components of Disney's success model, such as encouraging human ingenuity, internal customer service, employee engagement, and leadership. A key lesson from this chapter is that if a company that hosts well over 100 million guests in its theme parks annually can successfully engage its employees and customers, then so can any small, medium, or large company or nonprofit. Chapter 7 outlines how Disney creates an environment in its parks and resorts that facilitates cast member engagement with guests and uses physical place and environment to provide unforgettable guest experiences. All companies, whether in a large urban area or small, rural community, can benefit from delivering an outstanding customer experience. Therefore, we explain how Disney creates an environment that builds an extremely loyal fan base and brings people back to their parks year after year. The key lesson from this chapter is that companies who can successfully build relationships with their customers through employee engagement and world-class atmosphere will be successful. A Disney theme park provides an immense classroom where lessons about entrepreneurship, innovation, and company building can be learned firsthand.

Both sections tell the Disney story by examining the major entrepreneurial decisions and setbacks occurring in each era of the company's history. These major moments provide opportunities to reflect on why successes and failures occur in the complex and unpredictable lives of entrepreneurs and executives. Throughout the chapters, we will take time to pause and reflect on what you can take away from the stories from the Walt Disney Company over the years. Research literature from entrepreneurship and psychology will provide context for considering what did and did not work well for Disney. Further, by taking the time to reflect on Walt's journey, you'll be better prepared to handle the tough decisions you'll face when you take on your own entrepreneurial projects. It is our contention that Walt Disney and the Walt Disney Company are the perfect vehicles for gaining an understanding of how a person of modest means can attain great success in a capitalist system through entrepreneurship. As you will discover as you read this book, such pursuits have an epic quality to them. Knowing the Disney story and why the company has survived and thrived will better prepare you for the challenges you will face when you are pursuing your own entrepreneurial projects.

Whether you want to build your own business, be entrepreneurial in your job, enhance your efforts in your community work, or are simply a Disney fan wanting to know more about Walt and his company, this book will be helpful to you. Walt Disney created one of the most successful ventures in history. Coming from the most modest of upbringings, he accomplished this feat by blending entrepreneurship, creativity, and a relentless drive to bring out the best in his teams. The concepts Disney applied to building his empire still work today. It is no coincidence that the Walt Disney Company continues to lead the way in providing the most unique and satisfying customer experiences in the entertainment market. The lessons inspired by Walt Disney and practiced every day at the Walt Disney Company serve as beacons for anyone wanting to be successful in their life and work. Disney shows us what is possible when an entrepreneurial dream is pursued with total dedication and follow-through.

As you encounter our personal stories and experiences in this book, it's important to note that we have never received preferential treatment as guests in the parks and resorts. Our stories are authentic and demonstrate the magic Disney parks and resorts create for their guests every day.

Entrepreneurial Leadership Instrument (ELI): Discover Your Inner Walt

In this book, you'll learn about Walt Disney's mastery of entrepreneurship during the course of his life. You will also learn what types of entrepreneurial leaders have led the Walt Disney Company as chief executive officer in the post-Walt era. You'll read about different leadership styles that played a more prominent role at different times in the company's evolution. Below, we present to you the Entrepreneurial Leadership Instrument (ELI). Follow the directions to discover your unique entrepreneurial leadership style by using this assessment tool. Consider your style as you take the journey Walt and his successors took in building an entertainment empire. You may find that you connect more with specific eras of the company's history because the leadership style deployed in those eras matches your leadership lens. Reflect on why you find certain eras more exciting and consider how you can augment your abilities and perspective by building a diverse leadership team around you. As you'll discover throughout the book, Walt did, and we contend it was the major source of his success.

This inventory is designed to describe your entrepreneurial leadership style. The aim is to describe how you lead entrepreneurial ventures, not to evaluate leadership abilities.

Instructions:
In each horizontal set assign a 4 to the word which best characterizes your approach to the world, a 3 to the word which next best characterizes your approach to the world, a 2 to the next characteristic word, and a 1 to the word which is least characteristic of your approach to the world. Be sure to assign a different number to each of the four words in each horizontal set. Do not make ties.

	Column 1	Column 2	Column 3	Column 4
1.	____ Emotional	____ Inventing	____ Rational	____ Constructing
2.	____ Shy	____ Boastful	____ Driven	____ Thoughtful
3.	____ Inspiring	____ Researching	____ Meticulous	____ Carrying Out
4.	____ Enthusiastic	____ Questioning	____ Conscientious	____ Confident
5.	____ Pleasant	____ Rancorous	____ Jumpy	____ Spiritual
6.	____ Idealistic	____ Searching	____ Realistic	____ Decisive
7.	____ Philosophical	____ Discovering	____ Practical	____ Developing
8.	____ Loud	____ Excitable	____ Charming	____ Dissenting
9.	____ Imaginative	____ Designing	____ Logical	____ Completing
10.	____ Intuitive	____ Knowledge Seeking	____ Calculated	____ Profit Seeking
11.	____ Messy	____ Convincing	____ Organized	____ Introspective
12.	____ Outspoken	____ Inquiring	____ Careful	____ Executing
13.	____ Poetic	____ Researching	____ Pragmatic	____ Doing
14.	____ Fiery	____ Analytical	____ Judicious	____ Action-Oriented
15.	____ Proud	____ Careful	____ Fast	____ Direct
16.	____ Dramatic	____ Exploring	____ Empirical	____ Conquering
17.	____ Demonstrative	____ Victorious	____ Level-Headed	____ Peaceful
18.	____ Gung Ho	____ Studious	____ Methodical	____ Decisive

Scoring your results: *Cross out numbers 2, 5, 8, 11, 15 & 17.* These are distractors to keep you from finding a pattern. Add up each column. The total number should equal 120.

☐ + ☐ + ☐ + ☐ = 120

FIGURE I.1 Entrepreneurial Leadership Instrument

How to use the data:

Plot your total from Column 1 on Axis 1, Column 2 on Axis 2, Column 3 on Axis 3, Column 4 on Axis 4. Then, darkly shade in the biggest quadrant. Lightly shade in the second biggest quadrant(s).

Column 1	Column 2	Column 3	Column 4	
22	+ 28	+ 38	+ 32	= 120

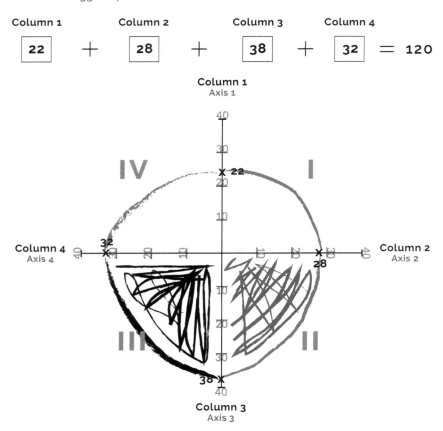

Your Entrepreneurial Leadership Profile: Quadrant __III__, Quadrant __II__

FIGURE I.2 Entrepreneurial Leadership Sample

How do you figure out your profile?

Instructions:
Plot your column totals from **Figure i.1** on the corresponding axis below. Connect each mark into an oval or distorted circle. Then, darkly shade in the biggest quadrant. Lightly shade in the second biggest quadrant(s). Shade all four if the scores for each column are exactly the same (30).

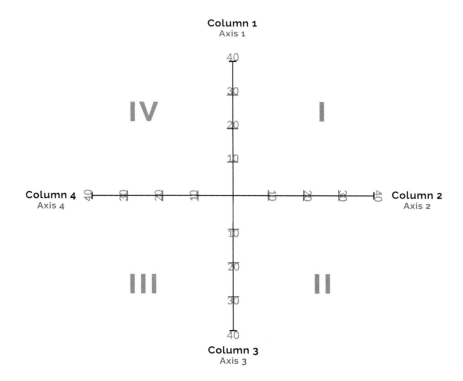

Your Entrepreneurial Leadership Profile: Quadrant _____, Quadrant _____

FIGURE I.3 Entrepreneurial Leadership Profile

Entrepreneurial Leadership Instrument Explained

Over the years, as entrepreneurship professors, we have come across four categories of successful entrepreneurs in the world. This categorization goes back to one key theme that defines entrepreneurship: opportunity. Seeking, recognizing, and acting on opportunities are what entrepreneurs do. We can further break down opportunity into two dimensions: how entrepreneurs think about opportunity and how they act on opportunity.

Let's look first at how entrepreneurs think about opportunity. Some devote a lot of time to abstractly thinking about opportunity. They like to work with big ideas. Abstract thinkers are skillful at moving people with their thoughts and connecting to their customers on a deep, human level. They're very in touch with the human condition and understand what drives people. These entrepreneurs build strong relationships with their customers by engaging their emotions.

Another group of entrepreneurs thinks about opportunity in a more concrete way. These entrepreneurs focus on the practicality of ideas. They seek a deep understanding of the reality in which they find themselves. Concrete thinkers look at the facts and test the feasibility of their ideas. Everyone does their share of abstract and concrete thinking, but most people tend to be more comfortable focusing on one or the other.

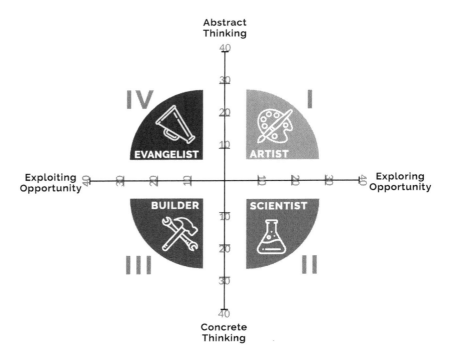

FIGURE I.4 What the ELI Measures

FIGURE I.5 Entrepreneurial Leadership Styles

Now let's examine how people act on opportunities. Some people enjoy exploring new ideas. They're comfortable with ambiguity and appreciate seeing what a creation can become. They follow opportunities—perhaps they actually chase them—even if they're not sure whether they will succeed or find a dead end. These entrepreneurs enjoy the challenge of looking at things others have overlooked or not recognized.

But other people enjoy exploiting opportunities. We don't mean exploit as in taking advantage of someone. What we mean is that when an opportunity has been recognized, they capitalize on it. These entrepreneurs make things happen on a grand scale. They marshal resources and motivate people to bring their vision into the world. Unlike the explorers who enjoy the subtleties and nuances of an area, exploiters follow the mantra "the bigger, the better."

Now when we take these two dimensions—how we think about opportunity and how we act on opportunity—we can create a profile of the categories of entrepreneurial leadership styles. You will see in Figure I.4 a grid with four quadrants. The top two quadrants represent people who think about ideas abstractly. The bottom two quadrants represent people who think concretely. To help remember this, you can imagine that concrete things are grounded here on earth, while abstract ideas tend to be thought of as things that float in the air. Now imagine that the two quadrants on the right represent people who act on ideas through exploration and the two quadrants on the left represent people who act on ideas through exploitation.

Putting all of this together, the top right quadrant consists of abstract explorers. We call these types of entrepreneurial leaders *artists*. The bottom right quadrant represents concrete explorers. We call these types of entrepreneurial leaders *scientists*. The bottom left quadrant represents concrete exploiters. We call these types of entrepreneurial leaders *builders*. And the top left quadrant represents abstract exploiters. We call these types of entrepreneurial leaders *evangelists*.

These are the four kinds of entrepreneurs that we have observed over the years. They're artists, scientists, evangelists, and builders. Let's go through each of these styles of entrepreneurial leaders in greater detail.

Artist

In the upper right-hand corner of the grid are the artists. They're leaders who think abstractly and enjoy exploring opportunities. They're like artists because they like thinking about big ideas and delving into the human psyche. Like artists, they're really in touch with the human condition. They're good at connecting with people. They explore what really drives people and what makes them

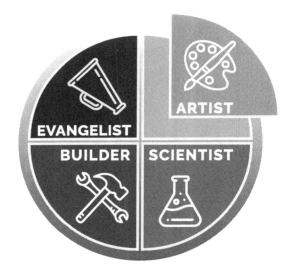

- Value creativity
- Love ideas
- Search for new solutions
- Empathize with and respect the customer
- Value the human condition
- Appreciate the subtleties of their craft
- Hard to predict

FIGURE I.6 Entrepreneurial Leadership Style—Artist

tick. An artist is in touch with people's subconscious minds. And they're very good at creating new things that people find gratifying. In the business world, a person with an artistic sensibility will have a great appreciation for the finer details of a product. Artists focus on quality. They consider the aesthetic content and features of a product: how something looks and how it is used. An artist produces products that people love. Above all, they see themselves as craftsmen.

Scientist

The scientist is in the bottom right-hand quadrant of the grid. Scientists are entrepreneurial leaders who think concretely and enjoy exploring opportunities. While the artist focuses on producing products that people love, the scientist focuses on making sure the product works. While they value new concepts, they're not impressed by pie-in-the-sky ideas. They want to make sure what they produce will work reliably and that it will be successful.

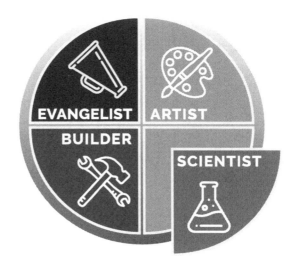

- Focus on reality
- Value deep research on a subject
- Search for supporting evidence of ideas
- Strive to perfect new concepts
- View modeling as a key entrepreneurial activity
- Study best practices
- Adapts and develops new technologies

FIGURE I.7 Entrepreneurial Leadership Style—Scientist

They're focused on the details of a design too, but they're more critical and try to find the shortcomings of an idea. They approach every idea as if it is a hypothesis that needs to be tested. After a scientist has worked with an idea, its economic and technical foundations will be solid. Scientists operate under the principle of understanding the reality of the world around them. Or to put it another way: scientists want facts. They have ideas about the world and they're interested in testing whether their ideas are accurate. Scientists also focus on things over people. They enjoy exploring the latest technology in their industry—often even creating their own—and considering how to elevate their core business with it. Scientists enjoy making insights that deepen their knowledge, always seeking an edge over their competition.

Builder

In the lower left-hand quadrant, we find the builders. Builders are entrepreneurial leaders who think concretely and enjoy exploiting opportunities. Now we call

- Scale businesses, ventures, and projects
- Desire efficient operations
- Build systems and processes
- Recruit multi-talented and multi-functional teams
- Lead and motivate to complete projects
- Value acquisitions and partnerships

FIGURE I.8 Entrepreneurial Leadership Style—Builder

these leaders builders because they get things built. Builders get things done, they make things real, and they like to grow organizations by scaling their operations to serve more of their market. If resources are needed to get the job done, they'll figure out how to get them. Builders are very well organized. They understand what's needed to get a business up and going and to sustain it and grow it. Builders manage others in order to meet deadlines. You could say they're the generals of business or—as we'll see later with Disneyland—the "admirals" of business. With this disciplined approach, they can take a good concept and turn it into a very successful enterprise.

Evangelist

And finally, in the upper left-hand quadrant, we find the evangelists. Evangelists are entrepreneurial leaders who think abstractly and enjoy exploiting

- On fire about their cause
- Use simple messages to connect with consumers
- Connect with employees through clear mission and purpose
- Able to charm the media
- Carry the banner for their organization and its initiatives
- Inspires followers and advocates

FIGURE I.9 Entrepreneurial Leadership Style—Evangelist

opportunities. They're very good at spreading an inspiring message about the organization, and they're great at getting others on board with their mission. While the artist connects with the customer in a more subtle and understated way, the evangelist is loud. They get the message out to the desired audience. Evangelists create excitement for their brand promise. Every person they meet gives them another opportunity to talk about the strengths of the company. Every venue is a stage where they can preach the story of their organization. When an evangelist has a compelling message, he or she can motivate others to change the world.

Concluding Thoughts

Entrepreneurs are very effective when they can dream up great products and services by thinking like an artist. Entrepreneurs that make technological breakthroughs by thinking like a scientist can revolutionize society as well. Both of these approaches can make an impact on the world. But perhaps the biggest and most sustained impact an entrepreneur can make on the world occurs when they build an organization that lives on long after they're gone. One of the key differences is this: the builder focuses on the business of the business. As you can imagine, being a builder of a large company isn't for everyone. Some entrepreneurs like being more like an artist and focusing on craftsmanship, or they prefer being like a scientist and tinkering with technology. However, being a builder provides a larger stage for the company to do more frequent and groundbreaking innovation. And the rare builder is one who can also evangelize their system to the world. Evangelizing opens doors into new markets as the entrepreneur seeks ways to expand the company's mission.

Now that you have taken the Entrepreneurial Leadership Instrument, you can discover what type of leader you are most like. We suggest you study other legendary entrepreneurs who fit that category to see what led to their success. Awareness of your entrepreneurial leadership style can also guide you in recruiting others to your team from the other quadrants in order to complement your perspective. Some leaders, however, are well-skilled in all four quadrants. We believe Walt Disney is the rare case of someone who moved among these quadrants with great success and created a legendary organization by doing so. In the first four chapters of this book, we explain how Walt mastered entrepreneurship by proceeding through the stages of artist, scientist, builder, and evangelist. You'll discover, as we have, that knowing Walt's journey can inspire you to better recognize and develop the opportunities that come to you. In Chapter Five, we examine the entrepreneurial leadership styles of the Walt Disney Company chief executive officers who followed Walt.

As you read the book, the perspectives of the authors' entrepreneurial leadership styles will likely be evident to you. Mike's style is artist/scientist. He enjoys exploring a variety of topics, and considers himself a modern renaissance man.

Mike is proud of his ability to quickly develop expertise in a broad range of topical areas. He also enjoys using evangelism to share this knowledge. Rob's style is scientist/builder. He loves entrepreneurship, innovation, creativity, and business that is done with excellence, and enjoys studying what makes the best the best. He was born to learn and apply those learnings. He is fascinated by tinkering with his ideas, concepts, and business models to make them as good as he possibly can. His passion and excitement for the topics he researches also allow him to evangelize his message. As a sidenote, we often compare our teamwork to that of Walt and Roy's.

Finally, it's important to note the ELI does not measure intensity or how good an artist, scientist, builder, or evangelist one is. Further, it does not measure if you are truly entrepreneurial. What is does measure is (a) your entrepreneurial perspective and style and (b) how you approach entrepreneurial ventures or activities. It's also important to note that leaders will have to "play" in each of the styles represented in the ELI at various times. Other instruments, such as Gallup's Builder Profile-10 (BP-10) and the Entrepreneurial Mindset Profile (EMP), have options for relative intensity scoring. These profiles, along with a talent assessment like StrengthsFinder, a functional work style inventory like the Basadur Innovation Profile, and a personality assessment like Myers-Briggs Temperament Assessment (MBTI) or DiSC, all pair very well with the ELI.

PART 1

Walt Disney, Entrepreneur

1

THE ARTIST YEARS

I had tremendous respect for my father. I worshipped him. Nothing but his family counted.

—Walt Disney[1]

A Window Into Walt

If you happen to go to Disneyland, take a moment to stop in front of the Emporium store on Main Street, U.S.A. Look up and you'll see a second floor window that reads "Elias Disney, Contractor." Elias Disney was Walt Disney's father. This tribute in the Happiest Place on Earth was given by the younger Disney to a man who by most accounts was not very happy. Harold Evans, the author of *They Made America*, describes him as "a disciplined man, a teetotaler and churchgoer, not very lucky in his enterprises. Elias was clearly not a bundle of laughs. He was straitlaced, puritanical, and humorless";[2] and Bob Thomas, the authorized Disney biographer, describes his parenting as overly strict, writing that "he thought nothing of taking a switch to his son or the fat part of his belt. Walt would bury his head in the bend of (his brother) Roy's elbow and ask if the man who beat him was really his father or just some mean old man who looked like him and wanted only to frighten or hurt him."[3]

Walt's charming and funny mother, Flora, on the other hand, kept the family home organized and ensured the children were educated and comfortable. She was also the peacemaker in the family, keeping the children and Elias's tempers under control. During many of the challenging periods the Disney family would encounter through the early twentieth century, Flora held the family together and offered a caring approach that counterbalanced her husband's sternness. By all accounts, she was adored by her husband and children.

So why would Walt Disney place a tribute to his stern father, instead of to his sensitive mother, front and center in the most heavily traveled area of Disneyland? After all, wouldn't it be more fitting to recognize the happiest Disney in the Happiest Place on Earth? Understanding this irony gives us insight into how Walt Disney became the premier entertainment entrepreneur of the twentieth century. Since Walt was obsessive, passionate, and purposeful in everything he did—a combination of traits often attributed to a high achiever—he would have surely given it a lot of thought as to whether or not to pay homage to his father in his favorite place. We believe this was Walt's way of telling us that if not for Elias Disney there would be no Disneyland. He recognized that Disneyland would not have happened if his father had not searched for a better life himself. Long before his son dreamed up the idea of the park, Elias started clearing the way for Main Street, U.S.A.

The Disneys serve as an example to us all how people from humble beginnings rise to great success. When you study the actual life of a "self-made man," you actually find the popular account of their ascent is more myth than reality. As Malcolm Gladwell has written in *Outliers: The Story of Success*, "People don't rise from nothing. We do owe something to parentage and patronage. The people who stand before kings may look like they did it all by themselves. But in fact they are invariably the beneficiaries of hidden advantages and extraordinary opportunities and cultural legacies that allow them to learn and work hard and make sense of the world in ways others cannot. It makes a difference where and when we grew up. The culture we belong to and the legacies passed down by our forebears shape the patterns of our achievement in ways we cannot begin to imagine."[4]

So, to gain insight into how Walt Disney became a great entrepreneur, we must first examine his father and the legacy he provided his son.

Elias Disney, Contractor

Long before Walt Disney produced *Snow White* and built Sleeping Beauty Castle, his father was chasing his own dreams. Elias and Walt Disney had much in common. They both came from humble origins and wanted to build a successful life. They both pursued opportunities whenever possible. Likewise, they both had a strong gut feeling that the next idea would be a lot better than the last. The world often delivered different plans for them. Each lost everything they owned a few times, but they both endured to give another business idea a try each time. This strategy paid off for Walt. His dreams eventually came true. His father's didn't.

If Elias had been born a half-century later and closer to an urban area, he might have been successful. Instead, he was born on February 6, 1859, in the small Canadian village of Bluevale. Alas, his childhood was spent in a remote region of Ontario that offered few opportunities to a farmer's son. The winters were brutal in Bluevale, and life was hard. When western expansion boomed just south of the Disney homestead, his father, Kepple, decided to move the family to Kansas in 1878, hoping for a better life. They bought three hundred acres from the Union Pacific Railroad and started a farm like many other immigrants who came to the region during that time. Although the conditions were better in Kansas, life was difficult for the Disneys. As immigrants, they were not afforded the same property deals as American citizens. The winters were still wicked, often bringing storms that caused ten-foot snow drifts on the barren plains. Even worse, money was tight. The family bootstrapped their existence with whatever resources were available to them, even resorting to building their house out of dirt and stone that they quarried from their land.[5]

Living off the land as a pioneer wore on Elias. He felt restless like his father, and, tiring of farm work, he decided to do something he would do many more times when life became difficult: he moved. His first job on his own was working as a machinist in a railroad machine shop. In an interesting twist of fate, he apprenticed alongside the future automobile tycoon Walter Chrysler. This would be the first of many Forrest Gump moments when a Disney unexpectedly crossed paths with a famous public figure or took part in a historic event. As the Disneys discovered, happy accidents seem to happen more when you move around. As we will see throughout this book, Walt's journey will have him working with many of the most acclaimed artists, scientists, and businessmen of the twentieth century.

Moving off the farm was a good step for Elias to learn a trade. He gained mechanical knowledge in the machine shop, but the routine of the work eventually bored him. When an opportunity arose to join a crew building the Union Pacific railroad through Colorado, he jumped at the chance to work outside and learn the construction trade. Unfortunately, the job was only temporary. Once the track was completed, he was out of work. He searched for other construction jobs but couldn't find any. With no other options available, he tried his luck as a fiddle player in saloons. Unfortunately, that occupation didn't pay well, so he returned to the family farm in Kansas. What looked like a bad turn of events actually brought Elias his happiest accident: he met his future wife Flora Call upon his return to the family homestead. Flora lived next door to the Disney farm. Her father, Charles, had given up teaching in Ohio and moved the family to Kansas. He apparently had buyer's remorse. He didn't like the winter blizzards that came through the plains and soon decided to move his family to Florida. Kepple had tired of the winters too, and, with Elias in tow, joined the convoy to the warmer state. The move for Kepple was short-lived. He returned to Kansas within a few months, but Elias stayed to be near Flora. Tired of his fate being determined by his father and railroad companies, he bought a forty-acre farm and took his first shot at being his own boss. He continued to woo Flora, and, after a long courtship, they married in 1888.

The year 1888 marked a turning point for Elias. He no longer wandered solo looking for fortune. He now had a travel companion in Flora. Photos of the couple capture their devotion to each other. In one picture they resemble the husband and wife from the *American Gothic* painting. Elias appeared a lanky man with seriousness etched over his thin face while Flora, with dark, coiffed hair, and in the somber clothes of the nineteenth century, wore a slight look of bemusement on her strong face. They appeared comfortable with each other. Flora stood behind Elias in the picture, just as she would do countless times in their marriage over the years.

While marriage brought companionship, it did not quell Elias's hunger for business success. By 1888, he already owned and sold a farm and a hotel, and turned to working as a mailman and owning an orange grove to make a living. Life became even busier on December 8, 1888, when their first son, Herbert, was born. As often happened to Elias, the family's situation took a bad turn in Florida. The orange grove was wrecked by a cold spell, Elias contracted malaria, and Flora's father died from injuries suffered in a farming accident. With new family responsibilities and a change in mood in the household, Elias determined it was time to move again. But where? The last move occurred because his father decided to move them to Florida. He didn't want to return to Kansas, where his father was. Maybe this time he would try his luck living in Chicago, where Robert, his younger brother, was.[6]

Robert Disney proved to be a fairly successful businessman and had moved to Chicago a year before with fortune on his mind. Robert was a speculator and entered nascent markets he thought contained the potential for a big score. He apparently possessed better luck than his older brother. Robert already traded in gold mines, oil, and real estate, and now his instincts told him Chicago was about to become a prime location for making a fortune. In 1893, Chicago would host the World's Columbian Exposition, which commemorated the four-hundredth anniversary of Columbus's founding of America.[7] The city experienced rapid growth in the nineteenth century, growing from two hundred residents in 1833 to roughly two million by 1890.[8] The world's first skyscrapers provided metropolitan views like no other place in the world, and leading thinkers were moving to Chicago to be part of this midwestern renaissance. Civic leaders wanted to showcase the city's merits, and the Columbian Exposition was to be Chicago's world debutante ball.

The exposition was masterminded by genius architect Daniel Burnham, a Walt Disney-like figure of the nineteenth century. Burnham's vision encompassed creating a model of what the ideal city should be, and Chicago would be his prototype of urban perfection. Majestic gardens, canals, lagoons, exhibits, and over two hundred classically styled buildings were built in the neighborhoods of South Shore, Jackson Park Highlands, Hyde Park, and Woodlawn. He imagined what Chicago could be, and by sheer will and salesmanship transformed the city. Burnham's resolve was further bolstered after consulting with legendary showman P. T. Barnum, who told him, "Make it bigger and better than any that have preceded it. Make it the greatest show on earth—greater even than my own Great Moral Show."[9] And he did. As Frank Lloyd Wright remembered him, "Burnham made masterful use of the methods and men of his time . . . (as) an enthusiastic promoter of great construction enterprises . . . his powerful personality was supreme."[10]

Burnham's example transformed the way Chicagoans saw themselves. His advice to others chasing their dreams is amazingly reminiscent of Walt Disney's approach to life. In an oft quoted rallying cry, he stated, "Make no little plans. They have no magic to stir men's blood and probably themselves will not be realized. Make big plans; aim high in hope and work, remembering that a noble, logical diagram once recorded will never die, but long after we are gone will be a living thing, asserting itself with ever-growing insistency. Remember that our sons and grandsons are going to do things that would stagger us. Let your watchword be order and your beacon beauty. Think big."[11]

Robert Disney decided to think big and built a hotel to prepare for the large influx of visitors who would come to see Burnham's creation. His instincts proved right. Over thirty million came to the fair. Elias and Flora moved to Chicago in 1890 because of its promising economy as well, but they put their focus on building something smaller upon their arrival to the city: their house. Flora drew up the floor plans and Elias employed the construction skills he had learned on the railroad. Their cozy home on 1249 Tripp Avenue in the northwestern section of Chicago caught the eyes of passersby, and before long they were building and selling houses to other new residents around the city. They functioned as a good team, and the house business was perhaps Elias's most successful venture during his life. Elias made the deals and built the homes while Flora handled the bookkeeping, supplies, and house designs. When needed, Walt said, "My mother would go out on construction jobs and hammer and saw planks with the men."[12] The household was being run by two entrepreneurs, and life was finally good for the Disneys.

The good times wouldn't last long. Business slowed a bit in 1893, so Elias turned to working seven days a week as a construction worker on the World's Columbian Exposition. This moment in his life is often provided as a footnote in other books, but we think it had significant influence on who Walt Disney became many years later. Boys often look up to their father, and we can imagine Walt thinking about his dad working on the Chicago World's Fair when he was building Disneyland. After all, a Disney theme park consists of half amusement park and half world's fair, whereas most other theme parks are focused on roller coasters. This combination is what brings us back to Disneyland throughout our lives. When we're younger we can't wait to get on the rides, but as we age we stroll a little more, taking in the sights and exhibits spread throughout the park. Elias's experience working on the exhibition and living in Chicago during that time may play as much a role in what Disneyland became as anything else that occurred in the family history.

Circumstantial evidence of this theory involves Walt's reputation for totally immersing himself in his projects. When he became interested in a topic, he sought to learn every detail that pertained to it. As his wife Lillian recalled when asked about his favorite topic of conversation, "His work was. He read a lot of things. Researched. He knew something about everything. I don't think he ever read a novel in his life but he was crazy about history. If he didn't know something he would ask. Walt always remembered everything."[13] He talked to experts in their respective fields and visited museums and historic sites whenever possible. He was also very nostalgic. Walt Disney liked to look at the past while he created the future. We picture Walt thinking back to Elias telling him stories at the dinner table about his earlier work experiences from around the country. It is likely that one of those stories consisted of his involvement in the construction of the world's fair, one of the largest entertainment projects of all time. When we retell stories, we often embellish them a bit. What we did becomes grander than it actually was. We emphasize the good parts, put ourselves in starring roles, and leave out the embarrassing moments. Erecting buildings for the most breathtaking showcase in history for a legendary architect would have given Elias ample material for entertaining his family. We think it is highly likely that Disney studied Burnham and the Chicago Fair for examples in creating his own utopian vision. As American Studies professor Michael Steiner has observed, "Sixty-two years after the Chicago Fair closed, another pleasure dome opened farther west among the orange groves of Anaheim. The master builders of these emulated lands had much in common. Daniel Hudson Burnham and Walter Elias Disney were midwestern idealists who etched deep signatures upon the land. Their utopian visions, bold plans, and deft orchestrations of other men's ideas have shaped much of the modern world."[14]

Walter Elias Disney

As expected, the Columbian World Exhibition boosted Chicago's economy, so Elias was eventually able to return to building houses. The Disney family continued to grow as well. Raymond Arnold was born in 1890, and Roy Oliver was born in 1893, but it would be eight years before the arrival of the most famous Disney.

Walter Elias Disney was born on December 5, 1901, and died on December 15, 1966. Very few people in history embodied the ability to achieve as much as Walt did. In a world revolving around entertainment and communication, it might be accurate to say that much of what we fill our days with is based on Disney's achievements. He was the first to put sound with animated cartoons (*Steamboat Willie* in 1928), the first to use color in a cartoon (*Flower and Trees* in 1932), the first to produce a feature-length animation (*Snow White* in 1937), the first major studio executive to develop material for television (*Disneyland* for ABC in 1954), the first to build a theme park (Disneyland in 1955), and the first to use robotic characters in a theme park (Audio-Animatronics in the Enchanted Tiki Room at Disneyland in 1963). His stories and characters live on as strongly today as they did on his passing in 1966. This legacy is a strong testament to both his creative genius and his business talent. How did Disney acquire such talent? The answer lies in his humble origins and how he persevered through the challenges of his day to reach the pinnacles of his later life.

The house on Tripp Avenue was small, and with the arrival of Ruth Flora Disney on December 6, 1903, Elias began to wonder if they should consider moving again. The family was doing financially well, but he cited concerns over the increased crime in the growing city. Elias appeared a very righteous man, and he wanted to ensure his family was raised in a more Christian environment. As Roy recalls, "Everything was going nicely up there. A neighboring family just like ours was very close to us. We woke up one morning and two of their boys were involved in a car-barn robbery, behind a bunch of railroad ties. They shot it out with the cops and killed a cop. One of them went to Joliet for life and the other got twenty years. These kids were just the same age as my older brother and my second brother. We had a nice neighborhood. A lot of good Irish and Poles and Swedes around there, but it was a rough neighborhood too. Up at the corner where we got our papers there were three saloons out of four corners. It worried Mother and Dad."

Given Elias's track record, though, it's possible he was getting bored as well. He always seemed to be looking forward to the next opportunity and challenge, traits his son Walt would later display as well. Elias mastered the construction business, and now it was time to try something else. The next challenge would be farming, and after looking at properties in Colorado and Alabama, he decided on Marceline, Missouri, in 1906, a place where his brother Robert owned land. The town was off the Topeka and Santa Fe Railway, contained rich pastures and farmland, and offered the stable setting he wanted to raise his family in. This backdrop set the stage for opportunities that would allow Walt Disney to thrive.

Main Street, U.S.A.

The street running by the "Elias Disney, Contractor" window in Disneyland is dedicated to the fond memories of two childhoods. It is a tribute by Walt Disney to his childhood hometown of Marceline, Missouri, where his family owned a farm. He credits it with being the source of all his future creative projects. Main Street, U.S.A., is also based on the look of Fort Collins, Colorado, where Harper Goff, its principal designer, grew up. While his creation resembles Marceline and Fort Collins in appearance, it stands for something bigger. Main Street, U.S.A., is Disney's version of the Parthenon. It's the good life, as depicted by Walt. Simple. Pure. Optimistic. Patriotic. It's commerce draped in warm feelings and friendly tones. The park encompasses the philosophy Walt tried to pass on to everyone entering his utopia.

Really, what made Marceline so special? After all, it didn't have a rich history or cultural legacy. It was founded only eighteen years before the Disney family moved there. The town was developed to be a division point on the Topeka and Santa Fe Railway between Kansas City and Chicago. The streets consisted of dirt. The buildings appeared rustic. The people were country folk making a simple living. Marceline provided a big change from Chicago. However, a more wholesome place to experience the age of innocence could not be found for Walt. As Walt remembered, "I guess Marceline must have made a deep impression on me. I can clearly remember every detail—just as if it had been yesterday. I even remember the train ride from Chicago to Marceline, and I remember the new things that I saw as I looked out of the window. You see, I had never been to the country before. Finally, we got into a wagon and drove out to the farm. It was a pretty farm with a good house and a big yard. Those were the happiest days of my life."[15] Roy's memories of Marceline were equally fond. He reminisced, "We had just a very cute, sweet little farm, if you can express it or describe a farm that way: Forty-five acres and five of it in wonderful apples, peaches, plums, and plenty of grapes and berries, and little pastures, and plots. We had a four-acre place where we raised hogs. And of course, we had chickens and then you had your pets. We had about four to six horses all the time and a few milk cows. It was just heaven for city kids. Walt loved it!"[16]

The farm animals and wildlife provided the most appealing aspect of living in Marceline. Many opportunities for passing the time in the woods surfaced. After all, many country boys love hunting and fishing. Not Walt. He enjoyed spending hours *with* the animals on the farm and in the woods. He didn't hunt them. He interacted with them. Walt gave them names and imagined having friendships with them. When he wanted to be alone, he sat beneath his "dreaming tree," a large cottonwood that stood beside a stream on the family property, where he spent hours lost in his thoughts and watching the wildlife. He found his bliss. This place of wonder would remain near to his heart for the rest of his life. However and whenever he could, Walt would try to bring Marceline back into his life and work.[17]

While in Marceline, Walt developed his first interest in trains. His uncle Mike Martin was an engineer on the Santa Fe Railway, and he enjoyed watching him pass by town on his legs between Chicago and Kansas City. Additionally, in Marceline, he was given his first positive reinforcement as an artist by his Aunt Margaret, who would bring him big tablets and crayons so he could draw pictures for her. Aunt Margaret raved about the pictures, as did a local physician, Doctor Sherwood. Doc Sherwood would pay him for drawings of his horse Rupert. Walt was hooked on drawing. With the encouragement of Doc Sherwood and his wife, Walt began to envision himself as an artist. Moments like this can have a large impact on someone's future. When an adult we respect tells us we're good at something, we often believe it. After all, when you're six years old, isn't everyone older than you an expert? How could they be wrong? In *Mindset: The New Psychology of Success*, psychologist Carol S. Dweck separates people into two groups: those with a fixed mind-set who believe people are born with a certain quantity of ability that determines their future and those with a growth mind-set who believe that through hard work and grit anything is possible. Disney embodied the growth mind-set. Much like Thomas Edison, who Dweck says "never stopped being the curious, tinkering boy looking for new challenges,"[18] Walt acquired a playfulness while a child in the tiny town of Marceline, Missouri, that would stay with him for the rest of his life. Even though he was living under the strict roof of his domineering father Elias, Walt's life was permeated by an insatiable drive to experiment, learn, and create. One famous story presented Walt drawing pictures on the side of the family farmhouse, much to Elias's consternation. As his sister Ruth recalled the gaffe, "My folks had gone to town, and we were left there alone, and we spied this big barrel of tar. We opened it up and were looking at it, and Walt said, 'Oh, this would be real good to paint with.' He said, 'Let's paint on the house.' It came to mind would it come off? He said, 'Oh, sure.' I can remember an awful feeling when we realized a little bit later the tar wouldn't budge. It stayed on the house until we moved."[19]

But Marceline wasn't fun for everyone in the Disney family, particularly Elias. He struggled with farming and running the estate. Market prices for crops were unpredictable, and he found it hard to make enough money to support the family. As he often did, he leaned on his sons to help out with the crisis. Elias expected them to work hard and put any money they had back into the family. Raymond and Herb's perspective differed on the issue. They decided they finally had enough and ran away from home in the middle of the night, leaving Elias and Roy to do the work. To make matters worse, Elias came down with typhoid fever and became bedridden. Walt and Ruth were too young to help, so he turned to Roy to run the farm and keep it afloat. Roy, at only sixteen years old, could not manage it. As a result of another stroke of bad luck, Elias made the tough decision to call the farm escapade quits and try something else. Having already gone north, south, and west, this time Elias looked east to Kansas City.

The Real World

In 1910, the Disney family moved from Marceline to Kansas City, Missouri, due to Elias's inability to manage the farm. The move made sense at the time. Kansas City was a thriving city of three hundred thousand residents in the early twentieth century. Because of his illness, Elias looked for a business opportunity that would allow him to make money while minimizing physical effort on his part. He settled on buying a newspaper route and forced Walt and Roy to deliver the papers.

Kansas City was a dramatic change from Marceline for Walt. He went from his idyllic existence in the countryside to one of drudgery in the big city. Delivering papers was hard work. Walt would have to rise for his shift at 3:15 a.m., which afforded him little time for play on a school day. If he was fortunate enough to get ahead of schedule, he could stop to take a nap in an apartment building's hallway or play with toys left on customers' porches. To make matters worse, he often needed to deliver the papers in freezing weather conditions. In one particularly grueling experience shortly after Christmas in 1916, he was wearing boots he had received as a gift, and made a gruesome mistake early on his route. His younger sister Ruth recalled, "Walt was delivering papers, during that terrible weather when the streets were just full of ice, and there was a block of wood there, a board, and it had a nail in it, and Walt had his heavy boots and he ran this nail right through his boot and about two or more inches into his large toe. They had several men get a hold of the board to pull it out of his shoe and he was laid up for quite a while with that, but he certainly was a brick, I never saw anybody like him. The doctor had to come out and scrape that every so often and put medication in it, and you never heard a sound of him, never a sound."[20] To make matters worse, Elias took the money Walt earned on the paper route and put it toward the family's needs and savings. To get pocket money, Walt worked at a candy store during his lunch recess at school. As he said later, "I had inexhaustible energy in those days, and I didn't mind being scolded by my parents for bad marks and beaten by my teachers for inattention. I needed the money. I ate candy like a mad fool."[21] He supplemented those earnings by delivering additional papers to neighbors of subscribers already on his route. He never informed Elias of these new customers, and he now got up at 3 a.m. to deliver the extra papers, but he was rewarded with more money.

Luckily, it wasn't all bad for Walt in Kansas City because he developed a second love: acting. Walt went to silent movies whenever he could afford them, and in the movie houses, he discovered Charlie Chaplin. Chaplin became Walt's biggest hero during his life. He would imitate him whenever he had the chance. Ruth recalled, "One time Roy got wind that Walt was going to be on amateur night somewhere, he never told us, and so we all hurried and got down to the theater a little ways away, and sure enough, he was acting like Charlie Chaplin. According to us, he was the best, but he didn't win the prize."[22] Friends and family said he had captured Chaplin's distinct Little Tramp walk and could put them in stitches.[23] He also recreated vaudeville acts with his best friend Walt Pfeiffer. Dubbed "The Two Walts," they would perform skits and tell jokes in foreign accents. They became very popular performers in the area. No doubt, these performances prepared him to act out scenes for animators during his studio days.

Another of Walt's interests in Kansas City involved amusement parks. For a future theme park developer, he could not have grown up in a better spot in the early twentieth century. Kansas City had Fairmount Amusement Park and

Electric Park, and both proved so popular that in 1920 a third amusement park, Fairyland, opened. One can imagine the parks trying to outcompete one another with increasingly magnificent attractions. And, indeed, that appears to have been true. Roller coasters, hot air balloons, beach areas, light shows, entertainment, and war reenactments on lakes were common attractions. As Brian Burnes, Robert W. Butler, and Dan Viets describe in *Walt Disney's Missouri*, "In pre-World War I Kansas City, the amusement park defined diversion. It's easy to understand how Kansas City residents, at the end of the gaslight era, were charmed by the sight of an estimated one hundred thousand electric lights outlining the various buildings and towers of the park. Electricity was employed in a variety of ways, most notably with the 'Living Statuary' attraction. Every hour after 9 p.m., young women appeared on a platform rising out of a fountain, posing while being washed by multi-colored lights. The effect of all this upon nine-year-old Walt Disney, who arrived in Kansas City with his family in 1911, can be imagined. The similarities between Electric Park and the Disney theme parks are several. At Electric Park there were fireworks at night. A train encircled the acreage. And just as brothers Walt and Roy Disney later built Disneyland Park, a trio of brothers—J.J., Mike and Ferdinand Heim, operators of Kansas City's Heim Brewing Co.—built Electric Park."[24]

While Marceline provided the ideals Disney would promote the rest of his life, Kansas City provided the experiences needed to bring them to others. Walt's boyhood friend William Rast recounts how much Walt loved amusement parks: "One time he came over to my house. He asked if I wanted to go over to the Fairmount Amusement Park. I told him I had no money. He said we didn't need any as he knew how to sneak in. We went over to where the entrance to Fairmount was. We carefully watched, looked around, and went under the boulevard where there was this big culvert. You had to crook over to get under. Luckily, it wasn't too slushy. On the other side there was this big screen, which some other kids had already opened. We just pushed it over and snuck in. We spent the whole day there. He made me promise never to tell that story while he was alive. He thought kids might use the excuse that if he could do it, then they could try to get into his park without paying."[25]

And Walt continued pursuing his passion for drawing. His identity as an artist was firmly ingrained by this point. He enrolled in art school and drew caricatures for friends and family.[26] His sister Ruth remembers he would be very busy at home doing drawings for the local barber Bert Hudson. She said, "He got his haircut for a drawing per week and it was comical in nature."[27] Walt remained in contact with Hudson for many years after he was famous. His Benton Grammar School classmate Nathan L. Bassin recalls, "Walt didn't socialize much because he was involved in drawing his cartoons. One time we were supposed to be studying geography, but Walt was slouched in his chair, drawing cartoons behind our big geography books. Mr. Cottingham came walking down the aisle. He stood beside Walt's desk and said sternly, 'Young man, you'll never amount to anything.'" How wrong Mr. Cottingham was; however, another stop on the journey of childhood would occur before Walt could go into the world and pursue his dreams on his own.

Walter Elias Disney, Cartoonist

The paper route in Kansas City paid the bills, but it didn't make Elias a rich man. So, in 1917, he moved the family to pursue a business opportunity at a jelly factory in Chicago. Elias was convinced that this venture would be the one that would make him a fortune. Flora, unconvinced of the wisdom of this idea, acquiesced in the end. Before moving to Chicago, Walt took a little time in the summer to pursue adventure on the Santa Fe Railway. He sold his portion of the paper route and took a job as a news butcher, selling candy and papers on the train. He loved the work, and it furthered his fondness for trains.

When school was ready to start up again, Walt transferred from Benton Grammar School to McKinley High School in Chicago. Work would continue to keep him busy, as it did in Kansas City, but it wasn't as brutish as the paper route. He worked in the jelly factory that Elias had invested in, and later became a postal carrier for a short while. Even with his jobs and school duties, there was always one constant for Walt no matter where he was—he never parted from his love of drawing. In fact, he drew whenever he could, and Chicago offered him many opportunities to broaden his artistic skills. He volunteered as the cartoonist for the school newspaper and took classes at the Chicago Academy of Fine Arts, which he paid for out of his savings from Kansas City. He kept his enrollment in the art classes a secret from Elias, but he believed it was worth the risk. It was a good decision. The academy's faculty had many on its roster who were employed at the very Chicago newspapers he hoped to work for one day. Walt looked up to them, and they enjoyed mentoring him. He especially enjoyed Carl Wertz's class. Wertz asked his students to draw from live models, both animals and people, and capture the way they moved and interacted with each other. He liked Walt's comical style of drawing the models and encouraged him to continue pursuing cartooning. Other teachers also served as excellent mentors in teaching young Walt the craft of cartooning. Carey Orr, a *Chicago Tribune* cartoonist, invited him to visit his office, and introduced him to his colleagues. They showed him the skills of the cartooning craft and gave him a picture of what life at a newspaper would be like. Walt loved the environment and what the men did. He was sure now. He would become a cartoonist.

Now that Walt set his mind on being a cartoonist, nothing at McKinley High School held his interest any longer, with the exception of one beautiful and energetic classmate he hoped to impress. Su Pitwoski, who had a brother fighting in World War I, was a very patriotic young woman, and Walt was determined to get her attention. He served as junior art editor for the school newspaper and placed his patriotic cartoons throughout each edition. Walt took his patriotic commitment one step further when he decided he wanted to join the military and fight in World War I. When he went to sign up, he discovered he was too young; however, he learned that at fifteen years old he could join the Red Cross. His parents weren't too keen on the idea, but they knew with his headstrong ways he'd find some way to serve overseas. Flora thought the Red Cross was the safest form of service and agreed to sign the papers that enlisted him in the ambulance corps. Finally able to leave the confines of the Disney household, like his older brothers Ray, Herbert, and Roy had done over the years, Walt was on his way to France.[28]

While Walt developed an identity as an artist, he was rapidly complementing it as a comedian. Even on his deployment over to France, he continued to entertain everyone around him by impersonating women in skits to pass the time. One can imagine Walt honing his comic timing and acting skills while receiving applause and encouragement for his antics. In later years, his artists would marvel at his ability to take on any character they were trying to draw, but the more we learn about his childhood the more we shouldn't be surprised by his acting skills. By the age of fifteen, he could perfectly mimic Charlie Chaplin, perhaps the greatest physical comedian of all time, and having lived in big cities he had come across a diverse group of characters he could imitate. This catalogue of personas would come in handy later in his life when he was creating cartoon characters. After all, animation literally means bringing something to life, and the only way to bring silly drawings to life is to imbue them with characteristics and movements with which we can relate. Such creating was not a problem for Walt. Understanding and relating to his audience gave him competitive advantages over other cartoon studios. Simply put, Walt Disney was always one of us.

The connection to the public would not have been possible without experiencing the good times and the bad times through which the average person lives. His journey to France and back was chock-full of his share of both. He enjoyed the excitement of romance and valor by writing to and receiving letters from Su. Another benefit of serving in France was that it afforded him more time to develop his drawing skills since he was no longer in school and he was away from his domineering father. Walt even set up a drawing desk next to his bed so that he could draw whenever possible. He gained notoriety in the camp for comical posters he drew that instructed corpsmen on hygiene and demeanor, and placed his image where everyone could see it by painting a caricature of himself on his ambulance. When he wasn't drawing, he was getting a sense of adventure, driving ambulances through the French countryside. Anyone serving in that job would have had good stories to tell their grandchildren because two other legends drove Red Cross ambulances as well. Forrest Gump moment two: Ray Kroc, who would later go on to build McDonald's into a multinational powerhouse, served in his unit, and Ernest Hemingway was inspired to write *A*

Farewell to Arms because of his time recovering from a serious injury incurred while driving a Red Cross ambulance in Italy.

Hemingway and Disney are evidence that a person's calling can be embraced in almost any circumstance. While Hemingway found inspiration to be a writer recovering in the hospital, Disney honed his entrepreneurial chops in the war-torn countryside. While his other comrades were spending their free time gambling, drinking, and chasing French women, Walt scoured the battlefields for discarded military rubbish. Items of interest were sold to soldiers as souvenirs to take home, with German steel helmets being the most popular item. Walt showed early signs of being a master salesman. He discovered that if he dressed up the helmets a bit he could get more money, so he would shoot bullets through them, scuff them up, and add hair and red paint to give the appearance that the helmets had once rested on the heads of downed enemies on the battlefield. The venture made Walt a lot of extra cash. As he said later, "Some of the boys would hand over every cent they had to get them. And the gorier they looked, the more they'd pay."[29]

Given the circumstances, things were going well. He found comrades, drew a lot, and he made good friends with another young man from Chicago, Russell Maas. The boys enjoyed each other's company, and they looked forward to the day when they would return to America and could take trips up and down the Mississippi River. But, his happiest discovery in France was a collie puppy he adopted. He named the dog Carey, after his hero Carey Orr at the *Chicago Tribune*. The pup slept at the foot of his bed every night. When he was off duty, he took Carey everywhere he went. The dog was also a good pupil, easily learning tricks and performing upon command. He even taught the dog to sit up and salute. Walt loved the dog, and they became constant companions.

By all appearances, it looked like Walt lived a charmed life in France; however, that would soon change. The downs were about to begin again for him. One day Russell got bad news that his mother was ill, and he decided to return home to Chicago. Russell told Walt he would take Carey back with him to Chicago and have him waiting for Walt upon his return from service. Now alone in France, without his family, best friend, and beloved dog, he finally decided it was time to go home. In a letter to his high school friends, he wrote, "Oh! I want to go home to my mama. I wanna go home. I do."[30] He soon got his wish. On September 3, 1919, Walt finally began his journey back home. Unfortunately, his return to Chicago was not a ticker tape parade. He found out Su had married another man three months before he arrived. When he heard of the news, he tore up her picture and threw it away and gave the gifts he'd bought for her to other girls he knew from high school. Sadly, the biggest tragedy was that Carey, his collie, had died of distemper while he was away. The loss haunted him for the rest of the time he lived in Chicago.

With the loss of romance and his faithful companion, he looked at work as the remedy to get his life on track. If he kept himself busy, he could bring stability back to his world. Elias was willing to help and offered him a job at the jelly factory, but Walt had different ambitions. He served his familial duty, putting in long hours for Elias in the past, and after serving his country, he decided to pursue his own dreams. Since drawing was his first love, he firmly decided he wanted to be an artist—or, more specifically, a cartoonist. He hoped that his idol Carey Orr at the *Tribune* would find him an opening at the paper. Unfortunately, there were no openings at the *Tribune*, but this didn't stop him from pursuing his dream. He wanted to be a cartoonist, and when Walt Disney made his mind up to do something, nothing would stand in the way of his going after it with all his heart. With no one else to turn to, he turned to the one person he could always depend on: his brother Roy. After World War I, Roy had taken back the job he had held at the Kansas City bank before the war. Walt decided he would go back there and find work in Missouri as a cartoonist.[31]

This decision proved to be a good choice. Cartooning, after all, was Walt's first love. It allowed him to employ his drawing skills and apply his comedy instincts to topics that interested him. As we will see in the following chapters, he enjoyed the process of putting his ideas on paper, and he especially took pleasure in making others laugh. Even more importantly, cartooning provided a cheap way for a poor kid to enter the entertainment world.

DISNEY LESSON 1: YOUR UNIQUE CIRCUMSTANCES PROVIDE UNIQUE OPPORTUNITIES FOR YOU

So, why did Walt honor his stern father on the window over Main Street, U.S.A.? We offer three reasons why Elias received this recognition. First, he exemplified an entrepreneurial spirit. True, Elias never struck it rich, but he was a seasoned risk-taker. He had owned and run a hotel, an orange grove, a construction business, a farm, a paper route, and a jelly factory with only moderate success, but like many small business owners, he put his family to work in the operations. As a result, Walt experienced firsthand the ups and downs of entrepreneurship at a young age. In our experience as entrepreneurship professors, we have found that students who grow up around a family business often go on to become very successful business owners themselves one day. In a sense, these students have already served an eighteen-year internship before they even step foot in our classes. Our main role when they come into our entrepreneurship program is to advise them to think bigger and more innovatively than their background may have allowed. Thinking big was never a problem for Walt Disney. Much of his success was due to his ability to bridge Elias's risk-taking ways with his own childhood dreams to create one of the most enduring and endearing companies in history.

Second, Elias ran his businesses with integrity. One way he did this was by always putting his customers first. While Elias never ran a business that brought in a lot of customers, he did try hard to satisfy the ones he did have. At a very young age, Walt learned that he was responsible for satisfying his customers on the paper routes. If the customer was unhappy, he would have to face Elias's wrath when he got home. Even as an adult, he would often wake up in the middle of the night in a cold sweat from nightmares about being late on a paper route or forgetting to deliver newspapers to customers. Walt was not alone. Elias held all his sons to these high standards. As a result, he was not their best friend when they were growing up, and their relationships were often strained. Raymond and Herbert ran away from the Disney household when Elias pushed them hard on the farm. Walt and Roy did the same when they got the chance too. Even still, the lesson was learned. If the customers weren't happy, they would go elsewhere. When Walt grew up to have his own company, he expected the same customer attention from his employees. This philosophy is still firmly adhered to by the company. Such ideas worked well in the twentieth century, and they continue to work well for the company in the twenty-first century.

In *How to Be Like Walt*, Pat Williams credits Elias's adherence to the Protestant ethic as the source of these standards. He states that "Elias possessed a number of good qualities that shaped Walt's life in a positive way. First, there was Elias Disney's Protestant integrity. He taught his children the importance of honesty and a good reputation. If Walt Disney had ever sullied his name with scandal, the trusted Walt Disney corporate identity would have become worthless. Second, there was Elias Disney's Protestant work ethic. Elias worked hard and usually earned a decent living for his family. When misfortune pushed him out of one business, he would start a new business, often in a different part of the country. Young Walter watched his father take risks and battle adversity, and he learned crucial lessons about hard work and persistence."[32]

Third, we think Walt recognized that had it not been for the journey Elias put his family through, he would not have gone on to accomplish what he did with Walt Disney Productions. Let's think about what that journey brought Walt. He experienced the good life in Marceline when he was a young boy. This part of his life provided the ideals and themes for his business projects. The Kansas City years built resilience in him to persevere through difficult times. The grit he harvested there would come in handy when he needed to overcome obstacles in his future entrepreneurial pursuits. We think people who grow up in difficult situations often go one of two ways: they either break from the strain, develop low self-esteem, and turn to destructive behavior to turn away from the pain they feel inside or they endure, build incredible resilience and grit, gain an indefatigable self-confidence, and go on to acquire in adulthood what they missed in their childhood. We think Walt was the second type of person.

Thus, the chief lesson Walt shows us is that within any obstacle is the opportunity to make ourselves better. Too many people stop short before learning the lessons difficult situations hold for them. That's unfortunate. In *The Last Lecture*, the late Carnegie Mellon professor and Imagineer Randy Pausch observed that "brick walls are there for a reason. They're not there to keep us out. The brick walls are there to give us a chance to show how badly we want something."[33] Disney faced plenty of brick walls, and he blasted through them all, chiefly because he had a very optimistic view of life. As his boyhood hero Carey Orr summed up his attitude: "You could tell that, unlike most cartoonists, he didn't really hate anybody. He had seen the carnage and stupidity of war in France, he had been betrayed by his girl, his best friend had let him down over his favorite dog, he was unhappy at home. But did this kid let his anger show in his attitude or his drawings? On the contrary, he was still the most amiable and forgiving of young men; there wasn't an ounce of bitterness or ill feeling in him, and his way of getting back at the world was to draw something that made you laugh."[34] We would all benefit from taking the same approach to life.

Going through tough times is never an enjoyable process, and yet weathering those moments can build one of the most powerful resources for an entrepreneur: grit. Angela Duckworth, the world's leading authority on the subject, says that grit is a blend of passion and perseverance. Those that have a firm commitment to what they're pursuing and endure the hardships along the way can outshine those with more natural talent in the long run. And here's the most powerful finding of her work: the more grit we build over time, the better we handle obstacles that come our way in the future.[35] Let's reflect on Walt's childhood again. Isn't it likely he developed a tremendous amount of grit working on the paper route as a child, living away from home overseas as a teenager in a military ambulance unit, and searching for artist jobs in Chicago? As we'll soon discover, he'll continue to build that grit capacity in his next living situation. It's a hard-earned resource, but as we'll see in later chapters, without it, it's not likely he would have achieved his great feats later in life.

The Return to Kansas City

Roy Disney looked out for his younger brother constantly. When Walt arrived in Kansas City, Roy helped him find his first cartooning job by connecting him with the Pesmen–Rubin Commercial Art Studio. After a short trial period, he was hired at fifty dollars a month. Much as newsrooms breed productive writers, an advertising firm expects its artists to work under deadlines every day. Pesmen-Rubin provided a good opportunity for him to advance his art skills while also working on projects that would be on display to the public. Walt diligently applied himself to his duties. In this pay-for-art environment, he learned about a variety of tools used for commercial art and produced drawings for a wide array of projects, ranging from farm catalogues to theater ads. He committed to keeping up with the more experienced illustrators in the firm, often taking only a short lunch break and drawing additional advertisements than were asked of him. However, like so many of Walt's ventures in his youth, the time at Pesmen-Rubin would be short-lived. After a particularly busy holiday season in which Walt worked on many Christmas sales advertisements, the firm let him go due to a slowdown in work. He was employed there only six weeks.

Fortunately, Kansas City thrived as a community in 1920. Opportunities proved plentiful for an industrious young person like Walt. Due to its centralized location and access to the Missouri River and train tracks, Kansas City maintained the second largest stockyard in the country, second only to Chicago. The massive livestock business put a lot of money in Kansas City, which spurred entrepreneurial activity and supported a modern cosmopolitan scene. The year 1920 was also the beginning of a boom time for the country. Although the end of World War I left an aftereffect of malaise in some quarters, overall the country was on the verge of transforming itself into a major global powerhouse. Modern chain stores, banks, movie theaters, and radio stations were springing up everywhere. If Pesmen-Rubin couldn't find commercial work for him, he thought he could arrange it on his own in this busy city.

Although he'd only been in the advertising world a short time, Walt felt he was fully capable of building a thriving business of his own. The stint at the advertising firm gave him some confidence that he could be a paid artist. He kept up with production demands, gained drafting and layout skills, and received confirmation from his bosses that his work was up to par. When Ubbe Iwwerks, another artist colleague of his from Pesmen-Rubin, visited him to commiserate about also being let go after the holidays, he saw an even bigger opportunity in front of him. Since they didn't have any job prospects at the moment, Walt and Ubbe decided to team up to form a new advertising firm called Iwwerks-Disney.[36] They believed that they could capitalize on each other's strengths. While Ubbe was an exceptional draftsman, he appeared very shy and socially backward. Walt, on the other hand, exuded enough personality for both of them. They decided that Walt would focus on lining up the clients and Ubbe would focus on the drawing. It was a good match, and in the first month they were already making more money than they had at Pesmen-Rubin.

As was the custom for Walt Disney, though, he always pursued the next best thing that came his way, and in a very short time he found another opportunity that piqued his interest. Another advertising firm called the Kansas City Slide

Co. was looking for an artist. The job required the new hire to draw simple animations for local movie theaters to play as warm-ups before their main shows were run. Although Iwwerks-Disney was off to a good start, the chance to work in a more entertaining medium had great appeal for Walt. Commercial art might bring in a nice income, but it wasn't the same as drawing funny pictures. After all, he desired to be a cartoonist, and the Kansas City Slide Co. afforded him the opportunity to get into the business. Iwwerks-Disney didn't immediately close shop. The duo decided that Ubbe would continue the operations of their nascent advertising firm while Walt pursued his dream of being a cartoonist during the day and pitched in at night on the commercial work when he could. However, with Walt out of the daily operations of the shop, it wasn't long before Iwwerks-Disney disintegrated. While Ubbe was a great draftsman, his awkward, quirky demeanor made him an awful salesman, so within only two months Iwwerks-Disney had to close its doors. Fortunately, Ubbe was able to get a job soon after at the Slide Co. as well.

DISNEY LESSON 2: BE HONEST WITH YOURSELF AND OTHERS ABOUT WHAT WORKS FOR YOU AND WHAT DOESN'T

Let's step back a moment and reflect on where Walt is now in his life. He's only nineteen years old. Already he has served overseas in an ambulance unit, and upon his return home he's quickly moved around from one city to another, trying to find work cartooning for newspapers. His first two stints in the advertising world lasted only a few months, he refuses to take a traditional job, and he's giving his artistic dream a third try in less than a year. With the exception of his older brother Roy, his family thinks he's delusional about his aspirations to be a famous cartoonist one day. What would be most people's state of mind given these circumstances? What type of decision would most people make if they were in Walt's shoes?

Our guess is most people would say they've given their dreams a good shot and the world is telling them that maybe they should do what everyone else expects them to do—but Walt Disney wasn't like most people. In fact, he relished the opportunity to give drawing another try and fully embraced his new job at the Kansas City Slide Co. As Disney biographer Neal Gabler observes:

> He had, in his short time at the Slide Co., begun redirecting his attention from commercial art and even from the dream of newspaper cartooning. . . .That was because Walt Disney, a young man who always seemed to be in the grip of some passion, had found a new

one: he had become intoxicated with animation as he had originally been with drawing back at the Benton School. "The trick of making things move on film is what got me," he would tell an interviewer years later.[37]

We often hear of artistic types being passionate about their work or, in Gabler's words, even intoxicated with their projects. For Walt Disney, once he was interested in something, he took it to almost addictive levels. His curiosity about animation drove him to think about it every minute he was awake. He worked hard at the Kansas City Slide Co. during the day, and in the evenings he experimented with animation techniques and cameras in a makeshift studio he set up in the garage behind the family house. Gabler describes Walt during this time as:

> Focused now on animation virtually to the exclusion of everything else. "Walt was a focused man from childhood," his niece, Dorothy, would say—he would repair to the garage after work each day, emerge for dinner, then return to his camera stand. "When he'd come home and long after everybody else was [in] bed," Roy remembered, "Walt was out there still, puttering away, working away, experimenting, trying this and that, drawing, and so on. He was just busy every second."[38]

While many people experience this type of enthusiasm for their interests when they're youngsters, Walt maintained this childlike approach to work throughout his whole life. What drove Walt to work so hard? Was he able to tap into an energy source that most people don't have access to? Perhaps. In an examination of America's wildly successful entrepreneurs since the Industrial Revolution, psychotherapist John Gardner claims that the fuel that drives these mavericks can be explained by a genetically based psychiatric disorder known as hypomania. Gardner states:

> Hypomania is a mild form of mania, often found in the relatives of manic depressives. Hypomanics are brimming with infectious energy, irrational confidence, and really big ideas. They think, talk, move, and make decisions quickly. Anyone who slows them down with questions "just doesn't get it." . . . Hypomanics live on the edge, between normal and abnormal.[39]

Let's look deeper at the hypomanic personality. It's possible Walt might have displayed some hypomanic traits given his incredible devotion to his work. Furthermore, he may have been the son of a manic depressive as well since Elias would often fluctuate between periods of risky business ventures and bouts of listless inactivity. As Gardner observes, people with hypomanic tendencies often are related to manic depressives. In a pilot study of internet entrepreneurs, Gardner wrote a list of hypomanic traits gathered from the psychiatric literature and asked them which of the following items described them well:

- He or she is filled with energy.
- He or she is flooded with ideas.
- He or she is driven, restless, and unable to keep still.
- He or she channels their energy into the achievement of wildly grand ambitions.
- He or she often works on little sleep.
- He or she feels brilliant, special, chosen, perhaps even destined to change the world.
- He or she can be euphoric.
- He or she becomes easily irritated by minor obstacles.
- He or she is a risk-taker.
- He or she overspends in both their business and personal life.
- He or she sometimes acts impulsively, with poor judgment, in ways that can have painful consequences.
- He or she is fast-talking.
- He or she is witty and gregarious.
- His or her confidence can make them charismatic and persuasive.
- He or she is prone to making enemies and feels that they are persecuted by those who do not accept their vision and mission.

Gardner was surprised by how enthusiastically the entrepreneurs said these characteristics described them, but he said he "shouldn't have been. As a psychotherapist, I am familiar with the way people become energized when they feel understood, especially when it helps them understand themselves better."[40] What about you? How well do you think the list describes you? If you find yourself agreeing with a lot of the items, you may have a psychological profile similar to Walt Disney's. You may exhibit many of the traits of the entrepreneurs Steve Jobs called "The Crazy Ones." Jobs extolled the great accomplishments of these types of entrepreneurs when he proclaimed:

> Here's to the crazy ones, the misfits, the rebels, troublemakers, the round pegs in the square holes . . . the ones who see things differently—they're not fond of rules . . . You can quote them, disagree with them, glorify or vilify them, but the only thing you can't do is

ignore them because they change things . . . They push the human race forward, and while some may see them as the crazy ones, we see genius, because the ones who are crazy enough to think they can change the world are the ones who do.[41]

Management scholar Ed Locke calls these crazy creators "Prime Movers," people "who move society forward by the force of their creative imagination, their own energy, and their own productive capacity."[42] But is there really something different about these "forces of nature"? Is there such a thing as an entrepreneurial personality? Are entrepreneurs born or made? It's a hotly debated subject in the field of entrepreneurship. Entrepreneurship scholar Norris Krueger states that, based on research from psychologists, sociologists, and human development theorists, "entrepreneurs like other experts are definitely made, not born."[43] While other scholars, such as Scott Shane, James Fisher, and James Koch, believe that behavioral genetics provides large-sample statistical evidence that entrepreneurial qualities are inherited,[44] it's likely that entrepreneurs are both born and made. As Locke notes, "There are, of course, degrees of any human trait. A small shopkeeper is a Mover—a creator of wealth—on a small scale. I focus on those who created on a large scale. . . . I reserve the term Prime Mover for them."[45] Consequently, a lot of people with the proper training and experience could open a business, but it's likely that the legendary entrepreneurs like Walt Disney are wired to pursue their ideas with more energy and obsession.

As Roy Disney described his little brother, "That was Walt all the time, driving himself frantic, day and night."[46] However, while this manic energy that is quite common among visionaries can drive projects forward, it can also strain relationships and create stress among those who are fulfilling the tasks and tactics of the visionary. Entrepreneurs like Walt Disney and Steve Jobs can be simultaneously mercurial and creative while bringing their visions from inside their heads into the world. Unfortunately for the ultra-committed entrepreneur, not everyone can keep up with their speed of thought or insistence on action. Notwithstanding, a hard-driving leader who has a team that can endure and raise their efforts to meet the project's goals can make extraordinary achievements. Creative tension, when channeled in one direction, can push people to achieve more than they think they are capable of accomplishing.

However, for the person with the hypomanic disposition, it's often hard for them to take orders from others. If left to their own way of accomplishing goals, they thrive. Meanwhile, as long as their team agrees to the same outcome, good results can happen. But, if a leader with hypomanic traits is challenged in ways they feel slow their projects down, problems are likely to arise in the organization. As Walt often told anyone who challenged his way of doing things, the name on the company was Disney. If someone wanted their own name recognized, he told them to start their own studio. For this reason, many Disney biographers think Walt was attracted to animation because he could control the production more. There were no movie stars to cajole into performances or elaborate sets to build. Entire worlds could be created on celluloid sheets (also known as "cels") by the animator's own hands.

Thus, if you're an ambitious, hardworking, aspiring entrepreneur who wants to change the world, there's much to learn from how Walt lived his life. Indeed, it's probably why Steve Jobs considered him a hero and role model for his entrepreneurial career. If you're driven to create great new products and services your way, you may have to strike out on your own with your own handpicked team. Or if you're inside a bigger company, you may require autonomy to fulfill your goals. This is a tradeoff for being innovative. You may create something great for the world, but some of your relationships may not last in the process. The hypomanic leader needs people who will work on the stated mission. Yet, for those who are on board with your mission for the whole journey, they may look back at that time with you as one of the most fulfilling periods of their lives. Indeed, as we'll see in the next chapter, while he didn't have a lot of friends outside the studio, Walt's inner circle remained true to him throughout his whole life.

Laugh-O-Grams

The year 1920 was a good one for a young person entering the animation field. Movie theaters were popular throughout the country, but animation was still in its primitive stages. For the most part, cartoons were considered a novelty at the time. The techniques and skills needed to be proficient in the field could be met within a fairly short amount of time. Working at his desk at the Kansas City Slide Co., Walt was able to work on all aspects of the production, from story concept to drawing to filming. However, the job didn't satiate Walt's appetite for animation. In his free time, he immersed himself further in the field by reading any book he could find on animation, drawing, and movement. He went to theaters regularly to watch others' animations, attended the Kansas City Art Institute in the evenings, and worked on side projects whenever he could wrangle extra film materials. Anything connected to animation was of interest to Walt during this time.

The pioneering stage of the industry also appealed to Walt. He deeply believed if he continued to work hard on animation he could one day end up at the top of his field. The competition seemed pretty slim in the early days of animation, and Walt could stand out in the field at a very young age. The dawn of a new industry emerged, and only a handful of people saw animation as a serious artistic medium or potential moneymaker. Another factor in his devotion to animation revolved around the studios providing him a social outlet. During this time, Walt's extended family started moving one by one out of Kansas City to different parts of the country. The most impactful absence to Walt was his brother Roy's move to various veterans hospitals to recuperate from tuberculosis, eventually settling in Los Angeles. With his biological family gone, his fellow animators became his source of companionship.

In 1921, the Kansas City Slide Co. changed its name to the Kansas City Film Ad Co. to reflect its focus on movie theater advertising. It had good reason. Movies were becoming big business in Kansas City and the rest of the country. Theaters were springing up all over town, and the locals were in love with the movie experience. The movie experience in 1921 was much different from the one in today's cineplexes. Walt kept his eye on one theater in particular: the Newman Theater. The Newman Theater was a work of art in itself. It had seventy-five-foot ceilings, was designed in Italian Renaissance style with terrazzo and white marble, and could seat a thousand movie goers.[47] If a Walt Disney cartoon could make its way into the Newman, he would have a big audience for his work. Walt approached his boss at the Film Ad Co. about using the latest cel animation techniques to create a short for the Newman, but they declined.[48] Undaunted, he created a one-minute cartoon reel on his own after work and showed it to the Newman's general manager. After viewing it the manager agreed it was quite good and promised to show it. He was only paid enough to cover his costs of production, but on March 20, 1921, the Newman ran the short film. Walt Disney was officially making cartoons under his own name. He called the shorts the "Newman Laugh-O-Grams." Since he still had his day job, he made the Laugh-O-Grams sporadically as best he could, but when the films did air the audiences liked them. The name "Walt Disney" was beginning to get recognized around town.

True to what we've seen already about Walt, once he took advantage of an opportunity, he very quickly started looking for the next one. Seeing his own name on the big screen was exhilarating. After only two years working for someone else, Walt was ready to quit the Film Ad Co. and make his own movies full-time. With his reputation for creating the Newman shorts, his experimental films, his enduring salesmanship, and his training at the Film Ad Co., he launched Laugh-O-Gram Films, Inc., on May 18, 1922, with $15,000 from local investors. The ambitious twenty-year-old was looking to make nationally distributed cartoons that would compete against the New York City studios. He very quickly put the resources in place to make it happen. He hired a few of his friends who had been working with him on his earlier experimental pictures in the garage. He also recruited a few people through want ads he placed for his studio. When production was ready to ramp up he had five animators, an "ink girl," a scenario editor, a business manager, and a salesman ready to go. The operation ran out of a two-room suite, housing inkers and tracers' tables, a superintendent's desk, animating booths, a still camera, a movie camera and stand, lighting equipment, and a copying stand.[49] Although it was a lot of people and equipment to cram into two rooms, Walt had everything he needed to make theater quality cartoons. Now he just needed to obtain a contract to keep his company busy and pay his studio's bills. This situation wound up being more challenging than he expected. Animated films in 1922 were not the major attractions they are today. For the most part, cartoons were just considered warm-up acts for the movie being shown that night.

There was not the huge demand for them there is today. Audiences liked the cartoons, but they weren't considered essential to the typical two-hour program. Walt placed advertisements in the movie trade magazines, hoping to line up a distributor, but he didn't receive any interest. Out of desperation, he sent Leslie Mace, his sales manager, to New York City to see if he could make a deal with a distributor face-to-face. Unfortunately, the major distributors weren't interested, but right before leaving town, Mace secured a six-cartoon deal with Pictorial Clubs, Inc., a very minor player in the industry. The terms of the contract weren't great ($11,100 for the six animations, with $100 up front and the remaining $11,000 paid upon delivery of the final product), but it was the best deal Disney could get. Perhaps the best outcome of the deal was that with a contract in place, Walt was able to entice his very talented friend Ubbe to leave the Kansas City Film Ad Co. to take part in the venture.

Now it was "go" time. With a deal in hand and little money to work with, the team worked feverishly to deliver the films. Since Walt wouldn't get paid until the pictures were completed, he had to get as much production as he could out of his team with the small up-front investment he had to work with. Further complicating the challenge was the fact that everyone on the team was young and learning as they went. For the most part, that was okay. They were excited about making a film for the rest of the world to see. Rudy Ising recalls that period as a charming time, where fun was mixed in with the pressure of the deadline: "Those early days were really something. We were in Kansas City and everything was done in Hollywood or in New York, where pictures were concerned. But we were learning so damn much at that time. So in a way, it was a lot of fun."[50]

Yet, as much fun as the team may have had making the films, Walt was feeling the pressure of running the studio. He was involved in every aspect of the operation; however, while he excelled on the creative front, handling the business side of the enterprise was a struggle. But Walt Disney wouldn't give up. He kept looking for further sources of financing around town and picked up little side projects whenever he could. Unfortunately, Walt's bootstrapping wouldn't be enough because just a few months after making the six-film deal, Pictorial

Clubs declared bankruptcy. With no revenue, Walt couldn't continue to pay his employees, so everyone quit on him. Still, Walt refused to give up. He took some of his earlier experimental work and sent it to New York, and while it was well received for its quality, no one would sign a deal with him. In one last act of desperation, he sent another letter to distributors in New York, declaring that he had discovered a new type of animation in which a live person interacts with cartoon characters in an animated world. This innovative idea did catch the attention of Margaret Winkler, a New York distributor, who said if the film was good, she would consider purchasing it.

With the possibility of saving the studio in mind, Walt went to work making *Alice's Wonderland*, which was to be an animated film where a real little girl lived in a cartoon world. No one had ever made a film like this before. He convinced a local family to let him film their talented and cute four-year-old daughter for the animated short and offered them 5 percent of the gross profit. He immediately went to work on the film, but his production faced an onslaught of obstacles. Without any income, he was eventually evicted from the two-room office setup he had; however, he was able to move down the street into a little office above the Isis Theater. His personal living arrangements were even worse. He had to endure one temporary housing arrangement after another until he was finally living full-time out of the tiny office. He was living day to day, sometimes only able to eat a can of beans for dinner. Still, he kept working on his film, and except for a little help from one of his friends, he filmed the live action sequences in the day, drew the animation at night, and spliced the live action and drawings together on the reel when he found extra time. Finally, though, the strain became too much for him. No matter how hard he worked, he couldn't complete the film on his own. With no money and no options, he finally succumbed and filed for bankruptcy.

After his best efforts in Kansas City failed, he decided if he wanted to make it in the movie business, he would need to pull up stakes and move to where the successful studios were. That meant New York or Hollywood. Since his brother Roy had moved to Los Angeles and he had an uncle who lived there as well, Walt chose Hollywood. Yet again, he had to scrap and hustle to figure out how to make his next move happen. All he had left was a movie camera and his salesmanship. He approached Carl Stallings, a friend who played organ at the Isis, and asked if he could do anything for him. Stallings offered him a little side work making song reels for the theater. Then, Walt looked for a little more money by going door to door through Kansas City, offering to make films of people's children. He found a few takers, and after he completed the jobs, he had enough money to leave town. He sold his camera and then bought a one-way ticket to Hollywood. And, in August 1923, Walt Disney arrived in California with a cardboard suitcase and forty dollars in his pocket, ready for his next adventure in the entertainment industry.

DISNEY LESSON 3: LEARNING TOUGH LESSONS OUTSIDE THE SPOTLIGHT PREPARES YOU FOR THE DAY WHEN YOU'RE IN IT

We often hear about the starving artist who's so dedicated to their work that they're willing to sacrifice their own financial well-being to pursue it. An artist takes great pride in learning their craft and then using their skills as a tool for expressing themselves. They feel compelled to take the pictures in their head and bring them into physical form in the external world. For some this is in visual form, for others it's verbal, and for some it's physical expression. Walt Disney fit this stereotype well during the first twenty-two years of his life. Animation provided him a way to express his ideas in all three forms. From an early age, he found his passion in drawing, and he continued that interest wherever he went, whether it was in the big city of Chicago, the small rural town of Marceline, Missouri, or the battle-scarred fields of post-World War I France. Indeed, his time in Kansas City provided him an apprenticeship in animation, the field he would one day conquer. Walt's drawing skills were good but not great. However, animation includes more skills than drawing alone. Animation also requires character development, storytelling, gag writing, inking, and photography. His timing in entering the field at a young age was of huge benefit to his career. The field was in its infancy when Walt was trained at Pesmen-Rubin and the Kansas City Slide Co., so he could work in all areas of a production. Theaters only needed two-minute animated films to entertain audiences before the main attractions played. A seven-minute animated short was even considered a major production in those days. So, the learning curve in the industry was fairly short. The equivalent situation in animation today would require a young person to create a ninety-minute computer generated film—clearly an impossible task for anyone. However, much like Steve Jobs and Bill Gates's entrance into the personal computer industry in the 1970s, animation in the early 1920s was very much in its tinkering stage. As Friz Freleng, one of his colleagues from the Film Ad Co. and an animator in his later company, said about the field at the time, "The art of animation was just something that you figured wasn't even going to last. I mean, they were just movement. The trick in the early days was just to make 'em move, make 'em run, make 'em turn around, make 'em talk to each other, in pantomime, of course. But you didn't distinguish one from another, they all did it the same."[51] It was clear that Walt loved animation. It gave him a vehicle to channel his creative energies, and he loved the chance to create his own world on film.

Walt paid his dues in Kansas City. That setting made the perfect classroom for him before making it big in Hollywood. He worked under the deadlines of the advertising firms, experimented on his own productions in the evening, and later built his own company. All these experiences provided him deep immersion in the field. By the time Walt left Kansas City, he was an expert on the entire animation process. He applied himself diligently to learning all aspects of the field in whatever way he could through apprenticeships, jobs, contract assignments, art classes, movie screenings, books, and experiments in the family garage. Research by Anders Ericsson, the leading authority on deliberate practice, would suggest that Walt was building his expertise on animation in Kansas City. This knowledge base would provide him the credibility for guiding others on projects he would later supervise in Hollywood. He knew what went into good animation because he was an experienced animator himself.

With regard to animation, Walt experienced the full range of this artistic medium. He enjoyed coming up with the story and acting out for his fellow animators what the characters would do in the film. Even though he wasn't a great drawer, he invested enough time in the practice to know what constituted good pictures. Thus, he could lead better artists in crafting the animation work. Therefore, it's safe to say Walt's best skill was as a *producer* of animated productions. While other individuals might excel at the specific skills of animation, Walt Disney would set himself apart as having the most expertise in bringing all those parts together into a better whole. From a young age, he managed entire animation projects, from story concept to the finishing touches. A "Walt Disney" production had Walt Disney's eye on every second of it.

Ericsson informs us that while natural talent can steer us toward our interests, it's the dedicated application of effort to those interests that ultimately determines success. Ericsson explains:

> Perhaps, for example, some children are born with a suite of genes that cause them to get more pleasure from drawing or from making music. Then those children will be more likely to draw or to make music than other children. If they're put in art classes or music classes, they're likely to spend more time practicing because it is more fun for them. They carry their sketchpads or guitars with them wherever they go. And over time these children will become better artists or better musicians than their peers—not because they are innately more talented in the sense that they have some genes for musical or artistic ability, but because something—perhaps genetic—pushed them to practice and thus develop their skills to a greater degree than their peers.[52]

Walt was probably the youngest producer of animated films in the world when he was leading his Laugh-O-Gram team; yet, he expected more out of his productions than his older bosses at the Kansas City Film Ad Co. asked of him. As we will see in upcoming chapters, he will maintain this artistic sensibility in craftsmanship, quality, and expression throughout all his future productions as well. Walt Disney always expected his employees to have the same commitment to their art that he did, and in turn, they will produce film classics that are still loved today. But he will not rely solely on pen and paint to do this work. To create these classics, Walt will experiment with new technologies and processes to take animated storytelling to new heights. It's as if he's acting like a scientist, making new discoveries and revolutionizing the way cartoons are created. The next chapter will demonstrate how Walt Disney used the studio as his own laboratory for inventing new forms of entertainment.

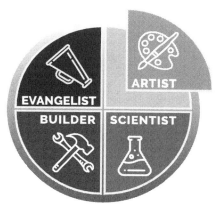

- Value creativity
- Love ideas
- Search for new solutions
- Empathize with and respect the customer
- Value the human condition
- Appreciate the subtleties of their craft
- Hard to predict

WALT DISNEY THE ARTIST

Learned craft of drawing and animation
- Chicago Academy of Fine Arts classes
- Cartoon drawings for troops in France
- Pesmen-Rubin Commercial Art Studio
- Kansas City Slide Co.
- Laugh-O-Grams

Skill development in animation
- Storytelling
- Acting through cartoon characters
- Drawing and editing animation for cartoons
- Directing cartoons
- Bootstrapping and fundraising for early startups
- Distribution of cartoons to market

Suffered for his art
- Financial and employee struggles making Laugh-O-Grams
- Living at boarding homes and office
- Bankruptcy in Kansas City

FIGURE 1.1 Entrepreneurial Leadership Style—Artist

Disney Principles

- Happy accidents happen more when you move around. Serendipity is the result of taking initiative and being mindful of the opportunities that arise.
- Enduring and overcoming difficult circumstances build grit and perseverance. These qualities help you to overcome the obstacles and challenges you face on your path to success.
- Follow your bliss. If you enjoy something, you will invest your energy and resources in it. With time, you will become good at it, which will bring rewards and satisfaction. Have patience that this will happen.
- Successful people are usually seen as a little crazy by people who know them well. That's okay. They are crazy by most people's standards, but by fully immersing themselves in their favorite pursuits they create treasures for others to enjoy.
- If you want to be a leading authority in your field, you'll need to pay your dues. If it's a new field, you may be able to reach expert level in just a few years like Walt did, but if the industry has a long tradition, you may need to dedicate many years to reach the top level of performance.

Work Like Disney: Exercises

1. If you had the opportunity to immortalize somebody on a window in Disneyland, who would it be? Why?
2. If you had a window on Main Street, U.S.A., what would it say?
3. How is your childhood similar or dissimilar to Walt Disney's?
4. If you had been born in Walt's circumstances, do you think you would have responded the same way? Why or why not?
5. Artists suffer for their art. Are you willing to pay your dues to learn your craft? What price are you willing to pay to get your foot in the door in an industry?

Notes

1. Williams, P., and Denney, J. (2004). *How to Be Like Walt: Capturing the Disney Magic Everyday of Your Life*. Deerfield Beach: Hearth Communications.
2. Evans, H., Buckland, G., and Lefer, D. (2004). *They Made America: From the Steam Engine to the Search Engine: Two Centuries of Innovators*. New York: Little, Brown and Company.
3. Thomas, B. (1974). *Walt Disney: An American Original*. New York: Disney Editions.
4. Gladwell, M. (2008). *Outliers: The Story of Success*. New York: Little, Brown and Company.
5. Gabler, N. (2006). *Walt Disney: The Triumph of the American Imagination*. New York: Vintage.
6. Ibid.
7. It was also known as the Chicago World's Fair-or sometimes, more simply, the Chicago Fair.

8. Timeline: Early Chicago History. (2003). *Chicago: City of the Century*. Boston: WGBH Educational Foundation and Window to the World Communications.
9. Greenhalgh, P. (1988). *Ephemeral Vistas: The Expositions Universeiles, Great Exhibitions, and World's Fairs, 19851–1939*. Manchester: Manchester University Press.
10. Wright, F.L. (1912). "Daniel Hudson Burnham, An Appreciation." *Architectural Record*, 32: 184.
11. Goodman, P., and Goodman, P. (1947). *Communitas: Means of Livelihood and Ways of Life*. New York: Vintage.
12. Davidson, B. (1964). "The Fantastic Walt Disney." *Saturday Evening Post*, 237(38): 67.
13. Ghez, D. (2008). *Walt's People*, Volume 6. Bloomington, IN: Xlibris.
14. Steiner, M. (2001). "Parables of Stone and Steel: Architectural Images of Progress and Nostalgia at the Columbian Exposition and Disneyland." *American Studies*, 42(1): 44–45.
15. Kent, G. (1938). "Snow White's Daddy." *The Family Circle*, 12(25): 11.
16. Ghez, D. (2008). *Walt's People*, Volume 6. Bloomington, IN: Xlibris.
17. Thomas, B. (1974). *Walt Disney: An American Original*. New York: Disney Editions.
18. Dweck, C. (2006). *Mindset: The New Psychology of Success*. New York: Random House.
19. Ghez, D. (2009). *Walt's People*, Volume 8. Bloomington, IN: Xlibris.
20. Ibid.
21. Mosley, L. (1985). *Disney's World*. New York: Stein and Day.
22. Ghez, D. (2009). *Walt's People*, Volume 8. Bloomington, IN: Xlibris.
23. Many years later, a mutual friend of Charlie Chaplin's introduced Walt to his hero. They remained good friends for the rest of Chaplin's life.
24. Burnes, B., Butler, R.W., and Viets, D. (2002). *Walt Disney's Missouri: The Roots of a Creative Genius*. Kansas City: Kansas City Stars Books.
25. Ghez, D. (2008). *Walt's People*, Volume 7. Bloomington, IN: Xlibris.
26. His drawings appear to be taken from the cartoons by Kin Hubbard, an *Indianapolis News* illustrator, who characterized Midwestern values through his character Abe Martin. Abe Martin was a likeable country guy who delivered homespun quips about life and America. Will Rogers was a fan of Hubbard's and called him "America's greatest humorist."
27. Ghez, D. (2009). *Walt's People*, Volume 8. Bloomington, IN: Xlibris.
28. Ford, B. (1989). *Walt Disney: A Biography*. New York: Walker and Company.
29. Mosley, L. (1985). *Disney's World*. New York: Stein and Day.
30. Burnes, B., Butler, R.W., and Viets, D. (2002). *Walt Disney's Missouri: The Roots of a Creative Genius*. Kansas City: Kansas City Stars Books.
31. Ford, B. (1989). *Walt Disney: A Biography*. New York: Walker and Company.
32. Williams, P., and Denney, J. (2004). *How to Be Like Walt: Capturing the Disney Magic Everyday of Your Life*. Deerfield Beach: Hearth Communications.
33. Pausch, R. (2008). *The Last Lecture*. Chatham: Mackays.
34. Mosley, L. (1985). *Disney's World*. New York: Stein and Day.
35. Duckworth, A. (2016). *Grit: The Power of Passion and Perseverance*. New York: Scribener.
36. Legend has it that they decided on this name because Disney-Iwwerks sounded like an eye doctor's office.
37. Gabler, N. (2006). *Walt Disney: The Triumph of the American Imagination*. New York: Vintage.
38. Ibid.
39. Gardner, J. (2005). *The Hypomanic Edge: The Link Between (A Little) Craziness and (A Lot of) Success*. New York: Simon & Schuster.
40. Ibid.

41. Isaacson, W. (2011). *Steve Jobs*. New York: Simon & Schuster.

42. Locke, E.A. (2000). *The Prime Movers: Traits of the Great Wealth Creators*. New York: AMACOM.

43. Fisher, J.L., and Koch, J.V. (2008). *Born, Not Made: The Entrepreneurial Personality*. Westport: Praeger.

44. Shane, S. (2010). *Born Entrepreneurs, Born Leaders: How Your Genes Affect Your Work Life*. New York: Oxford University Press.

45. Locke further reserves the term for anyone who grows a business into a major enterprise; thus, people working inside an organization who innovate and behave as corporate entrepreneurs can be Prime Movers as well. Therefore, you don't have to be a founder of the company to be considered an entrepreneur or a Prime Mover. One could argue that Steve Jobs played both roles at Apple during his time with the company. In his younger years, he was the founder of the company, but in his second run there he was hired from the outside to become a corporate entrepreneur and take it to new heights. In many ways, the Apple company he hired into in 1997 was a totally different company from the one he left in 1985.

46. Thomas, B. (1998). *Building a Company: Roy O. Disney and the Building of an Entertainment Empire*. New York: Disney Editions.

47. Burnes, B., Butler, R.W., and Viets, D. (2002). *Walt Disney's Missouri: The Roots of a Creative Genius*. Kansas City: Kansas City Stars Books.

48. The Kansas City Slide Co. preferred to use primitive drawing techniques where figures with moveable parts were filmed in stop animation style. However, the process of drawing the figures repeatedly on celluloid sheets and then photographing them one by one produced a richer and more artistic film short. It was a much slower process to create though, so the company Walt worked for preferred the more efficient production technique of re-using the poseable figures for the films.

49. Thomas, B. (1998). *Building a Company: Roy O. Disney and the Building of an Entertainment Empire*. New York: Disney Editions.

50. Ghez, D. (2005). *Walt's People,* Volume 1. Bloomington, IN: Xlibris.

51. Ghez, D. (2008). *Walt's People,* Volume 2. Bloomington, IN: Xlibris.

52. Ericsson, A., and Pool, R. (2016). *Peak: Secrets From the New Science of Expertise*. Boston: Houghton Mifflin Harcourt.

2

THE SCIENTIST YEARS

I'm just very curious—got to find out what makes things tick—and I've always liked working with my hands; my father was a carpenter. I even apprenticed to my own machine shop here and learned the trade. Since my outlook and attitude are ingrained throughout our organization, all our people have this curiosity; it keeps us moving forward, exploring, experimenting, opening new doors.

—Walt Disney[1]

Disney's California Adventure

The first chapter of this book opened with an exercise looking at the windows of Main Street, U.S.A., in Disneyland to better understand Walt Disney's youth. Walt's early years in Missouri instilled in him his values, provided an apprenticeship in animation, and supported his first entrepreneurial experience. However, the achievements we know Walt Disney by today happened in California. Therefore, if you took our Disneyland challenge, it's worth your time to take another day to venture to its sister park right next door. Disney California Adventure is a theme park that pays homage to Walt's earliest days in Hollywood. Buena Vista Street sits on the other side of the gate entrance and recreates the grandeur of Tinseltown in the 1920s with replicas of landmarks Walt would have seen when he moved there. Disney Imagineers designed the entrance to capture the excitement Walt would have felt arriving in California with only a suitcase, forty dollars in his pocket, and his dreams. After his struggles in Kansas City, Hollywood offered Walt a fresh start in a place more suited to his ambitions and temperament. Now Walt was putting himself in a much better place for potentially making his dreams a reality. Success is often a matter of being the right person doing the right thing in the right place at the right time. If any of these elements is missing, success will be much harder to attain. Kansas City wasn't the right place for being in the movie business, but California was. As Disney biographer Neil Gabler explains:[2]

> Walt Disney was made for Hollywood. He loved dress-up and make-believe, was boisterous, outgoing, self-aggrandizing, and histrionic, and craved attention. Hollywood was his spiritual destination. Even for the general public, roughly forty million of who, or one-third of the country's population, attended the movies each week in the early 1920s, Hollywood was more than a provider of entertainment. It was the capital of the imagination, the symbolic center of release and recklessness.

As we'll see in this chapter, Walt's early years in California were an extension of what he learned in Kansas City. His return to Missouri afforded him a safe and supportive place to learn the craft of animation among family and friends; however, the latter years in Kansas City turned him quite literally into a "starving artist." He sacrificed everything for his art, committing all his money, social capital, and energy to his animation enterprise. But in the end, he was left hungry, homeless, and alone.

So were the artist years a wasted time of his life? Would he have been better off going straight into the animation business in Hollywood after returning from France? Probably not. Walt was able to learn his craft and make rookie mistakes out of the limelight of Hollywood. Had he made the same mistakes in Hollywood, he may not have had the same legendary career. Although the business community in Kansas City may have seen him as a failure in his last days there, he was just a regular "nobody" in California. Or more appropriately, he wasn't a "somebody" yet because Hollywood was a clean slate where he could apply what he learned in Kansas City. As we'll see throughout this chapter, Kansas City afforded him an apprenticeship in the *art* of animation, but Hollywood is where he creates a new *science* of animation. The technical breakthroughs he makes will transform cartoons from being entertainment novelties to being serious works of filmmaking. However, before we learn about the inventions, technologies, and processes that made this shift possible, let's look closer at his first year in Hollywood.

Family Reunion

When Walt arrived in Hollywood in July 1923, he set his sights high. After moving in with his Uncle Robert, who happened to live in Hollywood at 4406 Kingswell Avenue, he pondered how he would break into the movies. But the studios weren't going to come to him, so early one morning he took a bus to Universal City Studios to look around. A press card from his Kansas

City newsreel days gained him admittance into the studio, where he could wander the movie lots late into the night. Over the next two months he also hung out in the Vitagraph, Paramount, and Metro studios, burning in his mind a template of what a successful movie operation looked like. Walt applied for jobs with the movie studios, but nothing materialized for him. However, he learned a lot about the movie business talking to producers, distributors, crewmen, and actors.[3] It was as if he were taking a self-taught course on motion pictures. Call it Walt 101.

Eventually, though, he became frustrated just hanging out on the studio lots. He wanted to get in on the action, so he fell back on his experience as an animator to see if that would open any doors. He shopped around the *Alice's Wonderland* reel he had started in Kansas City, but no one in California was interested in it. He then sent letters across the country to every distributor he could think of. Still, Walt's mailbox remained empty of offers. Then one day, just as in Kansas City, the New York distributor Margaret Winkler responded. She was in need of a new cartoon series and was willing to consider working with Walt again. Walt sent her what he had completed on the short, and on October 15, Winkler wired that she wanted twelve Alice comedy films. She promised to pay $1,500 upon receipt of each of the first six film negatives and $1,800 for each of the next six.

Walt was back in the movie business again. He no longer had to wander movie studios looking for work. Now he had a job to do delivering on the new contract, and he had to start on it fast. Per the contract, the first film was due in a couple months. But where should he start? Making films would require money, people, and a location to work. As in the past, Walt turned to the one person who was always there for him when he needed help: his big brother Roy. As it turned out, Roy was in a veterans hospital in Los Angeles, convalescing from tuberculosis. Walt ran to the hospital, shared the good news, and asked him for startup capital for a new production company. Roy was a bit apprehensive about being in the movie business, but he wanted to support his little brother. He promised Walt some money for the venture, and since he wasn't working anywhere, he offered to help with the business side of the enterprise too. Next, the brothers approached their wealthy, but conservative, Uncle Robert for startup funds. Robert wasn't excited about giving Walt funds for the venture, but he trusted Roy and relented. Now Walt was set to make movies again.

Back in the Game

With a contract in place with Margaret Winkler, the Disney brothers were ready to go; however, before they could start filming, they had to meet a stipulation in the contract. Winkler had been so happy about the performance of Virginia Davis in the demo reel that she wanted her to play Alice in the Hollywood films as well. Luck would once again shine through for Walt. It so happened that the Davis family was already thinking about moving to California so that Virginia could be in Hollywood movies one day. Since her father was a traveling salesman, the family could live anywhere. They saw the *Alice's Wonderland* series as a good segue into Hollywood and agreed to Walt's offer. With the money Walt and Roy had secured from Uncle Robert and a handful of other friends and family, they were able to set up a makeshift studio in the tiny office of a real estate business at 4651 Kingswell Avenue. They also rented an empty lot down the street to film movie scenes. After purchasing a new camera and equipment, they had everything they needed to start working on the film. Hollywood now had a new company in town: Disney Brothers Studio.

Disney Brothers was an appropriate name for the company in its earliest days of production. A typical day's work included Walt directing Virginia on how to act out a scene while Roy manned the camera. After filming the live action, Walt would draw the cartoon component of the film, splice the drawings into Virginia's scenes, and edit the film for release. Roy applied his banking experience to managing the business side of the little studio, something Walt didn't have in Kansas City. Although the operation was running smoother than the one in Kansas City, there was still a long way to go before Disney Brothers would be a respected production company. Case in point, Winkler was not always pleased with the quality of the productions, and Walt admitted to her that he was still learning how to deliver the films in the manner they both wanted. Still, the films were good enough to be released to the public, and Winkler honored the terms of the contract.

Walt did virtually all the animation on the first six pictures. The pace of meeting the production schedule alone was exhausting for him. However, the hard work paid off for him in steady revenue, giving Roy the confidence to allow Walt to hire three women to assist with the ink and paint duties of the animation and Rollin "Ham" Hamilton to help with the drawing. The increased manpower and division of labor inside the tiny studio improved the quality and speed of the production. And more importantly, Walt had proven that the Disneys could make films suited for a national audience. Pleased with their performance, Winkler requested that the delivery of the films go from one per month to two, instantly doubling the studio's revenue. Now Walt needed to up the studio's game even more. He turned to another important person from his Kansas City days: his old friend Ubbe Iwwerks. Walt and Ubbe had tried to make a go of it in Kansas City a couple years before, but they didn't have Roy working in the business then. Ubbe agreed to move to Hollywood to join Walt again, but he wasn't exactly the same person Walt once knew in Kansas City. For one thing, he shortened his name from Ubbe Iwwerks to Ub Iwerks, and, more importantly, he was a much more skilled animator than when Walt knew him the first time around. Ub had been a very busy animator in Kansas City. Although they started out together as nascent animators at the Pesmen-Rubin Art Studio in 1919, Ub was clearly a better draftsman than Walt now. Working on a lot of different projects over the last few years had greatly enhanced the pace and range of animation Ub could do. In Hollywood, Walt had the benefit of Roy handling the finances and Ub leading the animation team.

With Ub on board, the Disney films could now be more inventive and exciting, with each partner applying their strengths to the production. Ub had the ability to create situations and action that Walt couldn't animate on his own. And with Ub handling the chief animation duties, Walt could spend more time dreaming up funnier scenes and gags for the team to illustrate. The division of labor between Ub and Walt immensely improved the productions, further pleasing Winkler and her audiences. The blend of Walt's story writing, gag creation, and film direction with Ub's artistic craftsmanship led to a unique cartoon on the market. Additionally, no other cartoons had a real person performing in a cartoon environment like the Disney productions had in their Alice comedies.

With the art duties covered by Ub, Ham, and the women in ink and paint, Walt was now afforded the opportunity to upgrade the technology side of the productions. Walt and Ub invented new methods to make Alice's interactions with the cartoon characters more seamless. They tinkered with camera techniques that no one in the industry was utilizing, like using a matte that covered the edge of the camera lens to make it an easier medium for Ub to draw over.

As would often happen when Walt was finally hitting his stride, an unexpected setback would occur. In the case of the Alice comedy series, the setback was an unfortunate turn of events in the business arrangement he had with Winkler. Walt's excellent relationship with Winkler suddenly changed when she married an overbearing and manipulative man named Charles Mintz. The distribution of the Disney cartoons would now be in the hands of Mintz who also decided to take a more active role in the production side of the films. Mintz was a micromanager—a personality type that never fit well with Walt—and was very critical of the productions. He even sent Winkler's brother George to the studio to supervise and report back on the daily work of Walt and the animators. To make matters worse, Mintz began holding back full payment for the films, claiming that the cartoons were not profitable enough. Even with tightened budgets and the loss of studio autonomy, Walt didn't deviate from pushing everyone to meet their deadlines and bring more quality to the films.

The struggle to survive and meet payroll created a stressful atmosphere in the studio. It was like a replay of Kansas City all over again. But Walt pushed on, and when the sixteen-film agreement with Winkler was met, Mintz rewarded him with a better picture deal for eighteen more Alice comedies. It appeared the studio had weathered the storm and could up its game once again. With a little more capital in the company coffers, Walt promptly recruited and hired Hugh Harman and Rudy Ising, two former employees from his Laugh-O-Gram days in Kansas City, to the animation team. Instead of retaining the earnings like Roy would, Walt's mental default was to channel any money he could find back into his movies. Money was a reward that could be used on his next big idea. Given the option of saving cash for the future or investing in new technology and animators, Walt would always choose to put it toward expanding the studio's operations—much to the dismay of Roy. As Walt once said about his financial acumen:[4]

> Money is something I understand only vaguely, and think about it only when I don't have enough to finance my current enthusiasm, whatever it may be. All I know about money is that I have to have it to do things. . . . When I make a profit, I don't squander it or hide it away; I immediately plow it back into a fresh project. I regard it merely as a medium for financing new ideas. Money—or rather the lack of it to carry out my ideas—may worry me, but it does not excite me. Ideas excite me.

One of his later animators, Milt Kahl, confirmed this statement, saying, "It seems everything he touched turned to gold, like King Midas. It's amazing really because he didn't *think* about it. I don't think Walt ever in his life entered into any project because primarily it was going to make money. Quite a unique man."[5]

While the Disney movies were getting better, Roy and Walt's personal lives were on the upswing too. Roy decided to marry his longtime sweetheart Edna Francis on April 11, 1925. Always one to follow his big brother's lead, it didn't take long before Walt decided to do the same. He began dating Lillian Bounds, who worked in ink and paint at the studio, and just a few months later, they married. Lillian was a good match for her driven and energetic husband. She was a patient and willing ear for Walt to discuss his latest ideas and musings with, and wherever he decided to spend his time, she was willing to come along as his loyal companion. She also understood the business side of the enterprise as well, as she assisted Roy in the back office. Since the studio was a part of Lillian's life, she was sympathetic to Walt's obsession with his productions, and she also served as Roy's accomplice in steering his headstrong little brother away from making disastrous business decisions.

With their personal lives in place, the Disney brothers could now focus even more attention on their thriving studio. Audiences were clamoring for more of the films and critics were giving them positive reviews, but they had maxed out the capacity of what they could accomplish in the Kingswell studio. With the growing team of animators and increased production schedule, it was time to find a new location for the studio. On July 6, 1925, they made a $400 down payment on an empty lot down the street at 2719 Hyperion Avenue, and by spring 1926 they were able to move into a newly constructed single-story, white stucco building. Also during this time, the company's brand began to change.

Reflecting Walt's emerging status as an innovative movie producer, the company changed its name from Disney Brothers Studio to the Walt Disney Studios. Everything that came out of the studio now would have Walt's imprint on it, with Roy moving even more into the background—a place Roy was more than happy to be. Both the brothers calculated that the name change would persuade the public to believe that the quality films were the work of a lone genius named Walt Disney. It seemed to have worked, as over the years much of the Disney fan base thought Walt drew the cartoons himself. Walt and Roy knew this wasn't true, but they were savvy enough to understand that over time people would equate the name Walt Disney with innovative, quality family entertainment. As Walt observed many years later, "The studio was in the business of selling the name 'Walt Disney.'" To another associate he commented, "I'm not Walt Disney anymore. Walt Disney is a thing. It's grown to become a whole different meaning than just one man."[6] Even today, many people who visit Walt Disney World have no idea who Walt Disney really was.

A New Product

Although the name Disney was growing in popularity, money in the studio remained tight. Better quality meant more costs, all while still under the watch of Mintz. Mintz never gave the Disneys a break. He expected the films to be better, and he demanded they be completed at twice the speed as before. The pressure to deliver was intense for Walt, which affected his relationship with his team. By February 1927 the contract was fulfilled and Walt and Mintz agreed to end the Alice comedy series. But the business relationship between the two would not end there. Mintz was approached by Carl Laemmle of Universal Pictures with the idea of a new cartoon series featuring a rabbit. Mintz proposed to Walt that he create this new character for Universal. Walt took him up on the offer, and after Universal screened some early sketches of the concept, Mintz agreed to provide twenty-six cartoons featuring the new character of Oswald the Lucky Rabbit.

Why a rabbit? Cats had already been done before; even Walt had used one in the Alice comedies. A rabbit with long, exaggerated ears and a big, goofy expression offered a vehicle for new gags and visual acrobatics. And more importantly, a new, vibrant character would be featured in an all-animated cartoon series, rather than the live actor/cartoon concept that had been the focus of Walt's earlier films. Virginia Davis would no longer be the star of the show either. It would be Oswald, and, more importantly, a fully animated film would be the medium that Walt's studio would master for many years to come. In total, Walt delivered fifty-six Alice comedies to Mintz, but everyone knowledgeable of the enterprise—Walt, Roy, the animators, Mintz, and the audience—agreed it was time for the Walt Disney Studios to pursue a new animated series.

DISNEY LESSON 4: GO WHERE YOUR BEST PLACE OF OPPORTUNITY IS

As mentioned earlier in this chapter, success is often the result of being the right person doing the right thing in the right place at the right time. Walt's enterprise in Kansas City was not in the right place, nor was he doing the right thing. Hollywood, however, presented a different and unique set of circumstances that put Disney on a better path to making it in the movie business. A major difference between Kansas City and Hollywood was the presence of Roy. Think about it: if Roy wasn't recuperating from tuberculosis in Hollywood, he likely would have spent his life working in a bank in Kansas City, so Walt had the lucky break of having a devoted brother with eight years of banking experience available to join the enterprise. Additionally, Walt's Uncle Robert also provided cheap housing for him while he got established in California. He didn't have to live in poverty like he did during his last days in Kansas City. And to top it off, Walt moved to Hollywood just as it was becoming the entertainment capital of the world.

Yet, you might be saying, shouldn't Walt be given more credit for recognizing the opportunity that lay ahead of him in California? He was interested in movies and he had family living in Hollywood. Wouldn't that be an obvious place for him to go after his business failed in Kansas City? And even if he didn't go to Hollywood, with his entrepreneurial drive and intelligence, wouldn't he have ended up wildly successful somewhere else? Perhaps, but we'll never know. What we do know, though, is that Walt was willing to *move* where he thought his opportunities were. To Walt's credit, he was willing to put himself in what National Geographic photographer Dewitt Jones calls "the place of most potential" and creativity experts Rosamund Stone and Benjamin Zander call the "great space of possibility."[7] This behavior isn't to be taken lightly. Not everyone is willing to leave the perceived safety of what they know. However, assessing where you can apply your talent to make the most impact in the world is an essential ingredient of entrepreneurial success. We believe the formula for personal opportunity can be stated as:

Personal Opportunity = Talent x Work Ethic x Mobility

Talent comprises your individual skills, strengths, and intelligence that make you the unique person you are; work ethic is the philosophy and values you adhere to in pursuing your profession; and mobility is the willingness to move where you think your opportunities are. Becoming an expert on a topic and managing your resources of time, money, and reputation well are mostly personal matters you handle within yourself. Mobility, however, is a more external process that exposes you to new people, places, practices, and beliefs, which at first may make you uncomfortable. According to economist Todd Buchholz, it's the unwillingness to move to better opportunities that is causing many of the economic and social problems in today's society. Americans "are stuck in place literally and figuratively."[8] Walt Disney never allowed himself to be stuck. He was always willing to explore and investigate what was in the world around him. He would venture where he thought his next best opportunity was.

Making a big move can be a bit overwhelming for most people because there is so much to consider. How do you know where to start? Which possibility should you pursue? How do you know if you're choosing the right one? In *The Path of Least Resistance*, Robert Fritz advises readers to pick the easiest option that will get you moving forward. Fritz uses nature to explain how this process works. Water, for example, flows down to the lowest point of the terrain and energy moves through the structures that have the least resistance. It's like comedian Woody Allen once said, "80 percent of life is showing up." When you show up, things start happening. After Walt failed in Kansas City, he showed up at his Uncle Robert's house in California. Once in Hollywood, he tried to break into the motion picture business as an outsider, but he had no credentials there. However, that didn't keep Walt from getting on a bus and hanging out in the studios all day long, getting a feel for how the movie business worked. You can operate this way in your life too by following the advice of Gary Keller in *The One Thing*: when you're trying to achieve a big goal, you can begin by asking yourself, what's the one easy thing I can do now to get started on reaching this goal? That little step will set you up to do something a little bigger on your next move until eventually you achieve something of substance. Keller calls this process "the Domino Effect." A little domino can knock over a slightly larger domino, and if dominos are lined up in this fashion you can eventually knock down a gigantic domino. The story of Walt Disney's success is the result of his knocking over the next biggest domino. Oswald the Lucky Rabbit was the next domino Walt would turn his attention to on his way to becoming a Hollywood legend. And like every other endeavor he ever tackled, he would apply everything at his disposal to make it work.

On With the Show

The Walt Disney Studios got right to work in delivering the new cartoon for Mintz and Universal Pictures, and within a few months, the studio delivered its first Oswald cartoon. It was a bit of a rocky start, as Mintz and Universal were not happy with the initial design of the character—they thought Oswald appeared too old and frumpy—and said the film was a little repetitious and lacked punch. However, Walt worked with Ub to modify the character on the second attempt. In particular, they removed the sharp, angular features of Oswald and focused on drawing him with big feet and a round torso and facial features comprised of circles. This was a major advancement in the appeal of the character because circles gave Oswald a softer and friendlier appearance. Another bonus of the redesign was that the animators could draw circles fast, a major benefit when putting together the thousands of frames each film required.[9] This would be a technique Disney characters would exhibit in every cartoon and feature in the future, as noted by Disney biographer Bob Thomas:

> Oswald the Lucky Rabbit soon began to fulfill Walt's hopes. The rabbit became softer, more appealing, and the situations were funnier. Walt stinted on nothing. He refused to employ cycles—the repeated action which could save hours of work at the animation table. He insisted on photographing the rough animation and viewing it in a projection room. If it seemed to work, then Walt authorized the production process to continue. If not, the sequence went back to the animator. Such meticulousness was expensive and the cost of the Oswald cartoons climbed. But the added quality paid off.[10]

Walt Stinted on Nothing

Perhaps no sentence better described Walt Disney than "Walt stinted on nothing". Walt, like Steve Jobs a generation later at Apple, was obsessed with perfecting his products. He would sacrifice common practices in the industry, like re-using footage from a previous cartoon, to keep his animators focused on delivering a unique experience to the audience on every frame of film. He looked at the films from the perspective of his customers. He was one of them, and he knew what the audience would like. He relentlessly contemplated whether his animators were missing anything in making the films more entertaining. Could a gag be delivered better? Were there any flaws in the drawing or editing? This type of attention to cartoon detail was simply not found in those days. Cartoons were for kids. They were ephemeral warm-up acts for the main show. Why would anyone put so much effort into such a lightweight medium? And yet, as Walt studied the fine details of the cartoons, his animators adopted the same mind-set. He added more animators and ink and paint specialists to the studio's workforce, and he expected them to learn the studio culture and deliver excellence too. A Walt Disney production meant quality, innovation, and delight, and everyone needed to do their part to make that happen.

    The nation was taking notice of the studio's craftsmanship. After making the changes to the shaky debut of the first Oswald cartoon, *Poor Papa*, the improved second one, *Trolley Troubles*, received a much more enthusiastic response. *Moving Picture World*, for example, reported the series had "accomplished the amazing feat of jumping into the first-run favorite overnight."[11] Most people think Mickey Mouse was Walt's first hit. It wasn't. Oswald was nationally known too. One sign of the series' success is that Oswald began to be merchandised, in particular by a Portland, Oregon, candy company that co-promoted the series. *Universal Weekly* reported on August 10, 1927: "The chocolate bar immediately 'took' and is proving the biggest seller the candy company has ever had. Already shipments have been made to Honolulu and Alaska. Advertising and the wrapper on the candy bear a cartoon of the 'Lucky Rabbit' as he appears in the comedies and his face as well as his name is fast becoming familiar to fans. Wherever these bars are sold they form an ideal exhibitor-merchant tie-up which will benefit the theatre and the man selling the candy equally."[12] The Walt Disney Studios did not receive any royalties from the sales of the merchandise—Universal claimed those payments—but it did build the popularity of the character.

With the popularity of the series, the revenue model finally started looking good for the Disneys. Universal wanted an Oswald comedy every two weeks, and once the studio shipped the negative, the bigger company promptly responded with a check. The Disneys also received profit sharing on the theater rentals of the cartoons. The future boded well for the twenty-six-year-old film producer. The company was finally returning a guaranteed revenue stream and steady profit on every picture after their costs were covered. Year-end profits on theater rentals of the films were split sixty-forty between the Disney brothers, which enabled them to buy houses next to each other and live a comfortable life. In only four short years since living day to day in Kansas City, Walt Disney was finally starting to live the good life as the movie producer he'd always dreamed of being.

Betrayal in the Studio

Walt expected 1928 to be a breakout year for him. The year before saw the country fall in love with his Oswald cartoons, and upon nearing completion of the Universal contract, he fully expected that he would receive a bump in payments for their success. With a cartoon series that was getting more popular with each release, he'd proven he could run a successful studio. But all wasn't as it appeared. His old buddy and chief animator Ub Iwerks warned Walt that trouble was brewing in the studio. Ub practically lived at his animation desk and saw everything that went on in the studio when Walt was out promoting the business. And what he saw in January 1928 disturbed him greatly. George Winkler—Charles Mintz's handpicked plant in the studio—was wooing Walt's animators to abandon the Disneys and form a new studio to make the Oswald cartoons. Mintz was concocting a scheme to cut the Disneys out of the production and split the increased share of the profits with the animators. Mintz painted Walt as merely a middle man between the animators, who did the "real work," and Mintz, who lined up the business. By cutting out the middle man, everyone would make more money. George Winkler had seen firsthand that Walt never drew a frame of film, so what would be lost by cutting him out of the action? Walt, though, was in denial and wouldn't even investigate the claim. The thought was too disturbing to him. Ever the optimist, he couldn't imagine that the people he had hired, trained, and supported would do that to him. It didn't fit with how he wanted his world to work.

On February 2, 1928, Mintz renewed his relationship with Universal, signing a three-year contract for more Oswald cartoons. Walt and Lillian boarded a train to New York City shortly after the agreement was made to negotiate what his studio's cut of the action would be. Despite Ub's warning, Walt was upbeat about the negotiations. Since the films were a big hit, he hoped to get a 10 percent increase in guaranteed payments to go along with the profit sharing they had been receiving as well. If Mintz didn't agree to these terms, he planned to find another distribution company that would promote the films. The reality of this negotiation would actually be the exact opposite. When Mintz met with Walt, he didn't offer him a 10 percent pay increase for the new Oswald cartoons; he offered him a 38 percent *reduction* in payment for each picture. He was still willing to split the end-of-the-year profits fifty-fifty, and would throw in salaries for Walt and Roy as well. Under the old arrangement, Walt and Roy actually had smaller salaries than their animators, so the guaranteed salaries might have afforded them a bit more luxury before the end-of-the-year profit sharing kicked in. The proposed arrangement wasn't to Walt's liking, though. It basically meant he worked for Mintz, and the animators he had hired and trained would now be Mintz's as well. Walt's role would now be more like a frontline supervisor. This isn't how he wanted to work. After all, the opening credits said a "Walt Disney Production," not a "Charles Mintz Production." He wanted to keep it that way. When he threatened to take Oswald to another distribution company, he learned a hard lesson in intellectual property rights. Even though the Walt Disney Studios had created what Oswald was and produced all the films he was in, the rights to the series were retained by Universal. Mintz was legally within his rights to kick Walt out, sign away his animators, and oversee the productions of the Oswald comedies himself. Walt now had a "take it or leave it" decision to make.

Knowing that Mintz wasn't always truthful, Walt contacted Roy, who was back in the California studio, to see if the threat was real. Indeed it was. Roy told Walt that most of the staff were going to abandon him for Mintz. It was already in the works. Walt was in a tough bind, but he used his remaining time in New York City to pursue his options before making a decision. He approached Universal to see if they would drop Mintz and work directly with him, but they declined the offer. Mintz was seen as a mature, experienced distributor, and with the animation team intact, they believed they could continue the Oswald films with little disruption. With no other options, Mintz and Disney then recommenced negotiations over the terms of the Oswald series. Although the salary and guaranteed payment terms were flexible with Mintz, the condition compelling Walt to work for him was not. He could take the sure money and give up control or he could walk away from Oswald. Walt decided to turn down Mintz's offer and start over again on his own.

Riding back on the train to Hollywood with Lillian, Walt deliberated on what his next step should be. He still had his brother Roy running the business and his chief animator Ub, along with a few other artists, remaining on the team. The nucleus was there for something different to be created. He wondered, what if he came up with a *new* character to replace Oswald that he could build a series around? That was the answer. Forget Mintz. The next cartoon would be all Disney. When he arrived back with his faithful team in Hollywood, he gave them the challenge of coming up with a new cartoon star. After diverging on possible characters, they settled on a mouse. It was a good fit. Walt had an affinity for mice, as he'd treated some as pets in his Kansas City office. Plus, Ub found the character easy to draw, as he essentially took the Oswald character and changed the long ears into round ones and elongated the nose to give it the face of a mouse. Walt called the character Mortimer, but Lillian protested, saying it was too stuffy. She suggested Mickey instead, and the name stuck. Mickey Mouse was born. But Mickey couldn't exist alone in the cartoon world, so they also dreamed up a companion for him named Minnie.[13] Now it was time to bring the mouse to the rest of the world.

DISNEY LESSON 5: THOSE WHO ENDURE SETBACKS EARLY IN LIFE OFTEN ENJOY GREATER SUCCESS LATER

If you had been in the same situation Walt faced in Mintz's New York office, would you have made the same decision he did? In his memoir of his years in the White House, President George W. Bush called moments like these "decision points." He explained it was "the most important part of the job: making decisions. . . . Many of the decisions that reach the president's desk are tough calls, with strong arguments on both sides."[14] Facing the dilemma of deserting Oswald for a new and yet to be determined character was Walt's first pivotal entrepreneurial decision in the history of his company. It wasn't an easy choice to make: take a guaranteed paycheck and give up control of your studio or abandon the character you made famous and try again. While he had taken risky steps in the past, many of those situations were either impulsive or out of desperation. Hopping on a train alone to California after declaring bankruptcy in Kansas City was brave, but he had little to lose by doing so. Starting up the Alice comedies again was the only avenue he had to getting in the movies when he was kicking around the studios. But in this situation, he had a potentially viable path to stay in business that he turned down.

In hindsight, it's clear it was the right decision. Had he stayed with Mintz there would likely be no Mickey Mouse today. However, could the situation have gone more smoothly for him than it did? After all, Ub had warned him that Mintz was recruiting away his animators, but Walt ignored the information. Had he been more conscious of what was going on, the outcome may have been the same, but he may not have endured the psychological cost that came with feeling betrayed by his animators and disrespected by Mintz and Universal. Perhaps the psychological impact of betrayal taught him lessons about human nature that made him more perceptive about others he would face in the movie business over the years. As Merritt and Kaufmann note, "Disney had learned many important lessons about the film business during his years with Winkler and Mintz, and he had grown tougher. Previously he had simply followed standard procedure in his business dealings, where the producer served as a subordinate of the distributor, who controlled all the rights to the character and the films. Now Disney resolved never to make himself so vulnerable again."[15] Walt also wised up and relied on Roy to lead more of the negotiations in the future. Avoiding betrayal and entering into better partnerships warranted more due diligence in assessing what was actually going on around the studio, which Roy had a greater facility for doing. But more importantly, the moment of betrayal entrenched a hard-earned lesson Walt would follow the rest of his life: *he would never give up ownership of his properties again.* He vowed, "Never again will I work for somebody else."[16] A Walt Disney Production would be 100 percent Walt Disney.

On With the Show

The atmosphere in the Walt Disney Studios must have been awkward for everyone involved after the negotiations fell through with Mintz. Walt still owed Mintz three Oswald cartoons to fulfill the original contract, so the animators who were joining Mintz's operation were still on the payroll at Walt's studio. In the meantime, Walt and Ub needed to get working on the first Mickey Mouse cartoon in secret. After all, Walt didn't want another one of his ideas stolen by Mintz.

Setbacks like the Mintz affair often energize people in one of two ways: as fuel or poison. For some people, the disappointment poisons their spirit, and they sabotage their future by punishing themselves with self-destructive behavior. Others, however, allow the disappointment to serve as fuel, driving them to accomplish great feats. They won't allow themselves to be defeated by the circumstances. The fuel crowd follows the maxim that "success is the best revenge," and Walt and Ub were running on high-octane fuel during Oswald's last days in the studio. They would not give up. As Disney historians Russell Merritt and J.B. Kaufman said, "When Walt Disney made a decision, he acted quickly and decisively. Galvanized by the sudden loss of Oswald the Rabbit, he wasted no time on recrimination or reflection but went to work immediately on a new course of action."[17] Walt beat the street looking for distributors, and Ub worked day and night on the first Mickey Mouse cartoon. While the traitorous animators worked on Oswald, loyal Ub locked himself away in an office out of sight, working on their response to Mintz. Walt and Ub had to have Mickey ready for release to keep the studio alive when Oswald and his animators made the move to New York.

Completing the first Mickey Mouse cartoon, *Plane Crazy*, was a staggering animation achievement by Ub. In the Iwerks biography *The Hand Behind the Mouse*, written by his granddaughter Leslie, Ub's work style is captured:[18]

> He churned out more than seven hundred drawings a day on *Plane Crazy*—a feat that eclipsed Krazy Kat animator Bill Nolan's record of six hundred drawings a day. . . . Each day, Walt and Roy would take stacks of Ub's completed drawings—under the guise of going to get some work done on one of their cars—to Walt's home garage where Roy's wife, Edna, and Walt's wife, Lillian, along with Hazel Sewell, Walt's sister-in-law, would ink and paint the drawings onto cels. . . . In just two frenetic weeks, the first Mickey Mouse short was completed. Every frame of the film was animated by Ub Iwerks: storyboards, extremes, in-betweens, backgrounds, *everything!*

Let's assume Ub put in twenty-hour days during this frenzied production. That would mean he drew each individual frame in roughly thirty-five seconds—over seven hundred times per day for fourteen straight days. And this calculation doesn't include the other tasks he performed on the picture, which would speed up his drawing average even more. Walt may have lost a team of animators, but his retention of Ub was enough to save the day. As creativity expert Dean Keith Simonton maintains, the productive leaps of a genius can outproduce the product of an average group of people in a field.[19] In the case of Mickey Mouse, Ub kept to this rule. Mintz could have the other animators for Oswald. Walt had Ub for Mickey Mouse.

Why would Ub devote such energy to a questionable venture like Mickey Mouse when he had a sure thing with Mintz and Oswald? And what was the source of such a frenetic work pace? Remember, he warned Walt that the coup was coming. Perhaps loyalty and honesty were important values for him. Perhaps the mutiny of the other animators served as fuel to prove that the studio he'd taken a chance on could still make it. And it's possible that his obsessive and driven work style was the result of a genetic disposition geared toward thousands of hours at a drawing table. Consider that Ub was extremely shy and socially awkward—colleagues said he answered most questions with monosyllabic answers—and perhaps may have had behavioral traits resembling autism or Asperger syndrome. In the *Power of Different*, Dr. Gail Saltz states that "people with autism tend to exhibit 'hypersystemizing.' . . . They become fascinated by a particular subject and then inhale every detail about it to a degree far beyond what the neurotypical person could consume."[20] They also often demonstrate heightened visual acuity[21] and "exhibit enhanced perceptual abilities when engaged in visual search, visual discrimination, and embedded figure detection."[22] One can imagine that these traits would come in handy for an animator who has to recreate believable characters in an entirely created world on celluloid in such a short time span. While the more sociable Walt handled relations with the company's stakeholders inside and outside the studio, Ub was able to channel his energies toward the animation duties he enjoyed and did so well.

Environmental pressures may have also driven Ub to such amazing feats. As his daughter recounts:[23]

> Financially and emotionally, he had risked everything he owned on the studio's future success. At home, he and his wife, Mildred, were not only dealing with the responsibilities of raising their new baby son, Don, but they were also coping with the continued presence of Ub's mother. She had since moved in with the family and was under the direct care of Mildred. With his financial and family pressures mounting, Ub had to give this effort everything he had.

On top of that, Walt was exerting his own expectations on his star animator and everyone else still loyal to the team. "The first Mickey was made by twelve people after hours in a garage," said Walt.[24] After Iwerks finished drawing the scenes, Walt set up a makeshift studio in his garage, where Lillian, Edna, and Hazel put the ink and paint touches on the cels. The final negative was produced there as well. Spurred by Walt, everyone gave their all. When Walt Disney had his eye on a goal, nothing would derail him, and he had an uncanny ability to draw out of others what they didn't know they could do. It must have seemed surreal to be at the studio during that time. The regular animation team worked on the Oswald films during the day without knowing that Walt's friends and family were working around the clock to finish the first Mickey Mouse cartoon behind their backs.

In the meantime, the Mickey Mouse cartoon needed to find its way into theaters. While Ub drew, Walt looked for distributors for the debut cartoon. A few local theaters picked it up, but he couldn't find a major distributor willing to sign a deal. Part of the problem was that, due to the newness of the character and the rush to produce the film, the quality wasn't on the level of the Oswald cartoons. Clearly, there was room for a lot of improvement, but Mickey Mouse was now a reality—and more importantly, unlike Oswald, this cartoon character was his. And as he always did, Walt intended to improve the next Mickey Mouse cartoon very soon.

DISNEY LESSON 6: FIND A THOUGHTMATE TO PARTNER WITH ON YOUR WORK

Mickey Mouse saved the Walt Disney Company, but he wouldn't have become a reality without Ub's commitment to completing the cartoon for Walt. This kind of collaboration between two partners with different strengths is quite common in successful creative ventures. In *The Power of Twos*, Joshua Wolf Shenk documents that the most creative breakthroughs happen when two innovative people partner together to pursue a common dream. Shenk calls this chemistry "creative intimacy," citing Paul McCartney and John Lennon, Charlie Munger and Warren Buffet, and even Matt Stone and Trey Parker of *South Park* fame as examples of pairs who all shared this dynamic. Creative partners talk, think, and can even look like each other over time. And like other intimate relationships, conflicts often arise, and some partnerships even burn out. But in that cauldron of creative energy and competitive survival, great works can be created.[25] This cycle happened at Apple with Steve Jobs and Steve Wozniak as well, as they revolutionized the computer industry and eventually parted ways. Still, Jobs and Wozniak always viewed each other as brothers even as they pursued their own individual paths later in life. Finding a thoughtmate who can work with, shape, test, and help fulfill your ideas is one of the most valuable entrepreneurial lessons we can learn from Walt and Ub's partnership.

The relationship with Ub wasn't the only "power of two" Walt had going on in the studio. He worked closely with Roy to ensure money was coming in to pay for new projects. The relationship with distributors had to be given considerable time in order to make certain audiences were receiving a good product. Walt had to ensure that the production, money, and box office were all healthy, and each person in those areas had to be made to feel special. And as we'll see in upcoming chapters, every new venture the company would pursue in the future would require Walt to build deep relationships with other international players. All these relationships require time and energy to maintain. Is it any wonder then that entrepreneurs are often said to be "married to their work"? Many people are not willing to pay this price, but it's required to build a legendary company.

Iteration

Iteration is a common part of creating a hit product. The first attempt doesn't always quite hit the intended mark, and tweaks are needed to find the winning formula. The Mickey Mouse we've come to know and love today didn't appear in *Plane Crazy* and needed to be iterated too. His appearance wasn't fully formed yet. His personality even had a little cockiness and meanness to it that isn't present in the current version of Mickey. And unfortunately, the second picture, *The Gallopin' Gaucho*, didn't show much improvement over *Plane Crazy*. Mickey was just another cartoon character warming up audiences for the feature film to follow. There really didn't seem to be anything more special about this mouse than the rabbits, dogs, and cats that already starred in cartoons. Mickey Mouse was just another cartoon animal doing gags and stunts in comic situations. Walt knew he needed to come up with something special to make Mickey stand apart from his competition. He wasn't happy with the cartoons either, and he wondered what he could do to give Mickey more life. Then Walt came up with a big idea: put sound in the cartoons! It was a new technology in Hollywood, and no one had tried it in a cartoon yet. Disney biographer Neil Gabler tells how this idea came about:

> Roy said that they had screened a cartoon after *The Jazz Singer*, the Al Jolson film that is credited with being the first motion picture to synchronize the spoken word and the image. "That's it. That's it," Walt allegedly said. "It looks realistic, it'll be realistic. That's what we've got to do. Stop all these silent pictures." . . . Everyone was immediately energized, which may have been part of Walt's calculation to keep his crew's spirits from flagging. (Animator) Wilfred Jackson said he was so excited by the idea of a sound cartoon that he could not sleep that night.[26]

With that decision, the Walt Disney Studios now had to figure out how to get a cartoon to do something no one had ever done before: give an animal a voice. And if he could do that, he knew sound technology could also lead to another invention in animated films: giving a cartoon character a personality. If Mickey could talk, the audience could know what he's thinking and feeling. No longer would he have to act out his ideas physically. He could speak to others in a way no other character on the market could. But now Walt and his team had to overcome technical challenges unlike anything they'd ever faced before. It wasn't just a matter of churning out a production on a tight timeline. Now they had to figure out how to record and synchronize sound to the drawings. It was a big gamble, but Walt was willing to bet the company again that they could pull it off.

Steamboat Willie

When Walt was creating the first Mickey Mouse cartoons, he relied on a ragtag team of young animators to turn out the new product fast. Each team member was required to work at 100 percent capacity because financial ruin was lurking right around the corner. Walt spent day and night pushing the team and strategizing how to make the sound cartoon a hit. First, he had to come up with a catchy soundtrack to make the film fun. He chose two popular songs of the day, "Steamboat Bill" and "Turkey in the Straw," to be in the cartoon. The "Steamboat Bill" song then became the inspiration for the film's title, *Steamboat Willie*. Ub Iwerks continued his godlike pace of penciling up to seven hundred drawings a day, and Les Clark inked grays, blacks, and whites onto the cels to bring Ub's drawings to life. But perhaps the biggest challenge of the production was figuring out how to synchronize sound to the cartoon. This feature had never been attempted before, and it would require figuring out how to match the music and sounds of the characters with the action on the screen. There was no guide for how to do this. Walt and his crew had to invent it.

The first thing they figured out was that film was recorded at twenty-four frames per second. Walt then calculated how many frames of film equaled a bar of music. Given that the film had a musical element to it, Wilfred Jackson figured out how to synchronize the sound for *Steamboat Willie* by using a metronome. Now it was time to add the sound of the characters to the production, something never attempted before in a cartoon. Jackson described the breakthrough:

> A few scenes for the beginning of *Steamboat Willie* had been animated and were on film. Roy got outside the window with a projector (so the projector noise wouldn't be heard). Ub had rigged up a microphone and speaker, and it was placed behind a bed sheet used as a screen . . . What Walt was wondering was whether you could get an audience to believe that a drawing could make a noise. Would it seem that the sound was coming from the animation? . . . Walt and the boys ran the film over and over, trying to perfect the timing of the sound effects with the action on the screen. The animators were fascinated with the results. When a character opened his mouth, a sound came out. This was what we had been trying to achieve.[27]

With the mechanics of the new cartoon format developed, Walt next had to find someone who could help him record the sound onto the film, which would require the use of a complicated recording system. Sound in film was a new technology in the industry, so there wasn't a standard design yet. Like many new technology markets, entrepreneurs and companies provided a lot of choices to movie producers, each hoping to create the standard that would be adopted in future films. Walt examined sound systems offered by traditional movie companies like Fox and RCA but wasn't pleased with their quality. However, on a New York City trip, he met and was won over by Pat Powers, a charismatic Irish entrepreneur who had an independent sound company called Cinephone. Walt was fascinated with Powers, a born salesman with a lot of existing connections in the movie industry. He thought he'd finally found a partner who understood what he was trying to accomplish. Walt also expected Powers to be a power-broker for him, helping his films reach more theaters.

While the animation was completed in Hollywood, the sound had to be recorded in the Cinephone studios in New York City. It was a cumbersome process, with Walt crisscrossing the country by train to coordinate the animated and recorded elements of the cartoon. Walt worked frantically to make *Steamboat Willie* a reality. Believing the production rested on his shoulders, he coordinated and motivated all the parties to bring the production together, and with Powers's sound system *Steamboat Willie* was completed. Now all Walt had to do was find a distributor to sell it to. Walt's previous distributor Universal offered to pick up the Mickey Mouse cartoons, but they wanted to maintain control and ownership of Mickey like they had Oswald. Walt refused that offer. He would never again, in any situation, relinquish control of his films. The other distributors he shopped it around to found *Steamboat Willie* interesting, but none were willing to take a chance on a cartoon with sound. Finally, Walt's persistence paid off. Harry Reichenbach, a longtime New York City promoter, took a look at it and thought he had a winner on his hands. Reichenbach offered to show *Steamboat Willie* in his famous Broadway establishment, the Colony Theater. Now Walt had another pivotal entrepreneurial decision to make. He was happy Reichenbach was willing to show his cartoon at the Colony, but he was concerned that if he showed it before having a distributor, it would lose its chance to be picked up nationally. First runs are typically the most profitable releases, so distribution companies like to premiere a show. But with no other options, he took Reichenbach's advice to show it in the Colony Theater. Reichenbach was convinced his audiences would love it, so Walt gambled on the idea that if a sophisticated Broadway audience liked *Steamboat Willie*, it would serve as proof of concept to the major distributors. All he needed was one of them to sign him on for an extended series of Mickey Mouse sound cartoons. He was right. On November 18, 1928, *Steamboat Willie* was released as the opening short for a feature film that also had sound. As it turned out, the audience liked *Steamboat Willie* more than the feature film. Walt finally had a hit on his hands that was all his own. Sensing an opportunity to cash in on Mickey's new appeal, he quickly rereleased the previous two Mickey Mouse cartoons with sound too. The three sound cartoons turned Mickey into an overnight national sensation.

Walt's relentless refusal to give up in the face of the Oswald tragedy secured the studio a reprieve for the near future. The studio had a star character to build its productions around now. Having struggled and fought through the challenges of bankruptcy in Kansas City, the desertion of his animators in Hollywood to Mintz, and the loss of Oswald to Universal, it's understandable why Walt often said, "I only hope that we don't lose sight of one thing—that it was all started by a mouse." Mickey Mouse firmly established the Walt Disney Studios as its own enterprise. His time in the Cinephone studios and the success of Mickey Mouse also helped Walt recruit a crop of talented animators from New York

City. Talented people move where they think they can work on interesting projects with like-minded professionals, and it was clear that wasn't happening in New York anymore. Ben Sharpsteen, Bert Gillet, Jack King, and Norm Ferguson moved to Hollywood to join the Disney Studios, and would play major roles in the company for many years to come. In the meantime, the business side of the studio continued to develop as well. Brother Roy continued to manage the studio's money with a precision that helped it get through the cash crunch of this development period. Ub Iwerks continued his frenetic pace of drawing, and his fellow animators improved their techniques for putting the finishing touches of ink and color on the Disney creations. Had any one of these team members slacked off in their work habits, the studio would have collapsed. But with the completion of *Steamboat Willie* and the follow-up success of other Mickey Mouse cartoons, the foundation was set for the future success of the company. Walt Disney had weathered his first storm in Hollywood.

DISNEY LESSON 7: SUCCESSFUL ENTREPRENEURS ALWAYS FIND AN UPSIDE IN A BAD SITUATION

This period of Walt Disney's career holds a lot of lessons for entrepreneurs. First, the Walt Disney Company couldn't have happened without the help of other people besides Walt Disney. The company was a family business comprised of Walt's brother Roy and his wife Lillian and friends who were like family, such as Ub Iwerks, Les Clark, and Wilfred Jackson. Family businesses comprise 35 percent of the Fortune 500 list because family and friends stick by each other during the tough times. For example, Walt could be temperamental and pushy, but Roy never abandoned him. And when the company was on the line, Walt's family and friends went the extra mile for him when needed. As a result of their loyalty, all went on to have spectacular careers at the company. Walt became an entertainment legend, Ub won Oscars for technical achievements, Les put in a fifty-year career at the studios, Jackson became a film director, and Roy became Chief Executive Officer after his brother's untimely death. There are always kernels of opportunity for those who join a company at its ground floor stage.

But not everyone was loyal in the early days of the company. Walt learned a hard lesson when Mintz signed away most of his animators to work on Oswald without him. Sickened by the betrayal of many of his employees and the greed of the larger studio, Disney broke all ties with Oswald and decided to start anew. A new character would have to replace Oswald. It was out of these dire circumstances that Walt responded by creating his popular character Mickey Mouse. This is what successful entrepreneurs do when faced with setbacks. They find the upside by pivoting, adapting, and overcoming, and as a result, they're better prepared to face even bigger challenges in the future because of the growth and wisdom acquired in the moment. Entrepreneurship scholars Mike Morris, Don Kuratko, and Minet Schindehutte believe that's why the business shapes who the entrepreneur becomes every bit as much as the entrepreneur shapes the business.[28] Had it not been for Mintz's betrayal Mickey Mouse may never have been created and the Walt Disney Company may have been just an average animation studio.

Walt's Proof of Concept

Imagine you're twenty-eight years old. You've created a cultural phenomenon in Mickey Mouse. Everyone around the country is starting to know your name and is eagerly lining up for each new film you put out. Mickey Mouse Clubs are springing up around the country, with one million members packing Saturday matinees to watch your films. What do you do next? Do you focus all your efforts on producing more of what has made you famous? After all, it's sure money. Or do you take a chance and explore new projects to keep your customers and competition guessing? This is the situation that Walt Disney faced in 1929. Although the company was starting to be more established in the entertainment industry, money was still tight. The Disney brothers had a success in Mickey Mouse, so it made sense to keep making the Mickey Mouse cartoons. However, Walt was concerned that if he continued to just make Mickey Mouse cartoons the public would eventually get bored and move on to something else. And, like many self-made entrepreneurial legends, after any major achievement, Walt Disney always asked himself, what's next? Everyone outside of the animation team wanted Walt to stick to what was working. "No. No next! Just make more Mickey Mouse cartoons!" was the message he received from inside and outside the studio. In particular, his brother Roy didn't want Walt experimenting with a new series; he liked the steady cash flow of the Mickey Mouse cartoons. Plus, he was concerned that innovating while the company was still getting by week to week was very risky. Walt's wife Lillian agreed with Roy, and thought he was one bad idea away from bankrupting the company. Their distributor United Artists wasn't interested in anything experimental either. And business partner Pat Powers implored him to stick to Mickey Mouse by telling him, "More mice!"

Still, Walt believed that in the long run he had to explore new avenues to remain relevant in Hollywood. He didn't want to be just the best animation studio in the world. That would be like being the best tugboat in the navy. He had bigger ambitions than that. Walt wanted his studio to move into the hallowed ranks of United Artists, Paramount, and Universal. He wanted to be recognized with critical acclaim and be accepted in the elite crust of Hollywood movie producers. He wanted the name Walt Disney to mean more than just cartoons for kids. He wanted to be taken more seriously as a film producer, and Mickey Mouse alone wasn't going to get him there. He loved Mickey, but he needed something else more theatrical and eye catching to advance his craft. The world, after all, equated Walt Disney with Mickey Mouse. But how would they accept him as the auteur and movie mogul he desired to be if he stuck with Mickey? His only answer was to establish a proof of concept to his naysayers that the Walt Disney Studios could be a place for more serious and innovative filmmaking.

Walt decided he was going to take a chance and push his team in new directions that would catch the world off guard. The challenge now was to find a theme for the new films that would get the enterprise started. He had already made cartoons about a real little girl in an animated fantasy world with the Alice comedies, slapstick comedies about an adventurous rabbit with Oswald, and now a lovable character in Mickey Mouse. So what new idea could he come up with that was entirely different from his other body of work? He considered making live action movies like the bigger studios, but he didn't have the resources yet to do that, so that would have to wait. No, he would have to utilize his existing animation team to create something different from anything they had ever done before. Now, what could be more different than a young girl, a fun-loving rabbit, and an adorable mouse? How about death? How about a cemetery? How about skeletons, spiders, and withering trees? With these macabre themes in mind, Walt and his animators decided to create a musical cartoon called *The Skeleton Dance*.

The Skeleton Dance concept came from a couple of sources. Carl Stallings, Walt's longtime friend and composer for the Mickey Mouse sound cartoons, told him that he should pay homage to dancing skeletons in his little experiment. It was a common theme in other entertainment niches like silent films and vaudeville acts, but it had not been explored in cartoons yet. Apparently, adult audiences found the dark humor of skeletons dancing entertaining, but it was a little too scary a subject for young children. Walt had to wonder if the source material would be deemed appropriate for a cartoon. Could he make ghoulishness funny? Walt was going to find out. He wanted to surprise his audience.

Like the breakthrough with Mickey Mouse, Ub took the lead in crafting what *The Skeleton Dance* would be. After a visit to the local library to find source materials for inspiration, he began dreaming up scenarios for the graveyard in the film. And this time he would rely on the help of other animators to complete the task. No longer would he draw everything in the cartoon like he had in the early Mickey Mouse cartoons. As Ub explained about the process, "It was a different type of film from the Mickeys. I did all the animation, but I did it rough, in line form. Other guys put in the rib cages and teeth and eyes and bones."[29] However, *The Skeleton Dance* clearly came from the imaginations of the proven duo of Walt Disney and Ub Iwerks.

Due to its dark theme of death and dancing skeletons, it took Disney six weeks for a major theater to show it. In the meantime, the studio continued to release Mickey Mouse cartoons. It appeared maybe everyone was right about focusing on Mickey. But when Walt screened *The Skeleton Dance* for the owner of the Carthay Circle Theatre in Los Angeles, it was granted a limited run. The decision was a good one. *The Skeleton Dance* received a warm reception from the Carthay Circle crowd. They found it wildly entertaining and different from anything they had ever seen before. Whereas Mickey and Minnie would be caught up in some type of normal daily nuisance, *The Skeleton Dance* was otherworldly. Set in an eerie cemetery at night, skeletons come to life, groove to a spooky tune, and dance on top of their graves. It was a real stretch from what any animation studio had ever done before.

Keep in mind that Walt didn't *have* to produce this film. There was still plenty of demand for Mickey Mouse cartoons, but Walt wanted to push his team—and, more importantly, himself—into new creative territory. Walt's instinct for what the public would like was proven right again. *The Skeleton Dance* was eventually a big success with critics and audiences on both coasts; even the prestigious Roxy Theatre in New York City gave it a week's run. Walt's risky production convinced the country that he could make entertaining films that didn't include Mickey Mouse. *The Skeleton Dance* was a major step forward on his path to becoming a Hollywood legend. Now Walt Disney's name wasn't equated with only Mickey Mouse; it meant cutting edge entertainment. His fans were now open to waiting in line for *anything* that bore the Disney name—that is, as long as Roy could find the money to fund the new inventions and techniques needed to pull off Walt's ideas.

The success of *The Skeleton Dance* bolstered Walt's confidence to experiment to his heart's content, transforming his studio from a boutique art house into a high-tech lab that would create a new science of animation. Updating familiar themes and stories with new technology and advanced animation techniques enabled him to create instant classics. This formula worked well because the productions felt comfortably familiar but still novel enough to be interesting. Like Steve Jobs a generation later, Walt Disney borrowed, adapted, and improved already existing ideas. Anything that caught his interest could be grist for a future project, which also expanded the company's body of knowledge. Constantly experimenting and coming up with even better ideas helped him continually top his earlier work, which made it possible to move into new frontiers that other companies couldn't even imagine. Walt Disney's philosophy was to make sure the next production was always better than the last. As animator Les Clark recalled, "Walt was way ahead. He was so far ahead of us even then about what he wanted to do. We couldn't understand sometimes why he was giving us hell for something we thought was acceptable. Then later on we knew what he was talking about."[30] This mind-set was employed through every stage of Walt Disney's entrepreneurial life. If he couldn't be ahead of or do something better than his competition, he didn't do it. As Walt once told legendary director Cecil B. DeMille, "Never do anything that someone else can do better. That's why we ordinarily sidestep stories that could be done successfully in live action instead of animated action."[31]

Walt's Laboratory

With proof of concept firmly established with *The Skeleton Dance*, a new series called the *Silly Symphonies* was created to provide Walt with a vehicle for experimenting with new types of animation techniques. Each *Silly Symphony* could be its own experiment, with themes such as fairytales, existential crises, morality fables, and spiritual quests explored. More believable scenery and cinematography were crafted with innovative camera techniques. Also, when needed, fresh characters, such as Donald Duck, were created to bring new life to the Disney films. There was, however, a price to be paid for this innovation. Since each *Silly Symphony* production became its own distinct work of art, they couldn't be rolled out in a couple weeks like a Mickey Mouse cartoon. To further complicate the process, many of the animators who were well-trained to create traditional cartoons didn't possess the level of skill to pull off the new art form. That level of artistry was not in-house yet, and Walt wasn't capable of teaching his team what needed to be done. Therefore, he looked outside of the studio for someone who could help him develop the needed skills in his animators. Fortunately, the solution existed just down the street at the Chouinard Art Institute. In particular, there was a teacher there by the name of Don Graham who played a pivotal role in developing and advancing the artistic skills of the animators at the Walt Disney Studios. Graham held classes in color, composition, life study, and action analysis designed specifically for Walt's young animators. Partnering with Chouinard paid off, as Graham's instruction vastly improved the draftsmanship of the Disney animators. Walt was so pleased with the results that he even drove many of his animators to Chouinard himself to take the night classes. Eventually the numbers taking the classes got so large that Walt had to move Graham's operation inside the studio. Walt was so pleased with Graham's influence on his artists that he hired more Chouinard instructors to come on board.

Walt essentially created the world's first apprenticeship program in animation, with everyone taking Graham's classes and new animators shadowing more experienced ones. He even invited renowned artists, architects, and other big thinkers to visit the studio and offer seminars to expand the minds of his team and keep them in touch with the latest cultural movements going on in the world. On any given day, Salvador Dali or Frank Lloyd Wright might drop by to give a talk on their work. Walt obsessed on what animation could be, and the animators experimented in honing their craft.

The *Silly Symphonies* transformed animation into a serious business. Films with deep human themes and sympathetic characters were set to moving, classical music, and imparted age-old lessons of loyalty and perseverance. Characters seemed more lifelike and backgrounds more beautiful. Now, a Walt Disney cartoon was not only entertaining, but it also conveyed a distinct look and emotional feel. Many historians look back at the Hyperion days as the golden age of the Disney Studios. The company wasn't quite great yet, but everyone there could sense they were getting closer to doing something very special.

Another Bold Step

By 1932 Walt had gotten animation down to a science. The cartoon short moved through a well-established artistic assembly line he had built for meeting public demand for his productions. Animators apprenticed in training programs designed to deliver the Disney look. The animation steps became more compartmentalized, with assigned artists working on specific aspects of a production. No longer would a small team work tirelessly doing everything on a production. Cartoon production was broken down into steps, with quality control led by Walt. Walt even added his own story development team to help him flesh out ideas to make the films more entertaining. Everything seemed to be falling into place. But Walt never rested on his laurels; so once again he asked himself, what's next? What could be the next step for raising the studio's game?

Are you starting to see a pattern here? Are you getting it now? Do you understand why Disney inspired Steve Jobs and so many other entrepreneurs over the last century? Like Jobs, Walt never rested on his success. He was always on the lookout for the latest and greatest technologies to use in his own productions to up the animation game. The new breakthrough on the movie scene at this moment in time was Technicolor, but up until this point color was only used in major movie productions. Walt reflected on the success of adding sound to a cartoon (*Steamboat Willie*), and he wondered if he could do the same with color. However, Technicolor was a very expensive new technology. Consequently, just as before, with sound, Roy thought licensing it seemed a bad idea, as did his distributor United Artists. The added costs of Technicolor would definitely eat into the bottom line of a production. However, Walt was willing to sacrifice short-term profits to create a better product and thrill his loyal audience. He just needed to find a win-win situation with Technicolor where he could get access to the color process while also appeasing Roy. The solution emerged when Technicolor agreed to provide them exclusive rights for two years, establishing Disney as the only animation studio with the technology. Now, Walt had another game changing technology on his hands that he would challenge his team to figure out and use.

Great innovation requires significant investment in not only money but also time. The Technicolor method in movies was no different. There proved to be a steep learning curve for the studio that came with a largely untested technology. The early attempts at applying the Technicolor paint to the cartoon reels resulted in a lot of chipping and flaking. Each failed attempt required significant manpower and time to correct it. Walt knew if his team could master the Technicolor process, he'd have a huge advantage over his competition. Not only would a Walt Disney picture have better detail and more sophisticated themes, it would also appear more alive because of color. Walt's cartoons would be worlds apart from the black and white films of his competitors. Another benefit of adopting the Technicolor process was that the Walt Disney Studios was transforming from simply an entertainment company into a technology company as well. He and his team were learning how to experiment with new inventions and processes, problem solve, and introduce new breakthroughs into the industry, an ethic that the Walt Disney Company still adheres to today.

The first *Silly Symphony* to use the Technicolor technique was *Flowers and Trees* in 1932. The storyline is pretty basic. It's springtime and the flowers and trees in a forest are waking up at the end of a long winter. A good tree and a bad tree compete for the attention of a beautiful lady tree. The good tree is the victorious suitor, and the wildlife in the forest celebrate the outcome with the happy couple. The plot was thin, but the production was rich for its day; so rich, in fact, that the Academy Awards created a new division for best animated short to recognize the technical achievement of *Flowers and Trees*. Disney would continue to win the Academy Award in this category throughout the rest of the decade, and would ultimately win twenty-two Oscars in his career, the most among anyone in Academy of Motion Picture Arts and Sciences history.

Walt proved his detractors wrong again with Technicolor, and Universal responded with a six-picture agreement to produce more *Silly Symphonies* in color. Mickey Mouse, however, would stay in black and white another three years to keep costs down. The business model of the studio relied on the low-cost Mickey Mouse productions to serve as the cash cow for funding the *Silly Symphonies* experiments. Once the Technicolor exclusive agreement expired and the technology was available to all the other animation studios, Walt gave Mickey his first color treatment in 1935 with the release of *The Band Concert*. The days of black and white cartoons were over, but once again Walt had gotten the jump on his competition. The investment in Technicolor helped the *Silly Symphonies* become a showcase of Walt's technical and artistic prowess. Since his company was so adept at adapting new technologies and improving the quality of the art in the pictures, each *Silly Symphony* became an opportunity for Walt to ask, what's next? The Walt Disney Studios became a hit-making machine that profited from its increasing production efficiency and risk-taking experiments.

Walt's Assembly Line of Hits

Walt's team was on a roll now. The studio's assembly line approach rapidly released Mickey Mouse cartoons and *Silly Symphonies* to an eager national audience. So, what could he do to improve the productions now? Where was innovation missing in his process? What didn't have the Walt Disney stamp of originality on it? After studying his films, he decided that the musical numbers in the pictures had room for improvement. Up until this point, he used existing musical pieces to score his films. Adding their own songs to the cartoons would give his team another element of production to master. Plus, nothing gets in people's heads more than a catchy tune. What better way to spread the Disney name even further? Walt experimented with incorporating original music in the 1933 *Silly Symphonies* production of *The Three Little Pigs*. One song in particular, "Who's Afraid of the Big Bad Wolf," turned the cartoon into Walt's biggest hit yet. The country was in the depths of the Great Depression, and the public found inspiration in the three little pigs' stand against the formidable wolf. The catchy song rallied the nation to persevere through the tough economic times it was facing.

As with sound and color, Walt's musical experiment hit the right note on the first try, adding music as a new line of revenue for the company. The studio would continue to develop its musical department over the years, which would be an important ingredient later, when full-length animation classics were made. Walt Disney was now not only an entertainer and innovator but also a national public figure. Meanwhile, with the help of merchandiser Kay Kamen, the studio was able to capitalize on the Disney name by cashing in on song royalties, stuffed animals, children's books, newspaper comic strips, and a range of consumer products like Mickey Mouse watches. The influx of supplemental licensing revenue coupled with the boost in box office sales put the company in its best financial situation yet. According to Walt's daughter Diane Disney Miller, 1933 was a breakout year for him:

> I have to believe that 1933 was one of the most important years in my father's life. Technicolor had developed a three-color process for film that still was not perfected for live-action photography, but could be used for cartoons . . . It created a sensation . . . *Three Little Pigs* was a huge hit when it opened in 1933 . . . So many of the artists, musicians, and writers remember it as a uniquely exciting creative experience. The improvement in the work of the animators was astonishing. This was the result of the school Dad established on his lot under the supervision of Don Graham with the fine instructors from the Chouinard Art Institute. Dad worked closely with Graham in developing the curriculum for the school with action analysis, good draftsmanship, and knowledge of caricature stressed.[32]

A Sweeping Technical Achievement

Walt Disney's breakthrough year included huge hits in Mickey Mouse, the *Silly Symphonies*, and licensed products. He transcended what others thought was possible for an animation company, which put him miles ahead of the other cartoon makers in Hollywood. Not being one to coast on his success, Walt asked himself once again, what's next? How could he make the *Silly Symphonies* even better? The stories were good, the characters endearing, the musical scores popular, and the animation first class. Still, it seemed something was missing in his cartoons. Just as he turned to Chouinard for improving the artistry of his films, he now turned to engineers and scientists to create new tools for upping the studio's game again. As film historian Richard Schickel observed, "Disney's gift, from the beginning, was not as is commonly supposed a 'genius' for artistic expression . . . it was for the exploitation of technological innovation."[33]

Since the studio was on better financial footing, Walt felt he could be even more experimental in his productions. While filled with pride about what his team was creating, he felt his cartoons were still missing something technical that live action feature films had. He kept asking himself what traditional movies had that his cartoons didn't. What would give his cartoons the same theatrical experience that movies by great directors like Frank Capra and John Ford had in their live action films? Walt concluded that his films lacked the vibrant camera movement of the big studio film classics. The background scenery of his cartoons was adequately drawn and painted, but it wasn't dynamic. The camera shot appeared to move left and right but not forward and backward. His films lacked the rich cinematography and swooping camera shots that major motion pictures had. Directors give great thought to how to capture the scenery and characters with camera shots. The awe created by a swooping long shot capturing the natural beauty of a scene, the close-up of the star's face drawing us into their emotional state, and the kinetic movement of a chase sequence that helps us feel like we're part of the action are all tools of a live action film director. Yes, cinematography encompassed a major component of great filmmaking, and if Walt wanted to create art that would be judged to be on par with the great filmmakers, he knew he must figure out a way to bring a variety of shots to cartoons as well. After all, why couldn't a cartoon have a camera pan in for a close-up? or swoop in over a hill and descend into a town? or fly through a cloud and over the terrain? What was stopping his team from getting these shots? After diagnosing the problem, the animation team decided the constraint on their cinematography was the animation table where they filmed the cartoons. Essentially, an animation table utilizes a fixed camera that takes pictures of a two-dimensional world of celluloid sheets one at a time. The characters were drawn on cels, which were then laid on top of a background painting. One second of a cartoon is comprised of twenty-four cels captured one by one by the camera, with each frame being meticulously crafted. Live action films, on the other hand, could have their cameras on cranes, trucks, trains, planes, and dollies. Live action films and cartoons were markedly different in how they were put together, and in many ways cartoons were harder to make. However, cost accounted for another tradeoff made between the two movie forms. Walt didn't have to pay expensive movie stars to be in his productions; after all, he created them and they worked for free. He could also do the entire production inside his studio without expensive location shoots and sets. For now, he needed to accept the financial tradeoff of sticking to cartoons. But, still, wouldn't it be great if his cartoons could have the same dynamic effects he enjoyed seeing in live action films? He asked himself, how might I bring more energy and lifelike quality to these fantasy worlds I'm creating?

The answer to solving this technical achievement again would require an invention that would shake up the cartoon world like sound and color had before. What would that invention have to do? How could a camera move *through* a cartoon world, not just along it? How could a sense of depth be created in his scenes by his animators? This effect could not be attained from the fixed reference point of traditional animation cameras. The camera would have to move backward and forward to give the effect of swooping through the cartoon. Hence, this effect would still be limited because the camera would still be swooping toward the two-dimensional plane of the animation table that held the cels and backgrounds in place. You could get a close-up of the characters, but the magnificent cinematography found in major motion pictures still wouldn't happen. But, what if the camera could move through *multiple* planes in the cartoon? What if instead of one background painting, there were multiple background paintings spaced out, each one separated by actual physical distance to give the shot depth? Then the camera could "move through" the different planes and simulate the three dimensions of live action films. This insight led to the creation of the multiplane camera, an invention that revolutionized the theatrical quality of animation.

The multiplane camera was an engineering marvel. Unlike the standard animation table that placed a camera a couple feet above the cels, the multiplane camera was affixed atop an eleven-foot tower. Multiple planes of background were separated into layers painted on glass. The camera could then appear to move through a scene by changing the scope of what was being shot. The top plane could have a painting of a spider web with other background scenes like hills and towns still in the picture behind it. Moving the camera down the tower would focus the lens past the spider web and bring the other backgrounds more into the picture. In effect, the multiplane camera created the sensation of moving through the cartoon world. It was expensive and complex to operate, but the film effect was worth it to Walt. As Disney historian John Canemaker noted, "It allowed animated motion pictures a realism and vitality never before possible."[34]

Walt did it again. But he was particularly pleased with this technical achievement, reflecting, "It was always my ambition to own a swell camera, and now, goddammit, I got one. I get a kick just watching the boys operate it."[35] The multiplane camera created the effect he wanted, and his cartoon characters could now exist in more realistic settings. Better yet, the multiplane camera gave the cartoon shots a flexibility and nimbleness that live action movies couldn't even match. The camera could now go anywhere Walt dreamed up in his head. It could fly through space, submerge in an ocean, fly through the sky, or soar over land. The effect was only limited by what the animators could draw, and since Walt had the best team in the business, there was now little they couldn't do in a cartoon. The new camera movements also created a more dramatic effect in the cartoons, which enhanced the emotional experience of the films as well. A calm, slow, graceful shot brought tranquility, a fast-moving shot felt adventurous, and a shaky, violent shot was scary. Walt created a new tool to add to his film-making repertoire. He could now approach his movies the same way film auteurs he admired had. Better yet, he saw himself as one of those auteurs as well.

The multiplane camera was first employed in a *Silly Symphony* called *The Old Mill*. The cartoon opens with a long shot of an old, broken-down mill in a peaceful country meadow. The camera then moves through the meadow and into the mill itself. As it then proceeds to pan up the inside of the structure, a diverse collection of animals is revealed living inside the different parts of the mill. All seems good until a horrific storm sweeps through the meadow and plays havoc with the animals inside. The storm eventually passes and tranquility descends once again on the scene. The multiplane camera's shots, beautiful background paintings, lifelike animal drawings, and stirring musical score create a moving drama without a single word being said by a cartoon character. *The Old Mill* passed the test, winning Disney another Academy Award for technical achievement. Audiences and critics considered the film a critical achievement in elevating cartoons to a true art form. Even more importantly, the achievement confirmed for Walt and his crew that there wasn't a single subject or story that they couldn't tackle now. Walt now imagined what he could accomplish when he added characters, dialogue, and a good story to this camera work. So, with the technical achievement of the multiplane camera, Walt once again asked himself, what's next? Since he didn't see much room for improving animated shorts after the success of *The Old Mill*, the next logical step seemed to be scaling what his team had mastered into something bigger than a cartoon. He wondered, how could a Walt Disney production be the main attraction and not just the opening act? Walt was prepared and confident now to take on his biggest challenge yet. The Walt Disney Studios was finally ready to enter the big-time world of show business.

Conclusion

In the previous chapter, we saw how Walt behaved as an artist in his business. He took art classes, worked in an animation studio, and made movies with friends in his first venture in Kansas City. He put his time in as an animator. Even though there were others who could do it better, Walt came away from Kansas City understanding the animation process because he had paid his dues as an animator himself. His days in Hollywood would have a different tone.

He would no longer spend his time drawing the cartoons. Instead, he dreamed up the ideas that he would have others animate. Freed from drawing, he could now explore how to bring new technologies into the medium to improve the productions.

Now, there's nothing wrong with building a business around an art form. Master craftsmen can create excellent products, but it's hard to provide a lot of new products to customers relying on old technologies. Many entrepreneurs are not willing to invest in new technologies that disrupt the old way of doing things. Walt, however, was different. He was always on the lookout for anything that could bring better cartoons to his audiences. He was always asking himself, what's next? It was his time as a scientist, creating the science of animation, that took the Walt Disney Studios into a whole new stratosphere of the animation world. If Walt remained only in his artist phase, he would eventually have gotten bored. He needed new challenges, and there was only so much he could do with the existing state of animation. In this chapter, we can see that by tackling the challenges of sound, color, and enhanced camera techniques, and by building a school of Disney animation inside the studio, he was able to create cartoons like no one had ever imagined before.

Walt also took advantage of the fact that Mickey Mouse and the *Silly Symphonies* weren't the main features at a theater. This had its pluses and minuses. On the positive side, since the audience was paying for the main feature, the *Silly Symphonies* could be a testing ground for new animation techniques. Perfection wasn't required. Audiences expected more from the main feature than the warm-up cartoon. The minus side of this scenario was that the improved quality and experimentation of the *Silly Symphonies* incurred great costs for the studio. It took time to develop the new technology and techniques, which resulted in huge expenditures in manpower as well as longer production cycles. Additionally, the equipment that was required to pull off the effects, like the multiplane camera, was expensive as well. Fortunately during this time, Mickey Mouse maintained popularity and proved much easier to produce, which added to the bottom line. Also, with the help of merchandising whiz Kay Kamen, the studio received a nice cash flow from royalties on songs, toys, and books. Still, Walt's drive for innovation pushed Roy to figure out ways to keep the company in the black, even as the studio's films became more popular.

The *Silly Symphony* stage of Walt's life particularly embodied the practices and mind-set of a scientist. The *Silly Symphonies* were a laboratory for Walt to bring his new science of animation into the medium, which will lay the groundwork for all the masterpieces—most notably *Snow White*—that will come in the future. As Walt once explained when reflecting on the role of technology in his company:

> Our business has grown with and by technical achievements. Should this technological progress ever come to a full stop, prepare the funeral oration for our medium. That is how dependent we artists have become on the

new tools and refinements which the technicians give us. Sound, Technicolor, the multiplane camera, Fantasound, these and a host of other less spectacular contributions . . . have made possible the pictures which are the milestones in our progress.[36]

In the next chapter, we'll see Walt transition from being a scientist to being more of a builder. With the science of animation mastered, the studio can now

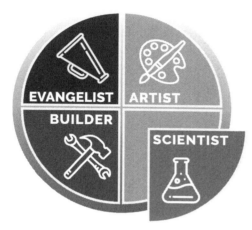

- Focus on reality
- Value deep research on a subject
- Search for supporting evidence of ideas
- Strive to perfect new concepts
- View modeling as a key entrepreneurial activity
- Study best practices
- Adapts and develops new technologies

WALT DISNEY THE SCIENTIST

Tinkering and adapting technology
- Putting actor in cartoon world: Alice's Wonderland
- Sound: Steamboat Willie
- Technicolor: Flower and Trees (Silly Symphonies)

Experimenting/Prototyping/Proof of Concept
- Giving cartoon characters personality (Mickey Mouse)
- Cartoon as dramatic piece: Skeleton Dance (Silly Symphonies)
- Invention of Multiplane camera: The Old Mill (Silly Symphonies)
- Adding show tunes to cartoons: 3 Little Pigs (Silly Symphonies)

Developed trainable methodology for animation
- Chouinard Art Institute classes
- Don Graham partnership leading Disney classes at studio
- Systematizing cartoon production into distinctive areas and specialists
- Recruited and trained new animators for future at Hyperion Studio

FIGURE 2.1 Entrepreneurial Leadership Style—Scientist

exploit its technical prowess to create bigger and bolder Disney products for the world. The next stage of the company will be about scale: bigger animation productions, a bigger studio, a big park devoted totally to the Disney brand, and, ultimately, a bigger company.

Disney Principles

* Success is often as much a result of where we put ourselves as what we do.
* In any setback, find the upside in the situation that you can capitalize on. There's always an upside to anything. It's your job to find it.
* When pursuing a big goal, ask yourself, what's the one easy step I can do to get this project going?
* Innovators expect things to change and take action to ensure it does. They are on the forefront of movements taking place in their industries.
* To have a legendary career like Walt, once you reach a milestone, immediately ask yourself, what's next? Legendary careers are comprised of a long series of accomplishments compressed into one lifetime.

Work Like Disney: Exercises

1. Why do you think the Walt Disney Company was so innovative? What can you take from Walt Disney's example that would transform your own company?
2. What keeps you from being innovative? How would Walt Disney have addressed these issues?
3. Walt Disney was in the trenches with his artists, working on stories and animation. Does the leadership of your company do this? Why or why not? If Walt were sitting down with you in a brainstorming session, how would it run differently than idea sessions go for you now?
4. How do your work habits resemble Walt's? Do you consider yourself creative? Why or why not? What approaches could you take in your job to get creative results like Walt did?
5. In Walt's famous memo to art teacher Don Graham, he stated that the qualities needed to be a good animator were good draftsmanship; knowledge of caricature, action, and features; knowledge and appreciation of acting; ability to think up gags and put over gags; knowledge of story construction and audience values; and knowledge and understanding of all the mechanical and detailed routine involved in animation work. If you were writing a memo to employees in your company, what would you tell them are the critical qualities needed to do good work in your industry? Now draft a memo stating what it takes to do creative, high-quality work in what you do.

Notes

1. Smith, D. (1994). *Walt Disney: Famous Quotes*. New York: Disney.
2. Gabler, N. (2006). *Walt Disney: The Triumph of the American Imagination*. New York: Vintage.
3. Ibid.
4. Disney Enterprises. (2001). *The Quotable Walt Disney*. New York: Disney Editions.
5. Ghez, D. (2008). *Walt's People,* Volume 7. Bloomington, IN: Xlibris.
6. Gabler, N. (2006). *Walt Disney: The Triumph of the American Imagination*. New York: Vintage.
7. Zander, R.S., and Zander, B. (2002). *The Art of Possibility: Transforming Professional and Personal Life*. New York: Penguin.
8. Buchholz, T. (2016). *The Price of Prosperity: Why Rich Nations Fail and How to Renew Them*. New York: HarperCollins.
9. Kaufman, J.B., and Merritt, R. (2000). *Walt in Wonderland: The Silent Films of Walt Disney*. Baltimore, MD: Johns Hopkins University Press.
10. Thomas, B. (1974). *Walt Disney: An American Original*. New York: Disney Editions.
11. Crafton, D. (1982). *Before Mickey: The Animated Film, 1898–1928*. Cambridge, MA: MIT Press.
12. (1927). "Universal's Oswald Cartoon Comedies Backed by Chocolate Bar Tie-Up." *Universal Weekly*, 32, August 20. Reprinted in Michael Barrier (2007), *The Animated Man: A Life of Walt Disney*.
13. Minnie was named after Minnie Cowles, a friend from Kansas City who had been very kind to Walt and Ub during the Laugh-O-Gram days.
14. Bush, G.W. (2010). *Decision Points*. New York: Crown.
15. Kaufman, J.B., and Merritt, R. (2000). *Walt in Wonderland: The Silent Films of Walt Disney*. Baltimore: Johns Hopkins University Press.
16. Thomas, B. (1974). *Walt Disney: An American Original*. New York: Disney Editions.
17. Kaufman, J.B., and Merritt, R. (2000). *Walt in Wonderland: The Silent Films of Walt Disney*. Baltimore: Johns Hopkins University Press.
18. Iwerks, L. (2001). *The Hand Behind the Mouse: An Intimate Biography of Ub Iwerks*. New York: Disney Editions.
19. Goldberg, S. (2017). "Genius Takes Many Forms. It's Time We Recognized Them All." *National Geographic*, May.
20. Saltz, G. (2017). *The Power of Different: The Link Between Disorder and Genius*. New York: Flatiron Books.
21. Ashwin, E., Ashwin, C., Rhydderch, D., Howells, J., and Baron-Cohen, S. (2009). "Eagle-Eyed Visual Acuity: An Experimental Investigation of Enhanced Perception in Autism." *Biological Psychiatry*, 65(1): 17–21.
22. Samson, F., Mottron, L., Soulieres, I., and Zeffiro, T.A. (2012). "Enhanced Visual Functioning in Autism: An ALE Meta-analysis." *Human Brain Mapping*, 33(7): 1553–1581.
23. Iwerks, L. (2001). *The Hand Behind the Mouse: An Intimate Biography of Ub Iwerks*. New York: Disney Editions.
24. Gabler, N. (2006). *Walt Disney: The Triumph of the American Imagination*. New York: Vintage.
25. Shenk, J.W. (2014). *Powers of Two: Finding the Essence of Innovation in Creative Pairs*. Boston: Houghton Mifflin Harcourt.

26. Gabler, N. (2006). *Walt Disney: The Triumph of the American Imagination*. New York: Vintage.

27. Care, R. (2016). *Disney Legend Wilfred Jackson: A Life in Animation*. Lexington: Theme Park Press.

28. Morris, M.H., Kuratko, D.F., Schindehutte, M., and Spivack, A.J. (2012). "Framing the Entrepreneurial Experience." *Entrepreneurship Theory and Practice*, 36(1): 11–40.

29. Iwerks, L. (2001). *The Hand Behind the Mouse: An Intimate Biography of Ub Iwerks*. New York: Disney Editions.

30. Ghez, D. (2009). *Walt's People*, Volume 8. Bloomington, IN: Xlibris.

31. Jackson, M.K. (2005). *Walt Disney: Conversations*. Oxford, MS: University of Mississippi Press.

32. Johnson, M. (2017). *Ink & Paint: The Women of Walt Disney's Animation*. New York: Disney Animations.

33. Schickel, R. (1997). *The Disney Version: The Life, Times, Art, and Commerce of Walt Disney*. Chicago: Ivan R. Dee.

34. Canemaker, J. (2014). *The Lost Notebook: Herman Schultheis & the Secrets of Walt Disney's Movie Magic*. New York: Welden Owen.

35. Gabler, N. (2006). *Walt Disney: The Triumph of the American Imagination*. New York: Vintage.

36. Disney, W. (1941). "Growing Pains." *American Cinematographer*, March.

3

THE BUILDER YEARS

Well, my greatest reward I think is I've been able to build this wonderful organization.
—Walt Disney[1]

Snow White: The Idea

By 1933, Walt Disney mastered the science of animation. Producing the most entertaining cartoons on the market established Disney as a global brand, with audiences clamoring for whatever the studio offered next. Yet, like always, Walt wanted a bigger challenge. The technical and artistic achievements of the *Silly Symphonies* proved that the studio could take animation in new directions. What if the quality of a Walt Disney production could be delivered for an entire feature-length film? The average cartoon in the *Silly Symphonies* and Mickey Mouse series consisted of approximately eight minutes. However, a feature-length film would require animating ten times the number of frames. Would audiences even be willing to sit through an eighty-minute animated film? Walt was willing to find out.

In the previous chapters, we challenged you to visit different theme park landmarks, in order to appreciate that stage of Walt's entrepreneurial career. A good exercise for this chapter is to watch one of the Disney cartoons from the early 1930s and compare it to *Snow White and the Seven Dwarfs*. The differences in the productions symbolize the changes that happened in the company. It's during this stage we see Walt transition from working like a scientist to more like a builder. Builders leverage skills of excellence and deliver more of it to their customers. For *Snow White* to achieve greatness on the big screen, Walt would have to scale everything the company was already doing. And since *Snow White* was a feature film, audiences would have higher expectations of its quality.

Delivering a bigger and better animated product would require more animators, more money, and more time while still continuing to produce Mickey Mouse and *Silly Symphonies* cartoons to cover the costs of the studio operations in the meantime. Walt's vision of what an animated production could become would also require him to reimagine what his studio was destined to be. Walt Disney Productions would have to become a much larger organization to make *Snow White* possible.

The studio maintained its innovative edge, even with its growth, because of the example Walt set for everyone. He was always enthusiastic about taking on new challenges. When he entertained an idea which excited him, his whole mood changed. He came alive, flamboyantly gesturing and talking about his exciting notion with whomever was near. He dropped everything else and focused his energy on building enthusiasm in the studio for the idea. Yet, following closely behind this excitement was a lot of hard work. Walt was as wholeheartedly committed to follow-through as he was ideas. Once he believed in something, he was compelled to turn his vision into reality. When it was time for everyone to give their all to a project, they knew their boss was doing the same. No one questioned whether Walt was working as hard as they were. Ben Sharpsteen, who animated and directed many of these projects, acknowledged:[2]

> There was no such thing as an "out-of-hours" with Walt. Every hour of the twenty-four in the day was a part of his routine. He never had his work off his mind; he never had time set aside for play. I wondered how he ever managed to get any sleep with all the problems that absorbed him. But evidently he did because he always came to the studio prepared to put in his day's work. To be at leisure with Walt outside of the studio was not to be at leisure. He was always preoccupied with the studio. It was his life.

Walt wasn't a totally unfeeling machine, though. He spent most of his time outside the studio with his family. However, he always brought work home with him. He was often reading scripts or tinkering with some new device in his home workshop. Additionally, he developed a voracious appetite for travel, going to exotic countries or historic towns, which served as source material for ideas for future productions. Sometimes, if he was really curious about something, he'd hit the road with employees from the studio, but any time with the boss was spent on business. As Sharpsteen recalls about Walt's travel habits:[3]

> He was not a man to relax. On a trip I never could separate him from his work at the studio; he was always either talking about the business or he was silent because he was preoccupied with problems. . . . We used

to say that he was a hound dog. He was hot on the trail, and we would follow him, but as he led us on, he would lose himself far ahead of us. We would plunge on blindly and find ourselves hanging on to the old trail, or as we put it, the end of the trail.

Walt had been on *Snow White's* trail for quite a while. He studied different versions of the Brothers Grimm story over the years. Finally, after working the storyline out with friends, he thought it was ready to present to his team of animators. On a winter night in 1934, Walt asked fifty of them to gather on a soundstage and wait for him to arrive. Once there, they proceeded to see him put on the performance of a lifetime. Walt acted out the whole story over three hours. Incredibly, he didn't just explain what the movie would be, he *became* the movie, even using different voices and mannerisms for each character. The performance was so masterful that it became the template for the entire production over the next three years. These exhilarating moments stirred the imagination of his employees.

DISNEY LESSON 8: ENTREPRENEURIAL LEADERS SET THE EXAMPLE FOR EVERYONE ELSE IN THE COMPANY TO FOLLOW

Walt and the story development team put great effort in the preproduction stage of *Snow White*, establishing the plot and characters. Once the story was established, the film was handed over to the animation team to bring it to life. Walt was as involved with the animators in this step as he was with his story people. The plot and storyboards provided the framework of what the movie could be, but it's the individual frames of the film that showcase Walt's attention to detail. If you want to know what Walt Disney was like, all you have to do is watch one of his productions. His mannerisms and personality are embedded in the characters, and the caliber of the production comes from his obsessive commitment to quality. When Walt had an idea for a scene, he didn't just tell it to everyone, he put on a show. No one slacked off in his presence because he expected his impromptu performances to one day be on the big screen. If they weren't paying attention, he'd know it when he saw the rough cut of a scene. Yet, that expectation brought out the best work of the most talented animators in the business, giving the Disneys another advantage over their competitors. His skills as an actor and storyteller coupled with his commitment to his productions set a high bar for everyone around him. As a result, everyone at the studio fed off his energy. As animator Wilfred Jackson attests:[4]

> Walt was my guru. It was a teacher-student relationship. He knew how to do what I wanted to do. By being the little finger on Walt's left hand, I could accomplish more than I could do by myself. I felt like I was being overpaid.

Bringing out the best of so many talented people is what made the hits possible, as animator Frank Thomas confirms: "He did what he did because of the men he had and what he could get out of them. He couldn't have done it without anyone else." Ollie Johnston, Thomas's best friend and collaborator in the studio, was amazed that Walt could even influence Roy, the person who knew him best. Johnston recalled a time Roy wanted him to tell reporter Richard Hubler about Walt's power of persuasion:[5]

> Roy said, "Tell him the little tricks that Walt used to play on all of us, tell him all the things that Walt did to us to get us to do what we didn't want to do." This is Roy saying this. Nobody escaped.

If Walt could get Roy, his risk-averse brother, to agree to his wild ideas, he could convince anyone. He needed to do this to get the movies made. He had confidence in his ideas, but he had an even greater awareness that he couldn't do the job alone. Frankly, as high as his expectations were of others, perhaps he demanded more of himself than anyone else. This drive to excel probably caused him to come off as moody and temperamental at times. The difficulties found in new challenges and obstacles brought a range of different emotions, ranging from quiet contemplation to manic eureka moments to frustration and angst. With so many projects circulating through the studio at once, Walt possessed little patience for small talk. Time wasted in one place prevented him from keeping other productions going. He expected someone seeing him to get to the crux of an issue so he could move on to the next concern on another project. His direct feedback appeared harsh to some employees but was effective in getting projects completed. His mannerisms were not intended to personally wound anyone, and he rarely held grudges. He was simply trying to get results. How else could he complete *Snow White* and keep the studio afloat at the same time?

Unsurprisingly, this range of emotions is to be expected from somebody who pushed themselves so hard in everything they did, as many creative legends do. The preparation, time, and hard work that go into realizing a powerful idea can at times be stressful and exhausting, but the payoff usually makes it all worthwhile. Such an outcome is often the price to be paid for the pursuit of perfection. And, for someone like Walt who had so many ideas in various stages of development, it would have been very normal for him to go through many different moods during the day. If you find yourself working for a driven entrepreneur, think about how you can make their job easier. What can you do to reduce their stress or fear on a project? In many ways, your job as an employee is to make your boss's job easier. Such an attitude will be greatly appreciated. After all, it's a common feature of human nature that people give you more responsibilities and privileges when they like and trust you. Walt's employees who understood and practiced this principle were afforded the opportunity to work on bigger assignments in the future. The pursuit of excellence can at times bring hardship to everyone in the enterprise. However, for a creative person, the chance to stretch their imagination and artistic skills on interesting projects can be a great reward in itself. Many of the Disney employees who understood and supported what Walt was trying to accomplish had careers in the company spanning decades.

In turn, if you're an entrepreneur, know that pursuing interesting projects will draw talented people to your company. Capable people not only want to be compensated well, they want the opportunity to apply their talents to meaningful and impactful work with other driven creators. The archetype of a lone genius with a breakthrough idea is a myth. Creative people do their best work around others who can inspire and motivate them. Consider Michelangelo, one of history's greatest creators. He produced his masterpieces in Florence, Italy, where other greats like Donatello and Giotto were located. He didn't sculpt David in the small rural village of Caldine. Michelangelo was near the action in his field. However, where that spot of opportunity for you is depends on your field of expertise. In *The Geography of Genius*, Eric Weiner chronicled the rise of innovative locations throughout history, and concluded: "Certain places, at certain times, produced a crop of brilliant minds and good ideas."[6] Great companies in an industry are the same. For Walt, guiding his teams on breakthrough projects during the golden age of Hollywood served as an immense source of pride for him. As he said, "Of all the things I've done, the most vital is coordinating the talents of those who work for us and pointing them toward a certain goal."[7]

Snow White: The Production

Imagine the challenges Walt faced even starting *Snow White*. A production team who never made a movie before now needed to generate a dramatic story that would hold an audience's attention for eighty minutes. New characters would need to be developed, and they wouldn't get a second chance to tweak the characters like they did with Mickey Mouse. The story and characters must be right the first time. Even so, to complicate the animation process, the fairytale would require drawing lifelike human figures, not just animals. Walt also learned from the success of the *Three Little Pigs* that a catchy show tune increased the entertainment value of his cartoons, but for a feature film an entire musical score would need to be drafted. With a small team of animators and story development people, Walt went to work figuring out what *Snow White* could be. Although the plot of the movie required several iterations, perhaps the issue consuming the team the most involved deciding who would star next to Snow White. The team explored many possible personalities for the seven dwarfs, including characters such as Scrappy, Dirty, Cranky, Sappy, Jumpy, Weepy, and Hungry, before settling on Grumpy, Happy, Sleepy, Bashful, Sneezy, Doc, and Dopey.[8] The next challenge involved deciding who would animate each of the dwarfs. To ensure authenticity of the characters, Walt selected artists whose personalities resembled those of each dwarf. After all, animators are actually actors themselves, performing through the characters they're drawing. So, for example, Grumpy was drawn by Bill Tytla, who was actually a grumpy person himself. The other dwarfs found their suitable matches too. Then Walt found radio performers who had voices that matched those personalities well.[9]

Another important element of the production was the background scenery. Since the movie required the feel of a fairytale, Walt hired European artists who knew that part of the world well. Walt and Roy even vacationed in Europe early in the film's production to hone their sensibility of what the film could be. During that trip Walt purchased fairytale books, absorbed European culture, and wandered the surrounding countryside, letting his imagination run wild. When Walt got back from the trip, he was inspired to move into full production and make the movie unforgettable. Unfortunately, Walt was understaffed for the making of *Snow White*. The studio continued to produce Mickey Mouse and *Silly Symphonies* cartoons, so making a feature film required a serious investment in new people. Walt turned again to his chief talent developer Don Graham. Graham worked overtime recruiting three hundred new animators to the studio as well as training them in the Disney style. The infusion of new talent would cost the company a lot of money, but such staffing was necessary to meet the production schedules for *Snow White* and the Mickey Mouse and *Silly Symphony* cartoons. The influx of new employees also put a strain on space in the already crowded and cramped Hyperion studio, which no longer resembled the tranquil artist paradise of previous times. Yet, many Disney historians compare this time in the studio to a Renaissance workshop, with people of various trades working closely together to produce great art.

Roy strongly felt the financial pressure of meeting the production schedule. Costs skyrocketed, and the cartoons and merchandise sales were barely keeping the studio afloat. The Disney brothers needed a bank loan to keep the company's cash flow positive. This proved to be quite a challenge, considering that the original budget of $500,000 for *Snow White* tripled over the course of the production. The cost overruns led many inside and outside the studio to call the *Snow White* production "Disney's Folly," and for good reason. If *Snow White* failed, the studio would go bankrupt. After all, Walt was the clear leader in the cartoon industry. Why would he need to stray from a successful formula, making the best cartoons in the world? But, it was that striving nature that put the studio in that leadership position in the first place. Reaching the summit of one medium compelled him to conquer another.

Walt and Roy were totally committed to *Snow White*, which meant everyone else in the company was too. The animators, ink and paint women, musicians, directors, and business team worked day and night to complete the production. The effort was there, but nothing they did could make up for the shortage of money they needed to meet their payroll. It seemed like Walt was always running the company in startup mode, working on new ideas, with Roy figuring out ways to keep the employees' checks from bouncing. Recognizing the financial crunch that the studio was under, Roy asked Walt to convince Bank of America to loan them more money. Walt didn't like getting involved in the money side of the business, but if he was going to continue putting the studio in the red, he needed to assist Roy. Walt appeared nervous meeting with Joe Rosenberg, the Bank of America executive who was coming to the studio. The current film was nowhere near ready for release. A rough screening wouldn't do justice to what Walt had in his head for the final production. However, he acquiesced after Roy said to him, "Walt, you have to. The only way we're going to get more money is to show them what you have."[10]

Sometimes an entrepreneur must improvise with what is available and paint a picture in the minds of investors of what's coming in the final product. The meeting with Bank of America proved another pivotal moment in the company's history where Walt's master salesmanship was put to the test. Walt told his team to splice together whatever rough pencil animations they had with the completed color scenes for Rosenberg to view. Since the movie wasn't complete, Walt would serve as a tour guide, explaining what the film would look like when it was done.

When Rosenberg arrived at the studio, Walt steered him to a dark projection room where the two men watched a rough version of the film. Where scenes were missing, Walt flipped through pages of pencil drawings and explained what the audience would eventually see. Rosenberg appeared quiet throughout the screening, which concerned Walt. If he wasn't excited about what he saw, Bank of America probably wouldn't give the Disneys the money they needed to complete the film. Eventually both men walked back quietly to Rosenberg's car in the studio parking lot. The tension in the air must have been thick as Walt awaited the decision that would determine if his dream could be completed or not. Rosenberg got into his car, and just before driving off he turned to Walt and said, "That thing is going to make a hatful of money."[11] Bank of America was in! Rosenberg liked the rough cut enough to know that the film was going to be a huge hit, and that meant that Bank of America wanted to be along for the ride. The studio received its loan, and production continued onward toward meeting the deadline. With the cash infusion, Walt could now go full bore in completing *Snow White*, but there was still the pressing deadline of getting it out to the public. Now time was his most limited resource, and he needed to drive his team with all the energy he could muster, not only to meet the deadline but also to deliver the quality that Bank of America expected from the Disneys.

In the summer of 1936, final animation took place on the production, and it wasn't until November 1937 that the last scene was completed. The final scene invoked the sorrow of the dwarfs and prince at Snow White's burial, which would prove to be the hardest challenge on the production. The scene was saved for last because it would require master craftsmanship in all aspects of animation and moviemaking. Every scene before this one helped develop the skills to make the final minutes work, which was critical to the film's success. After all, the first seventy minutes set the stage for this cinematic climax. The audience's ultimate reaction to the film would rest on whether those five minutes were emotionally satisfying before the final five minutes of credits rolled. The team did its best to meet the challenge, and completed the scene in time for its scheduled release date. Unfortunately, after piecing it into the final cut, Walt realized it wasn't perfect. Just a little more tweaking of a few scenes would truly make his creation the masterpiece he imagined in his mind. The scene in which the prince appears to shimmy as he walks to the casket particularly disturbed Walt. Walt pleaded with Roy to let him correct the error, but Roy refused this time, saying, "No, let the prince shimmy." Perfection would have to wait for future productions. Roy decided to settle for excellence and get the film to the theaters. It was good enough. Making money in the near future took priority over Walt's artistic perfectionism this time.

A lot of stakeholders incurred risks in making *Snow White*. Now they all got to see whether their decision to join the enterprise was a smart one. Even more importantly, had Walt made the right production calls to create a satisfying audience experience? With all this, perhaps even more curiosity was focused on the company. Did the Disneys build an organization capable of making such a grand production? Were animators who worked on Mickey Mouse cartoons capable of creating a movie that would entertain sophisticated audiences for eighty minutes? Would it be a sloppy production or would it look like a real Hollywood film? Did Walt and Roy possess the horsepower inside the little Hyperion studio to make *Snow White* work? Did Bank of America show sound business judgment in loaning the money? Was Joe Rosenberg even capable of making such a decision? Should Roy have given Walt more time to polish the final cut? All these questions would be answered at *Snow White's* premiere on December 21, 1937, at the Carthay Circle Theatre. It was an epic Hollywood event. After all, no one appreciates a creative risk more than the people who work in the industry. Movie stars turned out in anticipation to see if what Walt had been pursuing for the last few years would be something special or a disaster.

The final stage of the experiment took place when the curtain rose. As the movie played, the audience of Hollywood insiders was captivated by what it was seeing, and seventy-five minutes later, when the closing credits started to roll, the audience erupted in a standing ovation. Walt and his team had succeeded. The movie exceeded everyone's expectations.

The risk paid off. Three years of hard work rested on that audience's reaction. Imagine the relief and exhilaration everyone in the studio must have felt. Few people probably know the natural high Walt experienced at that moment. *Snow White* went on to win Walt an honorary Academy Award and gross eight million dollars at the box office. It played worldwide, and one theater in London alone grossed as much as the $500,000 original budget. People no longer called it "Disney's Folly"; it was now "Disney's Masterpiece." But, perhaps the greatest validation Walt got from its success was a congratulatory note he received from his boyhood hero Charlie Chaplin. The kid who was denied a job on a movie set when he arrived in town in 1923 was now a major Hollywood player. With a huge hit and plenty of money in the studio coffers, Walt could now animate more stories that beckoned him. The world awaited whatever he could dream up next. According to biographer Neal Gabler, "The nine months after *Snow White* debuted may have been the best months of Walt Disney's adult life."[12] He had proven his critics wrong and could pursue whatever ideas he wanted now.

DISNEY LESSON 9: YOU'LL FACE YOUR BIGGEST CHALLENGES ON THE WAY TO YOUR GREATEST ACCOMPLISHMENTS

Mickey Mouse and the *Silly Symphonies* introduced Walt as a legitimate player in Hollywood, but *Snow White* established his reputation as a creative genius. Not only did he and his team tackle the first feature-length animation, but they also invented new technology to bring it to the screen. People wondered in 1938 how it was possible to come up with so many excellent ideas to make *Snow White* work as well as it did. Additionally, they were further amazed, as many other classics came out of the studio over the years. So everybody asked what made Walt so creative. How did he dream up all these ideas? After all, Walt didn't take a creativity class to teach him how to do this. Seemingly, like so many innovators throughout history, he intuitively learned how to generate breakthrough ideas through hard work and informal experimentation. When something worked for him, he established it as more of a routine in his life. Fortunately, we can follow an easier path because of what we can learn from Walt's example.

Why did Walt have so many "eureka" moments when most people don't? Perhaps one reason is most people don't realize how hard he worked before having his flashes of insight. Walt sometimes spent years researching and mulling over a subject before he decided to move it into production. Most people who want to be creative like Walt aren't willing to sacrifice the amount of time he did in developing his ideas. While inspirational moments like the *Snow White* story pitch to the fifty animators are inspiring, we must always remember the immense preparation, hard work, and time that went into putting together the source material in the first place. He was patient during story development to ensure he had a good idea, but once he moved into production mode he pursued his deadlines with full conviction. Few people work as hard on the preparation side as they do on the execution side, and vice versa. Walt's willingness to embrace the uncertain, chaotic nature of creativity and then switch to disciplined follow-through is not found in most people. Meeting ambitious goals, however, requires equal commitment to both sides of the creativity equation.

Unlike production schedules, eureka moments don't adhere to a timeline. You don't know when you'll get one. Walt often got ideas while he was busy doing something unrelated to the studio. Sometimes, they appeared as a bolt out of the blue, but in most cases the answers surfaced in incremental fashion. Slowly but surely he formulated the solution, though. Walt didn't give up when he wanted to figure something out, which perhaps speaks to his strong drive for learning new subjects. He patiently learned from others when he was struggling with the ambiguity of a new idea. When something caught his attention, he dove deeply into the topic to better understand it, even to the point where he could have intelligent conversations with leading experts—not bad for a man who dropped out of school at the age of 15.

The following practices helped Walt develop his new ideas: 1) He daydreamed a lot, imagining the possibilities of future projects. Although he was around a lot of people during the day, he often spent quiet time after work reading books outside his expertise and wondering about the implications of them for his company; 2) he developed different hobbies throughout his life that allowed him to give his conscious mind a break and free up his subconscious to generate new ideas; 3) when he wanted to explore new topics, he removed himself from the studio to more leisurely environments (for example, at home instead of at the office); 4) he put new ideas on the backburner if they weren't strong enough yet to present to his team, but once he was sure his idea was ready, he moved promptly in fitting it into the studio's schedule; 5) he practiced being a voracious note-taker, recording ideas late at night or early in the morning on whatever he had handy; and 6) he took breaks from working, often going to foreign countries, which became places that later found their way into many of his movies.

Knowing some of the ways Walt obtained his ideas will assist you in becoming more creative. You'll have a better understanding of how to gather information, you'll trust that your subconscious is working for you in the background, and you'll develop more patience and persistence, traits that Walt had in abundance in his creative pursuits. If your good idea has yet to surface, be encouraged. You will know that it's not because of a lack of ability on your part. You simply need more information and time to solve the problem. Sometimes Walt spent years on ideas that didn't even appear on screen. In *The Disney That Never Was*, Charles Solomon observed:[13]

> Walt Disney frequently moved individual projects in and out of pro-duction as the studio's finances and the progress of competing ideas dictated. Some of the films were abandoned for obvious reasons—a lack of time, money, or enough trained artists . . . Some stories proved too weak to sustain an eighty-minute feature or a seven-minute short. Others were too long or complex, or centered on characters and actions that weren't suited to animation.

As we chronicled earlier in this chapter, the creative process can some-times be taxing. You're working hard, but the answer doesn't seem to be coming to you. Don't worry. Walt shows us that frustration and confusion are normal feelings during the creative process. Hang in there! When you come across pertinent information that might be helpful in solving a problem or creating a new product or service, your brain will let you know. Not only will it reward you with a boost of energy when you get a good idea, it will also give you an even bigger boost when you bring it to life. Unfortunately, you don't know if an idea will work for sure until you start it. Most people aren't willing to endure the chance that they might fail, but Walt was. He used to say, "The best way to get started is to quit talking and begin doing."[14] When you move out of the safety of the status quo into territory you don't know, you're bound to make mistakes. Walt did, and sometimes he even failed. But, he learned from his mistakes, and that knowledge became useful on future projects. Animator Joe Grant said, "After something went wrong, his basic attitude was 'Fine, that didn't work, what's the next project?' . . . He'd be disappointed, but you wouldn't find him grieving."[15] Walt's willingness to take creative risks put the studio on a bumpy path sometimes, but such efforts also built the company into what it is today.

A Clean Slate

Snow White consumed the attention of Walt and his production team between 1934 and 1938. Aside from some Mickey Mouse and *Silly Symphony* cartoons, no other projects were in the pipeline. Walt shouldn't be faulted for his monomaniacal focus on *Snow White*. The movie necessitated greatness. After all, if *Snow White* had failed, the studio would have gone under. For one time in his life, Walt didn't look ahead. He knew that if *Snow White* wasn't a phenomenal success, there would be no future productions. Fortunately, the gamble paid off, and the movie had a huge international run, making it the highest grossing film of all time. But now what? Now that audiences knew what a Walt Disney *film* was like, their expectations would be enormous. What story could Walt develop to ensure he didn't fall victim to a sophomore jinx? He struggled with the question over the next couple years, and while he did so, many of the animators sat around with nothing to do until he had made his decision.

Building the company around Walt's talent as a storyteller proved a strength and a weakness for the organization. On the positive side, it gave a competitive edge to the company. No one else in the industry had someone comparable to him. Clearly, there was now Walt Disney and everyone else. When people saw his name on a production, they knew it would be special. A Walt Disney production meant quality, innovation, and wholesomeness. On the negative side, that authority created a production bottleneck in the studio during the post-*Snow White* years. Everything started with Walt, and if he wasn't ready to move forward, everyone else had no choice but to wait. Imagine today if Pixar couldn't move forward with a film until current Disney CEO Bob Iger worked out a storyline. Yet, most times, the wait proved worthwhile, as Walt may be the best American storyteller of all time. We can get a glimpse into how he developed his stories by studying his memos to his creative teams. One particular note from October 6, 1938, provides the overall approach he followed:[16]

> The aim of the Disney Studio [*sic*] has always been to create a better product by improving on each improvement. Striving to top each picture with a better one is a difficult assignment, but this goal has been a major contributing factor to whatever success and advancement we have attained. . . . Our first job is to tell a story that isn't known to the audience. Then we have to tell a story that may cover several days, or years, in a little over an hour; so consequently we have to tell things faster than they happen in real life. Also, we want to make things more interesting than they are in real life. Our actors must be more interesting and more unusual than you and I. Their thought processes must be quicker than ours, and their uninteresting progressions from one situation to another must be skipped. Our main purpose is to entertain and amuse the audience.

Those who worked closely with him knew it was worth the wait too. As animator Ken O'Connor remembers:[17]

> The main thing was his story ability. We'd have a story meeting and we would be a bit bogged down on it, not knowing where to go. He was

very annoying to show a storyboard to, because you would start pointing along and you would look at him and he was down near the bottom. He was quick. But you would have to go through it anyway, and he would let you. Then by the time you got done, he would say, "Now take that part out. Develop this part. Now put this part up here." And then he'd go out and you'd say, "Why the hell didn't I think of that?" That was his intuition and judgment that worked all the time marvelously. He was a great story man.

His intuition for a story finally revealed itself in the fall of 1938, when he decided the studio would work on *Bambi*. However, after a brief attempt at the film, they discovered that animating deer was a formidable challenge, so Walt put it on hold and switched over to *Pinocchio*. *Pinocchio* would be easier to make because the animation style would be closer to the fairytale work they had already done on *Snow White*. Meanwhile, Walt continued to develop *Bambi* while *Pinocchio* was being made. He wouldn't have an empty pipeline again after his next release premiered. Contributing to the future workload, he developed an idea with famed conductor Leopold Stokowski for a film that would combine classical music with different animation sequences based on a variety of short stories. The working title was *The Concert Feature*, but it would later be called *Fantasia*. The sabbatical for Walt's animators was over. Now they would spend many long days and nights at their drawing tables as the studio entered the Golden Age of Disney animation.

After *Snow White*, the team continued to work away in the cramped Hyperion studios on *Pinocchio, Bambi,* and *Fantasia*, but Walt and Roy knew that if they were going to continue to make multiple productions at once they would need a new studio that could handle all their ambitious projects. With that in mind, Walt turned his attention to building a state-of-the-art studio worthy of a world-class company. With the development of three major films on the heels of the massive effort of *Snow White*, the company had greatly scaled up its workforce. They were running out of room, which required the purchase of buildings elsewhere around the city. *Bambi*, for example, was being developed in a building that could only be reached by car. Fortunately, *Snow White* provided the company with enough cash to make a studio move feasible. Additionally, the movie gave the Disneys more credibility in the business community. If their first foray into full-length animation could deliver such a hit, imagine what more experience and new technological advances could do. It made sense to deliver on those expectations.

A former military parade ground on Buena Vista Street in rural Burbank was chosen in February 1939 as the location of the new studio. Locating the new studio just over the hill from their current location worked well, as everyone could easily drive to it from where they currently lived. Abundant open space was another benefit of the spot for Walt. As Robert D. Field observed, "He conceived of the studio as a living organism, reaching out into the future, incapable of satisfaction with what already has been accomplished, forever watching for the opportunity to do something better."[18]

Walt threw himself into the studio project like he dove into *Snow White*. There was so much to learn and design for this facility. He wanted Burbank to be a major upgrade from the Hyperion studio, which was originally designed for cartoon production. Walt also didn't like his employees' working conditions at Hyperion. No commissary existed inside the studio where they could eat lunch. The Hyperion location required them to trek across the street to local diners or even drive somewhere to eat. He also wanted more comfort in the new facility. While the Hyperion studios were cramped and hot, the Burbank studio would be furnished with advanced General Electric air conditioning circulating through all the offices. Instead of jamming different departments into a cramped space, each specialty would have its own spacious building devoted to the needs of that particular unit. He responded to his animators' number one request for natural sunlight by providing windows with adjustable shutters. Walt also hired the best interior decorators and industrial designers to ensure all workspaces were ergonomic and aesthetically pleasing, making the many hours behind a desk or drawing board much more enjoyable. When studio employees wanted to take a break, they could relax, play games on grass lawns, or go to a coffee shop and hang out with friends before getting back to their desks. If they were hungry, they could go to an expansive commissary. There was even a barber shop if they needed a haircut. For the women who worked in the ink and paint department, courtyards with trees were provided in the middle of their building complex. Although Walt didn't go to college, he wanted the studio to look like a campus, so he planted beautiful trees and flowers on the grounds, with benches placed in spots where people could relax and enjoy the setting. Like everything else Walt did, he was ahead of his time, providing amenities none of the other studios had on their concrete lots. Practically perfect, this special place seemed the closest Walt could come to creating a worker's utopia for the people who made his masterpieces possible.

The corporate campus served a business purpose as well. Walt wanted his employees to feel they were special, and by doing so they would be more motivated to keep moving the company forward. He also wanted to attract the best talent from his competitors' studios. With the best talent in the Disney Studios, Walt knew if he organized and managed it well, he could produce great work for many years to come. Inspired by Henry Ford's example, he aspired to bring a scientific management approach to movie production to keep up with public demand. As Mindy Johnson explains in *Ink and Paint*:[19]

> As the animation process became more complicated, it took thousands of hours of painstaking work with production schedules, costs, and increasing staff numbers. One of Walt Disney's heroes, Ford revolutionized the world with his sturdy Model T and development of an assembly-line approach

to automotive production in an effort to reduce costs and increase efficiency. Leaders of other industries applied this approach to their own
methods of production—and that included the Disney brothers. . . . It
quickly became necessary to streamline the production process with a clear
and carefully planned pipeline.

Separate buildings eliminated distractions, helping each distinctive area of
production become better at their job. A tunnel system was another innovation
that ran throughout the campus. Since the drawings and animation cels weren't
under one roof anymore, the tunnels kept the artwork pristine and safe from
the outside elements as they were moved from building to building. These
tunnels would later be the model for the underground utilidor system constructed at the Magic Kingdom at Walt Disney World. Walt always thought
ahead on a project. Something used for today's purpose might find new expression when another opportunity arose. For example, Walt built a huge soundstage
on the new lot that was much bigger than what was needed for animated
productions. In the long run, the expense was not extravagant because those
soundstages were later used to film the live action sequence in the opening
scene of *Fantasia*, and would continue to be used for television shows like *The
Mickey Mouse Club*, comedy and adventure movies, and even as construction
facilities for building future attractions at Disneyland. Films, television, and
theme parks would all be run out of the Burbank studio for the rest of Walt's
life, and the studio continues to be used for the same purposes today. Since he
was going big on the design, Walt included anything that might serve as an
asset for future unforeseen projects. For example, he built a large theater on
the property so that the animators could see their work on the big screen like
their audiences would. The theater also served as a testing site where he could
invite the public to screen a film that was in production and assess whether
the audience was responding to the scenes like he hoped. Sometimes, he even
invited film critics to private screenings, which generated goodwill among many
of the tastemakers in the Hollywood media. Always considering his public
image, he knew critics would think it an honor to receive an invitation to Walt
Disney's studio. As a testament to Walt's aggressive building years, the company
today is still growing from the organizational footprint he put in place.

One thing that did not change in the bigger studio was Walt's presence in
the productions. Everything contained his fingerprint. Nothing left the studio
without his approval. In the old Hyperion studio days, Walt and his team screened
their rough cuts in a tiny projection room they called a "sweatbox." When they
moved to the Burbank studio, they built more spacious and air-conditioned
screening rooms but retained the name "sweatbox," perhaps because it's where
Walt turned up the heat on his team to improve their work. Although he created a more comfortable and pleasing setting for their daily needs, he still
demanded their best efforts in meeting his quality standard.

The first structure built on the property was the casting building, which was used as operational headquarters while the rest of the studio was being built. Some of the old buildings from the Hyperion studio—such as the animated shorts building that still remains on the property today—were also razed and moved to the new location. The animators moved into the new Burbank studio in October 1939, although many of the supporting functions remained at Hyperion for a while. The majority of the company moved in over the 1939–40 holidays, and by spring everyone was in their new home. Once in the new facility, the studio released its classic films *Pinocchio, Fantasia, Dumbo,* and *Bambi.* Although the movies were critical successes, they weren't box office hits like *Snow White.* The films were technically stunning, but the element of surprise *Snow White* had couldn't be met again in this genre. The productions were what audiences had come to expect from a Walt Disney animated film. To shock and delight his audience again, he would have to apply the Disney magic to new entertainment mediums. However, with the new studio and a crop of films released in short order, Walt managed to put a foundation in place to pursue such opportunities when the time was right.

DISNEY LESSON 10: ENTREPRENEURIAL LEADERS REACH THEIR GOALS THROUGH SUPPORTING AND FACILITATING THE WORK OF OTHERS

Disney animator Don Hahn calls animation a team sport, requiring the individual strengths and personalities of a wide range of talented people. Walt couldn't supervise everyone, so he delegated some authority to other leaders in the studio. The director he selected coordinated the writers, actors, animators, and musicians to fulfill his vision; the writers needed to create believable dialogue that was authentic to the characters; artists and storyboarders stretched their imagination and drawing ability to bring ideas to life for the first time; songwriters set the emotional tone of the film; and cinematographers ensured the grandeur of the subject matter was felt in the movie. If any of these teammates did not perform their job well, the production suffered and the finished film didn't reach its potential.[20]

Walt realized that having the best talent working at his company gave him a competitive advantage, and once there they found themselves in an environment which encouraged them to do their best work. As he once explained about his philosophy of filmmaking:[21]

> At first the cartoon medium was just novelty, but never really began to hit until we had more than tricks—until we developed personalities.

We had to get beyond getting a laugh. They may roll in the aisles, but that doesn't mean you have a great picture. You have to have pathos in the thing. . . .There is only one reason why "Walt Disney" has been played up: because it adds personality to the whole thing. It isn't "Ajax Films Presents"—it is a personality. Actually, "Walt Disney" is a lot of people. Let's put this in an honest way. This is an *organization*. Each man is willing to work with the other and share his ideas. This is an achievement.

The new studio sent the message that he was willing to invest in his employees' development. He took their comfort into account, ensuring the facilities had air conditioning, pleasant and ergonomic furniture, and adequate lighting. Walt recognized productivity would go up if the physical and emotional needs of his employees were met. While you may not have the resources of Disney at your disposal, you should provide areas in your company where people can get together to discuss ideas. If your location contains physical limitations, then organize salon-style get-togethers where colleagues can socialize and share their thoughts, whether that's at a home, coffee shop, or ball game. Demonstrate to your employees that you recognize their contributions make the outcomes you want possible. It will motivate them, even when you're not there to keep them moving forward.

Walt recognized the importance of training and developing talent well ahead of others in the industry. His partnership with art instructor Don Graham cannot be underestimated. Without the skillful instruction and pedagogical work of Graham, the studio would not have had animators capable of keeping pace with Walt's ambitious production schedule. Consider that Walt turned out forty-seven animated shorts during the company's critical growth period of the 1930s, and by the 1950s he had at his disposal on his lot a stable of the best animators and storytellers. Feature-length live and animated films, groundbreaking television shows, and Disneyland are some of his more well-known creations. However, training the animators in new job skills might be the most important innovation for making all those great feats possible. With the help of the best artists and instructors in the business, Walt performed feats that earned him the label of creative genius; but perhaps his real genius was his ability to see the potential of those around him. As he once said when reflecting on what he mainly did in the company:[22]

My role? Well, you know I was stumped one day when a little boy asked, "Do you draw Mickey Mouse?" I had to admit I do not draw anymore. "Then you think up all the jokes and ideas?" "No," I said, "I don't do that." Finally, he looked at me and said, "Mr. Disney, just what do you do?" "Well," I said, "sometimes I like to think of myself as a little bee. I go from one area of the studio to another and gather pollen and sort of stimulate everybody. I guess that's the job I do."

You can obtain the same effect with your people if you model Walt's inquisitive nature. When employees come to you with a tough problem, one of the smartest things you can do is admit you don't know. When moments like this occur, you have an opportunity to show others how they can get solutions to pressing issues. Take walks with your employees and search for answers together. Along the way, explain how you go about solving problems and let them observe you asking questions. Debrief after these sessions to discover what they saw and learned during the fact-finding excursions. As they learn the skill of inquiry, allow them to start asking questions of others too. Coach them on developing ideas and generating solutions. Before long there will be more little bees pollinating ideas in your workplace too.

The Strike

When it came to physical conditions, Burbank was a marked improvement over the Hyperion studio. However, one unexpected difference between the two locations was the working cultures inside them. Hyperion, while cramped and chaotic, was permeated with a family feeling in which everyone knew each other. Walt was a familiar person to all the crew there. But on the sprawling Burbank lot, specialties became more siloed in their own distinctive buildings. Many of the employees on the new campus might never meet Walt or get to know their colleagues in the other specialties. The expanded scale of projects taking place all over the studio required a different approach to work too. Walt and Roy tried to professionalize the company more during this growth. As Mindy Johnson explains:[23]

Efficiency experts were regularly brought in to structure the bourgeoning organization. Evolving from a freewheeling, all-hands-on deck approach to a chain-of-command assembly-line process, the production method at Walt Disney Studios developed into a continuous flow of results. This efficiency came at a price, as it isolated each department within focused areas of production, leading to a business of separate specialties rather than overall artists.

As the organizational structure became more hierarchical, many employees started to resent that they didn't have a personal relationship with Walt like others did. He even gave one group of animators their own nickname: the Nine

Old Men. Les Clark, Marc Davis, Ollie Johnston, Milt Kahl, Ward Kimball, Eric Larson, John Lounsbery, Wolfgang Reitherman, and Frank Thomas were treated as living legends because of their work on many of the animated classics. Although the Nine Old Men trained generations of animators over the years, their esteemed status gave them privileges and artistic license that others didn't have. Walt believed in a merit-based workplace. Rightly or wrongly, he thought the ones that contributed more to the success of the films should be given more latitude. Walt further separated himself from many of his employees by occupying a wing of offices in the animation building where he worked with his story development team and artists. Grumbling started to happen inside the ranks as some accused Walt of playing favorites, which was only exasperated by his use of a bonus system for rewarding work he thought was above the call of duty. It also didn't help that he requested everyone take a pay cut to help the studio get back on better financial footing. He reasoned that he'd taken a massive cut in his salary and hoped they would too, but this wasn't a good time to make such a proposal. Labor strife was spreading across the country, with workers organizing and challenging their employers for higher wages and recognition. Walt was somewhat naive in thinking those sentiments would stay outside the walls of his studio. Ever the optimist, he thought the labor movement wouldn't hit his employee paradise; however, the factory layout of the campus and the more hierarchical organizational structure that came with size played into the narrative labor leaders were whispering to his employees: "Walt's just another greedy capitalist making a fortune off your hard work."

Like so many other times in Walt's life, once he reached a milestone, setbacks sprang up to derail his progress. Similar to when his animators defected to Mintz and Universal, Walt was unaware of the labor issues brewing outside his office. He liked to believe his employees were willing to sacrifice for the company like he was. That optimistic outlook would change on May 29, 1941, when he showed up at his studio gate and discovered more than three hundred picketing employees blocking the path to his office. The timing was not good for the company. To put the studio back on solid footing, movies desperately needed to be made, but now that would have to be done with half the workforce. To make matters worse, many of the strikers were artists who had done some of studio's best work over the years. Walt couldn't believe the scenario. Hadn't he built them the best place in the world to work? Weren't they proud to know their handiwork went into masterpieces? Couldn't they see that he gave everything he had to the studio that made their jobs possible? What more could he do? Meanwhile, to make it all worse, Art Babbitt, one of his top animators, led the strike! Just as his experience of betrayal with Oswald changed how he approached his intellectual property, the strike of 1941 shifted the way he viewed the people in his organization. Before the strike, Walt displayed a cheerful, idealistic attitude about the studio. He saw it as a reprieve from the outside world; after the strike, he would look at the organization with a bit more detached oversight. The striking employees, whom he saw as part of his extended family, now cursed him and called him names each time he passed them through the gates. Walt took it to heart and would see many of his employees differently for the rest of his life. As Jack Kinney, one of Walt's top animators at the time, describes his boss's reaction to the strike:[24]

> Walt had hired a photographer to take pictures of the people on the picket line, and now these photos—blown up to poster size—lined the walls of his office. They were huge things that made each person exceptionally identifiable. . . . The strike became very bitter. Long friendships between "ins and outs" were destroyed. The hostility was brutal. Disney was required to bring a certain number of people back after the strike, but Walt never forgave them. He eventually fired every single one of them. The studio was never the same when it was over.

The strike lasted for three months, with hard feelings brewing on both sides. It could have easily led to the demise of the whole operation had it not been for Roy once again saving the day. Roy could see that his little brother wasn't going to reconcile very easily with the strikers, so he convinced Walt to take a goodwill trip to South America to promote the company. Roy knew that Walt was only going to escalate the conflict with his employees if he stayed in Burbank. The farther he was from the studio, Roy thought, the better. Removing himself from the fracas taking place at home helped Walt's health too. A victim of past nervous breakdowns, he needed to put his mind on something else while the calm and steady Roy handled the difficulties of the strike.

The South American trip provided more complications. Because Latin America was socialist, government officials feared Walt's labor difficulties might create a dangerous situation for him and a public relations crisis for the country. They didn't want things to look like a propaganda tour—even though for the United States it actually was—so it was billed as a cultural research trip for the company. Walt and the studio team did do actual research on the places and cultures of the countries they visited. Calling themselves "El Grupo," meaning "the group," they sketched, painted, and photographed source material they could use for future movie productions back in Burbank. Walt was a very curious person, so he loved these exploratory excursions. As J.B. Kaufman describes, "Walt would represent himself simply as a working artist, gathering research material for his films—which, of course, as far as it went, was the truth."[25] The trip was actually productive for the company as well, as it inspired the cross-cultural hit *Saludos Amigos*. And while Walt traveled, Roy settled the strike. Once things were cleared up with the employees, Roy told Walt to come back to the studio and get to work. The company needed to generate revenue once again to stay ahead of always looming financial crises.

While the strike took an emotional toll on Walt's psyche, it did serve a useful purpose in maturing the organization. The management style that worked at the Hyperion studio couldn't work in Burbank. In its aftermath, the strike brought more professionalism and less spontaneous organization within the ranks of the company. There was no way Walt could lead multiple major projects from his office and individually motivate all his employees on the ground at the same time. The Walt Disney Studios was a major corporation now, and Walt would need to add the builder skills of an executive to go with his experience of leading creative teams. As a builder, he took a more detached approach with many in the company. He also started to look the part, replacing the hip clothes of an artist with the suit and tie appearance befitting a Fortune 500 executive. As Ken O'Connor remembers the change:[26]

> When I went over to the studio on Hyperion, there was a very paternalistic feeling on his part. It was his family, sort of, and he could spank you if you went wrong. Half the time he'd say, if he spanked you, "Well if you weren't worth anything, I wouldn't bother spanking you, so that means you're worth something. Therefore I'm telling you did it all wrong." So you'd take it. He used to cut a melon, as they said, and give those he felt had most contributed to the pictures quite generous bonuses. This went on until the strike. And that changed the whole attitude. He was shocked and horrified by the strike and hardened up.

DISNEY LESSON 11: THERE'S A TREMENDOUS PRICE TO PAY FOR GREATNESS

Walt Disney was a beloved filmmaker, but he was not perfect. He developed some bad habits that ran contrary to his public image. For example, he was a chain smoker, he cursed, and he could be quite moody and pushy sometimes. As Ken O'Connor commented about Walt:[27]

> He was an unusual man. I don't think I ever fully understood him. Very few people did. . . . But he could be down to earth and just as regular a fellow as the next guy when he wanted to be. Half the time, he was forced by his position onto a pedestal, you know, "The Great Walt," with everyone bowing and kowtowing and saying, "Yes, Walt." I don't think he always enjoyed that either. I think maybe he would have liked to have been more one of the fellows, but I don't think he knew how. He had a different approach to life.

When studying the lives of great achievers, it can often be disillusioning to find out our heroes are actually very flawed people. We may ask ourselves, were we lied to? If they have these personality flaws, is there anyone we can truly admire? Do selfless people even exist in the world, and if so, can they ever be in leadership roles, shaping society? Consider that Thomas Jefferson pursued another man's wife when he was an up and coming political figure,[28] or that many of the Founding Fathers who embraced individual rights were also slaveholders, or that business icons like Cornelius Vanderbilt and Steve Jobs were sometimes viewed as combative tyrants by many of the employees who worked for them. And yet, without these people, society would not have advanced to where it is today. Instead, we can look at historical figures and find solace in knowing that if flawed people like these can bring forth creative feats, perhaps we can too. Studying the actual history of these legends informs us that flawed and imperfect people can rise above their situation in life and—while battling their inner demons—still make an impact in the world.

Walt Disney is no different. Like everyone else, he experienced some unfortunate events in his life that caused him pain, which he sometimes transferred onto the people who happened to be near him at the time. One particular physical ailment plagued him most of his adult life. During his younger years at the Hyperion studio, he enjoyed playing polo with celebrities at the Riviera Polo Club—that is, until one match when the ball hit him square in the neck. The injury resulted in pain he experienced for the rest of his life. In fact, he received treatment for it from the company nurse at the end of every workday before going home. Physical pain can affect mood, and coupled with the stresses of meeting production deadlines, skating ahead of financial doom, and pleasing the public, it's understandable that he could be irritable. As Ken O'Connor recalls:[29]

> He was always a gentleman to me. I'm not sure why, because he was not always to other people. He would wear what they called his "wounded bear suit," and everyone hid under the table when he was mad about something. But he was always nice to me. He was always reasonable, even when he turned down my ideas, which was fairly frequent. But he was a mercurial man. I gather that he could be exceptionally fierce. But he could also be absolutely charming to anybody.

Another source of pain that haunted Walt happened upon the death of his mother. As Walt and Roy experienced more success in the business, they decided to do something nice for their parents and buy them a new house. Unfortunately, in the summer of 1938, a faulty furnace caused his mother Flora to die of gas asphyxiation in that very same house. Imagine the guilt

Walt must have felt knowing that the home they bought had ended her life. His daughters were aware of the impact the tragedy had on his psyche:[30]

> As Diane recalled, "One of the greatest and I think only real tragedies in Dad's life was when his mother was killed. The little house that they bought them—it was the fault of the gas—the heating in the house." . . . Sharon recalled, "One morning I drove Daddy to work. I remember driving down Sunset Boulevard and asking Daddy where his mother was buried. All he said was, 'She's in Forest Lawn. And I don't want to talk about it.' Tears came into his eyes. Nothing more was said."

Part of Walt's difficult reputation stemmed from his not giving direct compliments to people on their work. He didn't dish out a lot of praise when he saw something great. Disney animating legend Floyd Norman said that if Walt liked what you did, he'd give you a simple "That'll work." But if he didn't like it, he might grunt or grimace a bit and move on. However, it didn't mean you never found out if your work impressed him because if he really liked something he saw, he'd tell people in another office that they ought to go see it. So, employees found out secondhand that Walt said something like, "Boy, you ought to check out what they did down the hall. That's some good work." While people appreciated knowing Walt approved of their work, they also found it odd. Wouldn't a compliment straight from the boss have gone further in motivating them? Maybe. Perhaps he thought he'd learned a lesson about such behavior during the strike. If he gave a compliment to someone in front of others, it might induce jealousy. So, one way or another, his employees found out when he liked something, but it's entirely possible he didn't want to appear to be playing favorites like he did when the company was a smaller operation. After all, with thousands of employees in Burbank, he needed to applaud studio outcomes rather than individuals, lest he induce negative repercussions like he did in the past.

His firm conviction in telling great stories also contributed to his orneriness. Imagine that you've devoted everything you possess to your product and you risked your financial well-being and future on paying employees and building a state-of-the-art studio to make your movies. You spent countless hours away from your family and pushed yourself so hard that you've had nervous breakdowns that required extended breaks from the very work you cared about most. Can it really be too much to ask that your employees be just as committed to the production before they go home to their family and put a check in the bank? It's likely Walt—like other obsessive entrepreneurs, such as Steve Jobs, who approached business like an art form—would want others to be as committed to excellence as he was. And, when people didn't live up to those expectations or made decisions that appeared to benefit themselves at the expense of the company, it's likely Walt took the behavior personally. It's similar to a great athlete who fails later at coaching. Why can't people work as hard at it as I did, they wonder. After all, they're just giving up their time. They're not risking their financial livelihood. Yet from the employee standpoint, they're not garnering the recognition from their hard work that the name on the picture is. For Walt, his productions provided everything. His productions consumed his thoughts. Walt oversaw every little detail of a production, including scripts, storyboards, rough animation, pencil tests, soundtrack scores, and final scenes. As Disney designer Bob Gurr describes working for him:[31]

> On the one hand, he was very serious. And on the other hand, when he was excited about something, that little eyebrow would just shoot up, and he had that little twinkle in his eye like, oh, I'm going to do something nobody else can do. Wait till I show the world this thing. So it was kind of a pixie-like thing. But day in, day out, I would say he was kind of slightly serious, slightly agitated a little bit. And I think the source of that was, like you run across a lot of people that are like that, they are thinking the whole time of what they're going to do. And it's such a consuming thing, almost like twenty-four hours a day. I think at night some of us—we think all night long and we wake up and go, "Oh, I got it! I got it! I better write it down real quick." Then I've got to go to work in the morning and hope I remember it. His mind worked like that. And a lot of people he collected in the company worked just like that too. It wasn't an eight-hour type of day.

Ward Kimball, one of the studio's top animators, confirmed Gurr's assessment: "Walt was a hard guy to get close to. He was a workaholic. His career was his whole life. I think I was as good a friend as he ever had."[32]

Walt matured into a better leader after each setback he faced during his career. The experiences of betrayal and personal injury could have tempered his youthful enthusiasm, but this is a common pattern for driven, hardworking people who are used to getting the results they desire. Eventually everyone is humbled when the world doesn't align with their intentions. When hundreds of employees protested his appearance at the studio gates, he was required to recalibrate his worldview and behavior. Fortunately, the South America tour gave him time to figure some things out, adapt to the new reality in the studio, and return better than ever. His optimism and hopefulness dwindled, but he became better prepared to be a more effective leader. He understood organizational issues in his growing company better and made wiser decisions suitable for an executive in his role. With a complex array of hundreds of distinct personalities, he couldn't just will everyone into action in face-to-face encounters. He needed to rely on other managers to get the job done for him. Although the strike was painful for Walt, without its occurrence, the professionalization of the organization may not have escalated as quickly as it did. Fortunately, it was this professionalization through the ranks that built the infrastructure to make the company the world-class enterprise it is today.

We all can learn very powerful lessons from Walt's years of scaling the business. Most importantly, he too was human and made mistakes, but he learned and adapted. Consequently, Walt's mistakes and disappointments provide us some of the most valuable lessons we can use in pursuing our own opportunities. As Joseph Campbell chronicled in his studies of the "hero's journey," rewards in life come to those who step into the unknown, endure their struggles, grow from the experience, and return to their work more mature for it. Wise leaders may lose a little of the naïve optimism that got them started, but the awareness of the complexity and realities of the world they live in gets them further down the path to success. That's the difficult lesson of growth Walt Disney learned when he was in his early forties, but it set him up to enjoy the best years of his life when he was older.

World War II

With the strike settled, Walt thought he could get right back into the studio and start making films again. However, his plans would be stalled once again when on December 7, 1941, the Japanese attacked Pearl Harbor. Not only did the crisis have national consequences, it directly affected every major company on the West Coast. The government reasoned, if Hawaii could be hit, would California be next? In preparation for such possibilities, the military commandeered many industrial locations to serve as outposts to protect the western shore in case enemy planes entered mainland airspace. With the magnificent campus the Disneys had, it was inevitable it would be one of the first places repurposed for the war effort. The U.S. Army immediately turned the spacious and well-designed Disney lot into a major support command post to protect the local Lockheed aircraft plant. Officers converted the soundstages into barracks, and antiaircraft guns, tanks, and other armory were repaired by soldiers and stored in the studio's buildings. Every employee on the lot had to carry special IDs in order to walk onto the once welcoming corporate campus. The Walt Disney Studios would be a military base first and a studio second for the next few years. However, the designation of the studio as a military base did allow a technicality to work in Walt's favor. Anyone working at the studio at the time was considered part of a military operation and therefore was exempt from having to fight overseas. In theory, if Walt could find space to make his films, he could continue to run his operation at full capacity as well. The reality of the situation was different, though. The Greatest Generation of the 1940s was immensely patriotic, and Walt's employees were no different. A significant amount of Disney personnel decided to fight overseas in the war effort. As John Baxter describes in *Disney During World War II*:[33]

> But even with the draft protection afforded Disney by the fact that they were working for the military, 174 Disney employees ended up serving during the war—more than a quarter of the total studio workforce at that time—though some were volunteers. Among those who served were future company president Cardon "Card" Walker and animators Wolfgang Reitherman and Frank Thomas (both members of the "Nine Old Men" fraternity).

Thus, the war took a toll on the human capital side of the business after all. Between the sharing of facilities with military personnel and the dilution of production talent by patriotic service, it was very difficult to make the feature films Walt planned after the strike. To make matters worse, there was also less demand for films worldwide since much of the international market would not be going to theaters in their war-torn countries. Financially speaking, the timing was devastating. While Walt and Roy exhibited great patriotism, having served their country in their younger years, the repurposing of the studio was straining their economic viability. They invested a lot of money in the new studio, and they needed box office revenue to pay off their loans. The government provided some revenue to pay the bills by ordering that the studio make propaganda films, training videos for the troops, education shorts for the public, and military insignia for different combat units, but the contracts were miniscule in comparison with the revenue a feature film generated. They continued to make a few cartoon shorts for theaters, but the majority of manpower was used on the public work. Walt could have coasted a bit during the military occupation of the studio and gone back to work once it was under his control again; however, he was too proud to let that happen. He was very supportive of the war effort and appreciated the patriotism of his employees. If he could produce shorts that educated the troops, inspired people, and entertained the public during the war, he would ensure that whatever left the studio met the Disney quality standard. As Baxter explains:[34]

> Despite the departure of so much talent and experience, the studio sustained a level of productivity for three and a half years that rivaled any other period in its history. Yet because most of the Disney material produced during that time was not viable as postwar entertainment, it was put into the vault in 1945.

While these public service shorts fell far short in meeting the needs of the studio's budgets, Walt and Roy were saved once again by having a good relationship with their financial friends. Just as they did when the studio was hemorrhaging cash during the *Snow White* production, Bank of America stepped in once again to provide a much-needed loan to keep the company afloat. Bank of America's founder A.P. Giannini was not only a fan of their work but also recognized the business potential for the studio. He believed that the Disney brothers made a product like no other and that once the war was over they'd quickly make money again creating feature films. In the meantime, Walt also made another concession to Roy by loosening his vow to never give up any ownership of his company, issuing $3.875 million of preferred stock. With the war winding down, money in reserve, and debt under control, the studio had again endured another tough time and was primed for the new frontiers ahead.

Baby Boom

After World War II ended, Walt had full use of the facilities and most of his animators back again; however, the strike and the war took their toll on the studio's output. A full-length animation release would have to wait until the creative team had time to develop a story. In the meantime, Walt produced a series of anthology films comprised of animated musical segments that also mixed in live action sequences. The films included the stories *The Legend of Sleepy Hollow*, *Casey at the Bat*, and *The Legend of Johnny Appleseed*, as well as musical numbers like "Zip-a-Dee-Doo-Dah," but none of the movies were major hits. It wasn't until 1950, when *Cinderella* was released, that the studio had a feature film on the market. Fortunately, *Cinderella* turned out to be a much-needed hit for the studio, bringing back the classic storytelling and fairytale animation that had been missing since *Bambi* was released eight years earlier. Walt had endured many challenges up to *Cinderella*, but now the studio was in a prime position to enter its next stage of growth. Walt and the company needed a good break. The 1940s were a tough decade for him both financially and emotionally. He had felt betrayed before when his animation team left him for Universal during the Oswald debacle, but that had been just a handful of people who deserted him. The strike was an order of magnitude bigger. Hundreds of people walked out on him when he needed them, and then he had to rely on many of these same people again after the strike. But Walt handled these challenges as best he could, and that grit would finally pay off in the 1950s as the baby boomer generation came of age. A second renaissance at the studio was about to blossom as Walt explored new ways to offer more films to the millions who now wanted family-friendly Disney entertainment. Maybe now was even the time to make the live action films he always wanted to produce. Walt wouldn't abandon animation, but with a large organization in place, he could venture into new mediums.

Walt had always been interested in making live action films, but up to this point his creative opportunities were in animation. He had been successful at it, so it made sense that Roy and their investors wanted him to continue on that path. After all, he had hired and trained an animation workforce and built an expansive studio to make more hits like *Snow White*. The aftermath of World War II, however, provided a business incentive for entering live action films. Europe had always been a major market for Disney films, but post-World War II England was not allowed to spend money on American products until its economy rebounded. Finding the upside in a tough situation (like all great entrepreneurs do), Walt reasoned that waiting until the embargo was lifted to ship Disney films overseas was costing the company a lot of money. But what if they actually *made* the films in England? Wouldn't the films then be considered British, allowing the people there to see them? And since it would be too expensive to ship all his animators overseas, the films would need to be in live action format, using local talent to keep costs down. Plus, in the process of employing British movie crews, he could learn the fundamentals of live action from them. The company had always benefited from its overseas markets, and the move would reestablish the brand in those countries and expand the company's bottom line. After making a strong business case for live action films to Roy, he prepared the company for its next stage of growth (as well as giving him films as a new medium to explore).

The first live action film made in England was *Treasure Island*, based on the classic adventure book by Robert Louis Stevenson. Now that Disney was in the live action genre, the Burbank studio's soundstages needed to expand in preparation for the movies that would inevitably be produced in the United States. In fact, many Disney movies that appear to be shot in the wilderness were actually shot on the back lots of the studio, where berms—essentially dirt walls with trees planted on them—shielded the cameras from the surrounding urban landscape. Walt would later use the same technique at Disneyland to great effect, obstructing guests' views of streets and highways sitting outside the park. This is an example of how Walt's problem-solving ability changed the way live action films were made—just as it had animated films. Any medium he entered can be segmented into pre-Walt and post-Walt eras. He was always looking for a better way to do things around him—a technique he called "plussing." While he learned the best practices of others, he didn't treat them as sacred and was always willing to ask, how can we do this better next time? What's making our work hard? How can we make it easier? How can we get more done? What are we missing that we need to get good at? What are others doing we're not? Why not? What can we do that others can't imitate? How can we stand out from our competitors in ways they can't even imagine? What can we do to continue to delight the public and shock our competition? To Walt, every day was one long debriefing session, capitalizing on what was working and fixing what wasn't. As a result of his relentless drive to tinker and innovate, many accepted practices in entertainment today came from Walt improving his own production process.

The mood inside the studio was also starting to recover from the strike. Many of the combative employees who led the strike either moved to other studios or eased their way back into more quiet roles assisting productions. In fact, most people who stayed after the strike or who joined the studio later speak very well of Disney as a boss. They admit he was strongminded, but that he was also a creative inspiration to those who worked for him. He was clear about what he expected from his employees on a project, but he was respectful and not demeaning to them as people. As long as his personal rules of engagement were followed, he was generally good to them. He'd been in the business long enough to know what worked for him, and he expected others to trust his judgment.

The live action films had a huge impact on expanding Disney's cultural influence on the country. Since traditional movies could be made more quickly than animated films, the studio could increase the frequency of productions released to the public. More movies meant more Disney, helping the company build a library of movies and characters that could be used in future ventures like television and theme parks. Live action also expanded their market share in the movie industry by directly taking on other studios in their own territory. The Walt Disney Studios grew to be more than a cartoon factory. While animation helped the company establish its footprint in the industry, the move into live action was a defining moment in transforming it into a major corporation. Walt had built a major movie company that could now recruit traditional entertainment talent and industry executives to complement the animation enterprise. Walt Disney Productions was not limited by animation any longer. It was in many ways a new company, offering Walt the opportunity to continue to learn and grow. He could utilize live action expertise to improve his animators' work, and, in turn, bring spirited animated musical numbers to live action filmmaking. This stable of cross-purpose talent afforded Walt the ability to pursue stories his competition couldn't.

Although he moved into live action filmmaking later in his life, like anything else he pursued, Walt was a quick learner and rapidly rose to the top. It's quite a compliment to his creative legacy that both business leaders and artists today look to Walt as their standard of excellence. Steve Jobs, for example, aspired to create in Apple a company like Disney, and filmmakers like Steven Spielberg and George Lucas judged the quality of their films based on whether they believed Walt would have liked them. Walt's humble Midwestern upbringing and down-home values may account for a lot of his success. His core audience was American families. He could put himself in their shoes. And even though he had ascended to the top of Hollywood, he still saw himself as one of them. Walt knew what they valued and enjoyed. He figured if he liked it, then they probably would too. But he took it a step further by pursuing an attention to detail and excellence that respected the audience as well. He didn't patronize his audience, knowing they could tell if he didn't give a production his full attention. Walt knew something about the people between the two coasts that writers and directors raised in New York or Los Angeles didn't: people in the heartland can spot a phony. As a result, Walt Disney may be the most authentic filmmaker in history. What you see on screen or in a Disney theme park is the embodiment of Walt's values, interests, and dreams. His philosophy of life is embedded in everything the company does. Although today's company may not always ask, what would Walt do? it does ask, would Walt approve? And while some film critics disparage his films as being "hokey shtick," Walt Disney truly believed in the themes of family, honor, friendship, perseverance, hope, hard work, and patriotism that run through all his productions. He didn't apologize for his approach and he didn't overthink what he wanted to give his audience. Other filmmakers may have made more serious movies, but as America entered a "New Frontier" of optimism for new technology, transportation, and economic growth, Walt Disney became the top producer of entertainment for his time.

Always up for learning new subjects, live action brought Walt unique challenges that animation didn't. Locating sets, managing crews, mastering cinematography, and directing actors were much different than painting animation cels and recording actor voiceovers, so Walt hired esteemed filmmakers who could meet the quality standard the public had come to expect from a Disney production. He drew talented writers, directors, set decorators, actors, and technical experts to his productions. As a result, Walt impacted live action productions like he had his cartoons. The special effects and set construction on movies like *20,000 Leagues Under the Sea* were revolutionary for their day, and still hold up on screen decades later. Creative professionals knew they would have the opportunity to work on interesting projects at the Walt Disney Studios. Further, many of the crews would bring their expertise and use of camera techniques (like forced perspective) to the construction of Disneyland years later.

One established director who built a great partnership with Walt was Robert Stevenson, who directed *Mary Poppins* and a stable of other hits for the studio. Stevenson had made some distinguished movies during his career before coming to the Disney Studios, but Walt gave him the opportunity to stretch his talent in new directions by working on fantasy and comedy films. Stevenson directed *The Absent-Minded Professor, Herbie the Love Bug, The Shaggy D.A., Bedknobs and Broomsticks*, and *The Son of Flubber*, among others, which all became huge hits for the studio. He in turn appreciated working for Walt because he could see his boss committing as much energy and focus to a production as the crews did working on the set. Walt knew what was going on and could have deep conversations with his production teams about how to improve whatever movie they were making. He didn't sit in his office in Burbank giving a distant thumbs up or thumbs down to a scene. He set the tone by working as hard as the crew on a film, and as a result his teams responded with equal commitment and effort. The unspoken message sent was that if a legend cared about this film maybe everyone else should too. In the evenings, Walt went over scripts line by line with his grease pencil, and the next day he'd have his writers create entirely new scenes if the film wasn't working as well as it could. Ken O'Connor describes his work style:[35]

> Walt was not a guy that anyone—perhaps his family's an exception—got very close to. He was not an ordinary man. You really didn't get close to Walt as a rule. He could come in and be very friendly, but you knew at the end of the conference it would shut off. Bang! And he's gone and you're working and that's it. He got to be so damn busy with the diversification of his empire that he was running like hell all the time. Even during vacations, he'd read scripts by the dozen. But he had the bull by the tail, and he couldn't let go. I don't think he wanted to let go. But the result was a terrific strain on him, after the thing grew very large. It was a strain all the time, but he was not without a sense of humor. And he was a good actor, too. He could act in story meetings a keen way of doing things. He would get up, take off his coat, and act like the devil, and pour out ideas. He was marvelous. And sometimes he was throwing out lines and sometimes just fishing. He couldn't express it perhaps or he expected you to do some detective work. But I think it must have taken it out of him, because any sort of creative effort is a strain. It can wear you out quicker than ditch digging.

The people who enjoyed long careers with him were the ones who were sympathetic to the work schedule, deadlines, and financial constraints that were always pressing on him. They also admired his exceptional skill as a storyteller. He had perhaps the best sense of storytelling of anyone who ever worked in the business. Story development meetings with Walt are the stuff of legend. From his years in animation, he could envision in his head what a scene could be. Then he could act out what the characters might do in it. He was always thinking about how he could improve the process of making films, like catching a mistake in preproduction storyboarding rather than discovering on a set something didn't work.

Although many people were involved in the physical creation of a Disney film, what went on screen was entirely guided by what had originated in Walt's wing of the studio. But once it left his office, he entrusted the talented team he had in place to make it happen. For as much as his image is one of being a bit overbearing during the making of the animation classics, with regard to the live action films, once a shooting script was approved by him he took a very hands-off approach to the filming. He left it to the directors to do their job shooting the footage. He would, however, get more involved again in the editing stage to ensure the story flowed well; and he kept tabs on everything going on in the studio, watching whatever scenes were completed on a shoot. Walt's involvement in all types of entertainment made him an expert on every stage of a movie, and he would step in if something didn't seem to be working well. Walt, after all, was the quality controller of the Disney brand, and everyone in the company knew it. His repository of entertainment knowledge and obsessive attention to detail kept his teams sharp throughout the entire production process. But that commitment to quality was respected by those who worked for him because they knew he held himself to the same standard he expected of them. If there was a better way to do something, he was willing to flex his vision to take a picture in a new direction or alter a scene from the way it was originally envisioned. Consequently, he was always open to a lot of ideas and viewpoints on a project, but once he decided on something, that was it. Walt didn't revisit anything again, and he expected others to respect his final decisions. He didn't have time for second guessing something once it was filmed because he always had a lot of projects going on at once. He had to keep things moving, so although he appreciated people who were willing to argue with him and offer different views, at the end of the day Walt Disney had final word on a Walt Disney production. Anyone who questioned it didn't last long at the studio. In short, the studio was ultimately the expression of what he loved and did best: inventing stories that entertained the world. As long as the company rolled out movies that made money, he could work on new stories and develop new approaches to telling them.

Conclusion

In the previous two chapters, we discussed how Walt mastered animation by thinking like an artist and then made technological breakthroughs, creating a science of animation. But perhaps the biggest and most sustaining contribution Walt made to the world is the organization that has lived on and thrived after his death. A lot of entrepreneurs would love to have a fraction of Walt's success, but it's not common, and it's not for lack of trying. The main difference between an entrepreneur who thinks like an artist or scientist and the entrepreneur who thinks like a builder is their approach in professionalizing their company. A builder sees the company and its brand, as opposed to a specific product or service, as their chief concerns—or put another way, a builder focuses on the business of the business.

The success of *Snow White* allowed the Disneys to build an impressive studio, but the company changed as a result of the growth that came with it. Walt was slow to admit that that change had happened, but the strike sent a strong message that he would have to modify his management practices. He learned the difficult lesson that being an executive of an established company is different from running a startup. When the company was small, Walt maintained personable relationships with most of his employees. But as it grew, the interpersonal dynamics changed. Some entrepreneurs can't make the transition into the executive role and step down—or sometimes are even asked to leave by the shareholders and replaced with a more experienced manager. Walt didn't walk away, though. He accepted the brutal reality of the new organizational culture and, as always, made the necessary adjustments in his approach. It should never be forgotten that not only did Walt evolve creatively over his career but he also evolved managerially as well. Walt's appearance working in striped T-shirts at the Hyperion studio and in a business suit in Burbank vividly demonstrates that difference.

What accounts for Walt's success in making the transition? What did he do so well that other entrepreneurs often don't? The simplest answer is he grew up. He entered the industry as a teenager and was very successful at a young age with Mickey Mouse, but he later matured and managed the company like a seasoned professional. In the early stages of the company, Walt was involved in the day-to-day activities of a production. More projects on the bigger corporate campus, however, forced him to codify what the business actually offered customers and how he delivered it to them. With that formula in place, the business evolved into a major corporation. By building a professional company, Walt was able to give his audience more movies while doing it more efficiently, and with discipline and planning he eventually built an entertainment empire. This is what builders do. They continue to provide great products their customers want even as they get bigger, which is the hardest challenge an entrepreneur can face.

Since this is such an important topic for entrepreneurial success, let's review it one more time. Building a growing company is fraught with dangers at every turn. If you don't continue delivering what customers expect from you, they'll turn to others who can. But this becomes more and more difficult when there are more variables to manage. Many entrepreneurs panic in this situation, or worse, they don't make any changes. Legendary entrepreneurs like Disney, Ford, and Rockefeller make the needed changes. How do they do this? They scale their operations—but that's really hard. It takes a lot of time, thought, and money to put all the right pieces in place. But, if done properly, scale is the ticket to an entrepreneur's wealth and provides the opportunity to work on even bigger projects. To make this happen, the entrepreneur must add a new skill set to their repertoire: they have to learn how to build a professional business. If the entrepreneur continues to run the company like they did when it was a startup, chaos will break out. So in this stage of the company, the entrepreneur has to build a system that runs like a machine. They also have to build a workforce that grows and maintains the company's reputation. And since new hires aren't part of the founding team, they have to be educated on how the company does business, what it stands for, and where it needs to go. Nothing can be taken for granted. This requires systematizing as much as possible what you want the employees to think and what you want the employees to do. If you don't spell it out for them *and* tell them how you'll monitor it, it won't get done. The fact that he was able to make the changes needed to handle the success that came with *Snow White* is a testament to Walt's skill as an entrepreneur.

This chapter has covered the builder stage of Walt's entrepreneurial career. By building an organization and studio large enough to house the best talent and technology in the industry, he finally was able to pursue whatever ideas caught his fancy. However, attaining this position did not come easily for him.

- Scale businesses, ventures, and projects
- Desire efficient operations
- Build systems and processes
- Recruit multi-talented and multi-functional teams
- Lead and motivate to complete projects
- Value acquisitions and partnerships

WALT DISNEY THE BUILDER

Scale projects
- First feature length animation: Snow White
- Expand production of feature length productions: Pinocchio, Fantasia, Bambi

Scale production
- Burbank studio
- Assembly line layout of buildings on Burbank lot
- Entry into live action films

Professionalization of company
- Post-strike management style
- Mature organizational structure
- Increased reliance on Roy to work with growing executive team

FIGURE 3.1 Entrepreneurial Leadership Style—Builder

He endured betrayals and setbacks, but the lessons learned from each episode moved him a little closer to reaching the top of the industry. As we'll see in the next chapter, he'll be able to leverage that position as an evangelist, entering new frontiers only he could imagine.

Disney Principles

- Walt produced the best cartoons in Hollywood during his scientific years, but his greatest animation came as builder. Large companies provide opportunities for being innovative because significant resources and well-established networks support collaboration on big projects.
- Walt invested the profits from *Snow White* into a state-of-the-art studio. You can do the same by keeping your employees' physical, mental, and emotional needs in mind when designing their workplace and schedules.
- Walt was inspired by everything. Examine new opportunities from different perspectives, think of the possibilities, and let your imagination run free.
- Walt could be temperamental at times in the studio, but that's common on high-stakes projects. Creative activities can often result in emotional swings as you go through periods of hard work, frustration, and achievement.
- Walt was willing to change the company and his management style when needed. Opportunities for creative change are possible in any segment of your company. Be open to the possibilities. You never know what might end up being the revenue generator of the future.

Work Like Disney: Exercises

1. Walt's path to success wasn't always smooth. What challenges have you overcome in your life? How did overcoming these challenges help you to live a better life?
2. Walt built his company around what he did best. What unique skills do you have? What unique skills do your employees have? Are there any new trends in the world where you could apply these skills?
3. Walt felt betrayed by many people he trusted. Who has been a difficult presence in your life? Who has been a source of disappointment for you? What did you learn from these encounters? With the passage of time, do you look at these people differently now? Why or why not?
4. Walt lived for his work. If you could do any job in the world, what would it be? What would you need to do to attain this position? If you're not pursuing that job now, why not?
5. The strike in 1941 was difficult for Walt, but he and the organization matured because of it. Has any event happened in your life that at the time was rough but in hindsight helped you be more successful? Why was this event good for you in the long run?

Notes

1. Smith, D. (2001). *The Quotable Walt Disney*. New York: Disney Editions.
2. Peri, D. (2008). *Working With Walt: Interviews With Disney Artists*. Oxford, MS: University of Mississippi Press.
3. Ibid.
4. Ghez, D. (2014). *Walt's People,* Volume 15. Lexington, KY: Theme Park Press.
5. Ghez, D. (2009). *Walt's People,* Volume 8. Bloomington, IN: Xlibris.
6. Weiner, E. (2016). *The Geography of Genius: A Search for the World's Most Creative Places From Ancient Athens to Silicon Valley*. New York: Simon & Schuster.
7. Shields, C. (2016). *The Disney Apprentice: Lessons Learned From Inside Disney*. Lexington: Theme Park Press.
8. Hollis, R., and Sibley, B. (1994). *Snow White and the Seven Dwarfs: The Making of the Classic Film*. New York: Hyperion.
9. Gabler, N. (2006). *Walt Disney: The Triumph of the American Imagination*. New York: Vintage.
10. Thomas, B. (1974). *Walt Disney: An American Original*. New York: Disney Editions.
11. Gabler, N. (2006). *Walt Disney: The Triumph of the American Imagination*. New York: Vintage.
12. Ibid.
13. Solomon, C. (1995). *The Disney that Never Was: The Story and Art of Five Decades of Unproduced Animation*. New York: Hyperion.
14. Smith, D. (2001). *The Quotable Walt Disney*. New York: Disney Editions.
15. Solomon, C. (1995). *The Disney that Never Was: The Story and Art of Five Decades of Unproduced Animation*. New York: Hyperion.
16. Hahn, D., and Miller-Zarneke, T. (2015). *Before Ever After: The Lost Lectures of Walt Disney's Animation Studio*. New York: Disney Editions.
17. Peri, D. (2008). *Working With Walt: Interviews With Disney Artists*. Oxford, MS: University of Mississippi Press.
18. Johnson, M. (2017). *Ink & Paint: The Women of Walt Disney's Animation*. New York: Disney Editions.
19. Ibid.
20. Hahn, D. (2008). *The Alchemy of Animation: Making an Animated Film in the Modern Age*. New York: Disney Editions.
21. Thomas, B. (1974). *Walt Disney: An American Original*. New York: Disney Editions.
22. Smith, D. (2001). *The Quotable Walt Disney*. New York: Disney Editions.
23. Johnson, M. (2017). *Ink & Paint: The Women of Walt Disney's Animation*. New York: Disney Editions.
24. Kinney, J. (1989). *Walt Disney and Other Assorted Characters: An Unauthorized Account of the Early Years at Disney*. New York: Harmony.
25. Kaufman, J.B. (2009). *South of the Border With Disney: Walt Disney and the Good Neighbors Program, 1941–1948*. New York: Disney Editions.
26. Peri, D. (2008). *Working With Walt: Interviews With Disney Artists*. Oxford, MS: University of Mississippi Press.
27. Ibid.
28. Meachem, J. (2012). *Thomas Jefferson: The Art of Power*. New York: Random House.
29. Peri, D. (2008). *Working With Walt: Interviews With Disney Artists*. Oxford, MS: University of Mississippi Press.

30. Johnson, M. (2017). *Ink & Paint: The Women of Walt Disney's Animation*. New York: Disney Editions.
31. Gurr, B. (2015). *Bob Gurr, Disney Imagineer/Talks at Google*. Retrieved from www.youtube.com/watch?v=q_60AEmnMUA.
32. Gabler, N. (2006). *Walt Disney: The Triumph of the American Imagination*. New York: Vintage.
33. Baxter, J. (2014). *Disney During World War II: How the Walt Disney Studio Contributed to Victory in the War*. New York: Disney Editions.
34. Ibid.
35. Peri, D. (2008). *Working With Walt: Interviews With Disney Artists*. Oxford, MS: University of Mississippi Press.

4

THE EVANGELIST YEARS

There's a great big beautiful tomorrow, shining at the end of every day.[1]
—Richard and Robert Sherman

Look around. The world can be a chaotic and stressful place. Many people are lost and confused. They're looking for something in which to believe. People are in pursuit of something that will give their lives meaning. Some people find what's missing in their life by going to churches. Still, a lot of people find meaning watching Disney movies and going to a Disney theme park. Wait a minute. A company can change lives? *Really*? Are we *really* comparing a company to a church? Well, yes, we are. There's actually a lot of commonalities between a successful company and a thriving church. Let's think about it. A good ministry can improve the lives of its congregation, and a good company can provide products and services that improve the lives of its customers. Both organizations often have charismatic leaders that people want to get behind. In the case of a church, a minister will be a great communicator that connects with her followers; in the case of Disney, the company had Walt.

Walt generated excitement by honing an honest and authentic image with which people connected. They appreciated the values he expressed, and, like a church, the projects of Walt Disney Productions celebrated and encouraged the better side of humankind. In the case of a church, charity, helping, and compassion are the key activities of the institution. But with Walt, it was the celebration of human achievement and the good that can happen when people live with virtue. We introduced exercises at the beginning of the first three chapters to help you understand the stage of development Walt encompassed at that time of his life. For this chapter, we recommend you visit the Carousel of Progress at Walt Disney World and watch the twenty-minute show there. A celebration of human ingenuity and technological achievement, it features the song "There's a Great Big Beautiful Tomorrow." Those who worked with Walt said the attraction embodies everything Walt believed in and dedicated his life to. The song's composer, Richard Sherman, said the catchy tune served as Walt's theme song. Walt's message was, hey, look at what great minds have achieved over the last century. And we're doing something special here too. There's so much that can be accomplished with technology and human ingenuity to make the world a better place. Don't you want to be a part of it? American audiences were indeed drawn to that message—and still are today.

Walt provided everyday Americans the hope that better days lay in the future. He assured them that things were okay. And the more people watched his shows, the better they felt; and the more they watched, the more successful Disney became. In the previous chapters, we've explained how Walt succeeded by thinking and acting like an artist, scientist, and builder. Each stage of his entrepreneurial career took the company to higher heights in the marketplace. In this chapter, we'll explore how operating like an evangelist brought Walt his best experiences in business. Up to this point in our story, the Disney magic could only be seen in theaters every few months or so, but in the evangelical stage, Walt actually comes to them in their homes via television—and as we'll see at the end of this chapter, the audience eventually even gets to meet Walt face-to-face in his. After all, when you've inspired and entertained generations of families through the Great Depression, World War II, and the Cold War, why wouldn't you want to deepen your relationship with them?

Television

The new entertainment medium of television gained rapid popularity in the United States in the 1950s, and perhaps no other company benefited more from it than Disney. Between 1946 and 1964 the number of children in the United States doubled to seventy-six million. Walt Disney was already known by this demographic because of Mickey Mouse and the studio's animation classics. Using television brought Walt the opportunity to reach his audience in their own homes. Now kids wouldn't have to wait until a Saturday matinee to watch a Disney production. While other movie studios avoided television, believing it was a medium of low standards, Walt embraced it with gusto. Just as he had embraced sound and Technicolor in his cartoon days, he moved into television ahead of his studio peers once again. He believed so much in the future of the new medium that he filmed many of his shows in color at a time when most homes had black and white television sets. Thinking ahead, as he always did, he imagined there would be a day when television would move to a color format, and when it did people wouldn't want to watch black and white programming as much. Since Disney reused most of its past intellectual property, Walt didn't want to let good work go to waste. He reasoned that if shows were shot in color, he could reuse them in upcoming projects. Filming in color cost more, but to Walt it was an investment.

The company's first production was called *Disneyland*, which premiered on October 22, 1954. The show gave the viewing public an early look at the Disneyland theme park that would open a year later. Not only did it serve to demonstrate the ingenuity going on in the company, it also created interest in the park before it opened. Building Disneyland was going to cost the company a lot of money, and it needed to generate revenue as soon as its gates opened. But perhaps Walt's biggest breakthrough in television happened in 1955 with *The Mickey Mouse Club*. The hour-long variety show ran each weekday at 5 p.m. Comprised of songs, dance numbers, comedy skits, cartoons, and miniseries, *The Mickey Mouse Club* kept kids' attention while their mothers prepared dinner for their households.

Walt was now a part of the daily lives of Americans, which required him to dream up more ways to keep them entertained on a regular basis. It was clear that Disney was going to become a regular presence on television. As a result, he looked for any way he could cross-promote his products, promoting characters on other shows he had. On *The Mickey Mouse Club*, *Disneyland*, *Walt Disney Presents*, and the *Wonderful World of Color*, series such as *Davy Crockett* and *Zorro* attracted huge followings. Merchandise and books related to the shows were sold and brought the company millions in additional revenue. Additionally, if a new movie was being released, Walt could promote it and take viewers behind the scenes to see how the show was made. Unlike many artists who prefer not to reveal their secrets, Walt wanted his audiences to appreciate the technology and craftsmanship that went into his movies. He saw it as a way to inspire audiences to embrace technology as well as appreciate the care his company put into entertaining them. Walt would often open shows by spending a few minutes introducing what would happen that night. It was a window into what held his attention, and since Walt was always in tune with the latest advances in the world, his audiences grew in their sophistication and tastes too. It was like looking into the mind of a genius, stretching minds to consider what's possible with imagination and a little pixie dust. As Richard Rothrock remembers in *Sunday Nights with Walt: Everything I Know I Learned from "The Wonderful World of Disney"*:[2]

> Walt used these segments to share what he was most interested in. And since most of what he was interested in was cutting edge (pushing the boundaries of animation, movie-making, robotics, theme park design), we kids were interested in them as well. And if it was not clear why we should be excited, Walt was able to demonstrate in his intros why we should be. The message we eagerly took in with our youthful eyes and ears was that the world was a marvelous place filled with adventure and

beauty and love. The past was an intriguing time populated by people who helped make our today possible. Nature was something to experience and treasure and keep safe. The future was here and it was going to be better than today. And, most important of all, we children could be a part of it all. All we had to do was dream.

The 1950s was a tremendous time for dreaming big. The space race was in its infancy, and the government needed the country to get behind its efforts to keep pace with the Soviet Union. Always at the cutting edge of new frontiers, Walt stepped in to help educate and excite the public to dream big about space by producing shows that showcased it. Featuring rocket pioneer Wernher von Braun, three 1955 television programs examined different aspects of the national endeavor. Animators worked with scientists to create realistic depictions of topics like spaceships, the effects of weightlessness, and space colonies.

But space wasn't the only topic explored on his shows. Progress and the world of tomorrow were themes he continuously explored in the last decades of his life. Walt always felt he was racing against time to make his impact on the world, and he devoted himself to whatever topics he thought might have lasting influence on future generations. When President Eisenhower developed the concept of the interstate highway system, Walt sold it to the public in his shows. He even explored what future cities could look like. He imagined a better future for his audiences and inspired them to go and make it possible. Most importantly, he based it in science, preferring that approach over science fiction. Actually, building things excited him more than fantasy now. Walt understood the power of entertainment to engage and shape minds by stimulating people's imaginations and curiosity. It was as if he were teaching them to approach the world like he did, and in the process he showed people how to change the world. Yet at the same time, he had great respect for the pioneers and innovators that came before him. Walt believed we should honor the world around us and show gratitude for the past. One series that paid particular tribute to the world around us was the *True-Life Adventures* series.

True-Life Adventures

Another popular contribution to society that Walt worked on alongside the live action movies and television was a nature series called *True-Life Adventures*. The *True-Life Adventures* are normally only accorded a footnote in the life of Walt Disney, but the series was actually one of the most innovative ventures he ever undertook. Cartoons, live action films, and television were mediums he revolutionized that already existed, but the *True-Life Adventures* created a new genre. Creating a new genre is a very risky endeavor. Just like with full-length animation, traditional studios didn't think people would sit down for an hour and watch animals. Wouldn't people who want to do that just go to a park or a zoo? How could animals on a screen compare to seeing them in nature? And aren't animals kind of dumb and boring? That's why cartoons and animation classics had to give them human traits—to make them interesting. So, what do you do? Train the animals to be entertaining? It didn't make sense to most people who heard the idea, but Walt wouldn't be deterred. He responded by saying, well, then let's make the animals interesting to the audience. Since people go to the movies for a good story, let's create some drama and humor around what they do. Let's use some of our expertise in storytelling and filmmaking to entertain people in a new way, and maybe in the process of entertaining the audience we can even educate them a little bit on animals and the environment around them. Following this formula, Walt created a new form of entertainment: "edutainment." Walt's theory was that people learned more when they were also entertained.

People today aren't as familiar with the *True-Life Adventures* as they are other Disney shows, but in its day it brought the company a lot of positive attention. Nature documentaries are common on television today—even entire channels are devoted to the genre—but it took Walt to make it possible. He called the series *True-Life* because he wanted the films to be true to life, providing audiences the experience of seeing the wonders of nature on a big screen. Having grown up on a farm, Walt had a strong affection for animals and wildlife. He got the idea for a nature series during the production of *Bambi*, when he sent camera crews to forests to film animals in the wild as reference material. Like many other ideas he envisioned, he let it simmer in his mind for years until the timing was right to do it. Plus, since it was subject matter no one had ever explored before, he would have to give the concept a lot of thought and preparation before seriously pursuing it. Still, something gnawed at him for years, telling him this idea was worth pursuing. Always curious to learn new things, he used his network of friends and collaborators to help him identify animal experts who could help him develop the idea. He was eventually referred to Alfred and Elma Milotte, a married couple who specialized in filming the grandeur of Alaska. The Milottes turned out to be the type of people Walt liked to work with on projects. They were down to earth, competent photographers with a sincere passion for the outdoors. Ben Sharpsteen, who directed and produced many of the *True-Life Adventures* for Walt, recounts how his boss first shared the idea with him:[3]

> At the transition period (from war to peace time) in 1947, Walt spoke to me about doing something in Alaska. It was a new thought to me. I had not known that that was on his mind. "What are we doing about it?" he asked. I said, "Nothing that I know of." "Well," he said, "we should look into it. We should look into the possibilities and probably send somebody up there, or anyhow, we should look into the possibilities first."

Possibilities. This is an impactful word Walt frequently used with people. Psychologist Judith Glaser's work in conversational intelligence suggests that speaking about future possibilities places the brains of a leader's followers into an aspirational state. Using aspirational language got his team excited about the project. Instead of telling Sharpsteen what the production would be, he included him in the process of creating it. Walt was essentially saying, let's explore this; let's see where it goes. He understood that sometimes the hardest part of a new project is just getting started. Thus, when it was time to move into the unknown of a creative project, Walt became a teacher, working at their level to get the first steps going. Once the basic framework was in place, his employees could develop the details that they would later show him for his approval. Think of Walt's leadership style as an early version of management by walking around (MBWA). Executives who don't interact with their employees sometimes unknowingly get the ranks thinking, "If they don't care about this, why should I?" For all of Walt's faults, he could never be accused of not caring. His employees knew Walt cared about what they were doing—and they better too.

The studio's first attempt with *True-Life Adventures* was the short film *Seal Island* in 1948. Walt invested $84,000 in the film.[4] The assignment was pretty straightforward. The Milottes filmed seals for a year on the Pribilof Islands off the coast of Alaska, and then the studio edited the footage and included music and narration to make it more entertaining. But once again Walt faced some pushback from the old Hollywood guard when he tried to release it. As Sharpsteen recounts the struggle:[5]

> Our distributing agent, RKO, said, "Never mind if anybody likes it or not; it's an impossible length. It's too long for a short subject and theaters won't run that with a double feature because it makes the program too long. It's no good; you're going to lose money on it." In typical "Walt manner," he completely ignored RKO's attitude. He knew what the public wanted and he was willing to gamble on it. Independent of RKO, we had the picture run for a week at the end of the year in Pasadena. We let the theater have the picture for a week in return for the privilege of passing out postcards in the lobby and asking for reactions. The audience was asked a very pointed question, besides the usual one, "Did you enjoy the movie?" They were asked, "If you enjoyed this picture, would you accept it in lieu of a second feature?" The response was almost unanimously affirmative.
>
> So we decided to enter it in its class for the Academy Awards in 1949, which it won. I attended the ceremonies, and I accepted the Oscar for the studio. Walt wanted to send Roy to RKO with the Oscar so he could hit those fellows who had predicted that nothing would come from *Seal Island* over the head with it. Now RKO could advertise it as an Academy Award

winner, and they were truly happy to take it. This was the beginning of the highly successful *True-Life Adventures* series.

The *True-Life Adventures* had a good run of fourteen films in theaters from 1948 to 1960. Film critic and historian Leonard Maltin explains the impact of the films on audiences:[6]

> You have to try to remember before National Geographic came to television, before there were entire documentaries and wildlife films and nature films, before there was IMAX, before any of that, Walt Disney started the *True-Life Adventures* series. He saw some of this amazing footage that a couple named Alfred and Elma Milotte had shot in Alaska, and he thought it was interesting, fascinating, and with a little polish from the studio could be made even more entertaining. So it was the start of a long-running series that eventually gave birth to two very highly praised and Academy Award winning feature films, *The Living Desert* and *The Vanishing Prairie*.

The *True-Life Adventures* provided audiences another escape from daily life, and they liked the satisfaction that came with learning something new from Walt's edutainment approach. The series took audiences to exotic locations where they could see animals behave in ways they never knew possible. It was fun and informative. We take nature films for granted today, but these films were revolutionary in their day, as Maltin further observes:[7]

> No one had really done this before. No one of his stature certainly had ever done this before. There had been many documentaries, and some had been successful with audiences over the years, but for someone of Walt Disney's great renown to put his stamp on documentary films and put his studio to work to popularize and make palatable this kind of entertainment was almost revolutionary. They were eclipsed somewhat by a newer generation of documentary filmmaking, which has even more high-tech capabilities than those photographers had then in the 1950s, but they still stand up awfully well, and they were much honored in their time.

Walt wasn't pleased with everything he produced in his career, but he thought the *True-Life Adventures* had hit their mark. As he explained in 1954, "In all my years of picture making, I have never had more satisfaction or felt more useful in the business of entertainment than I have in making the *True-Life Adventures* features."[8] And the films were good for the company's bottom line as well since there were no actors or expensive sets to fund. *Seal Island*, for example, earned five times more than it cost.[9] The *True-Life Adventures* also stand alongside Teddy Roosevelt's efforts in the twentieth century to increase public awareness of environmental issues. Walt raised awareness in other areas as well. Along with the

True-Life Adventures, he produced a separate documentary series in the 1950s called *People and Places* that transported the viewer to exotic locations with different cultures, showing audiences how other people around the world lived. Science, technology, and history were other short film subjects that received his attention. Edutainment was a vehicle Walt used to evangelize topics he thought the public should learn and endorse.

The edutainment legacy continues today with the *Disneynature* movies that come to theaters every year, and the company's support of conservation programs can be experienced firsthand at Disney's Animal Kingdom theme park. While today's Walt Disney Company dominates media with ESPN, ABC, and movie properties like Pixar, Marvel, Star Wars, and of course Walt Disney Pictures, Walt's reach might have been even greater in his day. Consider that during his evangelist years of the 1950s and 1960s, his films and shows were in nearly every household and classroom in America. Baby boomers were exposed to Disney entertainment (and edutainment) during school, after school, and on the weekends. Walt Disney's influence on society was now much greater than movie theaters, and it would only continue to grow on his next projects.

DISNEY LESSON 12: A COMPANY IS A PLACE FOR APPLYING YOUR STRENGTHS

Motivational writer Dale Carnegie once said that people become successful when they are themselves and know who they are. Perhaps no better instrument exists today in revealing who someone is than the CliftonStrengths assessment by Gallup. The CliftonStrengths assessment works from the premise that everyone has psychological talents that if recognized and developed can become a source of strength in a person's life. Focusing your time on what you're naturally comfortable with and good at will open doors of opportunity for you. Gallup's research has identified thirty-four possible talents a person can have, and each person has a handful that, if harnessed, can make them very effective in their work. While it's impossible to know for sure what Walt's strengths were since he didn't take the assessment, we can speculate on some he may have had, such as futuristic, significance, strategic, belief, ideation, maximizer, and achiever. Moreover, one strength that many people might not suspect, but that we think played a major role in Walt's life, was learner. Gallup states that a learner is someone who "has a great desire to learn and wants to continuously improve. In particular, the process of learning, rather than the outcome, excites them." If you want to understand what motivated Walt to continuously explore new markets and mediums, it was the opportunity to absorb a new body of knowledge, understand it, and then apply it to a new idea. The outcome didn't matter as much as the process. Of course he wanted to get his projects completed, and he made sure of that by driving his teams to meet deadlines. Nonetheless, the outcomes were simply a means to do more new projects in the future—the chance to learn. Consider that he didn't care about money other than as a resource to pay for his ideas, and he didn't like to repeat himself with the same type of project twice. Most people couldn't enter as many different areas as he did if they tried. His insatiable curiosity and desire to travel, study, and design inspired his creative activity. Therefore, his company not only satisfied his creative needs but also provided him a vehicle for learning. Space, nature, literature, fairytales, history, and technology are just a few of the areas he immersed himself in by working on his creative projects. Whatever Walt was interested in at that moment in time was what the company did as well.

Walt encountered immense organizational challenges in the 1950s and 1960s as his company ventured into new territory, but the new areas also kept him fresh. As the ultimate learner, each new genre, whether it was space, live action movies, television, or theme parks, gave him something new to master and creatively innovate. Along with his name recognition and supporting talent, he shaped what these mediums would become. The last two decades of his life allowed Walt to make contributions to the world that last to this day. Building on the hard lessons learned in the animation industry, he transformed other parts of American society too.

Clinical psychologist Dr. Jordan Peterson observed in his creativity research that people really successful in business are highly intelligent, pursue interests they're well suited for, and work incredibly hard (also known as conscientiousness or industriousness).[10] Walt exemplified all these traits from a young age. He worked in mediums he was interested in, he worked incredibly hard all the time, and he motivated others to work hard too. Most people who reach the heights of success retire or sell their business, but not Walt. He maintained his intense pace over a lifetime in the entertainment industry. If you wish to have a career like Walt's, it's unlikely you'll get as far as he did, but if you know what your strengths are, hone them, and use them in an industry that interests you, you can build a career you'll be satisfied with too.

Disneyland: The Concept

Walt traveled the world, finding inspiration for new movies in locations ranging from Europe to South America. He would often gaze out at the sight of majestic natural settings like the Alps or the Pacific Ocean and let his mind wander. When he wasn't exploring the exotic locales of the world, he would simply sit and watch people in his daily life. Walt was hyperaware of his surroundings because he was always on the lookout for something that would inspire his next big project. Always wanting to top his past accomplishments, he never liked to do the same thing twice. He exhibited strong traits of what economist Israel Kirzner calls "entrepreneurial alertness," meaning he was always open to what his next opportunity could be.

Walt even used outings with his family for inspiration. One trip that on the surface looked fairly mundane even prompted the idea for Disneyland. Walt always looked forward to Saturdays, which he called "Daddy's Day," when he spent time exclusively with his daughters Diane and Sharon. He would get away from the worries of the studio and catch up with them on their lives. One Saturday, while taking his children to an amusement park, he contemplated why the experience wasn't very satisfying. He was disgusted by the dirty conditions and lack of activities for parents at the park. No one working there seemed to care if he was happy or not. Everyone just seemed to be putting their time in while the kids kept themselves busy on rundown attractions. Sitting on a bench, he observed the situation and thought he could design a better amusement park. While he was always interested in the concept of an amusement park, it was the quiet, solitary moment on the bench that prompted his subconscious to go to work and imagine a cleaner, more family-oriented place. Walt said this moment ignited the spark that lit the fire under him to begin working on Disneyland.

Walt started small with the idea. Disneyland was originally going to be in Burbank on a ten-acre plot of land across the street from the studio. First conceived as Mickey Mouse Village, and then changed to Mickey Mouse Park, it would be a place where children could meet their favorite Disney characters up close in a fantasy setting. He had some of his designers draw preliminary sketches of what it could be. The park had a canal boat, a spaceship, a submarine ride, ponies, and a railroad that surrounded the grounds. He started to get excited about the idea and began thinking out loud with others about it. As animator Milt Kahl recalls, "Every time you had a meeting with Walt on something else, why, the Park would come up. Especially if you were in his office, where he had all his drawings and stuff."[11]

Walt began acquiring information and buying gadgets and toys to tinker with to help him develop the concept better. Even his hobbies served as inspiration for his next creation. His work and personal life worked together to develop his concepts. Everything served as a way to learn something that could be used in the park. Animator Ollie Johnston introduced him to one hobby in particular that would become one of the loves of his life and a huge inspiration for Disneyland: train memorabilia. Ollie was such a train enthusiast that he maintained a one-twelfth scale steam locomotive and railroad layout in his backyard. He enjoyed giving rides to people on his miniature trains, and Walt began spending a lot of time at Johnston's house, learning the trade. Walt was so impressed with

Ollie's creation that he soon followed suit and built an even grander one on his own property. The duo continued to exchange information and tips on model building and rode real trains cross country for fun. So, it should be no surprise that as Walt developed his theme park concept, it had to have a train circling the premises—just as Walt and Ollie had on their own home properties. Nevertheless, a train wasn't enough for Walt; now he needed to build a special hometown for the train to belong to. He crafted miniature buildings and even dug a tunnel for the train to traverse. He loved locking himself in his barn behind the family house and whiling away the hours, working with wood and metals to expand his train set and create his little version of an ideal town. Eventually he wanted to display what he had built to the public, so he came up with an idea he called Disneylandia, which would pay homage to the values of small town America. Some thought it embodied his fond memories of his hometown Marceline. Animator Harper Goff shared how Walt introduced the idea to him:[12]

> He said, "I've got something that I think you'd like." It was Disneyland. It wasn't called Disneyland then, but it was totally a different operation. One idea that he had in mind and that I was put on immediately was a traveling exhibit that would travel around the country. He wanted to have something here permanently, but he also wanted to put a show on the road. It would be called "Walt Disney's Americana." In those early days he was interested in animatronic figures, although the name "Audio-Animatronic figures" had not been created. He wanted something like, as he put it, a series of jukeboxes that could be loaded on express cars, and in little towns people could walk through the train, starting at the last car and walking up to the front, and see miniature scenes, beginning with the discovery of America right up through recent times.

The Disneylandia exhibit didn't come off exactly as he had planned. The logistics of putting a show on a train and stopping in one town after another were too impractical to be worth the effort. After all, how many people could actually see it that way? Still, many of the little experiments were shown to the public at small community events around his home. Walt had crafted much of the exhibit himself, stunning crowds with the detail he put in his work. Disney biographer Neal Gabler explains:[13]

> Hedda Hopper, who had visited the festival, marveled at Walt's handiwork and asked, "Why does he do it?" To which Walt answered, "Damned if I know." But he knew very well why he did it. Beyond the psychological benisons of control and the tactile exhilaration of his own craftsmanship, beyond the way it preoccupied him while the studio seemed to wobble, he did it because he harbored an even larger, more

audacious plan—a plan for which Disneylandia was only a trial run and a plan that seemed to sustain him even as he was losing interest in the rest of the company.

It's easy to see the connection to Disneyland, both in name and philosophy. The ideas of Mickey Mouse Park and Disneylandia became Disneyland, and the model town became Main Street, U.S.A., the entrance to the lands in the park. Although Disneyland took only a year to physically build, it was the result of many other projects, both small and large, that Walt worked on both professionally and at home over many years.

Once Walt got more serious about the idea, he started exploring what the park's layout could be. People at the studio would see him walking around the lot, mapping in his head where things would go in Disneyland. It didn't take too many walk-throughs for him to realize that he'd need more land to build his park. Ten acres wouldn't be enough for a town, train, and other assorted vehicles and attractions, not to mention (if he so decided) serving food and putting on shows. With the concept better developed and his decision to go forward made, the park became his personal mission. All his time and energy were devoted to getting others on board to make it happen. Unfortunately, as with his other big ideas, he experienced a difficult time getting the support he needed to get started on the project. Even his brother Roy and wife Lillian were reticent to back the idea of the theme park. After all, nothing like it had ever been built before, and to make matters worse, the amusement parks and fairgrounds of the day were not very family-friendly. Why would a family-friendly company want to get into that dirty business? Walt had a vision of something completely different from what they thought the park would be. Disneyland would be clean, friendly, and fun for both children and adults, but he had to convince others to buy into his dream.

Roy also thought a theme park was a far stretch from their core business of movies. After all, what did a bunch of animators and moviemakers know about physical projects? Not one to take no for an answer, Walt realized he'd have to develop a proof of concept to get others to come along for the ride. If words didn't work in communicating the idea, he'd turn to drawings and models. He wouldn't just tell them about Disneyland, he'd show them what it would be, then maybe they'd have a better understanding of what danced in his head. If the company wouldn't put any money into the idea, then Walt would use his own to develop the concept. Remarkably, on December 16, 1952, Walt founded WED Enterprises on the outskirts of the studio lot as a private company responsible for designing Disneyland. W.E.D. were the initials of Walt's full name, Walter Elias Disney. He even hired away some of the most creative minds in the studio to work for him, drawing pictures and building models that represented what Disneyland could be. Bill Cottrell, Dick Irvine, Marvin Davis, Harper Goff, and John Hench were the first WED employees to come on board—later Walt would call his WED team "Imagineers," combining the words "imagination" and "engineer." It was like Walt was starting over again with a new company, paying for their time out of his own pocket.

Now Walt needed to move on to due diligence, learning more of the business of amusement parks, before finalizing his decision. First, he had to learn what worked well and not so well in existing amusement parks. Todd James Pierce's *Three Years in Wonderland* covers the exploratory road trips Walt took to gather intelligence for building his theme park:[14]

> On Saturdays and Sundays, Walt and his new WED employees began their great experiment: the quest to see if men with absolutely no experience in the amusement industry could teach themselves how to build an amusement park that would rival the most famous parks in the world. They visited parks in Southern California, including the Los Angeles Fair in Pomona and Knott's Berry Farm in Buena Park, both for inspiration and to better understand the site layout of such facilities. "Funny thing," Imagineer Marvin Davis later revealed, "we visited Knott's Berry Farm, and at this time they had no idea of what was going to happen. They were so congenial and pleasant to Walt and all of our group, you know, and showing us *everything*." Walt was particularly interested in traffic flow, the way people moved through open space and narrow streets, what grabbed their attention, how landscape architecture affected their mood.

DISNEY LESSON 13: EMBRACE HUMILITY IN THE CONCEPTUAL STAGE OF A PROJECT; BE CONFIDENT WHEN YOU ACTUALLY LAUNCH IT

Although Walt got quite excited in the early stages of a new project, he was humble enough to know he still had a lot to learn to make it work. While seemingly contradictory to what we think achievement requires, humility properly understood leads to better results. It's a misunderstood topic with the public, but for empire builders it's a way of life. As Charles Koch, CEO of Koch Industries, told us, "Humility doesn't mean looking down at your shoes and saying, 'Aw shucks.' It means knowing what you don't know and turning to those who do. It's being willing to admit to yourself and others that you don't have all the answers. From that state of mind, you can get the answers you need to get things done." WED Enterprises was Walt's way of working daily with the experts from the studio on Disneyland, and the team went on frequent excursions to research what the park could be. You might not have a team of artists and engineers to work with on your new idea, but there are practices you can use to get the results you need. Consider what specific issues you need to know more about to proceed further on your project. Remember, experts are busy people, so they'll appreciate your consideration of their time by coming to a meeting prepared with a list of questions. Showing up with a clear agenda will make the most of your time with the expert, and if you're well prepared, you may find the expert enjoying herself too. Since the chance to self-reflect and share insights is rare in most busy people's days, you may find the expert quickly warming up to you, which might open the door to follow-up meetings in the future.

At the end of a meeting, an interesting question to ask is what book, video, website, or film they've found interesting recently. The answer will cue you into places to find other resources that will benefit your work. Most significantly, never forget the most important phrase you can utter at the end of a session with an expert: "Thank you for your time. Is there anyone else you know that might be helpful to me on these issues?" Walt applied this method before he made his final decision to move forward with Disneyland. He gathered a small focus group of amusement park operators to share their honest opinions about some of the concept drawings and models his team had hatched for the park. For a couple of hours the group provided reasons why Walt's vision was impractical and too costly to be a successful business, giving a detailed critique of what would go wrong with Disneyland. Walt appreciated their honest feedback and said he'd consider their input, but the session actually confirmed for him that he wanted to move forward with Disneyland. As Sam Gennawey explains, "Rather than being dissuaded, he was even more certain that his idea would work. Instead of another amusement park, Walt knew he was creating the first theme park."[15] Walt wanted to ensure there weren't any blind spots about his idea he may have missed. He wanted to temper his optimistic instincts with the knowledge others might be able to provide to help him refine his idea. Still, once he believed he had made an informed decision, he fully committed to the Disneyland project and released it confidently to the world. Backstage he was often cautious, but onstage he displayed boldness and confidence.

Empire builders like Walt Disney apply humility as a way of life when exploring new possibilities. Chip Heath and Dan Heath tell the tale of how this type of thinking helped Sam Walton build a retail giant that generated $485 billion in 2016. They explain: "Again and again in his career Walton found clever solutions by asking himself, 'Who else is struggling with a similar problem, and what can I learn from them?'"[16] This is an amazingly powerful question and one that can guide you in finding answers to problems that spring up on your own entrepreneurial journey. Imagine you're having a hard time finding a good supplier. You could ask yourself, who has the best supply chain? What can I learn from them? How did they build it? What benchmarks are they setting in their industry? Or maybe you're having a hard time getting your team to be more creative. You could ask yourself, which companies keep creating breakthrough products? How do they do it? How can I learn more about them? Here's how the Heath brothers explain how Sam Walton used this question to turn Walmart from a small business in Arkansas into the corporate giant it is today:[17]

> Throughout Walton's career, he kept his eyes out for good ideas. He once said that "most everything I've done I've copied from someone else." In the early days of discount store chains, he crisscrossed the country in search of insights, visiting discounters from Spartan and Mammoth Mart in the Northeast to FedMart in California. Through conversations with one of FedMart's leaders, Walton clarified his thinking on distribution, which would eventually become a defining strength of Walmart. And he admired the merchandise mix and displays in Kmart, founded in Garden City, Michigan, by S. S. Kresge. "I'll bet I've been in more Kmarts than anybody," Walton said. Again and again in his career, Walton found clever solutions by asking himself, "Who else is struggling with a similar problem, and what can I learn from them?"

A helpful twist on this question is, who's already doing something I want to do, and what can I learn from them? Do I have to make any modifications to what they do to make it work for us? What's not so good about the way they do that? How would I do it differently? What could I do better than they're doing? How would I do that? How can I work it in with what we already have or do? How can I combine it with something else outside our company and make it our own?

As proud as Walt was of the company's past achievements—reminding people that "it was all started by a mouse"—he displayed humility when starting new projects. Walt recognized that great achievements are built on the foundation of the hard work of others that came before him. He immersed himself in the traditions and practices of what already existed so that he could reimagine it to work for him. If a humble mind-set of learning from others is good enough for Walt Disney, it should be good enough for us too. Embrace what you don't know as the starting point for exploration, learning, and creation. Treat it like your own personal adventure. Eventually you'll have insights that others will want to copy too.

Disneyland: The Place

Recall that Disneyland was met with resistance when Walt first introduced the concept. But, as WED Enterprises did more research and crafted eye-catching artwork and models, Walt got more people on board with the project. It helped that he was able to articulate a simple concept of what Disneyland would be. As he summed it up:

> Physically, Disneyland would be a small world in itself—it would encompass the essence of the things that were good and true in American life. It would reflect the faith and challenge of the future, the entertainment, the interest in intelligently presented facts, the stimulation of the imagination, the standards of health and achievement, and above all, a sense of strength, contentment, and well-being.

Again, notice the aspirational language of the concept. Who wouldn't want to be a part of a project like this? Imagine you're an artist who's sat over a drawing table for years—wouldn't this be something you'd want to make happen? Wouldn't a business person love to figure out a way to finance and build this? And what would Disneyland ultimately provide the customer? Walt said:

> The idea of Disneyland is a simple one. It will be a place for people to find happiness and knowledge.

With this optimistic vision in mind, Walt wanted nothing sacrificed in ensuring the happiness of the customers who visited his park. From that sentiment, all the other details could fall into place. The landscape had to create awe, the buildings had to be beautiful, the rides had to be fun, and the employees—or what Disney calls the "cast members"—had to be friendly. The customer—what Disney calls a "guest"—comes first. As Walt generated more enthusiasm for the idea in the ranks, Roy allowed him to start pitching the idea to the rest of the company leadership. After all, Roy carried a fiscal duty to the board and investors to ensure Disneyland would be a wise business decision. Following careful consideration, it was decided that Walt had made a good case to warrant the next stage of development: finding the right location for the park. This challenge was outside Walt's expertise, so he realized he needed help in locating land that would accommodate Disneyland. The project required land that was accessible to the local market as well as suitable for handling the traffic he expected to come to the park from outside the region. Help came from Harrison "Buzz" Price of Stanford Research Institute (SRI), an expert in big project forecasting and analysis. Price had worked with many of the area's biggest companies but was especially excited about working on Disneyland. Walt put him right to work on the project, and after scoping out various locations around California, he advised that Anaheim held the best potential. Anaheim was a fast-growing area with good weather and easy access from major transportation routes, and it was rural at the time; the company would just have to purge some orange orchards and raze a few buildings to house the theme park.[18]

Although WED helped Walt sell his concept to the other powerbrokers at the company, there was still the matter of financing the park's construction.

Something this big would require other partners to share the risk with the Disneys. Walt started thinking, who else might benefit from being involved with us? It was unlikely he would partner with other movie studios. Were there other companies in the entertainment industry that Walt could create a win-win partnership with? The answer came, as it often did for Walt, by turning to new entertainment mediums, and in this case that was television. In the 1950s, television was still in its infancy, and companies didn't know if it would catch on. To gain credibility and a larger audience, the networks were courting Disney to create a show for them. They reasoned that Americans would embrace television more if Walt Disney was a part of it. Walt opened himself to the possibility and saw this as a chance to promote his brand, but he also used the opportunity to raise money for Disneyland. If a network would help pay for his theme park, he would provide a show for them. It would be even better if a broadcast partner needed him as badly as he needed them. ABC turned out to be that company. Unlike CBS and NBC, ABC was a neophyte company, struggling for identity, and was very open to whatever terms Walt would propose in order to have his presence on their network. To stay in business, ABC sorely needed Disney to draw audiences. The deal was a good one for both sides. Walt agreed to provide original television content to ABC, and in turn the network provided $500,000 cash that Walt could invest in the park. ABC also provided a $2 million ten-year bond and a guaranteed loan of $4.5 million and was given 34 percent ownership in Disneyland. By providing ABC with what they wanted he was able to get enough cash flow to begin building his park. The win-win deal also supported the growth of ABC television—a company that was later purchased by the Disney organization.

The ABC deal helped start the project, but it still wasn't enough money to meet construction and operational estimates. Walt once again turned to Bank of America for their help in closing the gap on the project. This ask would be different from past requests, though. With *Snow White*, Walt could show Bob Rosenberg some completed scenes and bank on his track record in Hollywood. Disneyland appeared to be different. Nothing like it had ever been created, so he had to find a creative way to communicate the concept. Evangelizing the theme park to stodgy New York bankers required Walt to go into artist mode. He would *show* them what Disneyland would be. Unfortunately, he hadn't actually put the complete vision to paper yet, so he enlisted the help of an artist to do so. With just a few days until the trip, Walt pleaded with and convinced veteran animator Herb Ryman to draw a detailed map of what Disneyland would look like from above. In a flurry of drawing, Ryman worked diligently in creating a captivating, realistic image of the park, and all the while Walt looked over his shoulder, explaining what needed to go into each part of the map. By the end of the weekend, Ryman produced a masterpiece that Walt liked. With map in hand, Roy met the bankers in New York and quickly closed the deal for the remaining financing to get Disneyland built.

Securing the money to build Disneyland, however, constituted only one challenge of many to bring the theme park to the world. Now Walt endeavored to build it, and to do that he hired a ragtag group of leaders from different segments of society, and to top it off they were only given a year to do it. If Walt were going to build a theme park from scratch in one year's time, he had to find a master builder to join the team. After considering different candidates, he hired Admiral Joe Fowler to lead the project. Fowler was responsible for building the Navy's fleet in World War II. Walt figured if Fowler was good enough to manufacture aircraft carriers, completing 160 acres of a theme park was within his wheelhouse. Fowler's military pedigree and stern countenance were well suited to working with the construction crews. While Fowler supervised the overall construction of the park, Walt hired other specialists who could supply the details to make Disneyland special. Bill Evans was a horticulturalist who transformed the orange groves into various landscapes, reflecting the different "lands" of the park. Evans also respected the construction budget by bootstrapping whenever possible, buying trees from the city and local residents for a good price and transplanting them inside the park's berm. He sometimes even planted trees upside down so that the root system looked like exotic branches. The company also bootstrapped by securing fifty corporate sponsors for attractions in the park and leasing store space to outside vendors. Merchandise, food, and beverages were largely sold by outside companies, something hard to fathom in today's Disney parks. Still, the tactic was effective in generating instant cash flow for the construction project. Additionally, for the park to run well, a new science of theme park management needed to be created. Figuring out what goals to accomplish in the park and how to get them done required new metrics and training programs. Once again, Buzz Price assisted the company with the needed numbers to make the operation happen. As he explains:[19]

> Over time, for Walt and his brother Roy, and those that followed, we invented an all-new vocabulary that is today the mathematical language of attraction development. It would include subjects like:

- Site analysis
- Concept development
- Market size; resident, tourist, and pass-through
- Market penetration
- Attendance target
- Seasonality, a veritable lexicon of indices when people come
- Length of visitor stay
- Design day attendance
- Peak on-site crowd at design day
- Ride, site, and facility capacities
- Projected rational development cost, hard and soft

- Per capita expenditures
- Probable economic performance (planned gross and net revenue, operating expenses, EBITDA operating profit, return on investment).

And Van France, an experienced human resources expert, was recruited to launch the now famous Disney training programs. As Doug Lipp describes France's contribution in *Disney U:*[20]

> Walt Disney had plenty of architects for the buildings. What he desperately needed now was someone like Van—someone to be the *human architect*, someone who could be as creative designing the employee orientation and training process as the *real* architects had been with their landscape and building designs. It was up to Van and his team to develop employees who could "create happiness." . . . By helping Walt Disney create The Happiest Place on Earth, Van France and his dedicated team started a business revolution in 1955 that eventually became the Disney University—an institution that forever changed the profession of employee training and development.

So many company legends were a part of the construction of Disneyland: Ryman's artistic achievement over a weekend, Evan's landscaping, Price's creation of theme park science, France's training programs, and Fowler's discipline pushing the project, among many others. Yet, even with all those incredible accomplishments, the journey was a tough one, mainly due to the tight deadline. Imagine: one year to build an entire theme park! Today, it takes theme park companies years to expand an existing operation. Disneyland was given only a year—from groundbreaking to opening day—to be built, and it seemed that just about anything that could go wrong did during construction. The construction teams that were hired from the outside, for example, encountered an assortment of structural issues to solve. After all, a theme park was a new design; there wasn't a manual to turn to for guidance. Unions went on strike at inopportune moments. Only three months out from opening day, many of the buildings were not even started yet. Still, Walt and his team pushed forward, and on July 17, 1955, the park opened. Opening day didn't go smoothly, and to make matters worse it was broadcast live to a national television audience. The day came to be known as "Black Sunday," but the company learned from its rookie mistakes and, in the weeks ahead, fixed them. Most people would have caved from the disastrous opening day, but Walt expected there would be problems. They just needed to find out what they were and address them, and the only way to really know what they were was by giving the system a stress test by opening the entrance gates.

By the end of the year, operations were smoother, and Disneyland became very profitable. Buzz Price estimated that Disneyland would have between 2.5

and 3 million visitors its first year, but the figure actually ended up being 4 million guests.[21] Reality exceeded the team's most optimistic prediction of success, but Walt didn't sit back and let the park run on automatic pilot after that first year. He was very committed to improving it. Once again he used aspirational language to guide others in making Disneyland into what it *could* be. Walt liked to think of it as an endless work in progress, reminding everyone that "Disneyland will never be completed. It will continue to grow as long as there is imagination left in the world."[22] Unlike a movie that's captured on celluloid forever, nothing in Disneyland was so sacred that it couldn't be "plussed" to provide a better experience to the guest.[23] He believed that[24]

> Disneyland is like a piece of clay. If there is something I don't like, I'm not stuck with it. I can reshape and revamp it. Whenever I go on a ride, I'm always thinking of what's wrong with the thing and how it can be improved.

It's practically a miracle that Disneyland exists. It was such a tough challenge and there were so many times where it could have failed, and yet Walt pulled it off. As Ken O'Connor sums up the accomplishment:[25]

> I thought of him most of the time as a great showman, because to me he was like Barnum of Barnum & Bailey. He had an intuitive, instinctive feeling for entertainment, and in his case, he thought all the time of entertaining the whole family—not children as he is generally credited with. The fact that he succeeded is brought out at Disneyland where I understand that four adults to one child attend. That was his objective, to entertain the whole family.

While Mickey Mouse, *Snow White*, and *20,000 Leagues Under the Sea* are amazing accomplishments, Disneyland may be Walt's greatest achievement. He always challenged his teams on movie projects, but Disneyland took the company way out of its comfort zone. For that reason, we now share a substantial lesson that can be drawn from Disneyland.

DISNEY LESSON 14: RECOGNIZE AND DEVELOP YOUR EMPLOYEES' TALENTS AS MUCH AS YOU CAN

Walt once said, "You can design and create, and build the most wonderful place in the world. But it takes people to make the dream a reality." He wasn't just spinning a feel good message for the public. He knew having the best talent working for him made it possible for his ideas to come to life, and he challenged them to be innovative. This process was not always easy, often pushing his employees out of their comfort zone. Consider the example of pioneering Imagineer X (Xavier) Atencio. X was an animator who worked on such classics as *Fantasia* and *Mary Poppins*. In 1965, in the middle of Disneyland's expansion into more complicated, dark rides, Walt relocated X to the Imagineering group in order to bring his creative talents to the projects.[26] X was a bit nervous. He was an experienced animator and writer, not a ride designer, but Walt encouraged him to stretch himself and develop material for the rides like he had for movies. Walt reasoned that rides were simply physical manifestations of stories. If X could tell a story in two dimensions, he could do it in three dimensions as well. X gave it a shot and ended up writing dialogue and music for the all-time classic rides *The Haunted Mansion* and *Pirates of the Caribbean*. His legacy lives on in the theme songs "Yo Ho, Yo Ho, A Pirate's Life for Me" and "Grim Grinning Ghosts," now classics sung by nearly everyone who walks through a Disney park. Had Walt not encouraged X to stretch his creative abilities, we would not have the same Disney park experience today. X credits Walt with tapping his hidden talents for dialogue and song. As X notes, "In my case, being a writer, I fell into it. It's a talent I didn't realize I had in myself. Walt put his finger on me and said go and do it. I went and did it and it was one of the greatest things that ever happened to me."[27] Animator Les Clark explains this method further:[28]

> I think that first of all he would evaluate what a man could do. And then gave him the job to do, and probably gave them a job they didn't think they could do, and that brought out more of what they were capable of doing. I know that this happened time and time again where he'd give someone an assignment and they'd be frightened of it, but he finally pulled out what he wanted from them, because he recognized possibly first that they had the ability to do so.

Consider the story of Rolly Crump. When Rolly was a young animator, Walt moved him to Imagineering to work on rides and attractions like the Enchanted Tiki Room. The Enchanted Tiki Room was a breakthrough attraction, as it was the first one to use the new technology of Audio-Animatronics. Walt knew animators were good at coming up with ideas and meeting movie deadlines. Why couldn't they do the same with theme park attractions? Rolly shares how Walt started a project with him:[29]

> Walt got that sly smile across his face and said, "Oh, we're going to have birds chirp to each other." You can tell he was really starting to like the idea, and how it was evolving. That was part of the beauty of these sessions. Ideas would come out, and just flow and evolve

into these wonderful things that would eventually make their way into Disneyland. Out of that first meeting, we were all assigned to do different things to get this off the ground. Walt came up to me and said, "Rolly, we're going to have this preshow area for people who are waiting to get in. I want to have some Tikis out there, and I want them to tell stories. I want you to design them." I had no choice but to say okay to him, but I didn't know a damn thing about Tikis! I had no idea what I was going to do. Luckily, John Hench was a good friend of mine, so I went to him and said, "What the hell do I do?" "Well," he said, "the best thing you can do is some research. Go get a book out of the library about the Gods of the Pacific." So, off I went to the library.

Rolly checked out a book about the mythology of the Pacific Islands called *Voices on the Wind*, which inspired a series of Tiki gods he designed for the attraction. After Walt approved his ideas, the next step was to sculpt some models of them. Rolly continues:[30]

I went to the head sculptor at the time, Blaine Gibson, and told him that he needed to get started on them as soon as he could. Blaine just looked at them and said, "I don't have time!" "Well, then, who's going to sculpt them?" I asked. He looked at me and said, "You are!" I said, "I am?" I'd never sculpted before in my life, so Blaine had to give me a real down and dirty lesson on how to do it. . . . Once the Tikis were sculpted, they were sent over to the Studio where molds were made out of them. . . . I ended up painting them myself. When I was finished, I had them shipped to Disneyland, where I helped bolt them to the ground.

Imagine how much Rolly learned working on the Enchanted Tiki Room from start to finish. Research. Sculpting. Painting. Installation. But the main lesson Walt taught him on the assignment was how to learn what he needed to figure out a project. Walt often liked to say, "The way to get started is to quit talking and begin doing."[31] This motto wasn't only about procrastination, it was also about learning. Your first attempt at something is likely to be messy, but just taking action leads to learning, which makes the next try better. Sometimes you don't need to have all the answers in your head when you start a project, but action will reveal what you need to learn. Indeed, if you stick with a project enough, you end up with some unexpected solutions Rolly liked to call "happy accidents." It certainly worked for him. He ended up having a very successful and creative forty-four-year career at Disney.

World's Fair

Although Disneyland drew big numbers, only 2 percent of its gate traffic came from east of the Mississippi River. That meant there was a huge, untapped market waiting to be developed; three-quarters of the country's population was there. Certainly, it wasn't like he was the only person thinking he should set up another park on the other side of the country. Letters were streaming in from other cities, courting him to build a Disneyland East. Walt was famous for being a dreamer—and he was—but he was a *practical* dreamer. Before letting his imagination run wild as to what he could build in a new park, he wanted to do his due diligence in researching whether there was enough interest in the east to make it worthwhile. Walt wondered if New York and other eastern cities would be too sophisticated to go to Disneyland. Would that market look down on a park there? It would really help if he could run an experiment in that part of the country to test whether the Disney brand would be well received. Fortunately, an opportunity arose to test his hypothesis. New York would be hosting a world's fair in 1964. He could create some Disneyland-like attractions for the fair and see how the public responded. The company could even experiment with some new technologies for the shows. In a best-case scenario, crowds would confirm interest in Disney in the east; in a worst-case scenario, Walt would have some new attractions to take back to Disneyland. And it would be even better if he could get others to pay for the experiment, so Walt told his executive team to get moving on finding corporate sponsors. He reasoned:[32]

> There's going to be a big fair up in New York. All the big corporations in the country are going to be spending a helluva lot of money building exhibits there. They won't know what they want to do. They won't even know *why* they're doing it, except that other corporations are doing it and they have to keep up with the Joneses. That's where WED Enterprises comes in.

Co-developing shows with Disney wasn't too hard a sell, though. World's fairs often drew tens of millions of visitors during their yearlong run, motivating every blue chip corporation to host an exhibit or pavilion. Joseph Tirella in *Tomorrow-Land* explains how Walt persuaded these companies to purchase his design services:

> Disney saw an opportunity to develop new rides, new concepts, and—with the benefit of corporate subsidies—new technologies. In addition, he would charge corporate clients $1 million for the use of his company's name in their pavilions—his surname had become synonymous with his patented, unique brand of American entertainment. . . . When a company expressed interest, Disney would personally fly in on his private Gulfstream jet for further discussions.

Walt wasn't new to world's fairs. He participated in the 1939 New York World's Fair, producing *Mickey's Surprise Party* for Nabisco, and he made a big splash at the 1958 Brussels World's Fair with his *America the Beautiful* film. *America the Beautiful* was no ordinary show about the United States; it featured the Circle-Vision 360-degree camera and projection technology developed by his old friend Ub Iwerks. The audience sat with eleven screens encircling them, with spectacular moving images of the most beautiful spots America had to offer. Developing the attraction for Brussels also paid off for the company, as it was later installed at Disneyland. Walt also enjoyed attending the fairs, which exposed him to the latest developments in industry and urban design. In particular, the Brussels World's Fair featured an exhibit called *Industrial Parks USA*, which might have piqued Walt's interest in visiting other companies' research and development labs. Moreover, his visit to the 1962 Seattle World's Fair featured a science pavilion with a model of the *World of Tomorrow*, a popular exhibit that most likely prompted him to think about designing a city of the future.[33]

The 1964 fair would be different from others in which he had participated. It was planned and hosted by Robert Moses, a charismatic figure every bit as influential as Walt Disney. While Walt transformed the entertainment world, Moses shaped the urban landscape of America. In *The Power Broker*, Moses' biographer Robert Caro describes him as[34]

the single most powerful man in New York's history, the shaper not only of the city's politics but of its physical structure . . . he developed his public authorities into a political machine that was virtually a fourth branch of government, one that could bring to their knees Governors and Mayors (even the mighty La Guardia) by mobilizing banks, contractors, labor unions, insurance firms, even the press and the Church, into an irresistible economic force . . . Moses built an empire and lived like an emperor. He personally conceived and completed public works so huge that he was the greatest builder America (and probably the world) has ever known. Without ever being elected to office, he dominated the men who were; even his most bitter enemy, Franklin D. Roosevelt, could not control him.

Respectfully, both men had great honor and admiration for each other. As Tirella explains the relationship between the two, "From the get-go the Master Builder and Master Showman hit it off. . . . Both had outsized imaginations and egos; both were leaders who surrounded themselves with armies of technicians on whom they could rely; and both were intensely driven workaholics."[35] However, while Walt terraformed an orange orchard into Disneyland, Moses built modern day New York City. As Caro describes:[36]

When Robert Moses began building playgrounds in New York City, there were 119. When he stopped, there were 777. Under his direction, an army of men that at times during the Great Depression included 84,000 laborers reshaped every park in the city and then filled the parks with zoos and skating rinks, boathouses and tennis houses, bridle paths and golf courses, 288 tennis courts and 673 baseball diamonds. Under his direction, endless convoys of trucks hauled the city's garbage into its marshes, and the garbage filled the marshes, was covered with earth and lawn, and became more parks. Long strings of barges brought to the city white sand dredged from the ocean floor and the sand was piled on mud flats to create beaches. . . . no public improvement of any type—not school or sewer, library or pier, hospital or catch basin—was built by any agency, even those which Robert Moses did not directly control, unless Robert Moses approved its design and location.

Imagine the conversation these two titans had when they first met in 1960 to discuss Walt's involvement in the fair. Moses first pitched the idea of Walt building a permanent children's village that would remain after the fair closed, but that didn't have commercial appeal for Disney. Walt wanted to use his creations at Disneyland when the fair ended. Moses then suggested he design and build exhibits for other companies wanting a presence at the fair. Since Walt had already been thinking about that before Moses met with him, it was easy to accept that offer. The two continued to meet over the next few years, planning for the fair, because each needed the Disney pavilions to be successful. While Walt was a beloved American figure, Moses made many enemies from his heavy-handed building of the New York landscape. The fair was his chance to leave a positive legacy to his city while Walt would benefit from developing and testing technologies with other companies' money.

Walt's partnership with Moses played a pivotal role in preparing the Disney Company to make its move east. Moses "owned" New York. If Walt needed help there on his projects, Moses could see to it he got what he needed. After a lot of talks with potential sponsors, they lined up the Ford Motor Company for *The Magic Skyway*—which introduced the Mustang for the first time to the American public; Pepsi and UNICEF for *it's a small world*; and General Electric for *Progressland*. Three attractions proved enough to keep Disney and his Imagineers busy, but their biggest challenge was yet to come. During a visit to the WED workshops, Walt showed Moses an Audio-Animatronics prototype of Abraham Lincoln for the future *Hall of Presidents* attraction at Disneyland. When Moses approached the figure, it reached out to shake his hand. Moses was floored by the demonstration and said he had to have it in his fair. Walt said he didn't think he could have it ready in time, but Moses persisted until he got Walt's agreement to deliver it. Then Moses went to work finding a sponsor for the attraction, which he eventually lined up with the state of Illinois, Lincoln's home state. The pavilion was called *Great Moments with Mr. Lincoln*. Mastering the Audio-Animatronics of Lincoln was brutal. All the Imagineers had mastered before were the birds in the Enchanted Tiki Room show. Designing Lincoln was a huge challenge, but in the end they pulled it off. Audiences were awed to see the country's sixteenth president come to life, giving them a five-minute patriotic speech. In the end, all the Disney creations were a smashing success, as Disney historian Sam Gennaway reports:[37]

> In a Gallup poll that asked people which exhibits they would recommend, three of the top four were from Disney. The scale was ten for a strongly recommend to zero for attractions people could "just skip seeing." General Electric tied with the General Motors Futurama at 9.1. Ford was right behind at 8.9, and *it's a small world* was 8.1. The small capacity for *Great Moments with Mr. Lincoln* was the primary reason it could not score higher. When the fair closed, three of the four exhibits were disassembled, shipped back to Disneyland, and reassembled. The dinosaurs of *Magic Skyway* became the finale to the Disneyland Railroad.

DISNEY LESSON 15: TALK TO EXPERTS TO BECOME ONE YOURSELF

A lot of powerful people feel compelled to make sure everyone thinks they're the smartest person in the room. Walt was different. He came across as the most *curious* person in the room. Walt appreciated that a good idea can come from anywhere. While his famous name got him meetings with leaders like Robert Moses, he didn't act like he knew more than they did. As we'll see throughout this chapter, each project was inspired by the ideas he learned from others. Bob Gurr was a young Imagineer who tagged along with Walt at a lot of these meetings. He observed firsthand that the secret of Walt's success was getting people to talk to him. Walt knew that he was an icon, and that people might get nervous in his presence, so he did his best to put them at ease. It wasn't just to be a nice guy. He knew that to get things done he needed everyone's best ideas to make a project work. As Gurr recounts:[38]

> Now to a lot of people, let's say even as late as 1954 when I'm with the company, a guy like Walt would seem like a god. In other words, he knew he was a really famous, famous person. I would see times when there'd be executives from other companies visit, they'd get to be close to Walt and their lower lip would start to quiver. They didn't quite know how to talk to him because they're in the presence of Walt Disney. The god, you know. Walt did everything possible to

make himself approachable. He'd unloosen [*sic*] his tie and make himself kind of ratty, so as he could have a conversation. And he would always point that out to us. He'd say, "Well, you know, to get this stuff done, I have to talk to people."

The Experimental Prototype Community of Tomorrow

As Walt put the pieces in place to test his brand appeal in the east, he started exploring locations to place his next park. Some of the cities he considered building Disneyland East in were Niagara Falls, New York; Kansas City, Missouri; St. Louis, Missouri; and even his hometown of Marceline, Missouri. Of these cities, St. Louis came closest to winning the bid . . . so close in fact that had it not been for a contentious meeting between Walt and August "Gussie" Busch, Jr., the theme park could have ended up in the middle of the country. Card Walker, a Disney Vice President and future CEO, reported that Walt had made up his mind to build there and was looking forward to announcing it the next day at a press conference. With all the details of the deal ironed out, everything was rolling along fine until Busch pointed out something that he disagreed with: no alcohol in Walt's parks (even though it was common practice at amusement parks). In addition, this was St. Louis, the home of Budweiser and other Busch beers. The thought of not serving beer at a major venue in St. Louis was more than Busch could handle. Richard Foglesong describes the episode in *Married to the Mouse:*[39]

Busch said, "Any man who thinks he can design an attraction that is going to be a success in this city and not serve beer or liquor, ought to have his head examined." Hearing the remark, the mayor gasped, "Oh, my god." He turned to Admiral Fowler, who sat next to him, and apologized, saying, "I just can't control that guy." But the damage was done. Walt hated being challenged, especially in public. Upon returning from the dinner party to his hotel suite, he asked Card Walker, "What time can we have the plane in the morning?" Surprised, Walker responded, "But you know we've got—" He tried to say they had legal papers to sign the next day, but Walt cut him off. "It's all finished," said Walt. "We're not coming. Forget about it." Afterwards, local bankers made three trips to California trying to change Walt's mind, all unsuccessful. Busch's insulting remark had killed the deal. The park would not be in St. Louis.

Imagine if Busch hadn't said what he did. You might be vacationing in Missouri more often. But as it turned out, the decision was probably for the best. St. Louis, although in the middle of the country and close to Walt's childhood home, was famous for beer. Why wouldn't Busch want his products sold in

Walt's park? His company was a major contributor to St. Louis's economy, after all. In the end, it probably wasn't a good fit anyway, and better yet it drove Walt to consider putting his park farther south in Florida. Turning to Buzz Price again for market analysis, Palm Beach in southern Florida and Ocala in the center of the state were identified as the two best possibilities for the new park. Palm Beach came very close to being chosen because billionaire John D. MacArthur wanted to work with Walt in building a unique community there. Florida was a rapidly developing state at the time, with model communities popping up all over it. MacArthur wanted to partner with Walt and RCA to develop a four hundred acre theme park and a town center for seventy thousand people on a large tract of land he owned. They even had a handshake agreement on the deal, but it later broke down when the three parties had different ideas on how the project should be developed. Walt and Roy had second thoughts about the amount of land they needed, and when Roy broached the subject of requesting more land, MacArthur took offense to changing the agreement. And when RCA discovered the Disneys wanted to expand the project beyond the initial agreement, they backed out. The projected costs were much more than they were willing to bear. With the Palm Beach deal now in the past, Walt and Roy turned their attention to Central Florida.[40]

After numerous trips to Central Florida, researching possible locations, Walt and his team decided the Orlando area held the most potential for development. Buzz Price and his team from Economic Research Associates studied fifty properties and then did detailed follow-up studies on twenty-five. While Price investigated properties, Walt organized a secret team inside the company to buy the land and handle the legalities and regulatory challenges that would come with purchasing thousands of acres of property. Walt was a *practical* dreamer. Making Disney World possible would require handling matters many creative people might dislike, but Walt knew that to make his ideas real he had to recruit and facilitate experts who could handle the details of the plan. He didn't just hand it over to the lawyers, legislators, accountants, and realtors. He worked with them, lest they make decisions he'd later regret. No, if the experts were to complete the project the way he wanted it, Walt would ensure that what he was asking for was done well. Walt's family name was on the park, after all, and he took full accountability for the outcome. It's easy to imagine Walt asking a real estate lawyer, "Now what are you doing here? How's that work?" Or more likely, "Explain what's holding us up right now. What're our options?"

Buzz Price recommended tracts of land near Interstate 4 as the best location for the project, and with shell companies and fake identities in place, local real estate agents were entrusted to acquire the land for the company. It took two years to buy the thirty thousand acres—or forty-seven square miles—that Walt Disney World stands on today. People were obviously noticing the purchases taking place in Florida, but the company was able to maintain its secret identity until October 17, 1965, when the *Orlando Sentinel* broke the story that the mysterious buyer was Disney. By this time record world's fair crowds at the Disney pavilions confirmed Walt's hypothesis on the eastern market, so with the land purchased and due diligence met, it was time to think seriously about designing the new park. The chief factor in Walt's thinking was that he wanted his Florida Project to be more than another Disneyland. He didn't like to repeat himself, and while he agreed the project needed a theme park to generate revenue, he wasn't interested in working on that part of the plan. Essentially, Walt said, yeah, put Disneyland there. However, there were aspects of the theme park that piqued his interest—such as building the utilidor, dredging the lake and designing watercraft for transportation, and building a couple of resort hotels—but for the most part, he pointed to where he wanted the Disneyland clone to be and expected others to implement its construction.

Walt exemplified a prime example of Stephen Covey's Circle of Influence and Circle of Concern principles. As his circle of influence grew, his insatiable curiosity drove him to tackle new frontiers that concerned him. Cartoons, movies, television, and theme parks had been mastered, so in his elder statesman years, he felt compelled to be a major player in the modernist movement, improving the way people lived in cities. For Walt, if he could be a part of something fresh and innovative, he pursued it—which meant everyone else in the company would be a part of it too. In fact, it was the urban design component of the Palm Beach deal that interested him most in partnering with MacArthur. Designing a "City of the Future" would be his final medium for mixing what he learned from his experiences with urban planners like Robert Moses, modern artists like Salvador Dali, U.S. Presidents, NASA administrators like Wernher von Braun, and scientists from corporate R&D labs. Always the learner, Walt turned to experts who could direct him to the sources he needed to make his dream a reality. In the case of urban design, he was most influenced by Welton Becket, an architect famous for designing futuristic airports, music centers, and other community buildings. Becket had already made an impact on Disney design, serving as an advisor and confidant to Walt on the Disneyland project. In fact, it was Becket who advised Walt to use movie production designers and set designers instead of traditional architecture firms to plan the park aesthetic. Becket reasoned that movie people would better understand what Walt was trying to create in the park, and that Walt would have an easier time working with his peers than architects who didn't understand show business. Disneyland, after all, is a show first and a physical place second. Set designers would better understand what was required to make magic onstage. Becket also influenced the construction of the now gone (but not forgotten) House of the Future in Disneyland's Tomorrowland. Sponsored by Monsanto, the structure was manufactured from plastic, a material just finding its way into all areas of modern life at that time.[41] Although Becket's house concept didn't make its way into everyday culture, it's an example of a great mind willing to explore possibilities. Walt and Becket were good friends, even vacationing together with their wives, and spent many hours discussing the state of modern cities and how they could offer solutions to urban problems—however, whether people decided to implement their solutions was up to them. As Disney expert Sam Gennawey explains:[42]

> Walt was a visionary as well as a practical man. He knew he could not do everything. (Imagineer) John Hench said that Walt did not want to "change people's lives . . . only the environment in which they lived." Imagineer Marvin Davis suggested, "It was his philosophy not to build a city that would solve all the urban problems all over the world, but to give a chance to American industry to experiment and show the world just how the problems of traffic and housing could be solved."

American industry, and in particular the American free enterprise system, played a pivotal role in Walt's design of what that city would look like. Walt believed that only in America could he have risen from his humble beginnings on a Midwestern farm to where he ended up in Hollywood, and it was business that made that journey possible. He was willing to provide an urban alternative to traditional government-planned cities that were run by politicians and bureaucrats. What would a city look like if industrialists constructed one using the best ideas from businesspeople and scientists? Walt wanted to find out and he wanted the public to offer their judgment of it. Gennawey continues:[43]

> John Hench said, "Walt believed people could always read about ideas or see photographs of new concepts. But they would find it more compelling if they went through it themselves. Once people experienced something first-hand they could go home to their own communities and make changes." According to Hench, Walt said, "Experiences were the only thing that you really own. They were yours." Buzz Price said, "Walt wanted to try going beyond the park experience. He wanted to try improving the environment, the urban setting. He was full of ideas about what that place would be like. EPCOT would not be just a park, but an urban experiment where you could try to improve the way people live, creating alternatives to our frantic, automobile existence."

EPCOT. The Experimental Prototype Community of Tomorrow. That was what Walt wanted to build in Florida. A city to test out ideas. But not just his ideas. The best ideas his industry friends had to offer too. Walt visited a lot of corporate labs and R&D departments over the years, and he was always flabbergasted by how many amazing inventions never made it to the marketplace. Walt thought those ideas should be in homes, making American life better. As a businessman, he understood the rationale for sticking with proven products that were paying the bills and maintaining a stock price. Maybe he could help other companies innovate by providing a place for testing ideas with the public.

What if companies could try out those ideas in his experimental community? And if enough companies participated in the community, they could even examine the effect a new technology had on other products and services. Other areas of science, like horticulture, had access to places for developing inventions in natural settings. Why not have a place for technology, business, and urban design? If a new idea came along, it could be tested in EPCOT. If it worked, the discovery could be passed on to the rest of the country; if it didn't, an R&D department could go back to the drawing board and try again.

Progress is what Walt lived for, and if he could accelerate it throughout the country, he felt it was his duty to do so. In fact, every aspect of the city could be a source of experimentation: agriculture, entertainment, transportation, work, and energy, all configured in a concentric circle around a city center where residents and guests could shop, dine, and socialize. Always thinking ahead to the future, he was even considering the use of nuclear energy on the site. Fossil fuel and coal would have limited presence on the premises since most of the public transportation would be run on electricity. The city would also be designed to encourage walking, with automobiles only having access to underground roadways and garages hidden away from public view. He also planned to construct a major airport for international flights, as EPCOT was going to be a hub for companies and visitors to share ideas that could be taken back to other communities. Since EPCOT was an entirely new city concept, never attempted in the world before, Walt petitioned the state of Florida for regulatory concessions to allow more independence than a traditional town had. Politicians are often fearful of upsetting established constituencies, but the Florida legislature agreed to the regulatory experiment. After all, Disneyland alone had an estimated economic impact of $556.2 million on Anaheim through its in-park sales, retail sales outside the park, wholesale sales, construction, property taxes, and sales taxes.[44] Imagine what a theme park *and* a new community could do for the local economy in the little cattle town in Central Florida.

Recognizing the unique circumstances, the state granted Disney the right to set up its own special-purpose government on the site, which eventually became known as the Reedy Creek Improvement District. With the government's flexibility in approving the private municipality, even the state of Florida was participating in the grand experiment. Walt wasn't working around the state; he was working with the state, effectively changing the central region of it. As Richard Foglesong observes:[45]

> It's like a city . . . but it is no ordinary city, moreover, but a proprietary city—a "showcase for free enterprise," in Walt's phrase—founded upon two private-sector strategies: privatization and deregulation. As an experiment in privatization, municipal services at Disney World are provided by the Reedy Creek Improvement District, the governmental arm of the Disney Co. As an experiment in deregulation, the Florida legislature

eventually agreed in 1967 to Walt's request, rolling back state and local regulation of building construction, land use, and so forth, in return for Disney's promised $600-million investment.

It's also interesting to see how Walt's vision got translated into the nitty gritty details of construction. Imagineering executive Marty Sklar notes that the building code the company wrote for EPCOT reveals the thinking Walt had behind the project. In particular, EPCOT was:[46]

- To provide the flexibility that will encourage American industry, through free enterprise, to introduce, test, and demonstrate new ideas, materials, and systems emerging now and in the future from the creative centers of industry.
- To provide an environment that will stimulate the best thinking of industry and the professions in the creative development of new technologies to meet the needs of people, expressed by the experience of those who live and work and visit here.

Walt also masterminded the alignment between the physical layout of the project and his vision for a city based on American free enterprise principles—combining what he knew from his many years running a studio and Disneyland with what he had learned from urban design experts. Walt knew he had something amazing in mind for the public, but they would need to experience it first to understand what he was trying to accomplish. After all, a trip to a theme park is an easier sell to a family than a visit to a city. So, knowing the psychology of his target market, he understood he had to draw them to the theme park in order to get them to see the city. As Dick Nunis, head of Disneyland park operations at the time, reflected on Walt's strategy:[47]

> He said, "We've got to put Disneyland, which everybody will know, at the very upper end of the property because that will be the weenie." Then whatever we build after that, the public will have to drive by to get to the Park.

Walt used the image of a weenie to reflect his idea that you needed to construct something dazzling in a park to draw the crowd so they would move to where you wanted them to go. Walt based this practice metaphorically on dog psychology. He knew waving a hot dog at a canine would entice it to follow you anywhere; the same worked with crowd psychology. For example, at Disneyland, Sleeping Beauty Castle—placed behind the center hub at the end of Main Street, U.S.A.—was the theme park's weenie. Once there, guests filter to the different lands in the park, but you have to draw them in first; otherwise the town square would get congested with confused guests. But before they can even reach the theme park nestled north of EPCOT, he must persuade them to come to Florida. That wasn't an easy task. The tourist experience in America was much different in the 1960s than it is today. Airline deregulation hadn't happened yet, so most families couldn't afford to fly to Orlando. Instead, they drove, oftentimes on country highways and backroads since the interstate highway system was still being constructed. So, Walt had to convince them that making the trip was worth it, and to do that he turned to the medium that had always worked for him before: television. In his "Florida Room" in California, Walt evangelized to the camera about the miraculous place that would be built in the Sunshine State. He explained the vision, revealed a map of the layout, and displayed models of what the city would look like. He'd pitched ideas before, but this one was different. It wasn't something to escape to; it was something to be a part of. EPCOT was Walt's gift to humankind, a legacy intended to make people's entire lives better.

Unfortunately, Walt wouldn't live to see the public reaction to his greatest dream. He died on December 15, 1966, before the public saw the film. A lifelong habit of smoking brought lung cancer, a challenge even he couldn't overcome. Fortunately, Walt kept his legacy in mind up to his last days. Before he passed, he purchased the land for what is now Walt Disney World, shared a clear vision of what it could be with Roy, and left a footprint for future Disney executives and Imagineers to develop. In his last year, he declined a trip out east to accept an award because he felt he still had too much to do in the studio. Every minute making his future projects a reality was precious to him. He told his niece's husband, "I don't know how much time I have. I need to stay here to do as much as I can to keep this enterprise twenty-five years ahead of the competition."[48] Walt actually underestimated his impact. We're still enjoying new experiences that stem from Walt's vision from over *fifty* years ago.

Walt's last meeting with Roy was from his bed at Saint Joseph Medical Center. Pointing at the ceiling tiles of his room and employing them as a makeshift grid, he explained to Roy where everything in the park had to go. Roy nodded and comforted his brother during his last hours, assuring him that Disney World would be built.[49] After Walt died, Roy kept his promise, coming out of retirement to oversee Disney World's construction and changing its name to *Walt* Disney World out of respect for his brother. He wanted to make it clear to future generations that Disney World was Walt's vision.[50]

Would Walt's Version of EPCOT Have Worked?

A common parlor game among Disney aficionados is speculating over whether EPCOT would have worked if Walt had the chance to build it like he wanted. He was sixty-five years old when he died. What if he had lived to eighty-five? What could he have done if he had overseen the company another twenty years? Originally, he planned to do it, telling a newspaper a year before he died, "As far as I'm concerned I am just in the *middle* of my career. I have several years and several projects to go before my life story should be written." Unfortunately, those plans are now grist for others to debate. Many social critics believed that what worked inside the company wouldn't work in a city. In particular, would residents be willing to submit most of the decision-making to one company, or more precisely, to one person? In October 1966, shortly before he died, Walt laid out his governance structure for EPCOT:[51]

> There'll be no landowners, and therefore no voting control. People will rent homes instead of buying them, and at market rentals. There will be no retirees. Everyone must be employed. One of our requirements is that people who live in EPCOT must help keep it alive. In EPCOT there will be no slum areas because we won't let them develop.

Utopian experiments typically implode as human nature interferes with good intentions. Consider that Walt envisioned a worker paradise for the Burbank studio but was faced with a labor strike within a few years of opening. Yet, Walt adapted from the crisis and took the company to even greater heights afterward. It's likely he would have modified his EPCOT plans as well as he learned what worked and what didn't. Some of his employees thought Walt would have had a hard time convincing companies to publicly prototype new inventions. Why would companies want to share their secrets before going to market with a product? Wouldn't that lose the element of surprise that comes with product releases? And what about EPCOT residents? Would they really want to play the role of guinea pigs, having their living environment changed on them at the discretion of a company? Imagineer Carl Bongiorno recalls:[52]

> Even prior to his death, everyone knew that you couldn't have 25,000 people living in a community . . . and constantly change, upgrade, move, innovate, go into people's homes, take out appliances, put new ones in, control everything about the project when you have a one-man, one-vote democracy.

So is it impossible to find twenty-five thousand people who would live under this type of control? Maybe, maybe not. Consider that at any one time over one hundred thousand guests visit Walt Disney World, where everything they do is provided by the Walt Disney Company. When you visit Walt Disney World, you're essentially submitting yourself to a beneficent dictatorship, where security officers ensure safety and order at all times and managers and cast members oversee the smallest of details in the guest experience, all measured and modified by the Team Disney executives. It's definitely effective—so much so that many guests make multiple trips per year, *paying* for the privilege to be in that controlled environment, often by being members of the Disney Vacation Club timesharing program. When you check into a Disney resort, the front desk always greets you by saying, "Welcome home." For recurrent guests, this is not an empty platitude. Their "home" hotel becomes a part of their lives—truly a second home. The most loyal guests often know Disney managers and cast members better than their own neighbors in their hometown. It's as if their jobs are places they have to be until they can get back to Walt Disney World, where they feel more welcome and appreciated. Consider also that people move to the Disney-created community of Celebration, and they buy multimillion-dollar homes in the Golden Oak neighborhood on company property. And maybe Walt could have created a cleaner, better functioning city than what currently exists in today's world. After all, everyone imagined Disneyland would be a dirty amusement park like all the others, but he proved them wrong there. Maybe EPCOT would have worked too. Many Disney colleagues who knew him best thought it would have. Buzz Price, who oversaw the economic forecasting and market analysis of Walt's ideas, said of EPCOT, "He had a seed idea, attempting a Walt idea—'I want to do this.' And if he'd lived another decade, he would have done it." And before he died in 2017, Imagineering legend Marty Sklar told people we spoke to at Disney that he firmly believed Walt would have pulled it off because he would have gotten the buy-in from other major companies to participate.

Whether he would have made the reality of EPCOT match up with his vision is a matter of conjecture now. But what most people can agree on is that the spirit of the EPCOT dream was met. In *Power and Paradise in Walt Disney's World*, Cher Krause Knight vividly explains its appeal:[53]

> Walt designed Disney World as a personal paradise, believing others would share his vision. His intention was to provide a refuge from the messes of daily life, a place where he could continually tinker with his notions of an ideal society. In his worldview, the United States was the most noble of nations, unified by God-fearing, hardworking, and optimistic citizens. The virtues Walt perceived in his country were the same that he sought to foster at Disney World—freedom, ingenuity, bravery, and contentment. The public quickly responded to his concept: nearly eleven million visitors passed through Disney World's gates in 1971, its first year of operation. Clearly, Walt's vision of paradise resonated with many people.

His passion still resonates today for the same reasons. Over fifty million guests visit the park each year compared with eleven million in its first year; new lands, attractions, and hotels open every year; and attendance continues to climb. Guests return time and time again to their personal paradise to escape the daily stressors of work and politics—and distractions from the ideals they seek in their lives. Perhaps Walt's personal press secretary summed it up best when he said, "I've always thought EPCOT achieved the spirit of Walt's vision of creating a better understanding of today's world and getting people excited about the possibilities of the future."[54]

We hope the awareness of what Walt was trying to provide his guests will make your next trip to Walt Disney World more special. As you walk around one of the parks and enjoy all Walt Disney World has to offer, consider what the world would be like if one Missouri farm boy hadn't boarded that train to Hollywood in 1923. Reflecting on Walt's life story will help you appreciate the existence of each ride, restaurant, and hotel a bit more. Think about the creativity, risk-taking, and hard work that went into making each experience there possible. Who knows, by doing so, maybe you'll be able to channel your inner Walt Disney the next time an opportunity comes to you.

Conclusion

In this chapter, we explained how operating like an evangelist helped Walt promote his company to the world in new ways. Every project provided a chance to better connect with his audience. Using television and face-to-face interactions at Disneyland helped the audience feel like they actually knew him, and they appreciated what he represented. Walt put a lot of thought into how his audience saw him, and he convinced them to be a part of his mission to improve the world. In the process, Walt created the Disney brand based on his values— values that still guide the company today. After all, business evangelism is really brand building, and no one did it better than Walt. If you want to build a great company, you need to evangelize a great brand by demonstrating what's important to you and expressing how your products and services deliver on that message.

In the following chapters, you'll learn how the company continues Walt's legacy through corporate entrepreneurship. There will be only one Walt Disney, but many others in the company follow the example he set for them. Although these corporate entrepreneurs aren't as famous as Walt, many of their innovations are. You'll see they honor Walt's legacy every day, not by asking, what would Walt do? but rather, would Walt approve? After all, Walt Disney was one of a kind. He embodied all four areas of entrepreneurship we've covered over the last four chapters. That's rare. He was an artist, a scientist, and a builder, but perhaps his most impressive role was as an evangelist. Walt was known as the company's "Chief Imagineer," but we offer an additional title for him: Chief Imagineur. Walt Disney showed the world what is possible when a person brings an expansive imagination to their entrepreneurial pursuits. He spent as much time imagining what his company could be as he did the products that came from it. Significantly, as a legend, we'll see he was a tough act to follow, but new executives will arrive on the scene to make Disney an even better company than when Walt was alive. Walt Disney's mission of honoring the past and looking to the future is still alive and well at the Walt Disney Company.

- On fire about their cause
- Uses simple messages to connect with consumers
- Connects with employees through clear mission and purpose
- Able to charm the media
- Carries the banner for their organization and its initiatives
- Inspires followers and advocates

WALT DISNEY THE EVANGELIST

Charm the media and reach the public
- Television
- Edutainment
- True-Life Adventures

Company cathedral to interact directly with customers
- Disneyland

Missionary work
- Expansion to eastern United States: 1964 New York World's Fair
- Partnerships with business leaders, blue chip companies, and urban planners
- Florida Project (a.k.a. Walt Disney World)

Optimistic vision for the future
- Promotes scientific advances
- Promotes United States space efforts
- Promotes industry and free enterprise system
- EPCOT

FIGURE 4.1 Entrepreneurial Leadership Style—Evangelist

Disney Principles

- Walt often gave employees assignments that made them uncomfortable at first. Innovative leaders are mentors and put their employees in situations that provide them opportunities to grow.

- Each stage of Walt's success built on the previous ones. Work with what you have. Learn by tinkering and build on your successes as they grow.
- Walt wanted the best talent working in his company. Build a strong network of people who have your interests in mind. If you are starting new projects, bring aboard people who can help.
- Walt enjoyed socializing with the top people from other fields. Talk to experts and learn how they became successful in their respective fields.
- Walt would often work a long time on an idea before starting a project. When exploring an opportunity, fact find, incubate, be patient, and execute when the time is right.

Work Like Disney: Exercises

1. If Walt Disney held the position you have in your company, what would he change about *your workplace*? What would he do to bring about these changes in your workplace? Will you make these changes when you go back to work? Why or why not?
2. Consider your own company and the *products and services* it sells. Now imagine Walt Disney held the position you have. What new products and services would Walt offer your customers? How does this differ from what your company offers? What would you have to do to bring these products into reality?
3. If Walt Disney led your organization, what new technologies would he embrace to shake up your *industry*? Is your company leadership currently taking this approach? Why or why not?
4. EPCOT was Walt's attempt at alleviating many of society's problems. What new technologies do you think Walt Disney would embrace in *today's world*? How would he implement that into the Walt Disney Company if he were alive today?
5. Do you think Walt Disney would be innovative in today's world? Why or why not?

Notes

1. Moran, C. (2015). *Great Big Beautiful Tomorrow: Walt Disney and Technology*. Lexington: Theme Park Press.
2. Rothrock, R. (2017). *Sunday Nights With Walt: Everything I Know I Learned From the Wonderful World of Disney*. Lexington: Theme Park Press.
3. Peri, D. (2008). *Working With Walt: Interviews With Disney Artists*. Oxford, MS: University of Mississippi Press.
4. Van Piper, A.B. (2011). *Learning From Mickey, Donald and Walt: Essays on Disney's Edutainment Films*. Jefferson: McFarland.
5. Peri, D. (2008). *Working With Walt: Interviews With Disney Artists*. Oxford, MS: University of Mississippi Press.
6. Maltin, L. (2012). *Leonard Maltin Discusses the True-Life Adventure Series*. Retrieved from www.youtube.com/watch?v=X0sQpbeEAVk.

7. Ibid.
8. Korkis, J. (2017). *The Vault of Walt, Volume 6: Other Unofficial Disney Stories Never Told.* Lexington: Theme Park Press.
9. Van Piper, A.B. (2011). *Learning From Mickey, Donald and Walt: Essays on Disney's Edutainment Films.* Jefferson: McFarland.
10. Peterson, J.B. (2017). *Lectures: Exploring the Psychology Side of Creativity (National Gallery of Canada).* Retrieved from www.youtube.com/watch?v=KxGPe1jD-qY.
11. Gabler, N. (2006). *Walt Disney: The Triumph of the American Imagination.* New York: Vintage.
12. Peri, D. (2008). *Working With Walt: Interviews With Disney Artists.* Oxford, MS: University of Mississippi Press.
13. Gabler, N. (2006). *Walt Disney: The Triumph of the American Imagination.* New York: Vintage.
14. Pierce, T.J. (2016). *Three Years in Wonderland: The Disney Brothers, C.V. Wood, and the Making of the Great American Theme Park.* Oxford, MS: University of Mississippi Press.
15. Genneway, S. (2014). *Walt and the Promise of Progress City.* Lexington: Theme Park Press.
16. Heath, C., and Heath, D. (2013). *Decisive: How to Make Better Choices in Life and Work.* New York: Crown Business.
17. Ibid.
18. Ibid.
19. Price, H.B. (2004). *Walt's Revolution!: By the Numbers.* New York: Ripley Entertainment.
20. Lipp, D. (2013). *Disney U.: How Disney University Develops the World's Most Engaged, Loyal, and Customer-Centric Employees.* New York: McGraw Hill.
21. Genneway, S. (2014). *Walt and the Promise of Progress City.* Lexington: Theme Park Press.
22. Smith, D. (2001). *The Quotable Walt Disney.* New York: Disney Editions.
23. The Walt Disney Company still follows Walt's lead on this philosophy. As one executive told us, "Sacred cows make the best burgers."
24. Ibid.
25. Peri, D. (2008). *Working With Walt: Interviews With Disney Artists.* Oxford, MS: University of Mississippi Press.
26. Dark rides are rides that are enclosed inside a building. The name implies that the rides are lit by artificial means, not by sunlight. Most have a theatrical quality to them and may employ animated figures, lighting tricks, various atmospheric elements like fire and water, and other special effects to tell a story. The rider boards a car or boat and travels into a place of fantasy, such as a haunted house or a children's fable.
27. Frost, J. (2009). *Interview With a Disney Legend: X Atencio.* Retrieved from www.laughingplace.com/News-ID 500190.asp.
28. Ghez, D. (2009). *Walt's People,* Volume 8. Bloomington, IN: Xlibris.
29. Crump, R., and Heimbuch, J. (2012). *It's Kind of a Cute Story.* Kissimmee: Bamboo Forest Publishing.
30. Ibid.
31. Smith, D. (2001). *The Quotable Walt Disney.* New York: Disney Editions.
32. Tirella, J. (2014). *Tomorrow-Land: The 1964–65 World's Fair & the Transformation of America.* Guilford: Lyons Press.
33. Genneway, S. (2014). *Walt and the Promise of Progress City.* Lexington: Theme Park Press.

34. Caro, R.A. (1975). *The Power Broker: Robert Moses and the Fall of New York*. New York: Vintage.
35. Tirella, J. (2014). *Tomorrow-Land: The 1964–65 World's Fair & the Transformation of America*. Guilford: Lyons Press.
36. Caro, R.A. (1975). *The Power Broker: Robert Moses and the Fall of New York*. New York: Vintage.
37. Genneway, S. (2014). *Walt and the Promise of Progress City*. Lexington: Theme Park Press.
38. Gurr, B. (2015). *Bob Gurr, Disney Imagineer/Talks at Google*. Retrieved from www.youtube.com/watch?v=q_6OAEmnMUA.
39. Fogelson, R. (2003). *Married to the Mouse: Walt Disney World and Orlando*. New Haven: Yale University Press.
40. Emerson, C.D. (2010). *Project Future: The Inside Story Behind the Creation of Disney World*. Lexington: Ayefour.
41. Hahn, D. (2017). *Yesterday's Tomorrow: Disney's Magical Mid-Century*. New York: Disney Editions.
42. Genneway, S. (2014). *Walt and the Promise of Progress City*. Lexington: Theme Park Press.
43. Ibid.
44. Mannheim, S. (2017). *Walt Disney and the Quest for Community*. London: Routledge.
45. Fogelson, R. (2003). *Married to the Mouse: Walt Disney World and Orlando*. New Haven: Yale University Press.
46. Sklar, M. (2013). *Dream It! Do It! My Half-Century Creating Disney's Magic Kingdoms*. New York: Disney Editions.
47. Hahn, D. (2017). *Yesterday's Tomorrow: Disney's Magical Mid-Century*. New York: Disney Editions.
48. Gabler, N. (2006). *Walt Disney: The Triumph of the American Imagination*. New York: Vintage.
49. Ibid.
50. It should be noted that Walt left other institutions behind too that still contribute to today's society. The California Institute of the Arts (CalArts), which Walt founded shortly before he died, produced some of the greatest talent over the years for Walt Disney Animation, Walt Disney Pictures, Pixar, and the theme parks, such as John Lasseter, Tim Burton, and Brad Bird. Additionally, the company still runs its operations out of the Walt Disney Studios in Burbank.
51. Mannheim, S. (2017). *Walt Disney and the Quest for Community*. London: Routledge.
52. Ibid.
53. Knight, C.K. (2014). *Power and Paradise in Walt Disney's World*. Gainesville: University of Florida Press.
54. Ridgway, C. (2007). *Spinning Disney's World: Memories of a Magic Kingdom Press Agent*. Branford: The Intrepid Traveler.

PART 2

Corporate Entrepreneurship at the Walt Disney Company

5

LEADERS IN THE POST-WALT DISNEY ERA

Roy O. Disney: Life After Walt (1966–1971)

After Walt's passing in 1966, just prior to the start of construction on Disney World, Roy postponed his retirement to honor his brother by seeing the Florida Project through to completion. Roy's careful and calculated approach to business and financing had been a great complement to the creativity and aggressive and entrepreneurial nature of Walt for many years, but at that point Roy took on a very different role. He wrote in a memo to fellow employees the day after Walt's death on December 15, 1966:[1]

> The death of Walt Disney is a loss to all the people of the world. In everything he did Walt had an intuitive way of reaching out and touching the hearts and minds of young and old alike. His entertainment was an international language. For more than forty years people have looked to Walt Disney for the finest in family entertainment.
>
> There is no way to replace Walt Disney. He was an extraordinary man. Perhaps there will never be another like him. I know that we who worked at his side for all these years will always cherish the years and the minutes we spent in helping Walt Disney entertain the people of the world. The world will always be a better place because Walt Disney was its master showman.
>
> As President and Chairman of the Board of Walt Disney Productions, I want to assure the public, our stockholders and each of our more than four thousand employees that we will continue to operate Walt Disney's company in the way that he has established and guided it. Walt Disney spent his entire life and almost every waking hour in the creative planning of motion pictures, Disneyland, television shows and all the other

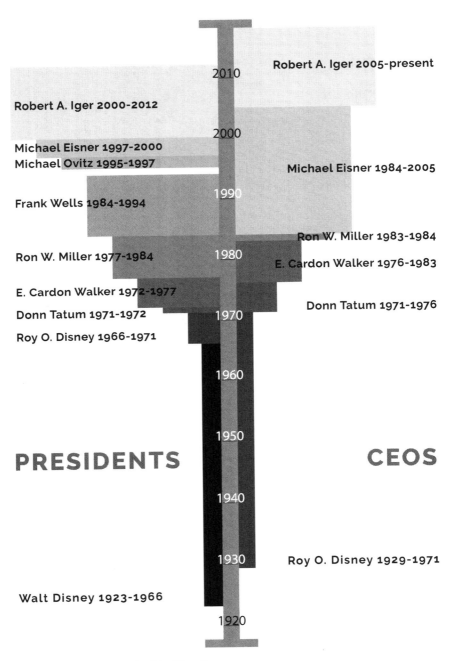

PRESIDENTS

Robert A. Iger 2000-2012

Michael Eisner 1997-2000
Michael Ovitz 1995-1997

Frank Wells 1984-1994

Ron W. Miller 1977-1984

E. Cardon Walker 1972-1977

Donn Tatum 1971-1972

Roy O. Disney 1966-1971

Walt Disney 1923-1966

CEOS

Robert A. Iger 2005-present

Michael Eisner 1984-2005

Ron W. Miller 1983-1984

E. Cardon Walker 1976-1983

Donn Tatum 1971-1976

Roy O. Disney 1929-1971

2010
2000
1990
1980
1970
1960
1950
1940
1930
1920

FIGURE 5.1 Disney Leadership Timeline

diversified activities that have carried his name through the years. Around him Walt Disney gathered the kind of creative people who understood his way of communicating with the public through entertainment. Walt's ways were always unique and he built a unique organization. A team of creative people that he was justifiably proud of.

I think Walt would have wanted me to repeat his words to describe the organization he built over the years. Last October when he accepted the "Showman of the World" award in New York, Walt said, "The Disney organization now has more than four thousand employees. Many have been with us for over thirty years. They take great pride in the organization which they helped to build. Only through the talent, labor and dedication of this staff could any Disney project get off the ground. We all think alike in the ultimate pattern."

Much of Walt Disney's energies had been directed to preparing for this day. It was Walt's wish that when the time came he would have built an organization with the creative talents to carry on as he had established and directed it through the years. Today this organization has been built and we will carry out this wish.

Walt Disney's preparation for the future has a solid, creative foundation. All of the plans for the future that Walt had begun—new motion pictures, the expansion of Disneyland, television production and our Florida and Mineral King projects—will continue to move ahead. That is the way Walt wanted it to be.

Roy was a builder—not an evangelist—but he lived on the fuel of Walt's Florida Project dream for almost five years—just long enough to lead the company to the October 1971 opening of Disney World. Sadly, Roy passed away just two months after the opening of Disney World. Some suggest he literally worked himself to death by pushing so hard to build Walt's dream resort, which he named Walt Disney World in honor of his younger brother.

Roy was a behind-the-scenes builder who financed and professionalized Walt's ideas and initiatives for nearly five decades. He creatively worked the deals that financed the opening of Disneyland, Walt Disney World, and countless other ventures Walt was determined to undertake. Roy was no doubt cautious in his approaches, but teamed with Walt he became an ambitious builder of the company. He was extremely uncomfortable being the face of the organization and preferred to not be in the public eye. Yet, after being the quiet and private brother of the charismatic Walt Disney for decades, he suddenly found himself about to address the crowd at the Magic Kingdom grand opening. So nervous he was paralyzed by anxiety, he asked an assistant for Mickey, and the character created by Walt came to his side, holding his hand as he addressed the crowd. The rest is history, as Walt Disney World Resort is now the premier vacation destination in the world thanks to the vision of Walt Disney and the execution of Roy O. Disney.

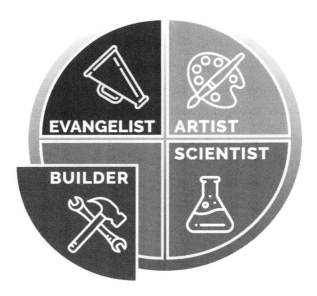

- Developed internal stability by professionalizing the Disney company
- Established company reputation with bankers, public markets, and stockholders
- Financed Disneyland with ABC grand opening broadcast
- Managed Walt's unpredictable nature with systems and financial analysis

FIGURE 5.2 Roy O. Disney—Builder

Donn Tatum, Card Walker, and Ron Miller: The Quiet Years (1971–1983)

The twelve-year period after Walt Disney World opened and Roy O. Disney passed away was very quiet for the Walt Disney Company. EPCOT Center opened as the second park at Walt Disney World in 1982 and Tokyo Disneyland opened in 1983, but not much else happened during that time frame. Because of this, the company became a vulnerable, corporate raider target due to its valuable collection of intellectual property (IP) rights and real estate holdings.

As we briefly discuss each of the three leaders during this era, it is important to note that while they were most likely artists or builders based on the Entrepreneurial Leadership Instrument (ELI), as we mentioned in the Introduction, the scale does not measure intensity. In other words, it measures one's entrepreneurial leadership style but not necessarily how strong an artist, scientist, builder, or evangelist a person is. Thus, these three leaders were not really what we would label entrepreneurial, as evidenced by their careful approach and more or less maintenance of the status quo.

DISNEY LESSON 16: CAUTIOUS ORGANIZATIONS CAN LOSE THEIR EDGE VERY QUICKLY

This era serves as a cautionary tale for established companies for a few different reasons. For publicly traded companies, organizations with rich traditions and strong corporate cultures, such as Disney, can be quickly decimated by leveraged buyouts. For small businesses, entrepreneurial ventures, and even social ventures, it serves as a reminder that merely surviving—or even having strong financials—does not exempt them from threats of competition and an ever-changing marketplace. It is critical that all organizations keep moving forward and making themselves better, which is why innovation and entrepreneurship are relevant to literally *every* organization on the planet. As we will discuss below, the world is a better place because of Roy E. Disney's (Roy O.'s son and Walt's nephew) interventions, which saved the Walt Disney Company from being split up and its valuable parts from being sold off to the highest bidders.

Donn Tatum (1971–1976)

Tatum, a lawyer by training, served as a production business manager and executive in the company for fifteen years before following Roy O. Disney as CEO in 1971. In fairness to Tatum, he followed Roy in what was a challenging time for the company. Walt had laid out the bulk of his vision for the Florida Project, so Imagineers and leaders had enough to work from to carry out that plan with the Magic Kingdom and the two initial resort hotels, but Disney leaders had little direction for advancing Walt Disney World, particularly for figuring out how to use the vast amount of land in Florida and reimagining the ambitious plan Walt had envisioned for EPCOT. Tatum's key accomplishments were his involvement in the development of EPCOT and Tokyo Disneyland, but overall, minor advancement of the company occured during his tenure as CEO.

Card Walker (1976–1983)

Card Walker started his Disney career in 1938 and quickly moved into production leadership roles. Walker, who had served as the President of the company under Tatum, stepped in as CEO after Tatum's retirement from day-to-day operations. His greatest focus was on developing and opening EPCOT and Tokyo Disneyland, but much like Tatum, his leadership represented a very quiet period for the company.

Ron Miller (1983–1984)

Ron Miller, the son-in-law of Walt Disney, started his career at Walt Disney Productions in 1954. After a brief hiatus due to the army draft and a short professional football career, Miller rejoined Walt Disney Productions as producer. Miller served as President of Walt Disney Productions from 1978 to 1983, when he took over as CEO of the Walt Disney Company. In Miller's brief tenure as CEO, he launched Touchstone Pictures and the Disney Channel, but there were some who lacked confidence in his leadership. After more than a decade of mostly cautious leadership between Tatum, Walker, and Miller, corporate raider leveraged buyout threats became heightened.

Those corporate raider buyout attempts got very real, as Saul Steinberg, a well-known New York investor at the time, organized a leveraged stock buyout. With Disney's stock price flat at about sixty dollars per share, the entire company, including all of its IP, physical assets, and real estate, could be purchased for a mere two billion dollars. Steinberg was banking on the fact that he could make his money back by selling the company's vast IP library, select assets, and select real estate, which would allow him to keep the U.S. theme park resorts, Disneyland and Walt Disney World, for himself. This move would have essentially broken up the company and forever diminished the longevity of Walt's living legacy in the organization. Simultaneously, Roy E. Disney, Walt's nephew and Roy O. Disney's son, was working on a leadership transition. After Steinberg publicly proclaimed that he was engineering a Disney stock takeover, Roy stepped in and escalated his efforts to fight for the future of the company—a fight that included new leadership and keeping the company as a whole intact. Disney resigned from the Board of Directors to set up the battle, where he teamed with oil and real estate tycoon Sid Bass and his brothers, Lee, Robert, and Edward, to organize a group of "friendly" investors that would allow the company to continue business as normal. This would preserve the opportunity for future generations to experience Disney entertainment as close to the way Walt had envisioned as possible.[2] Roy E. Disney's persistence was remarkable, and his ability to both thwart off a hostile takeover and organize a leadership transition at the same time was nothing short of amazing. As if that weren't enough, Roy rejoined the company Board as Chairman of the Animation Department with great success, including the billion-dollar hit *The Lion King*.[3] His artist style paired well with his evangelistic ability to influence key Board members and investors. As you will read about in the coming pages, Roy E.'s influence on the company at the highest level would resurface again roughly twenty years later.

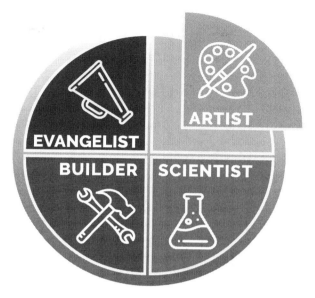

- Producer of True-Life Adventures
- Reinvigorated and saved Disney animation
- Upheld family legacy in company
- Committed to Disney's future success in 21st Century

FIGURE 5.3 Roy E. Disney—Artist With Just Enough Evangelist

Michael Eisner Part 1: Disney Renaissance Years (1984–1994)

Thanks to the work of Roy E. Disney, Michael Eisner (CEO), Frank Wells (President), and soon Jeffrey Katzenberg (Chairman of Walt Disney Studios) were ushered in as the new dynamic leadership team in 1984. All three came from outside the world of Disney, and Eisner and Wells were quickly dubbed a dynamic creative and business duo, much like Walt and Roy were in the past. Eisner was an artist extraordinaire at Disney, and Wells tempered him with checks and balances that resembled Roy's background builder approaches with Walt. Eisner also had just enough evangelist in him to rally the cast members, who had lost some of their fire during the quiet transition years, takeover rumors, and Board maneuvering to oust leaders.

Eisner's creativity and reverence for Walt instilled hope and injected energy into the organization. He quickly began to transform Disney from a fragile takeover target into a family entertainment and media giant. He leveraged

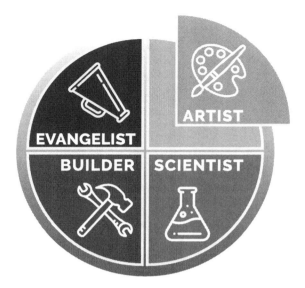

- Restored stability to avoid corporate raider buyout
- Launched Disney Vacation Club
- Built up the parks and resorts system:
  - Tokyo Disneyland
  - Animal Kingdom Park
  - Hollywood Studios Park
  - Disney California Adventure Park and Grand Californian Hotel
  - Disneyland Paris
  - Went from 3 resort hotels to 20 at Walt Disney World
  - Built 2 modern water parks at Walt Disney World
- Had strong enough evangelist talents to rally cast members

FIGURE 5.4 Michael Eisner—Artist With Just Enough Evangelist

Disney's vast and popular video library by churning out hundreds of millions of dollars' worth of cassettes and signing cable TV licensing deals. Eisner recognized Disney was underselling its premium theme park experiences and was able to generate billions more by raising ticket prices and creating premium experiences. Said Eisner, "Such a bounty has fallen into my lap. Every day a bounty falls out of the sky. Every time I open a door at this company, there's money behind it."[4] Jeffrey Katzenberg, whom Eisner brought in to run Walt Disney Studios, was also a huge success, as new shows and animated films, such as the *Little Mermaid*, *The Lion King*, and *Beauty and the Beast*, took theaters and cable networks by storm. A unit that hadn't produced anything of note since the late 1960s suddenly not only had life again but was also *the* major player in the industry. Eisner also leveraged the talents and opportunities available through Disney's subsidiary filmmaker, Touchstone, to generate new revenue.[5]

The former Paramount Pictures President also quickly recognized the untapped potential of Disney parks and resorts. This was particularly true of Walt Disney World, where the company owned tens of thousands of acres of unused land in Central Florida. Eisner saw this as a gold mine, and added MGM Studios (now called Disney's Hollywood Studios) as the third park at Walt Disney World in 1989. He also launched Disney Vacation Club (DVC), Disney's timeshare business, which generated an incredible amount of cash and drew new demographics to Disney's domestic parks. He added Euro Disney (now called Disneyland Paris) in 1992, and opened eleven new resort hotels (most were moderate and deluxe level hotels that commanded higher room rates) at Walt Disney World from 1984 to 1994. It was truly a magical time for the company, and profits and stock prices reflected the renaissance. Stock value escalated nearly nine thousand percentage points from 1994 to 2004, revenue skyrocketed from $1.5 billion to $30.8 billion, profits rose from $294 million to $4.49 billion, and market cap climbed to $69 billion in 2004 from just $2.8 billion in 1984.[6] Disney was flying high from 1984 to 1994, and was setting itself up for even greater heights in the next ten years with investments in capital assets, new ventures, and partnerships. Eisner's bold ideas, entrepreneurial discoveries, and ability to leverage the Disney brand and its IP and assets were virtually unprecedented. All was great with Eisner at the helm, right?

Michael Eisner Part 2: The Transition Years (1994–2005)

Eisner's expansion of Walt Disney World continued, with the company opening the massive Florida resort's fourth gate, Disney's Animal Kingdom, in 1998. The park was unique to the theme park world, as it focused on animals (it essentially included a zoo and African safari) and conservation. Eisner teamed up with now famous Imagineer Joe Rhode to sell the executive team and the Board on the new park by walking a Bengal tiger into the presentation room, making quite an impression on the Board. Rhode and Eisner wanted the Board to feel the presence of the animal.[7] He also showed great respect for the zoo and animal care industry, which helped him make connections in the field and attract quality cast members for the park.[8]

He continued to grow the theme parks with the once unfathomable 2001 expansion of the real estate-confined Disneyland Resort. Eisner's goal was to make Disney's Anaheim, California, location a true resort destination. As part of the expansion, Disney added a second park, Disney's California Adventure, along with the Downtown Disney restaurant and shopping district and the impressive Grand Californian Hotel & Spa.

Eisner also recognized Disney was falling behind in its water park business. Walt Disney World's River Country was a popular destination but outdated, dangerous (it relied on water and some space from Bay Lake), and low capacity. Disney opened modern, high-capacity water parks Typhoon Lagoon in 1989 and Blizzard Beach in 1995 and closed River Country in 2001.

Eisner's relentless capital investments continued, with nine more resort hotels and DVC sites opening at Walt Disney World between 1994 and 2004. Disney also added Pleasure Island in 1989 (a nighttime adult entertainment district in what is now Disney Springs), Disney's Wide World of Sports Complex in 1997, Disney-Quest (a gaming venue) in what is now Disney Springs in 1998, and Walt Disney World Speedway (a stock car racing facility and fan experience venue) in 1998, among other attractions at Walt Disney World. Disney's Wide World of Sports 220-acre sports complex (now named ESPN Wide World of Sports Complex) was a particularly brilliant venture, as the venue hosts a broad variety of travel sports tournaments as well as Major League Baseball spring training games and college basketball preseason tournaments, helping fill the Walt Disney World parks and resort hotels with families during traditionally slower times. It was truly an amazing time of growth for the Florida resort. Finally, Disney launched the wildly successful Disney Cruise Line as Magical Cruise Company Limited in 1996.

Eisner also engineered the 1995 purchase of Capital Cities/ABC. The nineteen-billion-dollar corporate takeover was the second largest of its kind and included ABC sports powerhouse ESPN. The acquisition provided turnkey distribution channels for its treasure trove of creative content while infusing ABC with much-needed creativity.[9]

Now let's rewind back to 1994, a pivotal year for Disney and the future of Eisner's leadership of the company. Frank Wells's financial brilliance as President had proven to be an excellent counterbalance to Eisner as CEO. And then tragedy struck. Wells died in a helicopter crash coming back from a skiing trip in 1994, meaning the most significant challenger to Eisner's bold ideas and ultra-aggressive business pursuits was gone.

Over the next few years, executives came and went, and it seemed Eisner had lost much of his diverse and highly talented team. In addition, many of the expansion decisions mentioned above ended up not being as well developed as originally thought. MGM, Animal Kingdom, and Disneyland Paris were viewed by visitors, Disney fans, and Disney insiders as incomplete parks. Further, Disney California Adventure was sorely lacking in Disney level theming and attractions and thus, underperformed financially. Locals and tourists alike were disinterested in the new park, and it showed in attendance numbers, as guests turned their attention back to Disneyland Park. Pleasure Island (a party venue for adults) did not match Walt Disney World's family atmosphere and mission. Finally, in moves that strayed well outside their core competencies, Disney started the Mighty Ducks of Anaheim (a National Hockey League franchise) for $50 million and purchased the Anaheim Angels (a Major League Baseball franchise) between 1996 and 1999 for a total investment of $170 million,[10] later selling it in 2003 for a reported $183 million.[11] After initial successes, both franchises lost well over $140 million under Disney ownership.[12] Eisner had also pulled out of

Disney's strategic partnership with Pixar, which had been a key factor in the growth and success of Walt Disney Studios.[13] At this point, the company needed a builder to take over and leverage the incredible work of Eisner.

Roy E. Disney stepped in again in 2003 with his second "Save Disney" campaign with his friend and fellow former Board member, Stanley Gold. Disney's revenue had been flat for several years, which ultimately gave the two the justification they needed to organize another transition in leadership. Their efforts again worked with the Board, who ramped up plans for Eisner's succession. Eisner had originally told the Board he would retire September 2006, but after the February 2005 release of James Stewart's *New York Times* bestseller *Disney War*, he escalated his departure to March 2005.[14]

DISNEY LESSON 17: SOMETIMES ORGANIZATIONS NEED NEW LEADERSHIP STYLES TO GET TO THEIR NEXT STAGE OF DEVELOPMENT

There are many lessons in the second half of Eisner's tenure. Entrepreneurs are often challenged by what's called the entrepreneurial ego.[15] Eisner, for all the great things he did, mishandled some key relationships. His long run of success led him to believe he had all the answers and that everything would always just work out as long as he had good ideas and the Disney name.

Though Eisner had some challenges the last several years of his tenure, it was more than worth it for the sake of the company when one considers Disney's current success and the marketplace demand for exceptional theme park experiences. Creative geniuses like Eisner only come along once in a generation, and, while talented, they naturally come with their quirks. Eisner not only reinvigorated the creativity and innovation of the Walt Disney Company, he was also Roy E. Disney's last piece of the original "Save Disney" campaign to rescue the company from corporate raiders. Further, as Disney is challenged today with how to navigate the declining network and cable TV industries, its parks and resorts are seeing significant growth, both in total revenue and in profit. Eisner's love affair with and investments in the parks and resorts provided much-needed infrastructure that is invaluable to the Walt Disney Company of today and its leaders.

I've tried to pull from the formula Walt created. He was an unbelievable futurist. But if you live too much in the past, you get stuck. Walt thought long term. I love that. You have to have some sense of what could happen and have some control over your destiny.

—*Bob Iger*

Bob Iger: Building the Leader in Entertainment (2005–Current)

Bob Iger officially took over the helm of the Walt Disney Company in September 2005. Iger's path to the role was interesting, as the Ithaca College graduate started his career at ABC in 1974, eventually serving as its President in the mid-1990s. He was promoted to President of Disney's International Division in 1999 while also retaining the role of Chairman of ABC. Iger proved to be a shrewd business-man and negotiator, and his ascension in the Walt Disney Company continued when he was elevated to President and Chief Operating Officer in 2000, assuming the post the controversial Michael Ovitz had vacated nearly a year and a half earlier. This move placed him directly under Eisner as the number two at Disney and would set the stage for yet another Roy E. Disney leadership intervention.

Roy E. Disney once again engineered a transition of sorts to replace Eisner as CEO and Chairman of the Board. As a result, Iger was put in charge of Disney operations in March 2005. As previously mentioned, under pressure resulting from the release of James Stewart's *New York Times* bestseller *Disney War*, Eisner resigned later that month instead of September of the next year, as he had origi-nally planned. Iger stepped into the CEO position at the mutual agreement of Eisner, the Disney Board, and Roy E. Disney and most of his fellow "Save Disney" supporters.[16] He later became Chairman of the Board in 2012.

Iger instantly went to work, starting with decentralizing Disney operations and quickly restoring confidence and workplace morale, which allowed Disney's talented workforce to once again thrive. Perhaps more importantly, he repaired the business relationship with Steve Jobs and Pixar, leading to Disney's 2006 acquisition of the popular animation company. Some view this as the key move that revitalized the Walt Disney Company. The Pixar purchase was the first of many strategic acquisitions and expansions under Iger's tenure, and it came at a great time, as Pixar was set to release the blockbuster *Cars* movie. *Cars* generated over $240 million in box office revenue for Disney right out of the gate in 2006,[17] with estimated merchandise revenue of over $8 billion through 2011.[18]

From early in his tenure, it was clear a major strategy of Iger's was to reinvigo-rate innovation and creativity by buying creative companies with underutilized people and assets. Into the mid to late 2000s, Disney was still challenged by its lack of targeted attention to teenage boys and men. Iger aggressively set out to fix this, and his first major move was to purchase Marvel Entertainment—a popular superhero comic and media production company—in 2009 for four billion dollars.[19] Though there were some rumblings about the possibility of an acquisition, it still caught the industry by surprise. This was largely due to existing exclusive Marvel and NBC contracts with Disney's most relevant theme park competitor, Universal Studios. The long-term agreement meant Disney could not use any existing Marvel characters in its domestic parks east of the Mississippi River in the United States or the Marvel brand name in any of its parks (per the agreement, Universal cannot use the Marvel brand name in its parks either). Despite Disney's lack of ability to use the Marvel brand name and its popular characters in its Florida theme parks, the return on investment of the Marvel brand has been impressive, and earning royalties from its theme park competitor puts Disney in a unique competitive position. Further, Disney is able to use Marvel characters at the Disneyland Resort, and as a result is scheduled to open a Marvel character themed land at California Adventure Park in 2020. This comes on the heels of the very successful conversion of the popular Disney California Adventure attraction Tower of Terror to Guardians of the Galaxy— Mission: Breakout! in 2017. In addition, Disney has announced plans for a Guardians of the Galaxy (a popular new franchise Disney introduced under the Marvel brand in 2014) roller coaster in Epcot in 2021.[20] Skeptics of the Marvel deal were quickly proven wrong. Disney has produced and distributed nineteen films under the Marvel banner in its ten years of owning the company, generating more than sixteen billion dollars in box office revenue. Industry experts and Disney executives agree there is no end in sight for the future potential of Marvel productions.[21]

In 2012, Iger and Disney shook up the world of entertainment again, purchasing Lucasfilm for what analysts called an incredible bargain at $4.1 billion. In the move, largely driven by the relationship Iger was able to build with CEO and Chairman George Lucas, Disney acquired the timeless Star Wars franchise along with Indiana Jones IP.[22] It is estimated Disney recovered more than one-fourth its initial four-billion-dollar investment with box office profits from just the first two Disney-produced Star Wars movies, *Star Wars: The Force Awakens* and *Rogue One*. Add another billion dollars of profit in Netflix licensing, merchandise sales, and TV shows in just three years, and the analysts were right— Disney walked away from the Lucasfilm deal with an incredible value.[23] And that does not even take into account the incredible potential impact of the Star Wars: Galaxy's Edge lands coming to Disneyland and Walt Disney World Resorts in 2019, the Star Wars themed hotel planned near Hollywood Studios at Walt Disney World,[24] future merchandise sales, spinoff series and movies, and licensing deals, among other opportunities to leverage the Star Wars brand.

While in the middle of a decline of traditional TV media, Iger has also placed a great deal of importance on building up the company's parks and resorts over the last several years. A key strategy in this plan included the 2008 creation of a fully integrated system called MyMagic+ that pulled together as many as seventeen independent legacy information systems. The system, which reportedly cost well over a billion dollars to implement, had its growing pains at first but today includes nearly all functions available to resort and park guests, including resort hotel, dining, and FastPass+ reservations, as well as account, pass, and ticket management. The impressive system allows Disney and its tens of millions of annual guests the ease of navigating their stay via the My Disney Experience web portal and phone application.[25] This technology was adapted in part for

Disneyland Resort as part of a system called MaxPass, which launched in 2017 (we cover these systems in Chapter Seven).[26]

Under Iger's leadership, Imagineers did a marvelous job of addressing the shortcomings of Disney California Adventure Park left behind from the Eisner era. The park was completely reimagined, resulting in the addition of the very impressive Cars Land. The transformation has put California Adventure on par with Disney's other domestic parks and has helped transform Disneyland into more of a destination resort. Disney also reimagined Fantasyland in Magic Kingdom Park into New Fantasyland and enlarged the center hub area at the park in an effort to manage crowds at the world's most highly attended theme park. The company also began to fully address its challenges at Disneyland Paris by purchasing the bulk of outsider-owned shares in the subsidiary in 2017.[27] Iger's regime is also in the middle of the process of addressing the lighter offerings at two Walt Disney World parks, Animal Kingdom and Hollywood Studios, by adding the Pandora—World of Avatar themed land at Animal Kingdom (spring 2017) and Toy Story Land (spring 2018) and Star Wars: Galaxy's Edge themed land (winter 2019) at Hollywood Studios. Disney recently completed the incredibly ambitious expansion and transition of its Downtown Disney restaurant and shopping district at Walt Disney World into Disney Springs. The multiyear project more than tripled the size of the destination and number of outlets it hosted, resulting in over 150 new tenants. The company also recently announced plans to open a new seven hundred room resort hotel at Disneyland Resort in 2021.[28] Disney worked with international partner, Oriental Land Company, to open Tokyo Disneyland's second gate, Tokyo DisneySea, in 2001 and the Chinese government to launch Shanghai Disneyland in 2016. Many theme park gurus call DisneySea and Shanghai the most impressive parks in the world. Iger has also initiated substantial growth in the DVC Division, adding non-theme park resort locations in Vero Beach, Florida; Hilton Head, South Carolina; and Kapolei, Hawaii—and introducing several new locations at Walt Disney World. During Iger's time as CEO, Disney Cruise Line has also added two more large capacity (four thousand occupancy each) ships, the Disney Dream and the Disney Fantasy.

In what could be Iger's last big splash, Disney's $52.4 billion offer to purchase the bulk of Twenty-First Century Fox appears to be on track to go through in 2018 or 2019,[29] though Comcast has reportedly come in with competing last-minute offers. The Fox deal includes a treasure trove of comic and superhero IP, the original Star Wars and Marvel movies, distribution rights to James Cameron's Avatar movies, and a majority ownership stake in alternative TV medium Hulu.[30]

Iger's pragmatic yet entrepreneurial strategies have proven to be extremely successful. Today, Disney's market capitalization is over $150 billion, with 2017 revenue topping $55 billion and net profits totaling nearly $9 billion.[31] Disney has soared to new heights under Iger, and this has mostly been driven by his

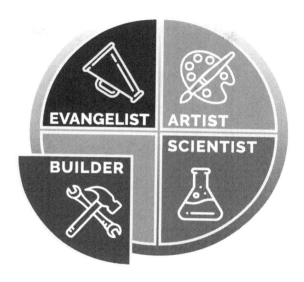

- Restored relationship with Steve Jobs and Pixar Studios
- Strategic Acquisitions and Target Market Expansion:
  - Pixar Studios
  - Marvel
  - Lucasfilms
  - 21st Century Fox (Pending)
- Created systems and processes to manage massive parks growth
  - My Magic Plus, FastPass+, My Disney Experience Application
  - MaxPass
- Massive growth in parks:
  - Redeveloped Disney California Adventure
  - Massive growth of Disney Vacation Club properties - Aulani
  - Magic Kingdom Expansions (New Fantasyland & hub project)
  - Added Pandora - World of Avatar at Animal Kingdom
  - Built Toy Story Land at Hollywood Studios
  - Added Shanghai Disneyland
  - Bought back Disneyland Paris stock
  - Added Star Wars Land At Disneyland and Hollywood Studios
  - Epcot attraction expansions
  - Maximized revenues through cutting edge pricing systems

FIGURE 5.5 Bob Iger—Builder With a Touch of Scientist

ability to balance aggressive business decisions while maintaining company culture. For instance, Disney Institute tells the story of Iger watching a parade at one of the parks, where he noted the age of the characters used in the parade. He recognized they needed to honor the original characters and heritage of the company while also integrating new properties that were more relevant to today's consumer. This initial insight and push led to an aggressive campaign to better leverage IP by integrating it into the parks. We see that today with the integration of Toy Story at the various Toy Story Lands at Disney parks across the globe, the conversion of Paradise Pier to Pixar Pier at California Adventure Park, the addition of Guardians of the Galaxy attractions at various parks, and the addition of Star Wars themed lands at Disneyland and Walt Disney World, among others. Iger, a visionary builder, shifted company priorities to match market demand for new characters and the business imperative of leveraging IP. He also invested heavily during recessionary times while most companies were just maintaining the status quo or retreating.

As evidenced by his strategic acquisitions, ability to leverage assets and intellectual properties, and willingness to invest heavily in systems and infrastructure, Iger is a prolific builder who has enough scientist talents to put the strategies together with great effectiveness.

DISNEY LESSON 18: EXTRAORDINARY PEOPLE CAN DO AMAZING THINGS, BUT SUCCESSORS STILL NEED TO BE IDENTIFIED AND GROOMED

Extraordinary people can accomplish just about anything. Just look at what Walt, Roy O., Roy E., Michael Eisner, and Bob Iger did for the Walt Disney Company over several decades. All faced unique challenges, and all delivered exceptionally well under some very difficult circumstances. Roy O. Disney faced the untimely death of his brother head-on to start construction of the massive Florida Project and see it through to completion. Being the face of the organization wasn't Roy's sweet spot, and it ultimately cost him his retirement and possibly even shortened his life, but he made that sacrifice for the sake of his brother's legacy. Roy E. Disney sacrificed mightily to fight for the leadership changes he believed were necessary to advance the Walt Disney Company. He certainly did not need or have to do this, as he was worth millions and could have just walked away, but he, much like his dad, did it for the sake of Walt's legacy and the sustainability of the company. Michael Eisner was a creative genius who forever changed the scope and reach of the Walt Disney Company. His bold and aggressive ideas and initiatives leveraged unused resources, uncovered new markets, and changed the profitability of the company long-term. Bob Iger's ability to mend and form relationships with key partners and acquisition targets has further increased Disney's target markets, and his sense for building systems to manage Disney's popularity among its guests is unparalleled. All of these dynamic leaders brought their unique perspectives to the table, but they didn't last forever in their executive roles. This is why it is so critical to identify extraordinary leaders at all levels, train them well, and coach and mentor them to lead the next generation. Disney is exceptional at this, and you can be too. The secrets for doing so lie in the next chapter.

The Next CEO: A New Generation

Iger had initially pledged to retire July 2019, but the pending acquisition of Twenty-First Century Fox in late 2018 is likely to delay Iger's retirement for a fourth time.[32] His run at Disney has been so successful that the Board has had a hard time letting go of him, and he has obliged by seeing Disney through some of the company's most impressive acquisitions and expansions. Thus, some suggest this has perhaps sent the message that the Board of Directors may be unsure about Iger's successor. Tom Staggs, who was elevated into the COO role three years prior to Iger's previously projected retirement of 2018, was once speculated to be a replacement but has since retired.[33] Some say the next CEO could be James Murdoch, son of Fox head Rupert Murdoch, should the Twenty-First Century Fox deal happen.[34] However, James announced that that would not happen, and that he planned to start his own company after the acquisition.[35] Others suggest Bob Chapek, Chairman of Disney's Parks, Experiences, and Consumer Products Division, is the likely successor, but some speculate that the Disney Board of Directors is looking for an outside candidate. One fact that is not in question is that Iger leaves dauntingly large shoes to fill, a challenge not uncommon for successful entrepreneurial ventures—whether corporate giants like Disney, gazelles, or growing smaller ventures that are privately held. Leadership succession is an incredibly challenging yet critical undertaking for entrepreneurial ventures[36] and one that has been particularly arduous for the Walt Disney Company since Walt's death in 1966.

The new CEO will most likely need to be an evangelist for the company. Charming the media will be a critical role in the C-suite moving forward, as Disney has focused on its pricing models and premium experience offerings a great deal in recent years—particularly in its parks and resorts—which has brought on some media scrutiny. The company has also been a target of news media attacks accusing Disney of corporate cronyism in Anaheim and fueling labor union battles. Warranted or undeserved, the new CEO will have to address these media issues. The incoming CEO will also have to continue to tackle the challenges of the rapidly changing network and cable TV markets. No doubt, tough

- Rally cast members to be creative
- Charm the media
- Reinvigorate the mission of the company
- Maximize people and assets through innovation and new markets

FIGURE 5.6 The Next CEO: What Is Needed? Evangelist With Just Enough Artist?

decisions will need to be made regarding ABC and ESPN, two once incredibly strong profit machines. Finally, the changing workforce, in conjunction with continued theme park, resort, and vacation properties growth, will be an ongoing challenge for the next CEO. Disney has built its premium experience reputation on exceptional service and engagement, so the new leadership team will have to be diligent in maintaining a service-oriented culture.

Disney Principles

- Disney went through a very quiet period the twelve years after Roy's death. Cautious companies or companies that rest on their brand image and don't innovate can quickly lose relevancy in the market.

- It takes some extraordinary leaders to have the kind of success Disney has enjoyed the last thirty-five years. It's important to remember that creative geniuses like Michael Eisner often have eccentric personalities. Value the talents these innovators bring to organizations.
- Exceptional leaders don't last forever. Sound succession planning at all levels is critical for sustained success.
- Emotionally invested leaders, like Roy O. and Roy E. Disney, are a great asset, especially in times of crisis.
- Both Eisner and Iger saw parks and resorts as the company's cash cow, and invested heavily in their infrastructure for the future. Those investments are of great benefit to the company today, particularly with the evolving TV industry.
- Entrepreneurial leadership styles play a critical role in projects, communications, and strategies.

Work Like Disney: Exercises

1. Have you thought about who will succeed you? What about who will succeed your key leaders? If so, what is your plan? If not, what can you do today to start the process?
2. Do you have emotionally invested people you can count on in hard times? Who are they? What makes them so invested?
3. If you could look into the future, what part of your business would be best to invest in right now? What is your plan for doing so?
4. Do you encourage new ideas and implementation of those ideas? If so, in what ways do you encourage innovative behavior? If not, what is stopping you?
5. What type of leader do you think your company needs heading into the future?
6. What type of leader did you assess as on the Entrepreneurial Leadership Instrument in the Introduction? How do you apply this perspective toward success? How can you use more of it? How can you augment your style with other leaders around you who have different approaches? How would you benefit from this? Which leader in Disney's history do you most identify with? Why? How can you learn from his tenure at Disney?

Notes

1. Letters of Note. (2011, June 4). *There Is No Way to Replace Walt Disney*. Retrieved from www.lettersofnote.com/2011/06/there-is-no-way-to-replace-walt-disney.html.
2. Taylor, J. (1987). *Storming the Magic Kingdom*. New York: Alfred A. Knopf.
3. Box Office Mojo. (n.d.). *The Lion King*. Retrieved from www.boxofficemojo.com/movies/?id=lionking.htm.
4. Masters, K. (2001). *The Keys to the Kingdom: The Raise of Michael Eisner and the Fall of Everybody Else*. New York: HarperCollins.

5. Riquier, A. (2014, April 14). *Disney Reanimated: How Eisner Brought the Magic Back.* Retrieved from www.investors.com/news/walt-disney-animation-stock-revived-in-1980s-1990s-under-eisner/

6. Epstein, A.J. (2005, September 27). *How Did Michael Eisner Make Disney Profitable?* Retrieved from www.slate.com/articles/arts/the_hollywood_ economist/2005/04/how_did_michael_eisner_make_disney_profitable.html.

7. Gunther, M., and McGowan, J. (1998, April 13). *Disney's Call of the Wild Michael Eisner and His Theme Park Wizards Are Counting on a Profit Bonanza From Their New $1 Billion Animal Kingdom in Orlando.* Retrieved from http://archive.fortune.com/magazines/ fortune/fortune_archive/1998/04/13/240839/index.htm.

8. Kober, J. (n.d.). *Looking Back on Disney's Animal Kingdom With Rick Barongi.* Retrieved from http://disneyatwork.com/looking-back-on-disneys-animal-kingdom-with-rick-barongi/.

9. Fabrikant, G. (1995). *The Media Business: The Merger; Walt Disney to Acquire ABC IN $19 Billion Deal to Build a Giant for Entertainment.* Retrieved from www.nytimes.com/1995/08/01/business/media-business-merger-walt-disney-acquire-abc-19-billion-deal-build-giant-for.html.

10. Emmons, S. (1995, May 19). *Disney Co. to Buy 25% of Angels: New Partner to Run Team's Daily Operations: Baseball: Plan Still Needs Approval of Major League Owners. The Entertainment Giant Will Have the Option to Purchase the Rest Later. News Gives Boost to Anaheim's Plans for Massive Sports Complex.* Retrieved from http://articles.latimes.com/1995-05-19/news/mn-3494_1_disney-angels-deal-gene-and-jackie-autry-california-angels-baseball-team.

11. CNN Money. (n.d.). *The Reign of Eisner.* Retrieved from http://money.cnn.com/pf/features/popups/disney_timeline/frameset.exclude.html.

12. Masunaga, S. (2015, November 12). *From the Mighty Ducks to the Angels: Disney's Track Record With Sports.* Retrieved from www.latimes.com/business/la-fi-disney-iger-20151112-htmlstory.html.

13. Stewart, J. (2005). *Disney War.* New York: Simon & Schuster.

14. Ibid.

15. Kuratko, D.F. (2014). *Entrepreneurship: Theory Process Practice.* Mason: South-Western Cengage.

16. Stewart, J. (2005). *Disney War.* New York: Simon & Schuster.

17. Box Office Mojo. (n.d.). *Franchises: Pixar.* Retrieved from www.boxofficemojo.com/franchises/chart/?id=pixar.htm.

18. Szalai, G. (2011, February 14). *Disney: Cars Has Crossed $8 Billion in Global Retail Sales.* Retrieved from www.hollywoodreporter.com/news/disney-cars-has-crossed-8-99438.

19. Goldman, D. (2009, August 31). *Disney to Buy Marvel for $4 Billion.* Retrieved from http://money.cnn.com/2009/08/31/news/companies/disney_marvel/.

20. Morris, C. (2018, April 9). *Why Disney Can't Use Spider-Man or the Avengers at Its Orlando Location—Even Though It Owns the Marvel Brand.* Retrieved from http://fortune.com/2018/04/09/disney-orlando-marvel-universal/.

21. Rains, B. (2018, May 10). *Marvel Movies Are Box Office Gold: Can We Expect Billions More From the MCU?* Retrieved from www.zacks.com/stock/news/303171/ marvel-movies-are-box-office-gold-can-we-expect-billions-more-from-the-mcu.

22. Krantz, M., Snider, M., Della Cava, M., and Alexander, B. (2012, October 30). *Disney Buys Lucasfilm for $4 Billion.* Retrieved from www.usatoday.com/story/money/business/2012/10/30/disney-star-wars-lucasfilm/1669739/.

23. Kline, D.B. (2017, January 4). *Disney Got a Bargain Buying Lucasfilm for $4 Billion.* Retrieved from www.businessinsider.com/disney-got-a-bargain-buying-lucasfilm-for-4-billion-2017-1.

24. Fickley-Baker, J. (2017, July 15). *Plans Unveiled for Star Wars-themed Resort at Walt Disney World.* Retrieved from https://disneyparks.disney.go.com/blog/2018/02/d23j-update-star-wars-hotel/?CMP=KNC-FY18_WDPR_DPK_ACT_DOME_ParksPortfolio_Brand-DSA|BR|G|4181000.WW.AM.01.02|NA_NA_NA_NA&keyword_id=aud-322878669822:dsa-144710043133|dc||256030976390|b|5053:3|&gclid=CjwKCAj wxZnYBRAVEiwANMTRX87OW96nXp8ldopaxSDWo1jSomEXyAPLF2_tbDn N5y29HD1Y00trlxoCadwQAvD_BwE&s_kwcid=AL!5053!3!256030976390!b!!g!! &ef_id=WtIA0AAAAMQQByvl:20180524231237:s&dclid=COKgw8y8n9sCFRVKX godhIIFQw.

25. Sekula, S. (2014, February 25). *Disney Gets Personal With New MyMagic+ System.* Retrieved from www.usatoday.com/story/dispatches/2014/01/27/disney-mymagic-vacation-planning/4582957/.

26. Glover, E. (2017, July 18). *First Look at Disney MaxPass Coming July 19 to Disneyland Resort.* Retrieved from https://disneyparks.disney.go.com/blog/2017/07/first-look-at-disney-maxpass-coming-july-19-to-disneyland-resort/.

27. Heiskanen, V. (2017, February 10). *Walt Disney Co. Ups Disneyland Paris Ownership Share, Eyes 100 Percent.* Retrieved from www.orlandosentinel.com/business/tourism/os-bb-disneyland-paris-ownership-20170210-story.html.

28. Glover, E. (2017, October 25). *New Hotel Coming to Disneyland Resort in 2021.* Retrieved from https://disneyparks.disney.go.com/blog/2017/10/new-hotel-disneyland-resort/.

29. Gold, H., and Riley, C. (2017, December 14). *Disney Is Buying Most of 21st Century Fox for $52.4 Billion.* Retrieved from http://money.cnn.com/2017/12/14/media/disney-fox-deal/index.html.

30. Snider, M. (2018, May 9). *What Could a Comcast-Disney Duel for Fox Mean for You . . . and the Marvel Universe?* Retrieved from www.usatoday.com/story/tech/news/2018/05/09/what-comcast-disney-duel-fox-means-you-and-marvels-universe/589721002/.

31. Walt Disney Company. (2017, November 9). *The Walt Disney Company Reports Fourth Quarter and Full Year Earnings for Fiscal Year 2017.* Retrieved from www.thewaltdisney company.com/walt-disney-company-reports-fourth-quarter-full-year-earnings-fiscal-2017/.

32. Barnes, B. (2017, December 6). *Murdoch Is Said to Want Iger to Stay as Disney C.E.O.* Retrieved from www.nytimes.com/2017/12/06/business/media/disney-fox-iger.html.

33. Bradt, G. (2016, April 5). *Learning From Disney's Staggering CEO Succession Failure.* Retrieved from www.forbes.com/sites/georgebradt/2016/04/05/learning-from-disneys-staggering-ceo-succession-failure/#31300489f1a0.

34. McAlone, N. (2017, December 5). *James Murdoch Has Reportedly Been 'Suggested' as a Successor to Disney CEO Bob Iger During Deal Talks.* Retrieved from www.businessinsider.com/james-murdoch-reportedly-suggested-as-a-successor-to-disney-ceo-bob-iger-report-2017-12.

35. Barnes, B. (2018, May 8). *James Murdoch Will Not Join Disney If Fox Deal Is Completed.* Retrieved from www.nytimes.com/2018/05/08/business/media/james-murdoch-disney-fox-deal.html.

36. Cascio, W. (2011). "Leadership Succession: How to Avoid a Crisis." *Ivey Business Journal*, 3. Retrieved from https://iveybusinessjournal.com/publication/leadership-succession-how-to-avoid-a-crisis/.

6

THE ENTREPRENEURIAL SPIRIT OF DISNEY PARKS AND RESORTS

> You don't build it for yourself. You know what the people want, and you build it for them.
>
> —Walt Disney

Walt occasionally took his family to amusement parks, carnivals, and fairs. Lillian did not care for these family adventures because she found these places to be dirty and creepy. Walt was fascinated that families would congregate in those places to be entertained, but she did not want to take her kids to those environments. When Walt shared his dream of opening a theme park with Lillian, she was very antagonistic about it because she viewed theme parks as dirty, crowded, and weird carnivals. Walt urged her to trust him that Disneyland would be different. She wasn't so sure, but as she had done many times over the years, she supported Walt in his entrepreneurial dream. As is well documented, Disneyland didn't go off without glitches, but overall people were amazed by the attention to detail, especially when it came to the friendliness and hospitality of the cast members. Keep in mind the extreme importance Walt placed on attention to detail and cast member excellence as we traverse this chapter and the next.

Walt had an eye for taking something with potential to a completely different level. His vision came to fruition at Disneyland and has continued at Disney parks and resorts all across the globe. The human, technological, and physical details are impeccable at Disney parks and resorts, and the emotions they create are amazing and carefully orchestrated. This chapter is the result of a 360-degree review of Disney parks and resorts over more than ten years. It's the culmination of a lifetime of triangulation, including visiting and studying Disney parks and resorts, asking cast members literally thousands of business-related questions, talking to executives, reading countless books on all things Disney, visiting the Disney Family Museum, and attending various training sessions. The following are our insights into what makes the Disney parks and resorts of today such a corporate entrepreneurial success story.

Mathews Entrepreneurial Insight: Redefining Entrepreneurship

After more than twenty years of owning businesses, reading business plans, teaching entrepreneurship classes, conducting a research study on entrepreneurship education for my dissertation, and coaching and mentoring aspiring entrepreneurs and students, I've come to the conclusion that most people really don't know what entrepreneurship is. Perhaps that's because we try to define it before we actually see it. I believe entrepreneurship is best defined by action; when we see entrepreneurial behavior, we typically recognize it. And entrepreneurship is just that: behavior. Entrepreneurship is not really an event, but rather a lifestyle, a way of behaving and thinking. It is proactive problem-finding before it is anything else because curiosity leads to innovation. It challenges the status quo. It asks why, and why again, and again, and again . . . until curiosity is mostly satisfied . . . and just when you think curiosity is satisfied, entrepreneurs continue to ask simple but great questions, such as why? why not? and isn't there a better way? Entrepreneurship is a mind-set and behavior that leads to solutions to problems, opportunities, and innovation.

Despite the massive size of the Walt Disney Company, life at Disney—at both the micro and macro levels—is largely what I described above. Human ingenuity is, by far, the most powerful asset any person or company has. Disney balances the need for systems and processes while leveraging this human ingenuity better than perhaps any company on the planet. This chapter outlines the key principles Disney uses to encourage this entrepreneurial behavior and how leaders, managers, and supervisors act on those principles. Disney's unique approach to business in its parks and resorts yields incredible results and has driven deep emotional connections to its products and services. In this chapter and the next, we outline those special things that set Disney parks and resorts apart from the rest of the entertainment, vacation, and even business world.

A noble purpose inspires sacrifice, stimulates innovation, and encourages perseverance.

—Gary Hamel

HIRING FOR FIT
- Outgoing personality
- Servant's heart
- Customer-focused
- Coachable

MANAGEMENT
- Responsibility
- Seeks information
- Coaching relationships with front-line cast members
- Extensive training & on-boarding
- Modeling: mission, values, company history
- Cross training & promotions/ movement to fit strengths
- Uses common language

HIRING FOR FIT
- Outgoing personality
- Servant's heart
- Job rotation
- Customer-focused
- Coachable
- Trusts the system

INTERNAL CARE & SERVICE
- Cast members serve each other
- Cast members own values, mission, company history
- Cast members encouraged to share problems and solutions
- Communication

LEADERSHIP
- Supports mission
- Ongoing/constant reinforcement and modeling of mission, values, company history
- Uses common language to emphasize values

MISSION
We create happiness by providing the best in entertainment for people of all ages everywhere.

CAST MEMBER ENGAGEMENT
- Model/Best-in-Class
  - Service
  - Attractions
  - Place & atmosphere
  - Experiences
- Innovation/constant improvement
- Operational precision
- Cast member retention

MANAGEMENT
- Modeling: mission, values, company history
- Accountability
- Team advocacy
  - Innovation
- Job rotation

GUEST ENGAGEMENT
- High profitability
- Return guests
- High market share
- Sustainable business model
- Lower competitive threats
- Synergy between business units

HIGH-END BUSINESS MODEL
- Premium price points
- "Take my money" attitude among guests
- Guests have emotional connection to the company
- Rite of passage for guests
- IP Integration

FIGURE 6.1 Disney Parks & Resorts Success Model

It's All About the Mission

Have you ever found yourself thinking vision, mission, purpose, and values state-ments were nothing more than corporate fluff? Sadly, you are not alone in this hasty judgment, and the reason is because it may not have been far from the truth for most companies. However, at Disney the company's mission and shared values not only hold deep historical meaning, they also centrally and emphatically drive *all* business practices for *everyone* in and involved with the company. Everyone means literally everyone—every cast member, from executives to custodial staff and part-time attraction operators, as well as partners and vendors.

> The mission of the Walt Disney Company is to be one of the world's leading producers and providers of entertainment and information. Using our portfolio of brands to differentiate our content, services, and consumer products, we seek to develop the most creative, innovative, and profitable entertainment experiences and related products in the world.[1]

The key words in this mission statement are "entertainment" and "experiences." As you discovered in Chapter Five, other key principles that have emerged from the Iger era are "differentiate" and "profitable." Disney Parks, Experiences, and Consumer Products has its own mission statement, which stems directly from the corporate mission: "We create happiness by providing the best in entertain-ment for people of all ages everywhere."[2] Again, we see entertainment and experience (i.e., "happiness") as the central themes, with an Iger-esque emphasis on people "of all ages everywhere" (market differentiation and complete family entertainment). However, Disney also added the word "best" to make it clear to its cast members and partners the expectation is still to deliver the pinnacle theme park, resort, and travel experiences in the world. As our Disney executive friends so appropriately often say, if you don't define your mission, others will define it for you. Further, Disney's brand promise for its parks and resorts (the commitment it communicates to its customers) is that the company provides special entertainment with heart. The internal promise is simply that they will create happiness for their guests.

How does mission statement relate to entrepreneurship, you say? The Disney Parks, Experiences, and Consumer Products mission quoted above essentially matches Walt's initial entrepreneurial dream and brand promise of over seven decades ago. In all organizations, mission should be central to the products and services the company is providing and to whom they provide them (but it's far from uncommon for companies to get derailed and even completely disconnected from mission while in the throes of seemingly mundane daily operations, or for the mission to be lost on what the contemporary marketplace desires). This is especially true at Disney, where customer experience is at the very heart and soul of the organization and everything they do asks the simple question, does this support the mission? This market-based approach is simple, with profit essentially being a byproduct of providing exemplary customer service. How does Disney consistently deliver top-notch customer service in its parks and resorts? It has a lot to do with how the company redefines the word "customer"—more on that later, but the simple fact that Disney's customers are strictly referred to as *guests* should provide a pretty strong clue. Disney fervently fights against the mission drift that plagues so many companies. This diligence has led to decades of consistently delivering the best entertainment and vacation experiences available anywhere.

The marketplace—the customer—is at the heart of this chapter and the next, and for good reason: successful entrepreneurship identifies needs, wants, and desires in the marketplace and delivers on them.[3] Good entrepreneurs leverage their knowledge of the market with the capabilities and skills of the teams they build. Corporate entrepreneurship (a.k.a., intrapreneurship)[4] takes it a step further, leveraging existing assets, human capabilities, brands, intellectual property, and opportunities to not only stay relevant but also thrive in competitive sandboxes. This chapter outlines Disney's formula for fruitful corporate entrepreneurial behavior. But don't be misled—corporate innovation is most often not glamorous and, in fact, is often hard to see and very difficult to duplicate unless you are willing to learn from a successful model. There's a reason why Disney is so successful and why its parks are the runaway leader in the industry—the company is meticulously intentional about how it does business, how it preserves Walt's legacy, and, perhaps most importantly, how it chooses what words to use in its internal and external communications. Though it may feel as if systems and processes are discussed a great deal in this chapter and the next, make no mistake, *well-developed systems and processes executed with precision and consistency facilitate the growth and smooth operationalization and delivery of the entrepreneurial dream.* Walt knew this, which is why he was so consumed by the details. While he was a big thinker, Walt had an eye for perfection. He was known for riding attractions, such as Jungle Cruise, and keeping lists of details that needed attention in terms of maintenance, script, cast member mannerisms, guest interactions, guest comments, and so on. In addition, he also had a reputation for knowing all Disneyland cast members by name. He would address them by first name, praise their efforts, discuss the shortfalls he observed, and then empower them to take ownership of the attraction and its successful operation. But his next course of action is an enduring lesson in entrepreneurial leadership. He would walk by the attraction in the mornings for as much as two to three weeks before revisiting it. He was sending the message that he trusted the cast members to address the issues and would give them time to work out the kinks. Walt was described as a kind man, but he was also crystal clear on his expectations, holding cast members to high standards of performance.

While radical innovation is a key part of high-growth entrepreneurship and is certainly prevalent in the Walt Disney Company, any Disney executive will tell you real corporate entrepreneurship lives in day-to-day operations. We will explore this concept in depth as well as other ways Disney is not only the entrepreneurial leader in both entertainment and theme parks (and really just about any market space in which they compete), but also perhaps the entire world of business. Our assertion is that the very *way* Disney—parks, resorts, and travel—goes about their business is entrepreneurial. Their methods, systems, marketing, guest engagement, research, and handling of cast members are strategic in nature, always focused on the brand promise to the end consumer, and, most importantly, in a constant state of improvement and enhancement.

> **You can design and create, and build the most wonderful place in the world. But it takes people to make the dream a reality.**
> **—Walt Disney**

Mathews Entrepreneurial Insight: From the Field

I grew up in the retail industry. My father owned multiple grocery and hardware stores my entire childhood. He was a wheeler and dealer beyond those businesses, and I picked up those skills along the way. We were the typical proprietor family; dad worked incredibly long hours, we talked shop over dinner, and every piece of our lives revolved around the family business. That carried into adulthood, as I have owned my own online sporting goods resale business, a retail home improvement center, a garden center, and a consulting practice, among other ventures. In the college setting I develop programming to train administrators, faculty members, and staff to be innovators, problem solvers, and entrepreneurial leaders. I also develop and lead management and leadership training programs for the retail home improvement industry, which provides me the opportunity to speak and work with hundreds of retailers and their emerging leaders every year. The story is virtually always the same in the service industries, as owners and leaders will almost always pose a question to the effect of, how do I get frontline (often hourly) employees to care about their work? There's no question the two most significant challenges service-based businesses face today are differentiating themselves from the competition and motivating *all* employees to fulfill the mission *all the time*. Disney's programs for training and motivating employees serve as a model for other businesses with frontline employees.

Connection to Something Special

Despite being more expensive than its competitors in nearly every space in which it competes (theme parks, cruise lines, resorts and hotels, restaurants, travel excursions, and retail), Disney Parks and Resorts enjoys extremely high customer satisfaction ratings and unparalleled success in each of those domains. Why is that? It's because everyone in the company operates within and honors a simple and clear purpose and shared values.

> **At the end of the day people won't remember what you said or did, they will remember how you made them feel.**
> **—Maya Angelou**

Purpose

Disney works diligently and intentionally to equip its cast members with a deep sense of purpose for their roles—a purpose that connects them to something much greater than themselves. The edict to create happiness for all who enter the gates of their parks and doors of their resorts and board their cruise ships is—above all else—what matters. How do they drive the message home? They start with an eight-hour cast member onboarding course called Traditions, where new cast members discover the legacy of Walt Disney, hear stories of cast members fulfilling the mission, and are given helpful tips for always keeping creating magic top of mind. This is what most in the company refer to as the Disney difference, or the Disney differentiating factor. When cast members feel deeply connected to the Disney company's history and reason for existing, they not only play their role with great energy to preserve the integrity of the organization's brand promise but they also go the extra mile to do so on a regular basis. How does Disney accomplish this? They use great storytelling to make it clear that Disney Parks and Resorts creates happiness for its guests. New hires tend to either latch onto the power of Walt's legacy of making dreams come true and stay for a lifetime or they roll their eyes and quit within a very short period of time. The Disney Traditions course for new cast members had such a profound impact on Caroline,[5] a new hire into the college program from the University of Colorado, that it inspired her to write a lengthy and enthusiastic blog post about the experience. The blog post was full of photos, everything she and her friend learned, and explanations of the meaning behind what they learned. This is not something you would see with new hires at other Fortune 500 companies—particularly college interns—but Disney is different, and the Traditions program and the rest of the Disney University[6] experience quickly connect new cast members emotionally to the purpose of Disney Parks and Resorts and their roles in the value chain. Disney's onboarding process is exemplary, but when one considers that only 12 percent of all companies actually do a good job of onboarding,[7] it makes Disney's efforts that much more impressive.

Disney empowers its cast members to fulfill that brand promise by making it clear that purpose always trumps task. Consider your last visit to a big box retailer. Perhaps you asked a clerk who was crouched down stocking the shelves to solve a problem you were having or where you might find a certain item. There's a very good chance you got a grunt and finger point with a hint (at least) of attitude for interrupting the task at hand. At a Disney park, that behavior would never be acceptable. At the very least, that person would stand up and talk at your level, asking questions to make sure he or she addressed all of your needs, not just the explicit one. In those brief moments, while in the process of transitioning you to another cast member, taking you to a different part of the store, or even walking you to a different part of the park, the cast member might learn something about you that becomes a point of conversation.

Mathews Family Moment: Curtis the Parking Lot Attendant

Why is it that my family and I still remember Curtis parking cars in the Animal Kingdom lot more than three years after it happened? To be sure, a whole lot of life has happened since then. Parking cars is a mundane, unimportant job, right? I'll tell you why we remember. Curtis, who was dancing and singing as he safely and efficiently parked a steady stream of vehicles in the hot and muggy Florida sun that morning, clearly and passionately understood his role in making magic that day. Curtis certainly could be an effective parking attendant at any other theme park, sporting venue, or hotel, but at Disney he is a part of something special, something bigger than himself. At Disney, he gets a chance to be himself and to shine in his role as part of the cast of the show. Yes, the task is important, especially for safety, but Curtis got it. If he delivered a smile and planted some positive thoughts in the minds of guests prior to park entry while performing a function such as parking, which most would see as a necessary hassle, then he had set the stage for his fellow cast members to delight those same guests upon entry to the park.

Given that Disney's internal research informs them that initial experiences, such as parking, hotel check-in, luggage assistance, etc., tend to drive strong feelings about the rest of the experience, they've learned they can't afford to ignore the seemingly mundane. If you want to be exceptional and provide best-in-class, holistic customer experiences, you can't ignore the engagements typically thought of as irrelevant or unimportant. It's often in these tasks where customers can experience hassles and frustrations if not delivered well. We implore you to examine how your mundane tasks impact the image of your organization. Stop viewing these roles as mere tasks that must be accomplished; instead, reframe them as a critical part of the show and your brand story. Customers may not always be aware when tasks are done well, but they will notice when service is poor. Many service-based companies lack discipline to deliver with excellence in the often overlooked tasks, but not Disney.

Mathews Family Moment: Tori at the Rock 'n' Roller Coaster Gift Shop

Enter Tori, a University of Alabama student in the Disney college internship program at Walt Disney World for one semester. My daughter and I met Tori coming off the Rock 'n' Roller Coaster in Hollywood Studios. Lindsey—seven at the time—immediately fixated on two specific pins on Tori's trading pin lanyard. At the very same time her excitement was building, I remembered my wife Julie and son Nate had split from us to ride Toy Story Mania! My wife handled all of the trading pins for the family. Tori listened to the conversation between my daughter and me regarding her mom having the trader pins and asked if my wife would be back in the area that night. She also asked my daughter what her favorite ride was. Lindsey enthusiastically said it was Rock 'n' Roller Coaster, and that this was the first time she was tall enough to ride it, which was very exciting for her. I said we planned to reconnect with my wife and son soon, and that we had a FastPass to ride the Twilight Zone Tower of Terror next. She said, "Perfect, have your wife meet you here in the gift shop when everyone finishes their rides." We reconvened at the Rock 'n' Roller Coaster gift shop about forty minutes later. I asked for Tori, and her fellow cast member said she was on break. I said it was no problem, and that I didn't want to bother her on break. She said—with a big, wry grin—"Oh, no, she's been expecting you; let me go get her. She's excited to see *Lindsey* again." Tori arrived with those two pins in hand as well as a lanyard full of pins with the same two themes of the first two: Princess Aurora and Minnie Mouse. She proceeded to break the rule of only two trades per person (remember, creating happiness trumps job tasks and most, if not all, standard practices not involving safety). Just when you think the story ends with the excitement of a personalized pin trading bonanza, think again. Tori told Lindsey what a pleasure it had been to meet her and pulled four Rock 'n' Roller Coaster FastPasses from her vest, saying, "I'm so glad you were finally able to ride Rock 'n' Roller Coaster for the first time, and now you can take whomever you want and enjoy it again on Mickey Mouse." Here's the part of the story Tori didn't know. Lindsey was in tears our last two trips to Disney World when she attempted to ride the coaster because she didn't quite make the mark at the dreaded height measuring stick. This wasn't just about being tall enough to ride a certain roller coaster—this was about something more. Riding this coaster was a big deal for her, as she was now on similar footing with her older brother. Tori, a college student only employed at Disney World for a brief time, could have easily forgotten about my daughter, and frankly, it wouldn't have even fazed me, but instead she made magic for her.

Why is it that the mission of creating happiness and the occasional magic comes second nature to Disney cast members? There is a great deal of intentionality that drives the desired behaviors that lead to creating happiness through outstanding experiences. This intentionality also encourages superior cast member-guest interactions that generate magical moments. These experiences are created not by chance but by a relentless dedication to empowering human ingenuity by leveraging cast member creativity, personalities, and a desire to serve. We will explore many examples of specific ways happiness and the occasional magic are created in this chapter and the next, but the following example demonstrates just how intentional Disney supervisors can be when it comes to empowering their cast members to deliver the unexpected. One of our colleagues at Ball State University, Brandon Smith, recounted his summer of working the whitewater rafting attraction, Kali River Rapids, at Animal Kingdom park at Walt Disney World:

> We had a daily rotation of jobs, like FastPass greeter, standby greeter, queue merge, ride operation, and load and unload. We rotated every half hour, which was nice because you got to see the ride from different perspectives and it made the day more interesting. The coolest job in the rotation was called "magic moments." For thirty minutes, your job was to create no-questions-asked magic, such as grabbing someone from the back of the standby line and escorting them to the front, taking a family to a photographer for a special photoshoot, granting people a second ride without having to go through the line again, giving kids merchandise, etc. It was so much fun!

This process-driven approach provides cast members with opportunities to deliberately deliver service that exceed guests' expectations.

Customers have grown to expect low engagement and virtually no care from "service" industry employees. However, the bare minimum expectation Disney has for its cast members is friendliness and a smile, but we implore you to ponder just how rare that truly is in today's supposed "service economy." That's why this is such a differentiating factor for Disney. While Disney cast members are great at asking questions, listening, and observing they won't always get the full story (like Tori in the example above); yet they know their job is to create happiness, and even make magic on occasion. While all Disney parks jobs require specific job skills, process and system skills, and knowledge sets (and those are all critically important to each role), Disney has simplified decisions for cast members, allowing them to always refer back to the mission and Four Keys (more on that later) and ask themselves if the answer they are about to give, the assistance they are about to provide, or the solution to a problem they are communicating fulfills the mission of the company. Remember, it's a relatively easy fix to coach an employee on going too far in what he or she gave your customer (which Disney leaders rarely have to do), but you can never recapture the opportunity to meaningfully engage with a customer. That moment in time is lost forever. On the contrary, consider how a magical moment like the one Tori provided enhances your company's relationship with its customer base.

Disney executives, past and present alike, will tell you the vast majority of fan mail the company receives from guests (regarding what they refer to as their most memorable moments from parks and resorts visits) involves a cast member turning the mundane into happiness, or even magic.[8] We've discussed the challenge of engaging frontline employees, but on the flip side, it's almost unheard of in service industries for customers to come back to a business and find an employee to give them a small token or gift of their appreciation, or even just a thank you and a smile. While it may seem odd to someone who hasn't experienced Disney magic, Disney parks and resorts guests do just that. They track down one of the seventy thousand cast members to thank them for their magical touch literally hundreds of times *daily*. Those actions speak volumes about just how at home cast members make guests feel.

Mathews Family Moment: Donald Duck

My son Nate adores Donald Duck. I think it's because they have similar personalities, as they both have great hearts but can be feisty and overly passionate on occasion. We had just waited in line at the Mexico Pavilion to get a photo with and meet Donald Duck. It was a typical hot and humid day at Disney World, which really makes you consider just what kind of a special person it must take to put on those thick and heavy outfits, which must feel like a human oven as much as a costume. I can see where it would be easy to just go through the motions until your thirty-minute shift is over, doing the bare minimum to get the guests through the line and appease your boss. But if you really want to see customer engagement that leads to meaningful guest experiences, pay close attention to the character lines the next time you go to a Disney park. The interactions are so genuine, and they create such lasting memories for guests. Further, those interactions are not limited to children, as many adults fulfill dreams when they pose for those pictures, hug their favorite character, or even get an autograph. Disney also makes it easy to capture those memories with photographers and helpers who are dedicated to keeping the line moving. Back to the story. Nate did not intend to ask Donald for an autograph, but Donald couldn't help but notice his crazy Donald Duck hat with the huge yellow beak (bill), and motioned to Nate as if to ask if it would be okay to autograph the underneath of the bill of his hat. Nate obliged, and Donald signed the hat. Five years later, that signed hat is still a treasure to Nate, so much so that he bought a second one with his own money to wear around the parks to avoid the risk of losing or ruining his coveted signed version. Disney, through the cast member playing Donald, made Nate feel like a Very Individual Person—or VIP, Walt's description of how he viewed all guests—that day, which made him perceive his experience as unique and special. Disney cast members seem to have a sixth sense about them when it comes to creating a lasting connection with guests.

Isn't it the entrepreneur's job to first and foremost meet the customer's needs and wants and then to engage with that customer in a way that creates connection and loyalty? It's not just the masterfully themed Expedition Everest roller coaster, the fresh coastal air aroma of the Beach Club Resort lobby, or the mystical lighting of Cars Land at night—it's the *people* of Disney parks and resorts who consistently deliver on the promise of happiness. Sure, all of those are critical components in the "show" that is the guest experience, but isn't it interesting—despite literally billions of dollars in investment in Disney attractions, physical environments, and assets around the world—that what guests really remember is the people?

Mathews Family Moment: Why We Keep Coming Back

Julie, who absolutely adores all things Disney, shared with me recently while walking through Disneyland Park on an "adult" trip that while the rides, sights, sounds, and smells are all great, what drives her love of Disney parks is the memories she can make with her family there. You see, the rides are no doubt fun, but what people really hold onto are things that make them feel good—experiences and memories.

Don't you want that kind of experience for your customers? How can you connect with them in a more meaningful way? How can you make them "fall in love" with your organization and be a loyal customer for life?

DISNEY LESSON 19: SUCCESSFUL ENTREPRENEURS AND LEADERS ALWAYS KEEP THEIR TEAMS FOCUSED ON THE MISSION AND BRAND PROMISE

What is the cost of not living up to your brand promise as close to 100 percent of the time as you can? The motto for Disney Parks and Resorts is to strive for perfection and settle for excellence. Notice their motto doesn't say anything about being good or about generating guest satisfaction—it says excellence. Sure, you will have moments when you miss the mark, but if you are excellent in most things you do, people will take the rare slipups in stride. How can you deliver excellence to your customers on a consistent basis, especially in the stereotypically menial tasks and "boring" business functions?

It is critical that you constantly reinforce just how important *each and every* role and job is and exactly how each role contributes to fulfilling the mission and brand promise. For instance, it's basically impossible to create happiness and magic if there is trash or a mess from spilled food on the ground, so the janitor's role is critical to the brand promise. The fantasy is instantly lost if the grounds are not kept immaculate, and the janitors, custodians, and maintenance professionals who keep the parks clean, presentable, and safe know their role is extremely critical to the brand promise and the show. A "one team, one dream" mantra is critical if you want *every* employee to *always* passionately defend the integrity of your entrepreneurial dream—your brand promise.

Guest Experience Recovery

Like any organization, things don't always go perfectly with Disney; thus, guest service recovery is carefully anticipated and handled. Disney cast members have learned that oftentimes a simple apology and a small gesture or restitution, such as a FastPass to an attraction, is enough to restore guest confidence in the brand promise. After all, above all else, most people just want to know they are heard and their concerns are respected and taken into consideration.

Mathews Moment: Group Experience at Boardwalk

Disney is not immune to big gaffes, and while we've experienced more than enough happiness in the parks to make me want to go back dozens of times, we have experienced those snafus on a few occasions. One at the top of mind is when we hosted our Ball State University staff leadership development group at Boardwalk Inn at Walt Disney World for a five-day trip to explore what excellence and a best-in-class organization looked like. The resort hotel planner, Matthew Harrelson, and his staff had been absolutely fantastic to work with through the months of meticulous planning leading up to the excursion. He had even asked the right questions and listened closely enough to know that my son and I loved golf, and that my son's favorite character was Donald Duck. When I walked into my hotel room for the first time, lo and behold there was a gift bag with a Disney golf towel,

Mickey Mouse golf balls, and, yes, Donald Duck ball markers for my son. Matthew took great care in his first on-site engagement with me, and I was blown away at the service and customization of the experience. That was a side story, though, because around midmorning on our Disney Institute training day, the piano and singing in preparation for a wedding fired up in the convention center room with which we were sharing a wall. It became incredibly distracting, to the point where I contacted Matthew, as did my colleague and co-writer, Mike Goldsby, and the Disney Institute trainer himself. Matthew had the noise moved by lunchtime, and we were happy, but clearly Matthew and the Disney Institute folks were not satisfied with their failure to deliver on the Disney brand promise. At the end of our session, a freezer with free Mickey ice cream sandwiches was rolled in, and Mickey and Minnie Mouse showed up for pictures and autographs. It's important to note this is normally a very expensive add-on experience, but Matthew had the authority and wherewithal to make the call so as not to leave any doubts in our mind about the integrity of the Disney product. What Matthew realized was that he had to fix more than just the problem; he had to fix the relationship with our team. Also keep in mind that while the incident may not have been his fault (it's highly likely he did not make the room scheduling error), he knew from his training and his empowerment to fulfill purpose over task that it was indeed his problem.

This is an important concept for your team to learn and embrace, as most customer issues will not be their fault, but they are their problem because they stand between the customer and the brand promise of your company.

We've all left a highly attended sporting event, amusement park, or concert only to realize that in our excitement to get into the venue we forgot to document where we parked. You're tired, it's late, and you and your family just want to get on the road toward home. It's a frustrating and embarrassing error that usually leads to mindlessly walking up and down endless rows of cars and ultimately just waiting around until most cars are gone so the task becomes more manageable. Of course this isn't the concert or sporting venue's problem, right? Why are they responsible for your absentmindedness? Disney reframes this very problem as a Disney concern because they don't want you to end your day in a negative fashion and thus leave with a tarnished experience. First, Disney has extensive signage with multiple identifiers in each parking lot (row numbers and character areas), and parking attendants and shuttle drivers remind you in which area you parked. Those are proactive solutions. Yet Disney knows this information will occasionally still be lost in the excitement of guests visiting their favorite park, so cast members are trained to spot lost families in parking lots. These cast members approach these families, asking a series of questions to efficiently get them to their lost car. If the family remembers within a thirty-minute window when they arrived, cast members will have them back to their car in very short order, and the guests are always amazed. Of course this does not magically happen but is instead the result of systems that log what sublots and rows were filled at specific times. Was this the cast members' fault? Of course not, but they not only made it their problem but also their job to solve the issue and recover the experience. Most companies would just write off parking as a necessary evil for the guests, but not Disney. While Disney tries to prevent experience snafus, the cast members provide guest recovery for situations that are not necessarily even the fault of the company. This kind of behavior requires a deep level of proactive problem-finding—a key entrepreneurial activity—that stems from understanding that *anything* that gets in the way of an excellent customer experience *is indeed your organization's problem*. Don't allow yourself and your employees to ignore customer stumbling blocks that create a less than ideal experience. Your entrepreneurial vision is worth protecting at every customer touchpoint, so reframe how you and your people view customer interactions with your brand.

Mathews Family Moment: Recovery at Wilderness Lodge

Another Disney personal recovery story that comes to mind stems from an atypical experience we had at Wilderness Lodge at Walt Disney World a few years ago. Our family has been really loyal to the Lodge and Beach Club Resorts over the years, and we've always had very good experiences at both resorts. This experience—particularly during the check-in process—just wasn't up to Disney standards and, in fact, was a downright rough series of encounters. I sent an email to the hotel explaining the situation. Having grown up in the retail business and having owned my own businesses, I always provide feedback in those situations, but I do it with a heart for helping rather than complaining or asking for restitution. In fact, I even mentioned that I was not asking for restitution in this instance; rather, I wanted to pass along the information for their benefit. I received, within hours, both an email and a follow-up phone call from Stacey Springer, the Rooms and Recreations Manager at Wilderness Lodge. I had also provided the information on the Disney post-trip online survey, and I received an email and phone call from Megan, a Guest Experiences Services person in that area too. Stacey had already looked up our future reservations (at Port Orleans Resort—French Quarter, a moderate resort) and offered a free upgrade to a Wilderness Lodge club level room with a Magic Kingdom park view for that trip. Remember, I had specifically mentioned I was not asking for reparations, but she had taken the time to look up our history, and she combined Disney protocol, her experiences, and her judgment to offer the free upgrade for the next trip. Also keep in mind that she did not offer the room for free, which is fine, and—in my mind—smart business. As Dan Cockerell, former VP of Magic Kingdom park, once told me, "Don't overreact to customer complaints. Solve the problem for the customer without destroying your staff for the one out of ninety-nine where things didn't quite go right. Learn from it, restore the customer relationship, and move on." It is also worth noting that the upgrade may not have cost the Lodge anything, as they likely had excess capacity (particularly in club level) the time of year that the follow-up trip took place. Stacey even followed up after our trip to make sure everything went well, and she thanked me for taking the time to provide the helpful feedback. The recovery experience left no doubt in our minds that Wilderness Lodge will continue to be—as it has always been—one of our favorite resorts, Disney or otherwise.

The lesson here is to not take customer feedback personally, throwing emotion and pride out the window when making amends with your valuable customers and protecting the reputation of your brand. As former Walt Disney World Executive Vice President for Operations, Lee Cockerell, often says, "You should always view feedback as a gift." Lee's message is to empower employees to always make things right with the customer. If employees are trained well and immersed in the culture and purpose of the organization, they will make a great decision just about every time an issue arises and repair not only the situation but, more importantly, the relationship with the customer.

If your employees aren't clear how their job contributes to or points toward the mission, then either the position is not needed or you haven't clearly articulated and consistently reinforced their role in fulfilling that mission—perhaps you haven't even clearly defined the mission or reinforced it with expectations, modeled behavior, and signaling regarding what is truly important in the organization. It's also critical that you give your employees the authority to take ownership of the customer experience, much like what Disney clearly did with Curtis, Tori, Matthew, Stacey, and, yes, even Donald Duck.

There has been a steady decline in quality of service among businesses over the last two to three decades. Why is that? No matter the reasons, there is great opportunity within this void. The exemplary service described in the stories above really stands out, and Disney knows it. People still seek out good service, and they are willing to pay a premium for it. How can you provide better service in your organization to take advantage of this unmet demand for premium customer experiences? There are significant entrepreneurial opportunities available to those who want to provide top-shelf service to today's experience-hungry consumers.[9]

Employee Engagement

It's perfectly sensible for you to be saying, but I still don't understand how they do it. To keep driving the point home, we repeat: Disney leaders are intentional and diligent with their approach to business, what they stress as important, and the words they use. They understand that an engaged employee is a productive employee, and at Disney that means an employee that not only performs the functional job duties as expected but also, more importantly, fulfills the mission with excellence on an ongoing basis. An engaged cast member—regardless of title, rank, or wage—is one that loves the job to the point where she has stopped viewing it as a job, which means she often goes above and beyond minimum expectations, becoming a cheerleader and advocate for the company, coworkers, partners, and guests. Gallup's research indicates that engagement drives performance and is influenced by four key human areas of need: basic, individual, teamwork, and growth.[10] Disney has worked with Gallup for many years, and these basic principles still serve as the foundation for their cast member engagement philosophy and efforts. Disney defines three levels of employee engagement: highly uncommitted, neither fully committed nor uncommitted, and highly committed.[11] Gallup similarly defines these levels as actively disengaged, disengaged, and engaged.[12] The bottom group (highly uncommitted or actively disengaged) typically represents employees who actually work against what you're trying to accomplish. Gallup and Disney both suggest you should have low patience levels with such employees, as they can do serious harm to your business model, culture, and customer relationships. The second group (neither fully committed nor uncommitted and disengaged) represents an opportunity space. They would likely do more if their mangers engaged them more by coaching them, building a relationship with them, involving them in decisions and solutions, and providing them with growth opportunities. The third group (committed and engaged) features exemplary employees who are internally motivated, passionate about their work, and consistently model desired behaviors that directly support the mission of the organization. The risk with this group is that they could actually become disengaged or uncommitted if employers are not intentional about keeping them engaged. As we explore this crucial concept of employee engagement, our hope is for you to see how creating a culture of engagement makes entrepreneurial dreams come to life. It preserves the entrepreneurial spirit of your team by allowing them to express and leverage their human ingenuity.

> **The biggest tip I could offer anybody who is leading full time employees or interns or executives is to really care about your employees.[13]**
>
> **—Kristi Breen, VP Disney Campus Programs
> & Disney Cruise Line Recruitment**

Internal Customer Service

Before we dive into the four elements that drive employee engagement and how they play out in Disney parks and resorts, let's first examine the crucial Disney imperative of *internal* customer service. After having the opportunity to hang around and learn from countless Disney cast members for the last decade, this concept of internal customer service finally registered with us the last three to four years. It's critical to employee engagement, external customer service, and customer engagement and thus paramount to business results.

As we traversed through a sea of literally thousands of ornate costumes and accessories recently in one of the backstage costuming areas at Disneyland Park near Tomorrowland, several Disney innovation insights began to emerge. Costumes are critical to the show Disney puts on in its parks. A great deal of care is put into the theming details in the costumes (notice they're not called uniforms—more on that later). Costume details and how they impact the show in the eyes of the guest are important, but we would like to focus on the business process particulars that make this story uniquely Disney. Because leaders have observed and been involved with operations at the ground level and also listened to cast member suggestions over the years, major improvements have been made to costuming functions.

There's no doubt improvements have been made to enhance durability, cosmetics, and other details of costumes, but we would like to hone in on the *care* put into the cast member's experience, as this is a very important piece of being "in character" while onstage in the parks and resorts. Disney used to heavily control costumes—perhaps rightfully so. Cast members would have to search through the endless racks of garments for their apparel for the day—often settling for a size or fit that was not ideal or overly flattering—change, and then rush to their post in the park for their shift. As you can imagine, this process was frustrating for cast members on many fronts, and they were often late to work because the process was unpredictable and cumbersome. Most companies would have a "too bad, that's just the way it is" attitude with their employees, but not Disney. Disney's culture says there must be a better way, so let's *proactively look* for problems and challenges, *listen* for frustration points, and *work together* toward *solutions*. The solutions, though not flashy, dramatically increased job satisfaction, engagement, and effectiveness of cast members. Why? Because they eliminated frustration points.

First, cast members can now visit a WALL-E themed (reinforce your brands every chance you get!) kiosk, select where they work and their role, and print a costume retrieval checklist. Second, they are now allowed to "latch onto" coveted sizes and take costumes home. Third, there are guest services cast members there to help them with questions and make sure they are getting what they need. Cast members are guaranteed a good fit; thus, costumes will be tailored if needed. Each costume piece has an RFID tag sewn into it, and as they exit, the piece is automatically checked out to the cast member. As they leave the costuming area, there is a counter for last-minute questions, problems, or requests bearing an overhead sign that reads "Guest Services." Finally, cast members return costumes that need deep laundering to a station that allows them to wave each item under a scanner that reads the RFID tags and then simply drop the items in laundry bins below. The items are registered on a computer screen above so the cast members can have confidence in knowing each piece was logged into the system as returned. The laundry bins are also very helpful to the textiles/laundry cast members, as they are on rollers and allow for ergonomically safe and efficient loading into the commercial washing machines and dryers. On top of all this, Disney now provides cast members with twenty minutes of paid walk time to arrive at their park or resort work location. Do you think an outside consultant, or even vendor, came up with the RFID idea and technology used for the costuming process? Of course not—it was conceived and developed by a cast member at the Disneyland Hong Kong Resort. This cast member's idea was heard, he was given funding to pilot it, and the process was perfected and then adopted across all parks and resorts. Keep this important entrepreneurial concept in mind later as we progress in this chapter.

Given costumes are sacred at Disney, the reduction in control that has taken place over the years is nothing short of amazing. The autonomy allows cast members to take ownership of the costuming process, increase accuracy and authenticity, and greatly reduce the time and energy it takes to retrieve their costumes and step on stage.

We tend to notice subtle outliers, and as you may recall, the "Guest Services" sign above the counter as cast members depart the costuming area was definitely not lost on us. Disney places extreme value on internal customer service, so much so that each unit treats its fellow cast members like *customers* (guests). This is a critical part of Disney's success and is a true differentiating factor. It's not nearly enough to serve just the external guests at Disney; each cast member is expected to treat their fellow cast members and internal and external partners with the same respect, reverence, friendliness, and unrelenting service they would give to the paying customer. They are just passing it forward by the time they interact with external guests. While this reframe of customer service and employee relations itself is innovative in nature, consider the *entrepreneurial behavior* that was both allowed and encouraged to take place to drive innovations every step of the way in the costuming process. This now hassle-free system has not only greatly increased the internal service levels that Disney provides its cast members but has also driven greater efficiency and thus improved business results. Corporate innovation leverages the vast amount of often untapped human intellect with customer needs, current business practices, and industry best practices to ideate better ways of doing things and activate new approaches that solve multiple problems.

DISNEY LESSON 20: INTERNAL CUSTOMER SERVICE IS CRITICAL IF YOU ASPIRE TO BE A FIRST-CLASS ENTREPRENEURIAL ORGANIZATION

Can you see how Disney creates an entrepreneurial environment by fostering new ideas in process improvements? How are you serving your employees? How are they serving each other? Is a culture of service throughout the value chain expected and explicit in your culture or is it every person for themselves? These questions are a critical first step toward creating and maintaining exemplary external customer experience and subsequent business results. Bluntly put, you cannot and will not have world-class employee engagement without an inherent and active environment of internal customer service that is deliberately woven into the company's culture. Disney's executives, leaders, managers, and frontline cast members all care about each other and serve each other as guests in an ongoing fashion. As you and your employees engage in any task, you should always first ask yourself who the *real* customer is in *that very moment*. We take our students and trainees through an important process of reframing who the customer is quite often, and it is always fascinating to see those aha moments where it starts to click as to just how often we are clueless with regard to whom we are actually serving.[14]

We'll now transition to how Disney addresses Gallup's four fundamental areas and twelve sub-behaviors that drive employee engagement.[15] You can think of the following section as sort of a "Disney's field guide to driving business results by championing a culture of engagement." As you work your way through how Disney Parks and Resorts succeeds at each of the elements of engagement, you ought to be considering how you can translate this proven formula to your organization.

Basic Engagement Needs

Clear Expectations[16]

Gallup research indicates that over 50 percent of all U.S. employees say they don't know what is expected of them at work.[17] While that statistic likely shocks you, we assure you it absolutely does not play out that way at Disney. Because of the simplicity of and care put into tying job task to mission, as discussed above, cast members are keenly aware that their job is always to default to simply creating happiness. If you're thinking, that's great, but my employees can't just run around randomly making wishes come true because they do have an actual job they're paid to do, that's certainly true, and it's no different at Disney. What is different about Disney is those jobs—and the way to do them—are very clearly defined by the company. Further, cast members are meticulously trained in those skills and processes before they ever set foot on stage in the parks. As we will discuss in the coming pages, this is why Disney does not focus its hiring efforts as much on specific job skills and knowledge nearly as much as other companies. The company has learned those functions are trainable.

Traditions

As referenced earlier in the chapter, new Disney Parks and Resorts cast members go through an emotional and rigorous course on the heritage of the company their first day on the job. This course tends to have a deep impact on these freshly hired cast members, and they often become instant fans of the company—and the mission—and the values for which it stands. Right away cast members are sent the clear message that creating happiness should be first and foremost on their mind, and they will be trained on the specifics of the job later. This direct tie back to the purpose and shared values of the company leaves nothing to question in terms of what the cast member is to deliver. Further, cast members will be constantly reminded of the purpose or the "why"[18] of their roles throughout the lifespan of their employment. Trainers and guest speakers tell their Disney stories, which instantly reinforce the purpose of the company. For instance, Disney Institute trainer, René Torrico, visits the Traditions class to tell them the story of what Disney parks mean to him. As a child, his father would randomly drive past his school on a Friday, which meant he was going to share a day of "hooky" with him at Disneyland. Torrico describes those as some of the happiest days of his life, and he delivers the story with emotion and passion. Stories like René's are great tools for making the mission of creating happiness come to life, and they also encourage new cast members to discover and begin to share their own stories.

Provide Your Employees With the Necessary Tools and Resources[19]

While excellence is expected of cast members, they are given the training, skills, tools, software, equipment, and other resources they need to effectively do their job, which is a key requirement of meeting basic engagement needs. Think about it, as a customer, when did you last hear an employee complain about not having the right tools to do his or her job? Did you hear and see the frustration? Did you think to yourself, I wonder when that person will just altogether quit caring about his or her job, if they haven't, in fact, already done so? We frequently encounter this is in the world of higher education, where budgets are tight and employees are too often expected to live without the proper equipment or supplies necessary to do their job, or they're expected to use a one-size-fits-all software package that inadequately serves students, partners, and other employees and departments on a variety of key tasks and functions. Disney recognized it had a software and system problem—particularly at Walt Disney World—several years ago, and the company set out to fix it. We will discuss the MyMagic+ project in the next chapter, but Disney recognized the problem and aggressively (both financially and from an implementation timeline standpoint) addressed it. Further, expectations and metrics are clearly set for each job at Disney, and safety processes are clearly outlined and rehearsed to prepare cast members for what is expected of them every day, including how to handle emergencies. Simply put, cast members are well equipped to do their jobs at a very high level. What's important about this is that the commitment of resources and investment in cast members are consistent with the goal of providing excellence in customer service. If you are not equipping your employees with the necessary tools for their jobs, you really need to ask yourself why (and then ask yourself why again to that response, and so on until you've gained understanding).[20] Earnestly consider how it prohibits your employees from playing their part to the best of their ability. If you say your vision is to deliver a world-class product, service, and experience, but you're holding back on investing in your employees or providing them with essential tools to carry out the role at the expected level of excellence, then you will likely never fully bring your entrepreneurial vision into reality.

> When I first arrived at the Walt Disney Company, I was surprised to find I had to go back to school—at Disney University! There, I learned the fundamentals of guest service that consistently gave Disney a tremendous advantage in the marketplace.[21]
>
> *Michael Eisner*

Training

Along with providing the necessary tools of the trade and financial resources, it is critical that you invest in your employees through creative and immersive training experiences. Walt made it very clear early in the life of Disneyland that training would be a priority in his company. He lured Van France, a renowned trainer and labor relations expert, away from Kaiser Aluminum to head up his training efforts. Walt liked France because he was a training expert and had not been tainted by the entertainment industry. Through France the purpose of creating happiness was born and cemented as the anthem by which Disneyland cast members were to live.[22] The commitment to cast member training continues today, as Disney invests a minimum of $3,000 per employee in initial training.[23] That's a significant investment, and even a sacrifice—one that most companies skimp on—but the results speak for themselves: Disney parks and resorts employees are thoroughly prepared to consistently perform their roles to near perfection. Today's Disney employees spend their first week on the job at Disney University. As you discovered earlier in the chapter, they first learn about the heritage of Walt and the history of the company in a one-day Traditions course, which instills in them Walt's values, which not only live on today but also drive unparalleled business results in the theme park, resort, cruise line, and vacation industries. After the Traditions course, they spend the rest of the week learning the specifics of their role and how to apply their personality to that role. For instance, if they are going to be a driver for the Kilimanjaro Safaris live animal savannah attraction at Animal Kingdom park at Walt Disney World, they will practice on a simulator and learn their lines and the story behind those lines. They will also learn how to handle safety concerns, such as a guest reaching over the edge of the safari truck to try to retrieve a lost cell phone. In addition, they get coached on how to bring their voice and character to the excursion. Disney wants cast members to put their personality on display in their roles. This is important because employees who are encouraged to use their strengths and put their personality on display are more fulfilled and engaged in their job.[24] Cast members are also trained in the other roles of the attraction, such as FastPass queue, loading, unloading, stroller duty, etc. Cast members are deeply trained on the extreme details of each task and process through experiential exercises, and the reasons why certain processes and procedures are used are explained as well. This allows for best practices to be followed, which drives a consistent but flawless guest experience, but it also allows the cast members to be so comfortable with those ongoing duties that they can focus most of their energy on just being themselves and serving the guests.

Disney takes training so seriously that it has an entire building, Disney University, dedicated to full-time preparation of cast members at Walt Disney World. The building is state-of-the-art, and training spaces are designed and themed with the parks and resorts in mind. Rooms are well organized, and everything is in working order. Trainers are professional and on time, have diverse experiences, and are extremely well prepared. Disney identifies cast members who are passionate, can relate to the average employee, and can model the purpose of the company to new cast members. The training environment is also fun and immersive. Finally, after an exciting week of training, new cast members earn their "Mouseters Degree"—one final reinforcement of brand—before heading out to their physical work environment. All of this professionalism and training excellence sends the message to cast members that, yes, we're very serious about this and committed to investing in you.[25] How many jobs have you had where training was either nonexistent, an afterthought, or very sloppily executed? Or worse yet, how often are you guilty of not making first-class training for new employees a priority? It's a common issue among organizations of all industries and sizes, but it's particularly customary in small and entrepreneurial firms. Do you really want to hire what you perceive as "skill" and just hope your new employees magically exhibit desired priorities and behaviors?

Disney also trains for the unexpected, the extraordinary, and even the unimaginable, such as lost children (which they refer to as "lost parents" so as not to scare the children), lost wallets, natural disasters, and even terrorist attacks. Their training and processes are so good, in fact, that they were able to evacuate well over one hundred thousand people from all four of the Walt Disney World parks in under an hour during the 9/11 crisis![26] Did anyone actually expect them to pull off a mass evacuation of that magnitude—with that much tension and stress attached to it—with such precision? Would anyone have held it against them if it had been a chaotic experience? Of course not, but this is the Disney difference. They wow you when you least expect it, and you walk away with an unexplained reverence for the company. Disney treats you like its royal guest to whom extreme care is given.

> ## DISNEY LESSON 21: DON'T CUT CORNERS ON TRAINING AND ONBOARDING
>
> Disney invests significant resources, time, and energy on training and onboarding new cast members. In fact, their commitment is so deep that they refuse to cut back for any reason, even in times of economic slowdowns. Cast members know their role, and they have the necessary talents, skills, knowledge, and processes to be successful in those roles. Are you throwing new employees into the fire with little to no training? Are you providing your people with the necessary resources and know-how to do their jobs with excellence? Are you onboarding them in a way that clearly communicates and ingrains in them the importance of your company's mission and brand promise?

Communication of Strategies

In an organization as large as Disney (there are over seventy thousand cast members at Walt Disney World alone), there are always changes and additions happening. Disney Parks and Resorts does an extraordinary job of communicating the changes every step of the way: as they are being planned, as they are announced to the public, during construction, during soft openings, during grand openings, and throughout the infancy of the implementation phase of the project. Not only does the company have a system for communicating such changes but they also explain the why behind the decisions. Many Disneyland Resort fans were furious over the conversion of the Tower of Terror to Guardians of the Galaxy—Mission: Breakout! Disney executives knew this would be the case, but they also knew the Disney California Adventure version of Tower of Terror was its lowest rated rendition of the popular ride in the entire Disney parks global system. They also needed a strategy to bring Marvel intellectual property to domestic parks, and this was their best opportunity to do so. While cast members and guests showed initial disappointment in the conversion, Disney gave cast members stories to tell, sneak previews, a glimpse into the long-term strategy of inserting Marvel and Pixar properties into the park, and insights about the conversion that they could at least partially share with guests. The insights also helped frontline cast members understand the reasons behind the strategy and thus get them on board with the decision and upcoming changes. The result? Within months of the opening of the remodeled and reimagined ride, Guardians of the Galaxy—Mission: Breakout! was one of the most popular attractions at Disneyland Resort. When cast members know how the decision relates to the mission, they get behind and reinforce the strategy.

Disney Parks and Resorts executives use a variety of avenues to communicate this type of key information to cast members. One tool is the *Disneyland Line*, a weekly printed brochure-type publication that outlines new merchandise, special events, park changes, construction, etc. The *Disneyland Line* is an entrepreneurial venture in its own right, as Disney sells advertising spots to cover development, printing, and distribution costs. Cast members love the publication, and it disseminates crucial information that empowers them to better understand the purpose of their job, how that aligns with corporate strategy, and how to communicate with guests. They also use a company intranet, bulletin boards, memos, texts, emails, phone applications, and video displays in backstage areas as ways to deliver timely information to cast members. Beyond those tangible delivery systems, perhaps the most effective tools are those of the face-to-face variety. They regularly hold "town hall" meetings where cast members can ask questions about process changes, new merchandise, and construction projects. They also encourage managers to hold regular impromptu meetings and one-on-one discussions with their cast members on upcoming changes and new offerings. These multichannel communication methods not only inform cast members of key initiatives and their purpose but they can also often turn animosity or insecurity about changes into enthusiasm with some intentional yet simple messaging around details and strategy.

There's little doubt Disney has a plethora of data points, guests, and history with which to build systems and processes with a great deal of predictability, but you need to ask yourself how you can further advance your vision and entrepreneurial dream by putting systems in place that will help bring the vision to fruition. Scalability of entrepreneurial ventures is not mystical, but rather achieved by systematizing and professionalizing roles and functions to reach the ideal outcomes you and your customers desire. In case you're concerned that heavy systems and processes will kill the entrepreneurial spirit of your company, we hear you, and we urge you to hang in there, as we will discuss the ongoing innovation of these systems and processes later in this chapter as well as the next. But in the short run, just keep in mind that precise and consistent systems and processes help make entrepreneurial dreams a reality.

Decision-Making and Touchpoints

Disney Parks and Resorts' Four Keys are fairly well known both inside and outside the theme park industry. Having said that, we're always amazed that more organizations—especially within the industry—don't imitate this highly successful decision-making tool. It's easy to understand, hierarchical, and gives the cast member the authority to make decisions with purposeful guidance. Disney's Four Keys are: 1) safety, 2) courtesy, 3) show, and 4) efficiency. Safety is always the number one priority, although most people are quietly surprised when they learn this. From Disney's perspective, though, nothing really matters without safety. Providing a safe environment for guests, cast members, and partners is the right thing to do, but it also reduces liability and negative media attention. It's also nearly impossible to create happiness and the occasional magic when people don't feel safe, or, worse yet, when people aren't safe. Thinking back to the concept of purpose, it's sensible to get confused as to why courtesy and show wouldn't be reversed in the pecking order. Again, it's nearly impossible to create happiness and magic in the entertainment industry (show) without simple courtesy and friendliness. Very few businesses, if any, come even remotely close to Disney's level of friendliness. Chick-fil-A comes to mind, as its employees are always friendly and seem very well prepared to serve the customer. Having said that, while Chick-fil-A is several notches above every competitor in its space, Disney service and experience levels are in yet a different class than the Chick-fil-A's of the world. Imagine every guest touchpoint between first contact and setting foot on that first attraction at a Disney park. These can include trip booking, hotel entry gate guards, hotel entry, front desk, parking, transportation, security, park access, photographers, merchandise carts, line queue greeters, and so on, to name just some of the literally hundreds of customer touchpoints of Disney Parks and Resorts. If each of these touchpoints isn't playing its role at a minimum acceptable courtesy level per Disney standards, the show of that first attraction visited is likely to be tarnished, not to mention the integrity and perception of the overall show and guest experience (we will go into the details of show experience and nonhuman touchpoints in more depth in the next chapter).

Work hard to reframe what a complete customer experience looks like. Consider going beyond what is perhaps your company's minimum responsibility but nonetheless affects the customer experience. For example, what do you dread the most about traveling? We're assuming, if we surveyed people (and I'm quite sure Disney has), luggage and taxis would rank near the top of the most dreaded travel realities list. Several years ago, Disney even went so far as to address these Walt Disney World guest vacation touchpoints that were seemingly out of its control. First, guests receive luggage tags with their travel paperwork about a month before their departure. They attach these tags to their bags, which allows them to skip the luggage retrieval belts at the airport. Disney delivers their bags directly to their hotel room within just a few hours of their plane touching down. Likewise, guests (or hotel bellhops) can deliver their bags for departure to the airline check-in station located at each Walt Disney World resort hotel, where they can check those bags and even receive boarding passes for their flight. Disney then delivers their luggage to the airlines well in advance of the flight, which also serves the airport and commercial airline companies. It's safe to say no one else in the industry would have even thought to address these customer touchpoints, and if they had, the idea would have been quickly dismissed because it is surely impossible to work with the airport, commercial airlines, and TSA, right? Disney is so good at listening to its cast members and guests and then reframing the problem into an opportunity to shine that nothing is ruled out as impossible. Because of this proactive problem-finding and problem-solving mentality and approach, guests no longer have to stress about the hassles associated with luggage. One complete category of hassle eliminated— genius! Guests also have the option of boarding a Disney Magical Express motor coach operated by Mears, a third party partner. There's no need for guests who take advantage of this option to battle the rental car counter or kiosk, unknown routes, and toll booths, services which they can also take advantage of on the way back to the airport. On top of that, families can watch Disney cartoons and learn about the resort and parks on the bus ride. This service comes at a steep price tag for Disney, costing literally tens of millions of dollars per year, but it accomplishes two things: 1) it keeps guests in Disney's on-site transportation system and thus most likely on Disney property for the duration of their stay and 2) it ensures positive guest touchpoints and brand promise reinforcement. Second hassle eliminated—again, genius! Consider just how much this exemplary service package enhances the customer experience and sets guests' vacations off on the right foot, keeping in mind it begins in the home mailbox! It's critical that you examine the minutia of your company's customer touchpoints. Examine even those touchpoints that you've always thought were either not your problem or out of your control. You can greatly increase the odds of your entrepreneurial dream thriving and delivering on your brand promise beyond your customer's wildest imagination if you simply ask everyone involved in the customer process what could be better. Show is at the very *heart* of Disney's business, but the greatest displays of entertainment mean nothing without delivery from—and meaningful interaction with—joyful, engaged cast members and business partner employees.

Disney makes the nonnegotiables very clear to its cast members. Name tags are an absolute must at all Disney parks and resorts. They always provide the first name only, as Walt wanted guests to feel at home, and he was adamant that being on a first name basis with cast members was the best way to accomplish that. They also send a message that cast members are approachable. Their name is tied to the quality of the company, and they are accountable for their behaviors and delivery of the Disney brand promise.

Finally, notice that efficiency, a much more business-like and performance-based term, is last in the priority list of the famed Four Keys. It's not as if Disney is disinterested in efficiency and maximizing revenue and profit, but the company is making a distinct statement about the prioritized delivery of the actual brand promise of Disney Parks and Resorts. If the company fulfills the brand promise of high-quality entertainment and *show*, producing happiness in its guests *safely* and in a friendly and *courteous* manner, business performance will naturally excel. Are you starting to see how Disney is able to charge far more than its competitors for virtually everything in its product and service offering menu?

A great example of this principle at work is the investment Disney Cruise Line made in inside cabins several years ago. Much like the Disney's Magical Express example above, not all investments will have a direct return. Some may not *ever* directly generate any revenue. Disney, since entering the cruise line market in 1996, has consistently disrupted the industry. If you've been on cruises, you know inside cabins and cabins below water level have traditionally been labeled the cheap, "armpit" experience of the cruise industry. Disney Imagineers didn't just accept this as fact, but rather sought a solution. Their answer? They installed video cameras outside the ship that would capture scenes of what guests in both the inside cabins and those below the water line would see if they were indeed on the outer level, above the water line. They fed the live feed to round, portal window-shaped TV monitors above the beds of those cabins and showed kid-friendly cartoon characters overlying the ocean views. Those Imagineers understood the purpose of their job (happiness) and the hierarchy of the Four Keys. And guess what? That seemingly costly innovation eventually led to greater demand and higher prices for inner cabins. How do you handle investments that have no immediate measurable return but provide benefit for the customer and thus the company in the long run? How can you leverage these strategic investments to create a more unique customer experience that is *more valuable* in the marketplace?

Onstage Versus Backstage

Cast members are given very clear guidelines for on-site protocol, specifically onstage versus backstage behavior. To preserve the show, cast members are expected to be in character, including costume, voice, mannerisms, language, conversations, and actions, at all times when they are within view or earshot of guests onstage.

Mathews Family Moment: The Big Box Store Visit

Not that long ago, I visited a big box retailer with my family. Aside from the parking lot being littered with trash, my first impression was that of two college-aged employees talking about their escapades at a fraternity party the night before. I asked if I could have one of the shopping carts (that was holding one of them up) and got a grunt and the invitation to serve myself. Of course, as luck would have it, the cart I was trying to retrieve was caught on the next one in the row. As I struggled to release it, the employees just went about their conversation as if we weren't even there, let alone laboring over the cart. It's the middle of the summer, and I'm actually dripping with sweat and agitated at this point, so I just gave up on the cart. This hurt the retailer in the long run, as I was now going to be carrying anything I reluctantly decided to purchase. My next encounter was a uniformed employee who was smoking while positioned right next to the entry door. As we walked into the store, no one greeted us and, worse yet, employees pretty much made it a point to ignore us, including the two cashiers talking about things my five-year-old daughter and seven-year-old son absolutely did not need to hear. As you have aptly predicted by now, the experience did not get any better. We finally decided to purchase just the essentials, all of which were loss leaders with low to no profit margin. As you can probably also predict, we haven't been back to that store since that day—over three years ago. What if I had pulled into a clean parking lot? How about if the two college students in the parking lot had been friendly and helped with the cart? What if the employee smoking at the entrance had either changed out of his uniform if he was off the clock or, better yet, smoked in his car or behind the store and out of sight of customers? How about those cashiers? What if they were tidying up their areas and greeting entering visitors while waiting to ring up the next customer? Perhaps if the stocker in the health and beauty aids aisle could have been friendly and helpful it would have at least somewhat recovered the negative image we had of the store.

With most customers, we have one shot to get it right. If we misfire badly, there are enough other options to ensure we will never see them again. You owe it to yourself, those invested in you, and your employees to provide the most thoughtful experience possible. Be deliberate about what the customer sees, feels, hears, and experiences.

DISNEY LESSON 22: DRILL DOWN TO THE FINITE DETAILS BY EXAMINING ALL TOUCHPOINTS FOR ALL CUSTOMER ENGAGEMENTS

Does the story above describe your organization or do maybe even just a few of these negative experiences persist? If you're not examining all of your customer touchpoints, you need to reconsider why not and realize you can't afford to fail to closely examine each and every one of them. When we say all of your customer touchpoints, we mean *all* of them. Disney examines and scrutinizes over *one hundred* touchpoints for *each* of its experiences, while other companies *might* passively consider just a handful of obvious touchpoints.[27] It's critical your people know exactly what is expected of them at all times and what image and brand promise they are expected to uphold. If you are near perfect or excellent at most of your touchpoints, customers will likely forgive imperfections or even miss one or two in select areas.

Individual Engagement Needs

Help Your Employees Use Their Talents[28]

With the help of talent mining tools provided through internal Disney surveys and by outside vendors, Disney is able to strategically hire and place cast members in the roles that best fit their abilities and passions. They also rely on personality instruments to match role to person. This is easily noticeable in cast members playing characters throughout their parks. Cast members obviously need to have an appropriate body size and shape to be able to play a specific character (such as a petite female likely playing the role of Minnie or Mickey Mouse), but those characters also need to have a warm personality that fits the expected actions and body language of a specific character. On the contrary, a cast member playing the role of Peter Pan is going to have a more flamboyant and overly energetic personality and naturally "springy" body action. There's also a significant difference in cast member qualities between those who play characters whose faces are hidden behind a mask and those who don't as well as ones who speak versus ones who don't. Disney doesn't just leave these connections to chance. Why? Because the authenticity of those characters translates directly to the quality of the show Disney is trying to put on, which either reinforces the company's brand or destroys its integrity. Getting these placements right the first time is critical to the brand promise, which is why Disney had Gallup develop assessments that specifically identified prime candidates for each character that roams Disney parks and restaurants. One would expect a tall and muscular young man to play Gaston, but it's equally important that the cast member also have a naturally brash and somewhat egotistical aura about him. In other positions, cast members are moved if they're lacking certain skills. For example, if a cashier fits the Disney personality preferences but struggles counting change, then that person will be reassigned to a different job.[29]

Gallup research indicates that employees who use their talents every day are more engaged and 12.5 percent more productive.[30] If you want to escort your entrepreneurial dream to the marketplace or grow your brand and your top and bottom lines, hire people who will be cheerleaders for your company and its purpose and defend its integrity as if it were their own. Bring in and invest in people who will form an army of innovators, representatives, and sales people who will propel your brand promise. If you aren't using reliable tools to assess talent and then using that knowledge to strategically place your employees in the roles that best fit with their talents and personalities, then you need to board the talent train, and quickly! In addition to using talent assessment tools, leadership expert, Roy West, suggests repeating what your people say verbatim to let them know you are listening and hearing them. They'll reveal their talents and passions in those conversations (especially if you ask the right questions) and you will learn a great deal about them as a person. Figure out what your employees are good at, in what roles and environments they shine, and exactly how they are fulfilled, and set them up for success.

Regularly Recognize the Value of Your Employees

Gallup's research indicates that employees need to be genuinely recognized for their positive contributions weekly, at a minimum.[31] Disney managers regularly praise their cast members, but the company also provides ways for cast members to recognize their peers. Cast members have the ability to recognize each other through the Four Keys Compliment Card and the Recognize Now! internal application. The company is also working on virtual badging as a form of recognition. Guests are able to recognize cast members through specific email addresses, phone numbers, and Twitter handles, such as @WDWToday and @DisneylandToday. Cast members are also recognized through a variety of awards, such as R.A.V.E. excellence in diversity, environmental excellence award, and a variety of individual awards per unit, but a favorite is the Disney Legacy Award, which recognizes excellence in "everyday" performers. Recipients of the Legacy Award are given a special blue name tag to replace the normal white name tags and are recognized at an annual gala banquet. The award, given to only around six hundred recipients system-wide each year, requires exemplary performance in the areas of customer service, support and engagement of fellow employees, and efficiency.[32] It is important that recognition efforts are specific and authentic in the Disney culture, as they reinforce company mission, values, and culture.

It is also critical that managers learn enough to know how their cast members would like to be recognized. Some people are easily embarrassed by public recognition while some revel in it. Other employees find it really important for their family to be there if they are being formally presented with an award. Get to know your employees and ascertain exactly *how* they prefer to be recognized. Disney also has special events and promotions. Dan Cockerell, former VP of Magic Kingdom park at Walt Disney World, initiated an internal marketing initiative called "just say yes" a few years ago in an effort to raise customer satisfaction scores. He did this despite Magic Kingdom Park being at the peak of global theme park popularity. Cast members were empowered to create more magical moments. They were asked to document their most inspiring stories from this endeavor, and managers submitted their top guest service success stories on a weekly basis. Dan, a cast member favorite, personally selected five of those each week, and recognized the units and cast members by telling their stories to their Magic Kingdom peers on his popular weekly podcast. The program was such a hit that they extended the window of the promotion. Dan's dad, Lee, refers to genuine employee recognition as "free fuel" because it costs very little, but everyone gains so much from a manager who simply recognizes his or her employees.[33]

Care About Each Employee as a Person[34]

Consider some of the stories mentioned above, such as the internal guest service provided to cast members in the costuming department. Do the services provided and the elimination of hassle send the message that the company cares about its employees? Of course they do! Former Executive VP of Operations at Walt Disney World, Lee Cockerell, tells several stories about getting to know his employees on a personal level in his book, *Creating Magic: 10 Common Sense Leadership Strategies from a Life at Disney*. He also tells the story about his supervisor, Al Weiss, *expecting* him to go to his granddaughter's recital. After days of fretting about asking Al if he could attend his granddaughter's event, Lee finally sheepishly took the plunge. Weiss's response was that he would have been *mad* if he had found out Lee did not attend![35] Lee said he was always a believer in managing your time in order to be flexible in such circumstances, but that moment made him realize the depth at which he and his supervisors in park operations needed to go to truly show care for their employees. Get to know your people, not only their talents but also their personal lives (or at least as much as they are willing to share). Don't be Ebenezer Scrooge, who didn't have any idea (or care, at the time) that Bob Cratchit's boy, Tim, had a dire health situation until he was forced to know. Encourage a healthy work-life balance and a family-first attitude. Not only is it the right thing to do, you will actually get better productivity out of your employees in the long run if you show them you care and give them the necessary flexibility to balance their lives. If they have positive feelings about their employer and their role, they will be more engaged and more creative.

If you are not sure how effectively you—as an entrepreneur and/or leader—or your people handle work relationships in your organization, you should ask yourself where you fall on the continuum of leader social behavior,[36] and then you should in turn ask other leaders in your company to also critically examine where they fall on the continuum. For example, let's see what this leader social continuum might look like if you were passing an employee in the hallway. This continuum of leader behavior bottoms out at no "hi" or eye contact; moves to eye contact and a quick and relatively obligatory "hi," or maybe even "how's it going," with no pause to actually caringly receive an authentic response; then to a caring and sincere "hi, how are you doing" followed by a quick conversation; then to the occasional longer conversation to really get to know someone; and, finally, to a lunch visit to get out of the office and truly get to know someone on a personal level. Just like Walt got to know the "Jims" and "Sues" of the company, you need to do so too.

Mathews Entrepreneurial Insight: Leadership Failures

I will admit that in my early days as a leader I used to get frustrated when my retail employees would start every fall and winter Monday morning with a ten-minute conversation about the Indianapolis Colts game the day before, and would start other days talking about their kids, grandchildren, spouses, or hobbies. I didn't mind it so much if they did so in brief fashion with customers, but even that grated on me a bit. Sure, there is a time and place for everything, but instead of being annoyed and forging ahead because I was "too busy" working, I've since learned to not only embrace our people using those conversations to build relationships but also that I, too, need to be authentically involved in those conversations on occasion.

At the CliftonStrengths Summit last summer, a United States military team-building facilitator told a story about a talent development and teamwork strengths workshop he conducted for the unit of a general with a reputation for being rather, shall we say, crusty. The facilitator said he expected to kind of go through the motions and just survive because surely this general was into control more than relationships. The trainer said the workshop went fine, though it wasn't spectacular by any means. He had survived but did not expect any earth-shattering results from the group, as the general was awkward and the team seemed uptight and rigid. About a month later, the facilitator was about to cross paths with the general in a hallway of the Pentagon. He anxiously drifted to the opposite side of the hallway from the general's path in hopes of avoiding an awkward encounter. The two passed each other without confrontation or too much discomfort—perfect!

Not so fast—the general quickly did an about-face, grabbed the timid trainer's arm, and proceeded to pull him over to an open spot along the wall. The general was toting an orange briefcase (such briefcases typically contain top secret documents and are never to be opened in public spaces, such as the hallway in which they found themselves). As you are probably already anticipating, the general—of course—begins to open the briefcase normally reserved for super-secret military files. The facilitator has beads of sweat running down his forehead and sideburns at this point. As his neck hairs begin to stand on end, the general pulls out a heavily handled pile of papers from an exercise the facilitator had conducted with his team a month earlier. The exercise, "The Best of Us," uses a sheet of paper to ask four simple questions of each member of the team: 1) You get the best of me when; 2) You get the worst of me when; 3) You can count on me to; and 4) This is what I need from you.[37] Each member of the general's staff had completed the form on the sheet of paper and discussed their responses with a partner during the facilitation. The general proudly told the trainer he was intrigued by the exercise; hence the "well loved" appearance of the stack of completed forms. He had been studying their responses to the prompts every day since the exercise. Despite the general's bristly reputation and the facilitator's assumption that the session was a waste of time for all involved, the general and his team had benefited from the exercise. The trainer reconsidered his preconceptions and assumptions and was reminded that people value your investment in them and the general's team likely knew he cared about them because this probably wasn't the first time he had done something similar to this.

How many theme parks or outdoor events (concerts, sporting, etc.) have you been to where you saw someone standing in the hot sun doing a mundane job and thought to yourself just how awful a job that must be. We've all experienced those situations and thoughts. Disney shows its cast members it cares by providing the little extras. For example, we passed by a very pleasant lady manning the stroller parking area just outside the SeaBase aquarium exhibit at Epcot at Walt Disney World. She was parked under an umbrella just outside the entrance, and she had a water cooler right next to her. This extra care, while not extremely expensive, demonstrated that Disney is serious about the values it espouses and cares for its cast members.

Mathews Family Moment: Keys to the Kingdom Tour

Hands down one of my favorite Disney leadership stories came from Michael, our guide for the Keys to the Kingdom Tour in the Magic Kingdom park at Walt Disney World. Michael very proudly told us about how the park's leader at the time, Dan Cockerell, would randomly pull into the cast member parking lot, which was located far enough away from the park that it required a shuttle just to get to the outer rim of the underground access corridors (called utilidors) of the park. Cockerell would then hand his parking pass, tied to a much more convenient (and cool!) spot inside the park, to a random cast member and proceed to park in the cast member lot and shuttle to the utilidor entry point. This is great leadership on so many levels. First, Dan humbled himself on a regular basis by doing this and other random acts of kindness, such as personally baking and handing out his famous banana (that he dubbed Danana) bread. Second, he sent the distinct message to his cast members that he cared about them and their role perspective. Third, he was intentional about seeing things from their point of view to better understand their mindset and their typical day. This is entrepreneurial in nature, as leaders learn a great deal by stepping into the shoes of their staff and customers, which often leads to process, place, or service innovations.

Encourage Growth and Development in Your Employees[38]

Disney Parks and Resorts provides endless growth opportunities for cast members. First, they provide cast members with opportunities to develop a diverse understanding of the company and operations perspectives by moving them around. You discovered earlier in the chapter that they do this in just about every department—even on the attractions—on a daily basis. In addition, they regularly rotate cast members to different departments and attractions and even completely unrelated jobs. Why? First, this gives cast members a deep understanding of the big picture business model. When cast members understand all roles and functions, each unit (and the organization as a whole) operates as a highly efficient, well-oiled machine. Second, it allows cast members to stay fresh and not get burned out. Third, it gives them an appreciation for the roles other units and their fellow cast members play. Perspective is powerful, and giving cast members plenty of opportunities to learn the perspectives of others and thus widen their own viewpoints is a very empowering gift that generates massive growth. Fourth, the cross-pollination that occurs leads to collaboration and joint solutions, the sharing of solutions that are already working but perhaps trapped in silos, partnerships, and ultimately both incremental and radical innovations. It's not uncommon to engage a cast member in a conversation and quickly learn that he or she has worked several jobs during his or her tenure. We mentioned René Torrico, a Disney Institute trainer, earlier. In more than ten years with the company, he has played a number of roles, such as cast member credit union clerk, marketer, cast member credit union manager, cast member ambassador, and, of course, trainer and facilitator, among others.

Job rotation is a great tool for broadening cast member perspectives at Disney parks and resorts, but the Walt Disney Company also employs other tools that enhance cast member knowledge, skills, and perspectives, such as optional advanced training, additional "library" resources, visits from outside speakers and facilitators, and regular cast member coaching by supervisors, managers, and leaders. We will talk more about these in the growth needs area of employee engagement in the coming pages, as this practice of Leader-Member Exchange (LMX) is a powerful tool for driving engagement and retention.[39]

DISNEY LESSON 23: PROVIDE CHALLENGES AND GROWTH OPPORTUNITIES FOR YOUR EMPLOYEES

Consider how the practices of role and job rotation and providing optional knowledge and perspective expansion lead to insights for entrepreneurs as well as encourage the entrepreneurial mind-set.[40] Perspective is a critical component of entrepreneurship. As an entrepreneur, you can have what you think is the greatest idea ever, but you need to confirm—and more than likely adapt—that idea based on in-depth market feedback, research, and information triangulation efforts.[41] To start the engine of your entrepreneurial dream, you also need to encourage your team to give you feedback on the processes and systems you've put in place. As your team starts to take ownership of your original vision, it also leads to your own people becoming entrepreneurs who are looking for opportunities to innovate and start new business units within your company. How cool is that? You don't have to be the lone entrepreneur (nor should you be)!

Teamwork Engagement Needs[42]

Rich Maloney, a very successful Division I college baseball head coach, always says, "Teamwork makes the dream work." This, one of Rich's favorite sayings, may sound corny, but as one Disney Institute cast member recently told us, Disney has been very successful with corny, but the corny is tied to a higher purpose, so it works. The same could be said of Rich, as the great success of his two programs at Ball State University and the University of Michigan over the last two decades speaks for itself.

Listen to Your Employees and Respect Their Perspectives[43]

Disney understands the power of perspective and human ingenuity better than anyone on the planet. Seeking feedback and ideas from guests and cast members is a significant component of the Disney culture. Thus, it should not surprise us when guests say they are delighted by the atmosphere, attractions, and service levels they encounter at Disney parks and resorts. Ideas, commentary on problems or challenges, and suggestions for improvement are not only listened to, they are actively sought out and engaged with within the Disney Parks and Resorts system. Some leaders and managers get nervous at the thought of supporting a culture of open idea sharing and aggressive vetting, but in the face of this pushback, creativity expert Jeff Stamp stated, "All ideas deserve to be heard, but not all ideas deserve a place in the market."[44] As you might have guessed, Disney obviously doesn't follow through and invest time and financial resources in all problems or ideas, but what the company does really well is intentionally and faithfully show sincere reverence for all problem-finding and idea generation activity within the company. Remember the story about RFID tags in costumes? The idea was implemented on a system-wide basis because Disney was aware of the problems associated with costumes, listened to a Hong Kong Disneyland cast member's idea for a solution, and funded prototyping and proof of concept beta testing. And what's perhaps even more intriguing is that one solution led to other internal customer service improvements in the costuming units at Disney parks and resorts. Successful innovation breeds more innovation because cast members feel empowered to be engaged in problem-solving and opportunity-seeking.

One creativity myth is that ideas always have to be completely novel and original. George Kalogridis, who was VP of Epcot at Walt Disney World at the time, brought a simple merchandise and guest engagement concept back with him from a trip to the Winter Olympics in Nagano, Japan, in 1998. Kalogridis and his team walked away with some great ideas, but one of them would forever change the way Disney did business. They discovered a culture of pin trading at the village and among exhibitors that opened up doors to not only commerce but also communication. The Disney delegation noted that athletes and exhibitors had even developed their own language for pin trading. Kalogridis brought the idea back to Disney World. Disney funded initial art and inventories and successfully launched pin trading at Walt Disney World the following year, selling three million dollars' worth of pins. If you follow Disney at all, you know pin trading has become a cultural phenomenon and a multibillion-dollar business. Beyond that, pin trading is a great way for cast members and guests to engage with one another—a true win-win for Disney. Again, we see how Disney leaders sent George on the research trip and *listened* to what he and his team saw and suggested as a result of that experience. The idea had merit, so the company followed through on proof of concept and implementation. It's worth repeating: pins are now a multibillion-dollar business that further immerses guests and cast members in Disney brands and culture.[45] It's important to note, as we mentioned earlier with regard to training and job rotation, that experiences and exposure to different ways of doing things are important pieces of the idea generation puzzle.[46] Disney regularly sends cast members and leaders to competitor locations, conferences, seminars, and even out-of-industry events, like the Winter Olympics. They do this because it exposes them to new perspectives and generates ideas. Inspiration for ideas can come from a variety of sources, and Disney recognizes and embraces that. Often the best business venture propositions come from adapting someone else's concept or even just a part of it, putting your own spin on it and leveraging your own assets, IP, and core competencies to make it work for you. Disney built on what was but a small part of the Olympic culture, matched it with its vast portfolio of intellectual property, successful Imagineering, and its network of parks and resorts gift shops, and built it into a huge business that added great engagement value to the company beyond just the direct profitability of the pin venture itself. Another concept that was "borrowed" from a competitor was Disney's original FastPass system, which was launched in 1999. Disney wasn't the first kid on the block to offer line reservations, but the company was the first to brand it as its own. It is worth noting that there are some great ideas out there that have never really caught on simply because they were either not tied to a successful operation or were not adequately branded. We discuss the evolution of the FastPass system at Disney parks with regard to customer experience in the next chapter, but it goes without saying that Disney is now several iterations removed from that original concept. They never rest on processes or ideas, as they are constantly looking for a better way to operate. Some would refer to Disney as a "learning organization"[47] because leaders are constantly seeking knowledge and perspective. Disney parks and resorts field ideas in a variety of ways, including cast member surveys, guest surveys, guest observation, anonymous emails, listening posts, roundtables, team meetings, and, most importantly, through manager and cast member coaching relationships and conversations. They close the loop by communicating back to cast members with a program called "You Said, We Listened," which highlights the implementation of cast members ideas—ideas that are often fixes to operational problems.

Another creativity myth is that ideas only come from high-level leaders. If you've been in the parks and ever paused to check out the sidewalk artistry of custodians, you're familiar with the way janitors engage with guests by creating Disney character faces with brooms and water on the pavement. Their work is captivating and impressive, to say the least. This practice originated in Tokyo Disneyland. A custodial cast member, who was an aspiring artist, started creating Disney characters on the sidewalks from fallen flower petals. His supervisor assumed positive intentions and was curious about his talents and positive guest reactions and engagements, so he learned from his custodian. In typical Disney fashion, they institutionalized this practice but added training and swapped flower petals for brooms and buckets of water—items that were readily available to custodians. The rest is history, as this is now common practice across all parks globally.[48] *Disney not only allowed the voice of the custodian to be heard but also invited it to be a valuable part of the company's strategies moving forward.* Success stories of such deep engagement by frontline cast members such as these send incredibly strong messages of inclusion, worth, purpose, and hope to every cast member in literally every role in the organization. The origin story of the water art is just another example of Disney living out the values it so boldly shares with its new cast members.

Just months before his death, Walt was talking to a group of janitors from the third shift as his historian, Bob Thomas, approached him to meet for a preplanned interview. Bob noticed the conversation, so he waited at a nearby table. Walt finished and walked over to Bob, questioning why he would spend his valuable time with janitors. Walt told him that you never know from where or whom the next great idea will come. He intimated that those guys knew how things worked around the parks and had knowledge and perspectives that he and other leaders just did not possess.

Sixty years later, Walt's legacy of respecting all roles and all cast members lived on through Dan Cockerell, former VP of Magic Kingdom park at Walt Disney World. Dan initiated a project to improve processes to handle the massive amounts of trash accumulating in a park that boasted nearly twenty-one million visitors annually.[49] True to the culture and leadership behaviors modeled by Walt, Dan proactively conducted problem-finding sessions with the entire custodial staff of the park. Disney also conducted fact-finding around what was and was not working well for guests, janitors, cast members, and external partners. All parties impacted were involved in the fact-finding discussions and exercises to gain diverse perspectives, and Disney also pulled into the sessions data from trash can and restroom sensors that were part of a Tomorrowland test. The end result was a much more efficient trash management system that resulted in better disbursement of janitors, significantly faster cleanup of spills, and virtual elimination of waste receptacle overflow. These results were made possible because Cockerell and his leadership team humbled themselves and actively sought out the perspectives of frontline employees—including those of union employees—much like Walt had done sixty years prior. From Walt to Dan Cockerell, *this is corporate entrepreneurship in action!*

It would be shortsighted to discuss idea generation and problem-solving at such length without mentioning some caveats. Disney uses the analogy of firefighters, arsonists, and fire marshals to describe problem-solving behavior. One could define problem solvers as "firefighters." However, leaders should be on the lookout for "firefighting arsonists", who enjoy putting out fires so much that they will intentionally start those same fires. This is not a healthy pattern. While this likely happens less at Disney than at other companies, there's little doubt that Disney deals with an overly ambitious cast member on ocassion. "Fire marshals (guardians of the system)," on the other hand, prevent fires, but they also often kill good ideas, which we discuss below. We don't want to overemphasize this point, though, because actively listening to ideas and challenges is certainly better than the alternative. Managers and leaders should ultimately assume good intentions and actively and intentionally listen to understand, reserve judgment, and assume something positive will come out of the idea or suggestion regardless of the likelihood of full adoption or implementation.

> **In large corporations innovation is not a methodology problem, it's a culture problem.**[50]
>
> —Steve Blank

DISNEY LESSON 24: SEEK INPUT FROM AND LISTEN TO YOUR EMPLOYEES—YOU'LL BE GLAD YOU DID

At Disney, seeking information is just a way of life. The company as a whole constantly seeks input, and supervisors have ongoing conversations with their people on a regular basis to keep a finger on the pulse of their team and area of operation. Frontline cast members are in tune with the guests and the day-to-day operations, so they generally know what is best for the company. That is why they get so many good ideas and solutions to problems.

We're convinced the concept of being heard and of value being inherently placed on ideas is central to engagement and, ultimately, business results because people withdraw when they feel like they're not heard. And when they withdraw, they are no longer a vital part of the business model and problem-solving and innovation process. Why do they withdraw? Well, it could be because managers never ask for ideas or for process improvement input or because employees simply think no one is listening, but more than likely there is no feedback or two-way communication on ideas (as in a communication system that responds to and documents ideas) or, worse yet, their ideas are quickly shot down with negative body language (such as eye rolls, looking down, sarcastic smirks, snarky sighs, or annoyed gasps, among others) or killer phrases ("we've never tried that before"; "things are fine how we're doing it now"; "sounds risky"; "the higher-ups will never go for it"; "it's not in the budget"; or "let's form a committee to discuss it," to name just a few).

When employees withdraw, not only does their productivity take a nose-dive but they also quit trying to actively find opportunities and solve problems and challenges. In other words, they simply go through the motions and collect a paycheck. Work life becomes a J-O-B to them, and you lose the great power of the mind and the passion associated with overcoming challenges and deep engagement with the purpose of the company. You simply cannot afford to let this happen. An organization full of teammates who are both individually and collectively solving problems and seeking opportunities in perpetuity is a force so strong it can't be stopped. If ideas are being directly or indirectly silenced in your organization, you have to—*you must*—find a way to course correct *right now*. Your organization's future—for profit or nonprofit—depends on it. As we mentioned earlier, engagement expert Roy West always reminds us to repeat verbatim what our employees are saying. When you do this, not only are you *truly* hearing what they are saying but they also know you are really listening.

Mathews Entrepreneurial Insight: Dylan Andreason

Whenever I think of the power of slowing down and simply listening to new ideas, I'm reminded of Dylan Andreason, a self-described "pretty green" twenty-something assistant manager who was a participant in one of our retail training programs this past year. He proudly told the class and facilitator (me!) about his recent proposal of a unique Instagram marketing campaign that aimed to engage employees and customers. His boss not only listened but also gave him a budget and full authority for and leadership of the project. Dylan shared the early successes of the six-month-old project with a huge smile on his face and pride in his voice and said how much he appreciated his manager listening to and considering his idea. He even emphasized getting the green light to launch it was just a bonus! What does that say about the importance of being heard? I can assure you of this—Dylan is an engaged employee who respects his boss and will continue to come up with ideas that support the mission of his company. Authentic dialogue with your employees *will* lead to a wealth of ideas. And nestled in that mountain of ideas are some real gems.

Two other myths that often plague organizations are that all ideas must make or save money and that new ideas must be big. As Karl Holz, President of New Vacation Operations & Disney Cruise Line, so "eloquently" articulated, "Sacred cows make the best burgers." Disney Cruise Line lived this saying when they reinvented the views of inner cabins. Under the category of no idea is too small or insignificant comes the story of the birth of the Mickey Spam Musubi at Disney's Aulani Resort in Hawaii. The snack was designed by an Aulani chef to honor local culinary traditions and is made from simple ingredients: sticky rice, soy sauce, seaweed, and, of course, Spam.[51] The treat is so popular the resort cannot keep it in stock. Further, its success led to another Aulani exclusive snack, the Tuna Poke with Avocado Mousse.[52] These huge successes that started as novel ideas created by world-class chefs are a great reminder that great ideas often have humble beginnings. The Tuna Poke is also a wonderful indication that embracing ideas leads to even more ideas.

How does such a large corporation manage the unimaginable number of ideas, problems, and requests that must bubble up every year? Let's face it, the number of fully or partially discarded ideas heavily outweighs the number of ideas that move forward in some fashion. As you likely suspected, yes, Disney has a process for managing the complicated nature of creativity. Each unit has an innovation budget. This budget enables managers to encourage idea sharing, problem-solving, and opportunity-finding. In other words, it reinforces the concepts we have outlined in this chapter. The budget is discretionary and gives managers and their teams the ability to decide what is most important and to act quickly. Thus, they are encouraged and empowered to fix pressing problems right away. They can also conserve those funds by teaming with other units when they are experiencing similar or even nearly identical problems. For ideas and new ventures that require capital beyond the modest discretionary innovation budget, teams can submit their "blue sky" requests for the year. This forces teams to consider what is most important to them and to do some vetting of ideas prior to requesting resources. This convergence of ideas requires teams to act entrepreneurially, such as conducting research on their ideas, estimating return on investment, confirming connection to company purpose, and pitching a venture proposal. A special committee then evaluates the proposals, considering mission impact, scope of the project, and return on investment. They also sort the proposals, looking for common themes. The common themes lead to efficient problem-solving, but, again, they also encourage managers and their teams to collaborate with other units prior to submissions. If two units can team up on a blue sky request, they've already done some of the work for the committee and likely have a stronger case. The committee either gives the project a green light or encourages the team to keep improving the proposal. Sometimes a caution flag comes up due to budget constraints, the scope of the project being too large or incongruent with other projects, or the committee already funding a number of projects from similar areas (i.e., attractions). This systematic approach to innovation has significant implications for company culture: It establishes a clear path to the expression, funding, and implementation of ideas. It allows everyone in the entire company to be heard. It places value on research, preparation, and stewardship. And finally, it encourages healthy competition inside the company.

In his book, *The Imagineering Process: Using the Disney Theme Park Design Process to Bring Your Creative Ideas to Life*, Louis Prosperi outlines in detail how Disney brings these new ideas to life. After the idea vetting process described above, Imagineering gets involved in the implementation of the selected projects by leading the following stages of the innovation process: concept development, design, construction, and epilogue (openings, evaluations, and show quality standards). In the concept development phase, the accepted idea is "more fully fleshed out" so as to provide enough detail regarding design and construction needs. The design phase brings in professionals to create specific documents (i.e., architectural drawings) with the goal of providing an implementation plan. Next is the construction phase, which tangibly brings the physical demands of the project to fruition. Through each phase, models[53] and storyboarding[54] are powerful tools used to provide visual representations and test the concept. Finally, Prosperi describes the epilogue phase as Disney's quest to continue making things better—even *after* opening. Disney constantly seeks feedback from guests, cast members, vendors, and partners, using cast member previews, soft openings, grand openings, and ongoing operations as various data points.[55] Another unique approach Disney takes is to heavily involve operational personnel in the Imagineering process. Disney has worked diligently to integrate operations and Imagineering through specific processes, social events, and design meetings. They work hard on this relationship in order to take advantage of the perspectives and talents of each of the units, knowing the best results only come from coordinated efforts.[56] These two critical components—building multifunctional entrepreneurial teams and getting projects, innovations, and businesses in the hands of teams of builders—drive actual results. Ideas without follow-through don't mean much and only represent the creation side of the entrepreneurial equation.[57]

Two other important concepts come out of Disney's penchant for innovaton. First, Walt saw Imagineering as a combination of engineering (technical expertise) and imagination (creativity). Second, he received advice while developing Disneyland to keep as much of the creativity in-house as possible, as his people would know the operation the best. He also received advice regarding how to fix problems, get better at what they were already doing, and create new experiences. Sure, seeking the input of outsiders is important too, but that advice given to Walt solidified the Imagineering arm of Disney then (Walter Elias Disney Enterprises; WED) and now (Walt Disney Imagineering; WDI).[58] Your people are your best bet for innovation—Disney is the living laboratory of proof of this concept.

As previously mentioned in Chapter Five, the 1970s and early 1980s were a very quiet period for the Walt Disney Company. While Walt and Roy Disney's family and company values were maintained, the company lost its innovative edge and, at best, merely hung on to its position in the market. For all his challenges—especially later in his tenure—Eisner's arrival, creative genius, and aggressive risk-taking, as we articulated in Chapter Five, revived Disney's entrepreneurial spirit. Current Disney executives are, without question, very appreciative of the parks and resorts infrastructure he built up during his tenure.

Are you suppressing the power of human ingenuity that exists in your organization or are you encouraging the active participation of open idea exploration? What if your most significant challenge led to years of no sleep, lost revenue, and declining productivity, and then you found out the solution to the problem was not being communicated by a frontline employee because she thought her ideas did not matter? When you look at it that way, it seems more like destructive and reckless behavior than an innocent misunderstanding. The best source of innovation comes from your people and your customers, not consultants (and often not executives or managers either). Further, problem-solving, opportunity-finding, and idea generation are not reserved for executives or other high-level leaders but rather should be at the very core of the culture of the entire organization. We implore you to use consultants as trained problem-solving facilitators instead of as doctors prescribing fixes for your company from the outside, looking in. We facilitate many sessions like this annually, and it's not uncommon to see companies completely transformed by the process. You will be astonished by the results of empowering key stakeholders to uncover the facts, reframe the problems, ideate and select solutions, and take responsibility for implementing those new ventures.[59]

Hiring

The same Disney cast member who told us Disney made a living from being corny also shared a hiring story with us that would shock a lot of people. An experienced professional went through a series of interviews to join the Disneyland legal team. He had worked his way through several interviews with top leaders; they all liked him a lot and recommended he be made an offer to join the team. The last interviewer, a seasoned leader of more than two decades at Disneyland, had the same experience during his time with the candidate until he mentioned something—almost just in passing, yet very intentionally—about it being a tradition for every Anaheim cast member to work on Christmas Day. The entire resort system—Disneyland Park, Disney California Adventure Park, all on-site resort hotels, and Downtown Disney—operate at full capacity on that holiday. The interviewee mentioned he wasn't sure that would work for him. The veteran interviewer again pursued the topic from a different angle, trying to explain the tradition of cast members teaming up to meet the demand of the busy day, but the potential cast member again indicated he had no plans to work on Christmas Day. Just like the other six interviews prior to this one, the interview went well and ended very pleasantly, but the final leader left the meeting wrestling with whether or not the candidate would fit in with the company culture. If you're thinking they must be crazy at Disney, you're not alone. The cast member who told the story could see the perplexed look in our eyes, and reiterated just how important togetherness and teamwork are at Disneyland. While you may think it's harsh that this candidate—a professional who nonetheless would have had an office job if hired—was essentially being pressured into working Christmas Day, she said it spoke to a bigger red flag, as the candidate was not willing to embrace the tradition, understand the need, and get in the trenches with his teammates. He just wasn't a cultural fit. Was he likeable? Absolutely. So be careful about hiring people you like just because they are similar to you. Oh, and just in case you're curious, they indeed did NOT hire the candidate.

Mathews Family Moment: The Hotel Airport Shuttle

We live about seventy-five minutes from the Indianapolis International Airport, so when the kids are with us, we typically stay at a hotel near the airport the night before early morning flights. We like the Hilton Garden Inn because it provides a package that includes free parking the duration of your trip as well as a reliable shuttle to and from the airport. We've had the pleasure of having Chris as our shuttle driver the last several times. I say this because Chris has a true servant's heart, does a great job, and truly loves what she does. Just the fact that we know her name speaks volumes about how Julie and I feel about her work. I vividly remember the first time she insisted on loading all of our bags onto the bus. My golf bag wasn't the only heavy one, but it was full, and it tipped the scales at 49.8 pounds at the ticket counter at Southwest. I felt bad the entire shuttle ride and tried to intervene when she attempted to unload our bags at the airport, but Chris again insisted that it was her job. Sadly, we are one of the few families who seem to tip in those situations, but it really doesn't seem to bother Chris, as she loves her job and loves serving people. As we dragged our bags to the Southwest (another great service provider!) counter, it occurred to me that I needed to *let* Chris do her thing. She was fulfilled when she was given free rein to serve other people, and on subsequent trips she has since told us she knows traveling can be stressful—especially with children—and she wants people to get off to a good start on their vacations or business trips. We are fortunate when we get to interact with the Chris's of the world, aren't we? I have no idea whether or not the manager at the Hilton Garden Inn got lucky when he or she hired Chris, but nonetheless, Chris is a great representative of that hotel, and she alone keeps us from even considering different preflight accommodations. Chris demonstrates that Disney caliber service is possible in environments far-removed from a theme park.

Almost all companies get the hiring function dead wrong. Even though leadership experts like Jim Collins stress the extreme importance of getting the right people on the bus,[60] even well-intentioned organizations with good leadership often miss the mark. Why? How does this happen? There are literally dozens of efficient hiring tools, surveys, and capable hiring managers out there, so it almost seems unacceptable to botch this critical function.

While most companies continue to make the same mistake over and over again (all the while expecting different results) by focusing on the end of the road—job skills to do a specific task only—Disney reverses the equation. Some would say this is a controversial practice, but Disney hires personality. They look beyond the resume, find creative ways to ask interview questions, and ultimately select generally extroverted people who have a heart for service. We love the "I am Disney" recruiting campaign they ran in recent years because the slogans, videos, and photos showed potential cast members what their role looked like and how important creating happiness is. The spots also used and reinforced Disney storytelling to intimate exactly what they were seeking in future cast members. For example, a bus driver was shown bending over talking to a young girl in a princess outfit, and the text overlay states, "To some I'm a bus driver, to this princess, I'm her coachman."[61] It doesn't take an HR expert to know this ad is most likely to attract someone who is inclined to service and is likely to embrace the Disney way and easily assimilate into Disney culture. Disney hires happy, helpful, kind people who are flexible and generally pay attention to detail. By hiring for cultural fit, they know employees are much more likely to be engaged from day one.

Disney leaders are confident they can and will train a new hire in specific job skills and knowledge after they've hired the right person and properly onboarded them into the company's traditions, service expectations, and culture. After all, those are the only people who can and will consistently deliver on both the internal and external brand promises of Disney Parks and Resorts. Do they swing and miss? Sure. But they are intentional when it comes to hiring for cultural fit and training for performance, so they get it right a lot more often than not. And as previously mentioned, the ones who slip through the cracks in the interview process almost always very quickly self-select out of the company because they realize they are not a fit. This is because a culture of engagement, friendliness, and service essentially scares them away. You can easily find many social media posts from short-stay cast members who intimated that while they loved being served as a paying customer in the parks, they struggled to identify with the whole happiness and magic mantra all the time as a cast member. Is it really any surprise they didn't last long at the happiest, most magical place on earth? The others either find a backstage niche or get coached up or are released from their duties (in Disney terms, they are asked to find their happiness elsewhere).

DISNEY LESSON 25: THE IMPORTANCE OF HIRING CANNOT BE UNDERSTATED; WHO YOU HIRE BECOMES WHO YOU ARE AS AN ORGANIZATION

Consider the why of these hiring practices. Disney is very intentionally supporting the customer service- and experience-based mission of the company by hiring people who can consistently and excellently deliver it. While other companies focus on specific job skills and financial results, Disney focuses on sustainable quality service and customer experience, and the results speak for themselves. Hiring is an opportunity-driven function. You're either advancing or systematically destroying your purpose based on who you hire and their fit into the company's culture. Don't hastily settle for job skills over purposeful fit if you want to pursue your entrepreneurial vision with excellence!

Help Your Employees See Their Importance[62]

We've discussed purpose at length already, but it's worth reiterating how tying all roles to the mission—a worthy and simple mission of creating happiness at that—of the company is at the heart of Disney's success. Cast members feel their job is tied to a greater purpose and that they play a vital role in that purpose. As we've outlined in this chapter, Disney Parks and Resorts constantly reinforces the value of each and every job and person through the context of tradition and heritage. They accomplish this through intensive training, storytelling, actively listening to all cast member ideas, caring for cast members as people, providing opportunities to use and grow one's talents through intentional placement and coaching, providing opportunities for growth, and encouraging new perspectives through job rotation, responsibility, and accountability. It's worth noting that contemporary research indicates that millennials place extreme importance on their work being connected to a worthy mission.[63] So, if you feel like you're having trouble connecting with your younger employees, it could be that you're missing the mark on articulating, executing, communicating, and relating the value of the organization's mission to every role and person in the company.

We will discuss storytelling and the incredible details put into the park and resort environments in Chapter Seven, but some details are so minute that they are almost more purposeful in engaging cast members than wowing guests. For example, Disney encourages Imagineers to embed their "signatures" in structures they design and build. The average guest will never see these clues, which tell a story about the Imagineer's journey, but they provide a sense of ownership, closure to the project, and pride in how an Imagineer's role on a given project interfaces with the purpose of creating happiness.

Help Your Employees Feel Proud of Their Team's Work[64]

After new cast members complete their initial training, they are brought into Epcot at Walt Disney World to begin their first official day "on stage" prior to the park opening. In Epcot, all of the new cast members are ushered to an area just inside the main admission gate, where they observe and begin to line up on the walkway, facing inward around a large circle made of pavers. This circle is a visual identifier of the actual geographic center of the entire Walt Disney World property. Unbeknownst to the new cast members, the guests awaiting entry to the park are told that just inside the gates are brand new cast members beginning their first day, and the guests are encouraged to recognize the newly minted cast members with cheers and clapping as they make their way inside the park. Mere minutes before the park opens, the new cast members are asked to turn around and face outward around the circle. As the park opens, guests begin to flood in and the new cast members are welcomed and cheered by the guests to commemorate their first day. The paradox is powerful, as this will be the only "curtain call" that cast members will receive during their time performing for the guests they will encounter each day inside the various parks. This experience serves as the unparalleled welcome provided by Walt Disney World to its newest employees.

Between the Traditions course and rituals like the one described above, Disney makes employees feel special and proud of what they and their fellow cast members do every day. They also offer special cast member events in the parks that allow cast members to experience an evening of happiness and magic as a guest. It demonstrates that all cast members are committed to providing unified excellence in guest service and experience. The personal time in the parks helps them see the business model through the eyes of the guest. It also serves as an unofficial army of "secret shoppers" for the company.

Are your employees proud to work for your organization? Is there a common bond among your team? How can you encourage a sense of unity, togetherness, and pride in the mission you are working so hard to accomplish?

> Words stick to you, and your words stick to others. Words spoken over you are sticky. Words create thought, and thought creates culture. Words drive creativity, and what you name you have authority over. Your words work; your words have power.[65]
>
> —*Joey Salinas, Pastor, Sunrise Campus,*
> *Phoenix Church for the Nations*

Common Language

Before we dive into this important concept, we caution you not to dismiss this topic. What business language do you speak? Does it match your purpose, shared values, and goals? Do you even use a common language in your organization? At Disney Parks and Resorts, the Disney language is not only real and readily used, it strongly reinforces the purpose and values of the company. We've already introduced several key words of this language, such as *guest, cast member, role, magic, happiness, show, fantasy, fairytale, costumes, onstage, and backstage,* but there are certainly others. Words such as guest, happiness, magic, and fantasy point directly to the customer experience while show, costume, onstage, backstage, and cast member describe the how of that experience. Other popular phrases and uses of words include acronyms for the many functions and locations of Disney parks and resorts, code words for challenges that don't fit the Disney fairytale story (such as "protein spill" for someone vomiting), and terms like immersive, escape from reality, mousekeeping (instead of housekeeping for the hotels), and Imagineering (instead of engineering), among others. This common language constantly reinforces the storytelling and purpose of the "creating happiness" culture of the company and is a creative driver of the success of Disney parks and resorts.

In our Institute for Entrepreneurship and Free Enterprise at Ball State University, we communicate using two key impactful languages. First, we use the CliftonStrengths assessment[66] and engagement[67] languages to understand each other's talents, perspectives, and key behaviors that promote role engagement and ultimately drive personal fulfillment. This is a helpful language because it allows us to understand ourselves and each other in deep and practical ways. Common words and phrases in the StrengthsFinder language include *psychological talent, perspective, fulfillment, conflict clues, flow, and "the how."* Everyone in our office—and those who take advantage of our services and training—understands these words and what they mean, which essentially boils down to understanding perspective and developing and operating in ways that are the most productive and personally fulfilling. We also use problem-solving language,[68] which is helpful in understanding functional perspectives and creating a safe and open environment for constant idea flow. Common words and phrases include *"just diverging here," problem-finding, reframe, converge, idea flow, scaffolding, building, trust, fact-finding, "what's stopping us," and "how might we?"* These phrases go a long way toward reducing idea stoppers and encouraging the reframing of challenges and both individual and team idea flow. For instance, "how might we?" is a great phrase for taking the pressure off immediate action or implementation. It signals to all involved that we are simply exploring an idea or possible solution and not trying to solve the world's problems at the moment, but perhaps even more importantly, it is aspirational. We start many conversations with "just diverging here," which signals to everyone involved in the conversation that we are merely tossing an idea into the air to start a discussion. It's a wonderful way to disarm those involved and encourage open dialogue. "What's stopping us?" is a great way to transition to aspirational and solution-inducing language, leading teams away from excuses and toward fact-finding and creativity. Again, both everyone on our team and those with which we regularly work understand and use this language. We can assure you a common language goes a long way toward team building and innovation.

DISNEY LESSON 26: DEVELOPING A COMMON LANGUAGE MAY BE ONE OF THE MOST IMPORTANT THINGS YOU EVER DO

Language makes a difference! It is a constant reminder and encouragement to steer your efforts toward a common purpose and shared values. Disney's common language keeps everyone on the mission of creating premium family entertainment through the medium of show. Language creates a common bond where coaching and leadership trump just managing people. How can you start to work into your culture a common language that reinforces what you aspire to be? We urge you not to cast this strategy aside as a corny Disney-ism. If you want people to catch onto and help you implement your entrepreneurial dream, then you have to give them ways to attach themselves to that dream, and language is a great way to do so.

Give Employees the Authority to Make Decisions

As discussed in stories throughout this chapter and the next, Disney empowers its cast members to create happiness and make magic on an ongoing basis. It's just ingrained in the company's culture. *It's what they do.* Employees who know their role and are prepared to be confident in their role are proud of their contribution to the mission. It leads to engaged employees, quick decisions, and seamless experiences for the guests.

Encourage an Environment of Trust[69]

Everything we have discussed so far points to trust. Disney cast members trust their supervisors and each other because ideas are openly shared, there is an extreme importance placed on service and care, everyone is trained and prepared to perform their functions at a level of excellence, and cast members are given responsibility and held accountable to expected behaviors and results. Corporate and localized communication channels are regularly used to keep cast members up to date on decisions, changes, and successes. In the absence of relationship, mistrust runs rampant and employees make decisions for personal gain, but at Disney, manager-to-cast-member coaching relationships lead to personal care and trust. Employees need to know there are people they can trust, particularly when they are encountering difficulties. If there is a lack of trust in your organization, you need to figure out why and institute ways to establish trust.

Growth Engagement Needs

Review Your Employee's Contributions and Progress[70]

Most companies and nonprofits conduct semiannual or annual employee reviews (this is even true of Disney). While those reviews are a good idea, they don't always work. This is because it is very difficult to evaluate six or twelve months of work in one form or one sitting, and most employees feel their reviews are not done in a fair manner.[71] This is why Disney's emphasis on coaching works so well. Managers have relationships with their cast members, and they are able to quickly give them both positive and constructive feedback on a daily basis. Disney supervisors are always willing to be a resource for their cast members, and they often share knowledge and resources with them that might sometimes be protected in organizations where leaders are more interested in self-preservation. Managers also have to be willing to hold their team accountable on a regular basis; otherwise, due to blowups, the trust mentioned above can quickly deteriorate. At Disney, emotional intelligence[72] is an expectation of managers. They are trained to keep their emotions and egos in check because compromising trust weakens the company values of service and happiness.[73]

Challenge Your Employees With Opportunities to Learn and Grow[74]

We've given examples throughout this chapter of how Disney provides its cast members with opportunities to grow and stretch. An additional approach Disney Parks and Resorts has adopted in recent years is the proprietor model. Instead of restaurants in a given park falling under geographical departments, they now report up the restaurant chain of command, which ultimately reports to the park VP. This allows for regional, categorical, and vertical accountability. For example, each chef, restaurant manager, and retail manager is treated as a proprietor, and each is responsible for strategies, guest satisfaction scores, and business results that are consistent with Disney's mission and expectations. All have more independence to work with other units and run their own business, but they are also held accountable to service expectations and results. This is a great system because it encourages entrepreneurial behavior within the benefits of a proven system. Even the hot dog stand, churro cart, and margarita shack have their own sets of financials and customer experience ratings, which allows for good stewardship and allocation of human, physical, and financial assets. The consumer research and numbers will also provide clues as to whether guest satisfaction issues are related to Disney issues, such as location, theming, and physical space, or to leadership issues, such as service, friendliness, and quality. As one finance person at Disney World told us, the financials don't lie—the market speaks through the income statement of a given restaurant or gift shop.

Lee Cockerell, who left an indelible mark on the entire Disney Parks and Resorts system, was a firm believer in giving cast members small challenges based on their talents and interests, and then increasing the level of those challenges as they grew their skill sets, developed their talents, and increased their confidence.[75] Disney also provides cast members with an enormous "library" of both physical and online resources to grow themselves, their impact, and ultimately their career. Over the years, we've met many executives in the company who started as hourly workers. How did they do it? First, they worked hard and made decisions with great integrity. They credited much of their success to always accepting new, difficult assignments that challenged them to learn and grow. However, they didn't take on these tasks alone. Senior leadership mentored their development on these difficult assignments. A common piece of advice we were given was, if you want to rise to senior leadership, look for those assignments other people are afraid to take. These executives are a great example of what integrity, hard work, problem-solving, a diverse perspective, and seizing opportunities can lead to, especially when you work for a company that values its people as much as Disney.

Wil Davis, who cofounded and served as the CEO and Chairman of Systems LLC—the leader in collections support software—for over two decades, is a master of helping employees and associates grow. He calls it the *stewardship of people cycle*, where, as a leader, you prepare your people for their role, provide opportunities that match their skills and talents, give them the authority to lead the project, and hold employees accountable to as well as reward them for the results.[76] John Maxwell refers to this as Level 4 (development of people) and Level 5 (long-term organization-wide impact: Pinnacle leadership)[77] while Jim Collins calls this level of engagement and investment Level 5 (commitment to company culture and others).[78]

Engaged employees will use their human ingenuity for the good of the organization. They will use their heightened concern and awareness to generate ideas to constantly improve and promote the cause of their company. There is no greater tool in our box or stronger asset on our balance sheet than our people. Are you tapping into the incredible human ingenuity of your people by doing everything you can to engage them? As a Disney executive shared with us, organizational vibrancy is the most important thing you can have. As an entrepreneur, if you have to do it all yourself, you're never going to get there. You have to rely on your people to get you there. You have to trust others with your dream. Exemplary employee engagement is achievable, but your leaders and managers will need some training and coaching to get there. Because of this, we highly recommend you work with Gallup to elevate your employee engagement efforts[79] and consider attending Disney Institute sessions on service and employee engagement.[80]

Leadership: The Key to Engagement and Business Results

If you were wondering, yes, all four levels of employee engagement needs are interconnected and build on each other. Leaders need to be cognizant of how these principles fit together. For instance, how can employees possibly use their talents or feel like they're a part of something special—or provide ideas—if they don't even know what is required of them in their everyday job? When you create an environment of engagement, you are inviting employees to be an integral part of your entrepreneurial dream and vision. You are actually *sharing* your dream with them and giving them the authority to take ownership of it too.

The practices outlined in this chapter that drive engagement are the result of deliberate and intentional execution of strategy by engaged and experienced leaders who are completely sold on the brand promise of the company. Disney executives and managers are expected to constantly reinforce the mission and how it ties to decisions and roles, and they're also expected to walk the Disney talk. You'll never see an executive or team leader walk past a piece of trash on the ground because that would signify that they don't really mean what they say. It's also commonplace to see executives and leaders at Walt Disney World or Disneyland trading pins with a guest, helping a frazzled single parent situate a bag of merchandise under an already packed stroller, working a frontline job on a peak day, or assisting a confused guest with a park map. These actions model the Disney way and demonstrate humility and openness, signaling they are a part of the team just like any other cast member. Lee Cockerell wrote that executives and leaders were expected to spend roughly 70 percent of their time engaged with their people, teaching and coaching them, and modeling expected behaviors.[81] This is a complete reversal (at best) of expected time allotment for typical leadership and management jobs in corporate America, where most lead through a position of command and title.

Chaordic Tension

Order. For some, the processes, rules, and systems that bring order cause angst and frustration. On the other hand, conscientious people love order. They thrive in a predictable world that highly values analytics, standards, pragmatism, and calmness. Chaos. Others function best when the world around them is unpredictable and adventurous. They are not bothered by unclear instructions or a lack of preplanning. Even the most creative of entrepreneurs, if they are going to enjoy success, at some point realize they have to systematize their vision to make it come to life. But what happens when the very systems that allow you to scale your business also become the chains that keep your venture from being the very best it can be, or worse yet, actually cause it to lose ground to more innovative competitors or emerging alternatives available to the customer? There's

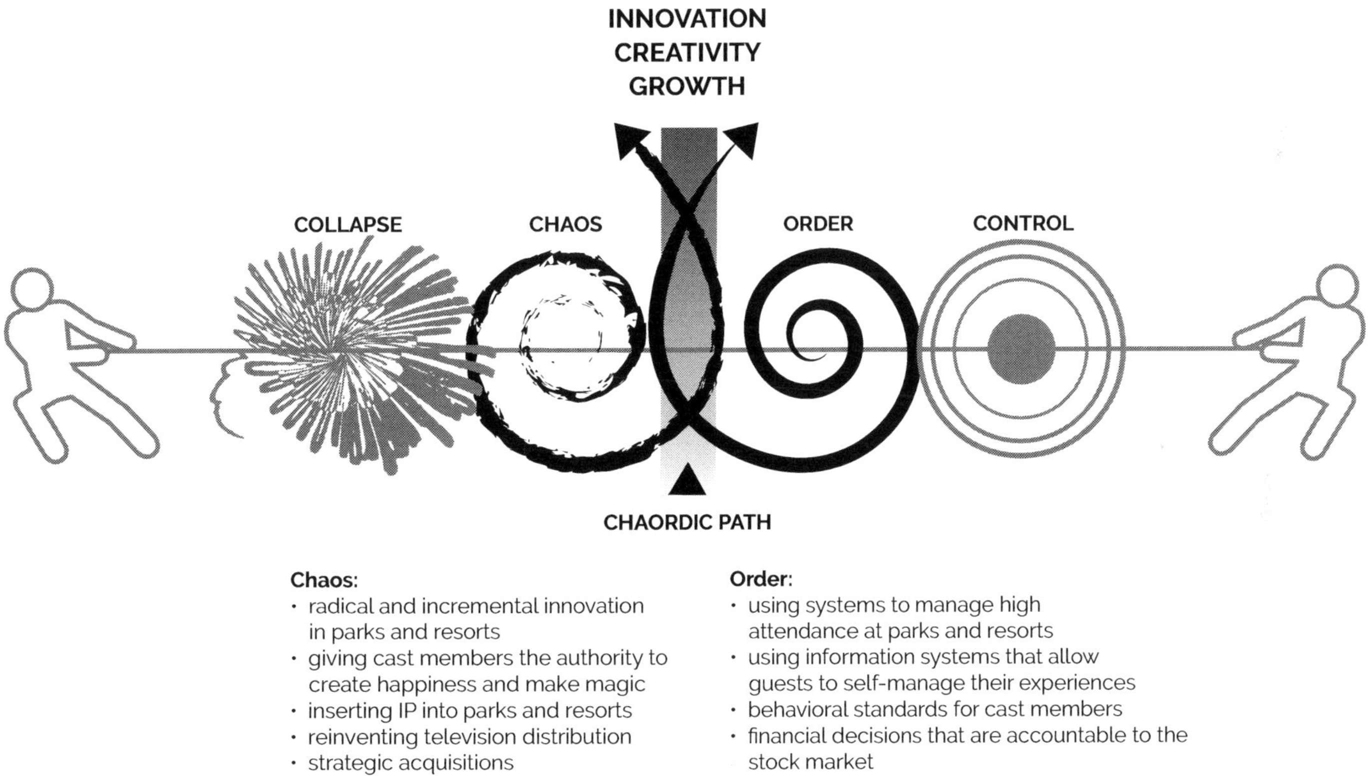

INNOVATION
CREATIVITY
GROWTH

COLLAPSE CHAOS ORDER CONTROL

CHAORDIC PATH

Chaos:
- radical and incremental innovation in parks and resorts
- giving cast members the authority to create happiness and make magic
- inserting IP into parks and resorts
- reinventing television distribution
- strategic acquisitions

Order:
- using systems to manage high attendance at parks and resorts
- using information systems that allow guests to self-manage their experiences
- behavioral standards for cast members
- financial decisions that are accountable to the stock market

FIGURE 6.2 Leading Chaordic Tension at Disney

no doubt standards and systems bring order to chaotic entrepreneurial ventures, but they also slowly take away the edge those ventures once had. This intriguing paradox causes what can become a toxic tug of war, if not handled with care. Think about how this plays out in our everyday lives. We crave and demand systems and consistency. Thus, systems and processes are created and implemented. We then complain about those systems and even exit them if they become too cumbersome. Good companies proactively listen and react, but they don't over-react. Great companies change processes and forge new paths, while bad companies die. This is why we endure so much anguish over government policies and processes. Without market pressures, there is little incentive to fix what ails them. After working with the Sante Fe Institute, founder and original CEO of Visa, Dee Hock, named this push and pull between chaos and order *chaordic tension.*[82]

Transformational leadership lives and thrives in the rough seas of chaordic tension, acting as a breakwater that keeps the ship sailing smoothly. It also simultaneously encourages the intentional and necessary disruption of the status quo. Leading firms through chaordic tension is a rigorous and never-ending challenge for those who desire sustainable success because the keepers of the system, such as accountants, lawyers, bureaucrats, and micromanagers, will fight hard to maintain order and often even oppress creativity and the questioning of the status quo. Their role is purposeful, but organizations that rely too heavily on optimization don't last forever. Why? Because someone else *will* come along with an untainted view of the market and the industry and the nimble feet of a player coming into the game with fresh legs. Processes got them there, but they are far from infallible. On the contrary, if their leader allows it, idea generators—the extreme creatives—are very often willing to live eternally in a sea of ideas and ambiguity. This tug of war between the machine and innovation is a critical dynamic for all sustainable organizations. Both are important. So how do good leaders navigate this messy proposition? Entrepreneurial leaders are all about people because people are their best and most enduring asset. As we've illustrated in this chapter, they remove hassles for both employees and customers. They listen and create safe cultures because they keep their emotions and egos in control. Great leaders learn from their employees and customers. They set their employees up for success and share with them as much knowledge and information as possible. They encourage growth through training, resources, job rotation, mentoring, and opportunities to stretch themselves and show their worth. They are humble enough to study competitors and world-class companies and operators. Exceptional leaders encourage freedom and flexibility and implore their people to be themselves while also maintaining the integrity of their offerings by exercising responsibility and clear expectations. Ultimately, entrepreneurial leaders honor and encourage *both* order and opportunity-seeking behavior.

Systems can and should be changed to keep up with—and hopefully ahead of—evolving needs and changes in the marketplace. It's essentially impossible to have employee engagement without a great deal of care put into balancing these two adversaries. But it's not for the faint of heart. Chaordic tension is uncomfortable, and no leader will manage it perfectly. Ironically, Dee Hock— even as cognizant of the imperative to live in the middle of chaos and order as he was—wasn't completely able to succeed, as Mastercard, a more crafty upstart in the late '90s, was able to sprint past Visa in terms of adoption rates and market acceptance. We've outlined the secret sauce for entrepreneurial leadership in this chapter, but in simple terms, Disney leaders demonstrate the balance of juggling the hard work of chaordic tension every day. Consider the role financial leaders at Disney Parks and Resorts play. Their job is to steward resources and be critical of new projects, yet if they are too cautious, the company fails to leverage opportunities before it, as happened in the post-Walt and Roy era. Remember Eisner's development of Disney's home video business? Today's financial leaders at Disney do an excellent job of balancing the role of scrutinizing expenditures while also being enthusiastic and supportive of new ventures within the company. Their ability to see the vision and value of scrutiny and processes while at the same time valuing innovation is the true recipe for enduring success. How these leaders balance chaordic tension in such eloquent fashion is a great anecdotal microcosm of why Disney is such an innovative machine. Did you catch that? "Innovative" and "machine" are paradoxical terms. Disney is as disciplined a company as you will ever encounter, yet it celebrates ideas and innovation as well as any large corporation out there. Clinical psychologist Jordan Peterson urges people to get disciplined while also actually seeking some chaos to keep growing as a person or organization.[83]

DISNEY LESSON 27: LEADERS AND THEIR ABILITY TO MANAGE CHAORDIC TENSION WILL MAKE OR BREAK YOUR ORGANIZATION

The true Disney difference lies in the ability of its leadership—across the company—to calm the sea of chaordic tension while also creating a safe environment that allows cast members to flourish. Patrick Lencione said that culture is either a multiplier or a diminisher; there is no in between.[84] Human ingenuity—through an entrepreneurial mind-set—is what drives entrepreneurial behavior and innovation. Disney constantly seeks feedback and ideas from its cast members through a variety of mediums, from surveys to ongoing coaching relationships. Disney's cast members are so in tune with their purpose of serving each guest with excellence that it empowers them to be creative in meeting that calling.

Think of all the companies that slowly wilted and died over time simply because order was maintained at the expense of exploring chaos—companies like Blockbuster Video, Woolworth, Borders, and so on. We are in a unique time in which many companies and industries—Sears, JCPenny, BlackBerry, network and cable television, and traditional retail, among others—are dying right before our eyes. Disney works diligently every day in everything it does to create a culture that values both order and chaos. Leading this tension takes humility but also discipline, responsibility, and accountability.

Humility and Leveraging Human Intellect

Humility is a key ingredient to Disney's success because when you admit you don't have all the answers, you are giving your people *permission* to—and are actually encouraging them to—bring their own ideas and ingenuity to the table. Further, when leaders *model* desired behavior, such as proactively looking for imperfections and picking up trash, cast members follow suit. Have you ever noticed a manager walking around a Disney park with a trash picker? No cast member wants trash on the ground at Disney, but it is just as important for leaders to demonstrate the habit of noticing and picking up debris while on the property. Walt Disney's legacy led directly to Dan Cockerell's respect and appreciation for the role of the custodian. As leaders, we have to know there is always a better way, and we need a broad range and depth of perspectives to find it.

Being in the middle of the action helps managers and leaders be observers, seeking to better understand each role, process, and system from the point of view of cast members, vendors, partners, and guests. It also allows them to ask questions and seek input regarding areas of hassle for each of the groups mentioned above. Leaders should be asking how they can better serve each of these constituents and where the imperfections exist in the business model. What do you typically see at the front of a retail store, professional office, restaurant, or even lobby to the main office of a department? You will almost always see some sort of suggestion box. While suggestion boxes are great, they don't always tell the whole story. Nothing drives process improvement like frontline conversations. These conversations also send a strong message to your people that they matter, and that their opinions, creative ideas, knowledge, experiences, and suggestions for improvement are valued and will help shape the future of the organization. In short, *this is innovation*. This is what entrepreneurship and human ingenuity look like. Problem-solving from all kinds of perspectives yields the best and most sustainable business results.[85] If problems and challenges are always reframed as an opportunity and with the customer in mind (both internal and external!), you have winning ingredients for innovation and entrepreneurial behavior.

Coaching, Teaching, and Learning

Walt firmly believed true leaders coached their people. This was evident in the Jungle Cruise story related earlier in the chapter. As Walt developed a relationship with the attraction manager, he coached him on what it would take to make the Jungle Cruise a first-class attraction and guided him on the why and how. He gave him time to make the changes, was on a first-name basis with him, and reinforced his accomplishments with praise.

Al Weiss and Lee Cockerell reinvigorated this coaching approach at Disney with their work at Walt Disney World in the 1990s and 2000s.[86] They made it a point to train their managers to spend a high percentage of their time teaching and coaching their teams. Executives were also expected to regularly encourage, "catch," and reinforce cast members modeling exemplary behavior.

Most companies tend to focus on upward movement as the natural career progression. While this makes sense on the surface, and Disney engages in this practice as well, as we examined above, Disney Parks and Resorts places extreme importance on the value of job rotation. In our interactions with hundreds of cast members over the years, we've heard similar stories of extreme role rotation within a relatively short period of time. All of these cast members say, without hesitation, that these diverse experiences and perspectives helped shaped them into who they are today. Disney wants its cast members to understand the importance and nuances of each role in an area before they are moved into leadership roles. Leaders also tend to emerge naturally and lead from relationships rather than position, so moving them around is a good way to see who shows leadership qualities from a variety of angles. *Perspective matters!* Great leaders and great entrepreneurs accumulate vast perspective through humility and diligence. This also reinforces the company values of never holding anyone back from opportunities to advance their career. Holding someone back from a promotion because he or she is too valuable to a manager is not acceptable at Disney.

Conclusion

Human ingenuity—through an entrepreneurial mind-set—is what drives entrepreneurial behavior and innovation at Disney Parks and Resorts. Feedback and ideas from cast members help Disney leadership to better understand how each role is tied to the company's brand promise. Serving each guest with excellence in entertainment is the job of *everyone* at Disney Parks and Resorts.

Disney's internal research has drawn emphatic correlations between cast member excellence and engagement and guest satisfaction. Given Disney is consistently rated as one of the best companies to work for[87] (clearly Walt's legacy is alive and well), the company has been successful at investing in and using the talents of its people, and ultimately in engaging its employees.

Consider this: Disney is best in class in theme parks, resorts and hotels, cruise lines, food service, retail, and stage entertainment. The company wasn't even in most of these businesses until the last two decades! Their relentless pursuit of excellence, creative approaches, reframing of problems and industry stereotypes into opportunities, ongoing innovation, and extreme engagement of cast members set Disney apart from each of its competitors in these market spaces. Couple their excellence in leveraging the people we discussed in this chapter with their quest to use that human intellect to create the ultimate guest experience through physical space, special effects, and atmosphere (which we will discuss in the next chapter), and it's easy to see why Disney is the undisputed leader in family entertainment.

Disney Principles

- Disney has a very simple yet well-defined mission statement. Really examine what you stand for and what your brand promise is. Keep it simple and point everything you do toward that mission. Repeat that mission over and over again and give your employees the authority to make decisions in an effort to support that mission.
- Disney's cast members make all the difference. Your people will be your differentiating factor. Invest heavily in them with training, coaching, and job rotation, and encourage entrepreneurial behavior.
- Eliminate hassle in everything you do. Disney is not excellent by chance. The company examines literally dozens—to even one hundred—touchpoints for each and every function and guest and cast member engagement. They pay close attention to the details.
- Strive to differentiate yourself through premium experiences. Anyone can come in and undercut you on price, but few, if anyone, will be willing to challenge you if you bring your best all the time.
- Disney relentlessly pursues continuous improvement. Always look for things you can improve and empower your employees to do the same. Innovation breeds more innovation.
- Leadership matters, so make sure you have the right people in leadership roles. You want leaders who will model productive and mission-fulfilling behavior all the time. You need leaders who will invest in your people through coaching and mentoring relationships. Your leaders need to be able to walk the tightrope between innovation and control (chaordic tension).

Work Like Disney: Exercises

1. What's the one thing you could do today to start operating more like Disney Parks and Resorts? How would you collect information on this? How would you get started?
2. In what ways have you been holding innovation and entrepreneurial behavior back in your organization? What immediate and long-term steps can you take to correct this course?
3. What is your mission statement or purpose? Is your mission statement and brand promise crystal clear to your customers and employees? Do you follow it and live by it on a daily basis? If not, what steps can you take to change that?
4. Are your employees fully engaged? If not, why? If so, how can you engage them even more? Examine the Gallup engagement model item by item and identify areas of strength and weakness in your organization.
5. Do you constantly look to improve toward excellence? Is your organization detailed and focused on all touchpoints? Find one thing (process, service, product) you could improve in the next month, six months, and year. What are those items and how would you improve each of them?
6. How could you start to develop a common language? What words would best describe what you want your organization to stand for? How could you begin to implement that language?

Notes

1. Walt Disney Company. (n.d.). *About the Walt Disney Company*. Retrieved from www. thewaltdisneycompany.com/about/.
2. Farfan, B. (2017, November 12). *Disney's Unique Company Mission Statement*. Retrieved from www.thebalancesmb.com/disney-mission-statement-2891828.
3. Morris, N.M. (2016, September). *Is There Content in Entrepreneurship?* Presented at the 17th Annual Experiential Classroom Conference, Gainesville, FL.
4. Kuratko, D.F., Goldsby, M.G., and Hornsby, J.S. (2012). *Innovation Acceleration: Transforming Organizational Thinking*. Upper Saddle River: Pearson/ Prentice Hall.
5. Collins, E. (2015, May 29). *Disney College Program Traditions Class*. Retrieved from https://collinsrace1.wordpress.com/tag/disney-traditions/.
6. Lipp, D. (2013). *Disney U: How Disney University Develops the World's Most Engaged, Loyal, and Customer-centric Employees*. New York: McGraw Hill.
7. Gabsa, R. (2018, May 16). *Why the Onboarding Experience Is Key for Retention*. Retrieved from http://news.gallup.com/opinion/gallup/234419/why-onboarding-experience-key-retention.aspx.
8. Cockerell, L. (2008). *Creating Magic: 10 Common Sense Leadership Strategies From a Life at Disney*. New York: Doubleday.
9. Pine II, B.J., and Gilmore, J.H. (2011). *The Experience Economy*. Boston: Harvard Business Review Press.
10. Gallup Press. (2016). *First, Break All the Rules: What the World's Greatest Managers Do Differently*. New York: Gallup Press.

11. Disney Institute. (2017). *Disney's Approach to Employee Engagement*. Lake Buena Vista, FL: Disney Institute.
12. Gallup Press. (2016). *First, Break All the Rules: What the World's Greatest Managers Do Differently*. New York: Gallup Press.
13. Breen, K. (2018). *Disney Recruiting LinkedIn Post*.
14. Basadur, M., and Goldsby, M. (2016). *Design-centered Entrepreneurship*. New York: Routledge.
15. Gallup Press. (2016). *First, Break All the Rules: What the World's Greatest Managers Do Differently*. New York: Gallup Press.
16. Ibid.
17. Nink, M. (2015, October 13). *Many Employees Don't Know What Is Expected of them at Work*. Retrieved from http://news.gallup.com/businessjournal/186164/employees-don-know-expected-work.aspx.
18. Senek, S. (2009). *Start With Why: How Great Leaders Inspire Everyone to Take Action*. New York: Penguin.
19. Gallup Press. (2016). *First, Break All the Rules: What the World's Greatest Managers Do Differently*. New York: Gallup Press.
20. Ohno, T. (1988). *Toyota Production System: Beyond Large-scale Production*. Portland: Productivity, Inc.
21. Lipp, D. (2013). *Disney U: How Disney University Develops the World's Most Engaged, Loyal, and Customer-centric Employees*. New York: McGraw Hill.
22. Storbeck, J. (2013, May 6). *Windows on Main Street, U.S.A., at Disneyland Park: Van France*. Retrieved from https://disneyparks.disney.go.com/blog/2013/05/windows-on-main-street-u-s-a-at-disneyland-park-van-france/.
23. Disney Institute. (2017). *Disney's Approach to Employee Engagement*. Lake Buena Vista, FL: Disney Institute.
24. Flade, P., Asplund, J., and Elliot, G. (2015, October 8). *Employees Who Use Their Strengths Outperform Those Who Don't*. Retrieved from http://news.gallup.com/businessjournal/186044/employees-strengths-outperform-don.aspx.
25. Lipp, D. (2013). *Disney U: How Disney University Develops the World's Most Engaged, Loyal, and Customer-centric Employees*. New York: McGraw Hill.
26. Cockerell, L. (2008). *Creating Magic: 10 Common Sense Leadership Strategies From a Life at Disney*. New York: Doubleday.
27. Disney Institute (2017). *Disney's Approach to Quality Service*. Lake Buena Vista, FL: Disney Institute.
28. Gallup Press. (2016). *First, Break All the Rules: What the World's Greatest Managers Do Differently*. New York: Gallup Press.
29. Cockerell, L. (2008). *Creating Magic: 10 Common Sense Leadership Strategies From a Life at Disney*. New York: Doubleday.
30. Sorenson, S. (2014, February 20). *How Employees' Strengths Make Your Company Stronger*. Retrieved from http://news.gallup.com/businessjournal/167462/employees-strengths-company-stronger.aspx?_ga=2.237096519.690721770.1517670481-197902642.1517670481.
31. Gallup Press. (2016). *First, Break All the Rules: What the World's Greatest Managers Do Differently*. New York: Gallup Press.
32. Kober, J. (2016, October 7). *Reward and Recognition at the Walt Disney World Resort*. Retrieved from http://worldclassbenchmarking.com/reward-recognition-at-the-walt-disney-world-resort/.

33. Cockerell, L. (2008). *Creating Magic: 10 Common Sense Leadership Strategies From a Life at Disney.* New York: Doubleday.
34. Gallup Press. (2016). *First, Break All the Rules: What the World's Greatest Managers Do Differently.* New York: Gallup Press.
35. Cockerell, L. (2008). *Creating Magic: 10 Common Sense Leadership Strategies From a Life at Disney.* New York: Doubleday.
36. Ibid.
37. Gallup. (2014). *Coaching Strengths: Accelerated Strengths Coaching.* New York: Gallup Press.
38. Gallup Press. (2016). *First, Break All the Rules: What the World's Greatest Managers Do Differently.* New York: Gallup Press.
39. Graen, G.B., and Uhl-Bien, M. (1995). "Relationship-based Approach to Leadership: Development of Leader-Member Exchange (LMX) Theory of Leadership Over 25 Years: Applying a Multi-level Multi-domain Perspective." *Leadership Quarterly,* 6: 219–247.
40. Kuratko, D.F. (2016, September). *Entrepreneurship Education Challenges: Innovate, Instill, Ignite!* Presented at the 17th Annual Experiential Classroom Conference, Gainesville, FL.
41. Blank, S. (2013). *The Four Steps to the Epiphany: Successful Strategies for Products that Win.* Sussex, WI: Quad/Graphics.
42. Gallup Press. (2016). *First, Break All the Rules: What the World's Greatest Managers Do Differently.* New York: Gallup Press.
43. Ibid.
44. Stamp, J. (2016, September). *What an Idea Needs to Survive.* Presented at the 17th Annual Experiential Classroom Conference, Gainesville, FL.
45. Cockerell, L. (2008). *Creating Magic: 10 Common Sense Leadership Strategies From a Life at Disney.* New York: Doubleday.
46. Basadur, M., Runco, M.A., and Vega, L.A. (2000). "Understanding How Creative Thinking Skills, Attitudes, and Behaviors Work Together: A Causal Model." *Journal of Creative Behavior,* 34.
47. Watkins, K.E., and Marsick, V.J. (1993). *Sculpting the Learning Organization: Lessons in the Art and Science of Systemic Change.* San Francisco: Jossey-Bass.
48. Disney Institute. (2017). *Disney's Approach to Employee Engagement.* Lake Buena Vista, FL: Disney Institute.
49. Themed Entertainment Association. (2016). *Theme Index Museum Index 2016: Global Attractions Attendance Report.* Retrieved from www.teaconnect.org/images/files/TEA_235_103719_170601.pdf.
50. Blank, S. (n.d.). *Why Big Companies Can't Innovate.* Retrieved from https://steveblank.com
51. Slater, T. (2015, August 11). *Discover With Me: Mickey-shaped Treats at Aulani, a Disney Resort and Spa.* Retrieved from https://disneyparks.disney.go.com/blog/2015/08/discover-with-me-mickey-shaped-treats-at-aulani-a-disney-resort-spa/.
52. Ramirez, M. (2017, May 30). *Recipe: Tuna Poke With Avocado Mousse at Aulani, a Disney Resort and Spa.* Retrieved from https://disneyparks.disney.go.com/blog/2017/05/recipe-tuna-poke-with-avocado-mousse-at-aulani-a-disney-resort-spa/.
53. Prosperi, L. (2018). *The Imagineering Process: Using the Disney Theme Park Design Process to Bring Your Creative Ideas to Life.* Lexington: Theme Park Press.
54. Prosperi, L. (2016). *The Imagineering Pyramid: Using Disney Theme Park Principles to Develop and Promote Your Creative Ideas.* Lexington: Theme Park Press.

55. Prosperi, L. (2018). *The Imagineering Process: Using the Disney Theme Park Design Process to Bring Your Creative Ideas to Life.* Lexington: Theme Park Press.

56. Disney Institute. (2018). *Disney's Approach to Leadership Excellence.* Lake Buena Vista, FL: Disney Institute.

57. Clifton, J., and Badal, S. (2018). *Born to Build: How to Build a Thriving Startup, a Winning Team, New Customers, and Your Best Life Imaginable.* New York: Gallup Press.

58. Prosperi, L. (2018). *The Imagineering Process: Using the Disney Theme Park Design Process to Bring Your Creative Ideas to Life.* Lexington: Theme Park Press.

59. Basadur, M. (2002). *Flight to Creativity: How to Dramatically Improve Your Creative Performance.* Toronto, Canada: Applied Creativity Press.

60. Collins, J. (2001). *Good to Great: Why Some Companies Make the Leap and Others Don't.* New York: HarperBusiness.

61. Disney Institute. (2017). *Disney's Approach to Employee Engagement.* Lake Buena Vista, FL: Disney Institute.

62. Gallup Press. (2016). *First, Break All the Rules: What the World's Greatest Managers Do Differently.* New York: Gallup Press.

63. Gallup. (n.d.). *How Millennials Want to Work and Live.* Retrieved from http://news.gallup.com/reports/189830/millennials-work-live.aspx.

64. Gallup Press. (2016). *First, Break All the Rules: What the World's Greatest Managers Do Differently.* New York: Gallup Press.

65. Salinas, J. (2017, December 31). *Your Words Work.* Talk given at Phoenix, Arizona Church for the Nations.

66. Rath, T. (2007). *StrengthsFinder 2.0 From Gallup: Discover Your Clifton Strengths.* New York: Gallup Press.

67. Harter, J., and Buckingham, M. (2016). *First, Break All the Rules: What the World's Greatest Managers Do Differently.* New York: Gallup Press.

68. Basadur, M.S. (1995). *The Power of Innovation.* London: Pitman Professional.

69. Gallup Press. (2016). *First, Break All the Rules: What the World's Greatest Managers Do Differently.* New York: Gallup Press.

70. Ibid.

71. Wigert, B., and Mann, A. (2017, September 25). *Give Performance Reviews that Actually Inspire Employees.* Retrieved from http://news.gallup.com/opinion/gallup/219863/give-performance-reviews-actually-inspire-employees.aspx?_ga=2.200395497.690721770.1517670481-197902642.1517670481.

72. Goleman, D., Boyatzis, R., and McKee, A. (2013). *Primal Leadership: Unleashing the Power of Emotional Intelligence.* Boston: Harvard Business School Publishing.

73. Cockerell, L. (2008). *Creating Magic: 10 Common Sense Leadership Strategies From a Life at Disney.* New York: Doubleday.

74. Gallup Press. (2016). *First, Break All the Rules: What the World's Greatest Managers Do Differently.* New York: Gallup Press.

75. Cockerell, L. (2008). *Creating Magic: 10 Common Sense Leadership Strategies From a Life at Disney.* New York: Doubleday.

76. Davis, W. (2005). *Creating a Culture of Excellence: Changing the World of Work One Person at a Time.* Bloomington: AuthorHouse.

77. Maxwell, J.W. (2013). *The 5 Levels of Leadership: Proven Steps to Maximize Your Potential.* New York: Hachette Book Group.

78. Collins, J. (2001). *Good to Great: Why Some Companies Make the Leap and Others Don't.* New York: HarperBusiness.

79. Visit https://q12.gallup.com/ for more information on Gallup engagement programs and access to the Q12 engagement survey.

80. Visit www.disneyinstitute.com/ for more information on Disney Institute programs.

81. Cockerell, L. (2008). *Creating Magic: 10 Common Sense Leadership Strategies From a Life at Disney*. New York: Doubleday.

82. Robinson, S., Robinson, M.M., and Kumar, S. (2014). *Holonomics: Business Where People and Planet Matter*. Edinburgh: Floris Books.

83. Peterson, J.B. (2018). *12 Rules for Life: An Antedote to Chaos*. Toronto, Canada: Random House Canada.

84. Lencione, P.M. (2012). *The Advantage: Why Organizational Health Trumps Everything Else in Business*. San Francisco: Jossey-Bass.

85. Basadur, M., and Goldsby, M. (2016). *Design-centered Entrepreneurship*. New York: Routledge.

86. Cockerell, L. (2008). *Creating Magic: 10 Common Sense Leadership Strategies From a Life at Disney*. New York: Doubleday.

87. Kauflin, J. (2016, December 7). *The Best Places to Work in 2017*. Retrieved from www.forbes.com/sites/jeffkauflin/2016/12/07/the-best-places-to-work-in-2017/#2668d55c8b16.

7

GUEST ENGAGEMENT AND EXPERIENCE AT DISNEY PARKS AND RESORTS

In a time where people—perhaps now more than ever—are searching for an escape from the demands of life,[1] Disney parks and resorts consistently deliver an impeccable experience, removing guests from reality and—if even for just a moment—making all their worries and troubles disappear into a world of fantasy. People remember what they can feel; Disney is the undisputed leader of entertainment because it understands the importance of invoking those feelings and emotions to transport its guests from their problems. World-famous restaurateur Danny Meyer said it best in his *New York Times* bestseller, *Setting the Table*:[2]

> You may think, as I once did, that I'm primarily in the business of serving good food. Actually, though, food is secondary to something that matters even more. In the end, what's most meaningful is creating positive, uplifting outcomes for human experiences and human relationships. Business, like life, is all about how you make people feel. It's that simple, and it's that hard.

We outlined the process and people aspects of Disney's world-class guest service in Chapter Six. We continue to examine this critical aspect of the Disney experience in this chapter, as we introduce ways in which Disney intentionally drives cast member engagement with guests. In the second half of the chapter, we cover the various ways Disney creates world-class "place" for its parks and resorts guests. The delivery of excellence in place brilliantly stands alongside cast members to support their mission of creating happiness and the occasional magic. As you have ascertained by now, Disney creates a truly unique guest environment with its cast members. There is little doubt Disney Parks and Resorts also deeply understands the value of creating the most incredible artificial physical environments on earth. Together, the people and places of Disney Parks and Resorts provide extraordinary experiences that lead to frequent and long-term guest engagement with the organization. In fact, Disney research has found that a high percentage of guests—despite spending a great deal of effort and resources on their current trip—start actively planning their next Disney vacation while still on their current Disney vacation. This behavior speaks volumes about the emotional bond the company creates with the customer through truly sensational experiences.

As you work your way through this chapter, keep the words of Danny Meyer in mind and continually ask yourself how you can reframe the way you think about your business, organization, or team. Disney isn't selling park tickets or renting hotel rooms; rather, the company is providing lifetime memories through first-class experiences that make people feel good. What are you providing that *really* sets you apart in the marketplace?

Customer Engagement

Disney works diligently and intentionally to create in its guests an emotional connection to its parks and resorts. As previously mentioned, all operations have standard processes to ensure consistency and quality in service and experience delivery because special care is put into the details of each guest touchpoint. We outlined the authority given to cast members to turn routine, process-driven moments in their roles (though still happy moments in the eyes of the guest) into magical moments.

Engaged employees positively interact with customers, which leads to engaged customers. Disney knows this, which is why the company goes to the great lengths mentioned in Chapter Six to engage cast members. Guest and cast member engagement plays a critical role in guest experience and is a key factor in Disney's success formula.

Cast members of Disney parks and resorts provide extraordinary care to guests every day—not because they are told to but because they have the authority to do so and the confidence and creativity to respond to customer engagement in ways that are not normal in traditional service industries. There are countless examples of this at work in the parks every day, but the following stories really stand out because of the great care the cast members put into creating a magical experience for the guests.

The first story sounds more like a fairytale than a customer interaction at a place of business. A cast member dressed as a princess at Cinderella's Royal Table restaurant in Cinderella Castle at Magic Kingdom park at Walt Disney World came upon a distressed young girl as the family was trying to leave. The family was trying to exit in a hurry to watch the fireworks show, which had just started, but the little girl—scared by the loud bangs of the fireworks—did not want to leave the restaurant. The princess crouched down and assured the young guest that she would protect her. She proceeded to put her hands over her ears and escort her outside to watch the fireworks.

The second story shows the power of dropping what you are doing to go the extra mile for a customer. A visually impaired guest asked a front entrance cast member at Hollywood Studios at Walt Disney World if she could meet Walt. The cast member thought quickly on his feet, telling Walt's story as they walked—arms locked—to the The Academy of Television Arts and Sciences Hall of Fame attraction in the park. Upon arrival to the attraction, the cast member guided the guest's hand along the bust of Walt.

Goldsby Disney Moment: Disney California Adventure With an Imagineer

When I visit Disneyland, I enjoy going to the Walt Disney Imagineering Blue Sky Cellar at Disney California Adventure. The little building hosts displays of concept art and models of upcoming attractions at the parks. Creativity and design are my specialties, and I especially like concept art. I can spend hours at the Blue Sky Cellar, examining the little details of the design work by the Imagineers. On one visit I was giving extra attention to an architectural model of Paradise Pier. A very nice cast member working at the Cellar came over to me and asked if I had any questions for him. He said he was an Imagineer trainee and thought he might be able to give me some deeper insights into what I was examining. Indeed I did, and we talked for at least an hour about Imagineering and the projects on display in the Cellar. It was a great encounter and made my visit at DCA even more enjoyable that day.

But the story doesn't end there. The next day I went to Disneyland. It was an especially busy day, so I found my way to an attractions board near the main hub that had expected wait times for the rides and shows. I was really engrossed in the display, contemplating what my day's schedule would be in the park. Then amidst the noise of the crowd, I heard, "Hey, Mike. What are you looking for? Anything I can help you with?" I turned and saw Mark, the cast member from the Blue Sky Cellar, except this time he was wearing a dapper outfit and hat. He could tell I was a little surprised to see him there and explained that he had Disney Ambassador duties at Disneyland that day. I told him what I was interested in doing that day, and he made recommendations for me, telling me the best times to go to each ride. Just as he had at the Blue Sky Cellar the day before, Mark made my day at Disneyland magical.

I've never seen Mark again, but I will always remember the encounters I had with him on that trip. Not only did he share information at the Blue Sky Cellar that was tailored to my interests but he also remembered and recognized me the next day amidst the thousands of guests flowing through the busy main hub. It felt like I was talking to a good friend I'd known for a long time. I always think of his hospitality and friendliness that day as indicative of the Disney Difference that makes the Walt Disney Company special to me.

Only Disney cast members could create stories like these. Why is that? It's because they are well trained, they understand what their purpose is, and they are empowered to take care of the guest.

DISNEY LESSON 28: ENCOURAGING CREATIVE LICENSE AND SERVICE SPONTANEITY DRIVES CUSTOMER EXPERIENCE AND LOYALTY

Cast members all across Disney parks and resorts make on-the-spot decisions, like the ones described above, every day to provide extraordinary guest experiences. Are you empowering your employees to make instinctual decisions to serve your customers in the best ways possible? Give your staff the creative license to drive your entrepreneurial dream by making your organization stand out with exemplary service, care, and experiences.

Guests Enter the Show

Disney does not reserve the stage for only its cast members. Guests also get to experience the stage in grand fashion. This provides cast members with a very impactful method for engaging with guests.

Mathews Family Moment: Disney California Adventure Rope Drop

Perhaps the most impactful of these engagements is when families are given the opportunity to "open" Disney parks. Rope drop and countdown ceremonies are common at Disney park openings in the mornings, and most parks also have cast members randomly select an opening family from the crowd each morning. These families are announced, and they typically lead the opening countdown. Think of this as the countdown to a big race or a shopping spree. Our family was fortunate enough to open Disney California Adventure Park at Disneyland Resort three years ago, and I can tell you that it was an exhilarating experience—one that our entire family will never forget!

Test Track, a popular ride at Epcot, was reimagined as a futuristic car testing attraction in 2012. This ride affords guests the opportunity to create their own car, which is later tested against other guests' cars in the areas of capability, efficiency, responsiveness, and power. Guests also receive an overall score to see how their cars fare against their competition as a whole. When riding this attraction, it is always fun to watch kids build their cars and see how they stack up.

We were fortunate enough to get a behind-the-scenes tour of the Enchanted Tales with Belle attraction with an Imagineer at Magic Kingdom park. The attraction, which features the storyline of *Beauty and the Beast*, opened in 2012 as part of the New Fantasyland expansion at the park. The experience starts with the preshow, where guests learn more about Belle's childhood. The scene in the first room ends with a small mirror transforming into a door right before the guests' eyes. Guests are then transferred to a room where Wardrobe (aka Madame de la Bouche), an armoire, and a cast member assign guests to parts in the upcoming show. Guests are given props and instructions, and they are called into the library by Lumière, the talking candelabra sitting atop the mantel, to play the scene where Belle falls in love with the beast. In typical Disney detail, the library is lined with over twelve thousand actual book spines. Lumière's face is illuminated with amazing graphics, and he moves as he speaks to the audience. He escorts Belle into the room, and the guests are queued to play their various roles with her as the storyline unfolds. The entire experience lasts about twenty minutes, and all audience members (about thirty per group) are heavily engaged. Guests who played specific roles are recognized, get a photo with Belle, and receive a bookmark signed by Belle. Enchanted Tales with Belle is an experience unique to Disney and is driven by creative technologies, special effects, and engaging cast members that set Disney attractions apart from the rest of the industry.

Mathews Family Moment: *Festival of the Lion King*

The highest rated show at Disney parks is *Festival of the Lion King* at Walt Disney World's Animal Kingdom park. Surely the top-rated show experience for Disney parks worldwide would not invite guests to participate in the show, right? This is where Disney surprises everyone, as a handful of children are asked to play a role in each showing several times a day.

Our daughter Lindsey was chosen for this experience, as she represented the lion portion of the crowd. My parents went on this trip with us, and out of countless magical moments we were fortunate enough to experience, the *Festival of the Lion King* held special meaning because my mom later said it moved her a great deal to see her granddaughter on stage in such a high-level production. My mom passed away shortly after that trip, but what a great memory we have of the excitement she experienced with our children that vacation and, particularly, that day.

Disney pushes the envelope when it comes to showcasing guests on the stage. Another Walt Disney World stage show at Hollywood Studios park, *Indiana Jones Stunt Spectacular*, has also become a fan favorite for guest participation, as several guests play the crowd in the exciting stunt show. One guest plays a major role and also becomes part of the demonstration of stunt illusions in movies. As we know from Chapter Six, Disney takes safety very seriously, so balancing the show with safety is something the company is willing to tackle to create memorable guest engagement and experiences. Yet another onstage guest experience available at one park at all global Disney resorts is *Jedi Training*. Parents can sign up guests aged 4–12 for this immersive stage experience where they get lightsaber training and become the star of the show against the dark side. Finally, guests can also form a team and join Agent P (Perry the Platypus from Disney Channel's extremely popular—but now retired—show, *Phineas and Ferb*) in stopping the evil deeds of Dr. Doofenshmirtz as they visit various World Showcase destinations in Disney World's Epcot. The adventure promotes engagement with cast members, Disney intellectual property, and Epcot (considered an "adult" park) itself. In addition, it provides a unique team experience for the groups it serves.

Sometimes the stage and the show are more simple but nonetheless very effective at making guests feel they are an integral part of the show. Guests can simply walk up to the sword in the stone—inspired by the tales of King Arthur— at Magic Kingdom and Disneyland parks and take a shot at pulling the famed sword from the stone. If you ever want to see a child's face light up—or an adult's face light up like that of a child—hang around the sword in the stone for a while and wait for someone to successfully lift the sword from its stone encasement. Occasionally Merlin will even come along and hold a special ceremony at the request of the king.[3]

In Chapter Six we discussed how Disney embraced a custodian's sidewalk artwork, creating a long-standing tradition of making janitors a regular part of the show by training them to create Disney character faces with brooms and water on the streets and sidewalks of the parks. Guests not only get up close and personal views of this phenomenon but they are also afforded the opportunity to get "trained" and play along by creating their own street caricatures with the custodians.

Mathews Family Moment: Shooting the Bow at Gaston's Tavern

Our family decided to take a break and get a cinnamon roll at Gaston's Tavern in Fantasyland at Magic Kingdom park. A young lady cast member outside the tavern was offering up chances to shoot suction cup darts (sets were conveniently being sold in the store in that area) from a toy bow at a large stand-up board with a bullseye painted on it. The location of the station encouraged cast member and guest engagement in a creative way, as guests passed right by to enter the busy dining location. The cast member was very inviting and patient and kind with the kids as she helped them learn to use the bow. The experience lasted about five minutes at most but provided some friendly competition between brother and sister and plenty of smiles, photos, and future memories, as we purchased a bow and arrow set for each of our two kids.

There are other simple engagements that invoke a smile and anticipation of future experiential opportunities for guests. A sampling of these guest interactions includes:

• Park entry posts that light up in different colors for special events or as guests tap their MagicBands (more on MagicBands later in the chapter, when we examine Disney's use of technology);
• Mouse ears, hats, mouse hands, and other toys that light up in coordination with nighttime shows;
• Pool parties and trivia time at resort pools;
• Marshmallow roasting at resorts.

These activities make it easy for cast members to engage with guests, but they also do an excellent job of "body management" (spreading guests out across resorts), thus creating deeper and richer guest experiences. Remember, the most relaxed engagements often create lifetime memories and a deeper connection to your company, so don't overlook simple opportunities to connect your customers to your organization. Highly successful entrepreneurs and their people figure out how to immerse their customers and get them deeply connected to their brand.

As we mentioned in Chapter Six, Disney's decision to simply listen to—and ultimately act on—George Kalogridis's ideas on pin trading paid huge financial dividends, as Disney pins became a near instant obsession with Disney novices and lifelong fans alike. Today pin sales are in the billions of dollars, but that tells only half the story. Nearly every cast member, including custodial and resort employees, wears pin trading lanyards or placards. These pin displays are an open invitation to guests to engage with cast members. For cast members, pins serve as a tool for starting countless conversations, minute by minute, at Disney parks, resorts, soda fountain shops, and retail stores all across the world literally every day. Not only do pins drive guest engagement with cast members but they also remind guests of the great memories of trips from the past and perpetuate ongoing intellectual property engagement. They brilliantly provide guests with whatever fits their style, such as well-designed replicas of their favorite characters and attractions, dated keepsakes, event markers, or highly collectible limited edition chase items. Other times, as you will see in the story below, guests become a part of the show on an impromptu basis.

Mathews Family Moment: Prince Charming

I'll share one of my favorite stories of turning the minimum expectation of creating happiness into making magic. Our family visited Walt Disney World's Grand Floridian Resort & Spa for dinner at 1900 Park Fare restaurant. The character dining experience, called *Cinderella's Happily Ever After Dinner*, features character interactions and performances that tell the story of the king's ball and Cinderella's introduction to Prince Charming. The dining room sets the stage, with ornate theming around a centerpiece of carousel horses. The dinner experience, a buffet with a lot of choices and select items unique to Disney (such as the famous strawberry soup) is well suited for children, as it also offers special buffet tables for children that are lower in stature or easy to access. The show started with Prince Charming escorting Cinderella to the center of the room for a dance, complete with music from the story. Toward the end of the dance, with the help of servers and bussers, children were invited to partake in a parade of sorts. After the dance, the Prince and Cinderella, along with Lady Tremaine, Anastasia, and Drizella, visited every table, carefully remaining in character. The interactions are both charming and engaging, fulfilling Disney's goal of removing guests from reality, even if just for a moment. These performances and interactions were all scripted, for the most part, and created happiness.

Where this story takes a Disney turn is when my daughter Lindsey, who was four at the time, decided to grab Prince Charming's hand as he escorted Cinderella to center stage for the dance. Keep in mind the music was going and the show was already on; this definitely wasn't in the script, but it didn't faze the tall and handsome prince. He quickly yet softly crouched down to our daughter and said, "Princess, I've already promised Cinderella this dance, but I will be back for you shortly. What is your name?" Lindsey told the prince her name while my wife and I kind of looked at each other with a "yeah, right" glance, and the show went on. Lindsey was enjoying the show, character interactions, and dinner, but whether explicit or implied, kids don't often forget promises, so I'm sure she fully expected the prince to magically appear at our table and sweep her off her feet. After the dance with Cinderella, it was time for the parade with the kids. Oddly, Lindsey didn't participate—I'm sure because she fully expected her special dance with the prince to come to fruition. There was a point where Julie and I forgot about the promise and, of course, that's when Prince Charming showed up and said, "Princess Lindsey, I've returned for our dance." He took her by the hand and subtly gave a look to someone to queue the music. The same music to which he danced with Cinderella fired up, and for the next three minutes our daughter was on center stage. The prince eloquently guided her through the impromptu dance, which was clearly off script. She was now in the show, and I could not take pictures fast enough. Julie was fighting back tears and Lindsey was smiling from ear to ear. Even her six-year-old brother Nate was excited for her. While I'm sure the prince had done this or something similar before, it was far from a forced interaction and was definitely outside the normal system and process and responded to a child's innocent request. The young man playing the prince was given the authority to create magic on occasion, and he exercised his charm and entrepreneurial spirit to seize the moment.

Julie and I were Disney fans at that point, but here's what I can tell you . . . we became Disney junkies in that instant, with a deep connection to the company, its parks and resorts, and, most importantly, its people. We've passed that emotional connection and ongoing engagement down to our children as well. Disney understands the power of human connection and the ability of people to deliver the brand promise better than any ride, attraction, or show ever could. To be sure, those pieces of the puzzle are important tools Disney uses with great success, but the cast members make the magic and create the emotional connection with the guests. That's why Julie recently said what she did about frequenting Disney parks and resorts for the family memories—not the rides, restaurants, and attractions. When I asked her—for the purpose of this book—if she remembered the 1900 Park Fare memory, she immediately said, "Of course, the Prince Charming moment is forever etched on my heart and in my mind."

Make no mistake, this market-driven approach, though seemingly simple in nature, is entrepreneurial because it grasps at the guests' hearts and turns their attention to Disney despite a crowded marketplace with an infinite number of entertainment options and attention grabbers with which the company competes. Customer engagement creates loyal customers who come back time and time again instead of going to the local park (at a fraction of the cost). As you consider how you can jump start your journey toward creating engaged, loyal customers, consider Disney's formula of common purpose and shared values, cast member engagement, internal customer service, and customer experience. You'll never get there without intentional, strategic, detailed, and consistent investment in your people.

Stories just like our Prince Charming tale play out every day at Disney parks and resorts. That's why families keep coming back. Those magical moments, along with the incredible attention to detail that creates indescribable happiness in guests, also make Disneyland and Walt Disney World a rite of passage for many American children. It's not uncommon to hear of families who have taken a trip to Walt Disney World for thirty straight years, even long after the kids have graduated from college and moved on to their own adult lives. As odd as it sounds, there's even a phrase—just take my money—that is repeated over and over across the internet on Disney fan forums when the company introduces new merchandise, lands, attractions, or vacation packages. How much would your business be changed if you could drive even a fraction of that kind of customer loyalty? What steps can you take today to start building stronger relationships with your customers?

Mathews Family Moment: Mad Hatter

A few key moments from our first trip to Disneyland a few years ago really stand out for me. Lindsey was five at the time. One of those moments happened as we were walking alongside the iconic Matterhorn Bobsleds. A cast member dressed as the Mad Hatter (Disney refers to him as "being a friend of" the Mad Hatter in order not to spoil the magic) came up from behind us, grabbed Lindsey's hand, and walked and talked with her ahead of us for a hundred yards or so to his picture-taking and autograph-signing destination. This was not really part of the script, which made for a great experience. The gentleman playing the Mad Hatter certainly could have just walked on by, but he chose to take advantage of the walk to his destination spot to make a little girl's day. Here's the funny part . . . up until that moment, Lindsey did not really care for the Mad Hatter, as she thought he was "kinda weird and creepy." However, since that encounter, she has had a special adoration for the Hatter and is always anxious to see him every trip.

Mathews Family Moment: The Kiss From Cinderella

Julie recently reminded me of the time we were partaking of the Princess Storybook Breakfast at the Akershus Royal Banquet Hall in the Norway Pavilion at Epcot at Walt Disney World. Lindsey, a lover of all things princess, was having a great time, but Nate (six at the time) was pretty bored. I should say he was bored until Cinderella came up and gave him a kiss on the cheek. Though he was embarrassed at the time, he waved off his mom's attempt to remove the lipstick from his cheek with a wet wipe. He sat there quite starstruck, with a comatose smile, the remaining thirty or so minutes of the breakfast. He was now engaged because the princess knew just what to do and had the authority to do it. There is great power in those moments when your employees authentically engage with your customers.

Backstage Becomes Onstage

Disney makes guests feel special by giving them opportunities to see backstage areas. While they accomplish this in a variety of ways, they are also careful not to tarnish the magic of their parks and resorts. Many of these experiences are included with park or resort entry, while others are sold as premium offerings. One of the included experiences is viewing animal surgeries at the Conservation Station at Animal Kingdom park at Walt Disney World. Scheduled surgery times are posted at the train station, and guests can take a short train ride to the Conversation Station to see them through a large glass window. The veterinarians provide insights into what the injury or condition is and how they are treating it. It is a great learning experience for children and adults alike, and also gives them a peak behind the curtain. It also reassures guests that Disney goes to great lengths to provide top-notch care for the animals in the park.

The Wilderness Lodge resort at Walt Disney World offers the Wonders of the Lodge Tour, which provides guests with a unique look at the Lodge. On the tour, guests get to see "hidden" areas; learn about architecture, construction, hidden Mickeys, and Lodge tales; and enjoy a visit to the Carolwood Pacific Room, which holds artifacts from Walt's train collection.

Sometimes the backstage becomes onstage out of necessity. For instance, during peak traffic times, backstage corridors are opened to allow extra space for entry into and exit out of Disneyland and Magic Kingdom parks. Disney dresses the walls of these areas with branding and scrims to hide the less aesthetic backstage views. At Disneyland Park, one of these extra routes also gives guests a behind-the-scenes look at the Jungle Cruise attraction boats.

Disney offers a wide variety of premium experiences, and backstage tours are some of their more coveted adventures. With dozens of tours offered across nearly all parks, there is something for everyone. The tours cost from around fifty to hundreds of dollars and range from two to eight hours. They are centered on trains, Star Wars, company history, company principles, aquatics, African savannah, animal care, and gardening, among others. Not only do these tours drive additional revenue, they also help disperse guests. Later in the chapter we further discuss how successful entrepreneurs can leverage their brands and experiences by offering premium add-on goods and services.

Atmosphere (Place) and Setup (Process and Systems)

Of course great customer service and engagement won't get a chance to fully shine without superb atmosphere, infrastructure, and processes. Disney provides world-class customer experience through immersive environments, amazing physical infrastructure, and near seamless processes that can effectively accommodate massive amounts of people. Exceptional experiences create an emotional connection. When you add emotion to a rational connection to a company, the end result is loyal customers. Gallup defines this emotional connection as customer engagement, and bases it on guests' confidence, integrity, pride, and passion in the company. According to Gallup, "Without a strong emotional bond, satisfaction is meaningless."[4]

Technology

As mentioned in Chapter Five, Disney has dramatically heightened its use of technology to preserve customer experience and engage the masses in its parks and resorts. CEO Bob Iger has made technology a key strategic priority, and it all started with My Disney Experience (MDE). MDE started as an online portal where Walt Disney World guests could create an account and make resort and dining reservations. The additions of MagicBands and the Walt Disney World phone application (My Disney Experience) to the portal system further streamlined the guest experience. Guests now have the ease of entering parks, redeeming FastPasses and paying for meals and merchandise on their wristbands and phones. Guests can book up to three FastPasses per day ahead of time (up to sixty days prior to their trip for Disney Resort guests), which allows them to skip standby lines. This system was a major undertaking, as one cast member told us the company retired at least seventeen legacy systems and merged them into one: MyMagic+. One Disney executive told us the growing pains were immense, as the system took five years to develop and test, carried a price tag of over one billion dollars, and featured only 30 percent successful dry runs during its unveiling and test year in 2013. Today the system runs over 90 percent clean, which is amazing considering Walt Disney World parks and resorts serve over fifty million guests annually.[5] Disney made this investment because of the massive popularity and growth of the parks and resorts system in Florida. The platform allows guests to customize and control their experience. The use of the phone application also serves as another tool to remove guests from the reality of answering texts, emails, and various life demands. Company executives knew they had to do something to manage the extreme crowds, various experience pain points, and park, resort, and restaurant operations planning on the back end. It was a bold entrepreneurial move by Iger and his team but one that has paid significant dividends in the several years since its inception.

Disney faced significant obstacles implementing My Disney Experience, MagicBands, and FastPass+ at Disneyland Resort in California. Unlike Walt Disney World, which features a disproportionate number of vacationers, according to one Disney associate, a minimum of over 50 percent (up to 80–90 percent on some days) of Disneyland's average daily attendance comes from local pass holders. Disney recognized it had to meet the needs of both locals and tourists in California. The solution? Disney came up with the MaxPass system, which was a brilliant answer that met the needs of both spontaneous locals and planning travelers. Guests can purchase MaxPass as a premium add-on to their annual passes or daily park tickets, which affords them unlimited photo downloads and the opportunity to start booking electronic FastPasses after park entry. We had the opportunity to test the new system in its first month of existence, and again a month later, and found that it greatly enhanced the Disneyland Resort experience for out-of-town guests while also preserving the expectations of local pass holders who prefer to take a more ad hoc approach to visiting the parks. This solution became a win-win for Disney because it met the needs of two very different customer groups and also managed to turn the new offering into a revenue booster. When you think you cannot serve two disparate customer segments, seek feedback from both groups, reframe the problem into an opportunity, and employ your staff to start ideating solutions. Once you develop the initial solution, solicit feedback from customers and employees on how it is going and adjust accordingly. MaxPass is a great example of the power of reframing and corporate entrepreneurship.

First and Last Impressions

One of our most favorite experiences at Disney resorts is when cast members greet us with "welcome home" upon resort hotel entry. This incredibly simple gesture puts us at ease, invites us to treat their resort as our home away from home, and sends the message that they are there to make our stay a great one. And because all cast members wear name tags with only their first name, our first impression is that we are instantly on a first-name basis with them. First impressions mean a great deal to a customer!

It is well known that a customer's first sight of—and interaction with—a business is critically important. My Disney Experience is typically the company's first interaction with the customer. That is why Iger so aggressively pursued major technological advancements. However, in essence, there are multiple "front porch" interactions with Disney parks and resorts, such as resort entry, hotel entry, park entry, and the unveiling of key park structures. When Disney introduced MagicBands at Walt Disney World Resort back in 2013, the rest of the business world thought Iger was crazy. However, the MagicBands park entry poles proved to be brilliant, as they cut entry times by one-fifth and greatly improved guest feedback on entry points, which were seen as much more open, inviting, and welcoming.

Disney also does an excellent job of providing dramatic and timely reveals of key structures. The most notable is Cinderella Castle at Magic Kingdom park at Walt Disney World. Guests cannot see the castle as they come up to the park because the train station acts as a curtain, hiding it. Once they get to the middle of Main Street, the castle majestically appears and is made to look even bigger than it is because of forced perspective techniques used on Main Street buildings (more on that later).

Providing stellar front porch encounters would be wasted without capping park visits off with equally superior closing experiences. The other theme park operators across the globe just cannot seem to understand why Disney is so adamant about doing nightcap shows—typically fireworks—at every park every night. This is a huge investment for the company. In fact, to put it into perspective, Disney parks represent 25 percent of the United States fireworks market. Why does Disney make such substantial investments in nightly shows when many midsized cities are actually cutting Independence Day fireworks from their annual budgets? You see, Disney knows who it is and is comfortable with who it is. Disney caters to guests willing to pay for premium experiences, and assumes that many people who go through the gates every day deserve to be treated to a once-in-a-lifetime experience. The company calls this its "kiss goodnight" to the guests.[6]

Successful entrepreneurs know first impressions make or break their brands because they create a lens through which their customers see the rest of their operation. They also know last impressions are equally important in driving customer referrals and return visits. These first and last impressions form an indelible mark on the customer's heart, ultimately shaping how they connect with the brand and experience and whether or not they choose to engage with the company over the long haul. Examine your first and last impressions and ask your employees and customers to give you honest feedback about those experiences. If you are building a new business, intentionally design those experiences to be excellent and continually refine them by seeking market feedback.[7]

Sensory—Lighting, Sounds, Smells, Touch

Disney parks and resorts do an amazing job of transporting guests away from reality through various sensory methods. No other company has mastered these techniques like Disney has. Disney uses "smellitzers" to add scents to areas to create atmosphere. They even pump the smell of freshly baked chocolate chip cookies through the Main Street bakeries at Magic Kingdom and Disneyland. Why? Because the cookies are baked off-site. The smell of coastal air awaits guests entering the Beach Club Resort lobby at Walt Disney World. Guests encounter various scents when riding Soarin', a flight simulator attraction located at Epcot, California Adventure, Shanghai Disneyland, and Tokyo DisneySea parks, including jasmine while flying over the Taj Mahal, fresh ocean breeze scents while visiting the Lau Islands, and fresh grass while looking down on elephants in Kilimanjaro National Park. Guests also smell fire as they traverse the room portraying the burning of the Library of Alexandria in Epcot's Spaceship Earth attraction. Finally, at Animal Kingdom park, one encounters various fresh smells on the revolutionary Avatar Flight of Passage ride. Sound is also strategically used in abundance in Disney parks and resorts. If you listen closely, you will hear piped-in sounds, such as crickets, crashing waves, and even voices, that are so realistic you'll swear they are indeed authentic.

If you have spent any length of time at Disney parks and resorts in the evenings, you know how captivating the lighting is. It sets an incredible stage and provides such a strong ambience that it is easy for people to forget they are in a theme park or resort hotel. The nighttime ambience creates a strong emotional connection between Disney's locations and its guests. While there are countless examples, let's hone in on a few that best illustrate the power of ambience through lighting.

The lighting at Cars Land at Disney California Adventure Park is captivating. The neon lights on the signs for the "businesses" take you in your mind to the Pixar-created town of Radiator Springs. The insects crawling up the trees, ultra-violet lights, and glowing sidewalks make you feel like you are on the planet of Pandora rather than in Animal Kingdom park. The lighting at Tokyo DisneySea transports you to faraway ports. The nighttime ambience of New Fantasyland in Magic Kingdom is largely driven by the lighting, which ranges from the strung lighting of a midcentury carnival at Storybook Circus to medieval lanterns around Seven Dwarfs Mine Train. The BoardWalk in the Epcot resort area glows bright, standing out as the landmark of the area and a place for entertainment. Seasonal lighting at the Disney parks and resorts is equally stunning, creating mythical Halloween, Thanksgiving, or Christmas experiences for guests for extended periods of time. In fact, at Cars Land, the street lights, which are designed to be on only one side of the road (just as they are in the movie), are modified with matching poles on the other side of the road to accommodate Christmas lights. Resort hotels, Downtown Disney, and Disney Springs areas also feature huge Christmas trees in November and December.

> You can get information about a changing environment through the soles of your feet.
>
> —*Walt Disney*

Texture changes are also commonly used at Disney parks and resorts to immerse guests in the environment. The next time you are in a signature park, such as Disneyland, Magic Kingdom, Disneyland Paris, Shanghai Disneyland, or Tokyo Disneyland, pay particular attention to the ground treatments and how they transition from one land to another. For instance, you will move from boards to cobblestone as you walk between Adventureland and Frontierland in the Magic Kingdom. Walt was extremely particular about all aspects of these transitions, and we examine them more closely later in the chapter.

Mathews Family Moment: Epcot Ambience

A few years ago, Julie and I were on a "kid-free" trip to Walt Disney World to attend Night of Joy, a two-night Christian concert series hosted at Magic Kingdom (it was later moved to ESPN Wide World of Sports and actually canceled in 2018). We settled into our room at Beach Club Resort and immediately ventured into Epcot. It was a typical warm September evening in

Central Florida and one of the few remaining slower times of year for Disney World. The nighttime ambience in the Epcot Resort Area is just special, and lays a wonderful "red carpet" for entering the park. One really nice perk of staying at one of the Epcot area resorts is that you have a special entrance to Epcot on the opposite end of the park from the main entrance. We were walking through the France pavilion when the atmosphere provided by the lighting seemed to hit us both at the same time. I said to Julie, "There's just something different about this place," to which she replied, as she grabbed my hand, "I know, I was thinking the exact same thing." Disney parks and resorts spark near indescribable emotions in people, and it's not by chance.

Immersion (Fairytale)

Storytelling

Just about everything at Disney parks and resorts is tied to a story. Sometimes the stories are subtle, while other times they are extremely well developed and forward-facing. An example of subtle theming is the Haunted Mansion attraction. While the attraction does actually have the story of a bride left at the altar and her fiancé dying a horrible death, the story is typically lost on most guests; thus, the content just helps to provide a good experience.[8] Some attractions tell stories straight from a movie, such as Radiator Springs Racers in Cars Land at Disney California Adventure Park. The ride train is the same one used for Test Track at Epcot, but the slow portion of the ride tells the story of the original *Cars* movie. Other attractions add to fairytales, such as the Enchanted Tales of Belle in New Fantasyland at Magic Kingdom park. Finally, some attractions develop entirely new stories, like Mission: Space in Epcot, which tells—and lets guests live—the story of astronaut training. Even the reimagined Disney Springs (formerly Downtown Disney) shopping and restaurant district at Walt Disney World Resort tells the story of historic Florida coastal cities and their natural springs.[9]

Further, some attractions use content to provide and/or enhance an experience. For instance, Disney recently rethemed California Screamin', a roller coaster in California Adventure Park, to Incredicoaster, themed after the Monsters, Inc., movie franchise. There really is not time or sufficient opportunity to build a true story for this ride, but the movie content does provide familiar theming to enhance the guest experience. Test Track at Epcot is an example of content driving the experience, as the sponsor of the ride, General Motors, provides models of futuristic car designs to add to the experience. This is what sets Disney parks aside from amusement parks across the globe. For example, while Cedar Point has an impressive lineup of excellent roller coasters, it doesn't attach stories, content, atmosphere, or experiences to them like Disney.

Disney still uses storyboards—step by step drawings—to depict the story of a resort hotel, attraction, restaurant, or other experience to develop each and every buildout. These storyboards become the basis for decision-making, answering questions such as why are you building this, why are you doing it this way or that way, why are you adding this element, or why is this aroma, lighting, or sound being used? In other words, how does every element enhance the story and/or guest experience?[10]

Disney recently reimagined the Twilight Zone Tower of Terror attraction at California Adventure Park into Guardians of Galaxy—Mission: Breakout! As we mentioned last chapter, the California version of Tower of Terror was widely known to have the weakest rated guest experience among all versions of the ride globally, and Disney had not yet used the newer Marvel IP in its parks, so the conversion was logical and strategic. Despite the initial uproar the repurposing of the attraction caused among locals, it has quickly become one of the most popular and beloved attractions at Disneyland Resort. The main reason the California version of Tower of Terror was rated so low was because the story was not very well developed due to a lack of space. Further, younger guests could not easily identify with the Twilight Zone themed story. On the other hand, the simple, upbeat, and positive (the ride features popular, uplifting music and a fun story featuring Rocket Raccoon and the other ornery heroes) story of Mission: Breakout! connects with children and adults alike. This is a great example of the value of Disney anchoring itself to its brand promise of providing great guest experiences through storytelling and content.

Entrepreneurs can bring their vision to fruition with stories. Stories are aspirational and informative and teach lessons and values. Stories augmented with exceptional details of place, as we discuss throughout this chapter, can and do transport guests away from reality. As an entrepreneur, are there ways you can emotionally connect with your customers through storytelling? Think of ways you can immerse your customers in your stories and content and thus connect them more tightly to your brand.

People can feel perfection.

—*Walt Disney*

Details That Lead to Immersion

Walt's legacy of obsessing over extreme details still lives on in the company today. Today's Imagineers consider and plan for every element of every portion of a land, attraction, resort, or restaurant. They even go so far as to heavily theme both attraction line queues (preshows) and exit areas (postshows). Everything from props to cast member costumes to working parts is created down to the smallest detail. Line queues are a key component of this and are often overlooked by other amusement park companies. Disney makes these lines enjoyable, with interactive games, facts and information, and entertainment. They employ the principles of tapping into the guests' emotions, eliminating confusion, keeping people occupied, and starting and ending strong to make wait times as painless as possible.[11] The Enchanted Tales with Belle attraction at the Magic Kingdom, which we discussed earlier in the chapter, is a great example of this. This, along with extreme details, quality, and craftsmanship, is why Disney takes so long, relative to the competition, to build new lands and attractions. The company is extremely patient and takes a long-term approach to almost all projects.

Walt was obsessed with how the physical environment evoked the emotions of the guests. He was a true visionary, but even his Imagineers found themselves impressed with his attention to detail. As mentioned earlier, Walt was extremely innovative when it came to ground up land-to-land transitions in Disneyland. Consider the challenge of transitioning from Adventureland (themed around pirates and the jungle) to Frontierland (theming centered on the early western frontier settlements). Walt was very particular about guests feeling, seeing, and sensing the transitions in such a way that they felt almost seamless. Another great example is Walt being so insistent on reworking the tiki bird animatronics in the Enchanted Tiki Room to make sure guests believed the birds were actually breathing. Thinking back to Chapter Six, yet another great example was his persistence in coaching cast members to fully achieve and maintain his vision of how the Jungle Cruise attraction should be experienced through the senses of the guest.

Walt even had Stanford University conduct a study to see how far people would walk with a piece of trash in their hand before discarding it on the ground. Today's cast members still take these iconic stories to heart and it shows in the quality and care put into the details of the principles and projects outlined below. Stanford's research led Walt to place trash cans no more than twenty-seven paces apart. While Walt was pretty obsessed with image control through waste management, today's Imagineers have taken trash cans a step further, as they are constantly maintained and ornately themed to match the areas in which they reside. For example, trash cans in Cars Land have different logos and inscriptions on them, such as "RS 1909 PLEASE KEEP OUR TOWN CLEAN," and receptacles in the Grizzly River Peak area in California Adventure (more on this area later in the chapter) have the "park" logo, with the inscription "Keep Grizzly Peak Clean." Consider this: Why would you work so hard to build up your entrepreneurial dream only to have it defined by trash on the ground, ugly trash cans that are not maintained, or smelly trash cans that are not cleaned out often enough? Control the little things so that you are remembered for the image and experience you set out to achieve.

The next time you visit Animal Kingdom park at Walt Disney World in Orlando, Florida, spend some time absorbing the details in Asia. Imagineer Joe Rhode and his research team spent several months studying the Tibetan culture and collecting artifacts to build this area and the amazing Expedition

Everest roller coaster. The area is so well themed that Tibetans who have visited it say they feel at home. If the area and ride are that well themed, you can bet the average guest is transported from reality as they walk the paths, eat at the restaurants, interact with the cast members, and experience the attractions.

We mentioned the storyline of the Radiator Springs Racers attraction in Cars Land above, so let's take a closer look at the details of this magnificently themed land in Disney California Adventure Park. Cars Land was added to the park in 2012 and covers twelve acres. Its featured attraction, Radiator Springs Racers, was Disney's most expensive attraction buildout at the time, costing over $200 million. You enter the mythical, once downtrodden southwestern town of Radiator Springs depicted in the original *Cars* movie via the "real" Route 66 Highway. The Imagineers spared no expense with the details, as street signs, manhole covers, street lights, and road markings begin to transport guests in their minds and hearts to the actual town of Radiator Springs. Guests look up to see the mountains on the horizon of the Radiator Springs Racers attraction. As they approach the attraction, the details on the ride and the mountains are accurate to both the geography and the movie. The town also features restaurants that are exact replicas of movie landmarks, including the Cozy Cone Motel and Flo's V8 Café. Other attractions in the land include Luigi's Rollickin' Roadsters (depicting Luigi's Casa Della Tires store) and Mater's Junkyard Jamboree (showcasing Tow Mater's propensity to collect all things car and tractor parts-related). Retail stores are heavily themed as well, such as Ramone's House of Body Art, Sarge's Surplus Hut, and Radiator Springs Curios. Street shows, dance parties, and photo opportunities with characters from the *Cars* movie also happen with regularity along Route 66.[12] As mentioned above, at nighttime, the land transforms into an unbelievable spectacle, complete with illuminated neon signs from movie landmarks on the buildings. Guests describe the land as being done so well that they actually *believe* they are in the mythical town of Radiator Springs as they walk down Route 66.

Tokyo DisneySea, often referred to as the most impressively themed park in the Disney system, was added as the second park at Tokyo Disney Resort in 2001. It covers 176 acres and was the fastest park in the world to reach ten million guests, doing so in just over three hundred days. DisneySea has a nautical theme and features "lands" including Mediterranean Harbor (featuring Italy and gondola rides), Mysterious Island (featuring Mount Prometheus volcano), Mermaid Lagoon (palace of King Triton and the Little Mermaid), Arabian Coast (Aladdin themed), Lost River Delta (Aztec pyramids and Indiana Jones theming), Port Discovery (futuristic Weather Control marina), and American Waterfront (old Cape Cod and New York Harbor). Mediterranean Harbor even features a resort—Hotel MiraCosta—inside the park. Experts describe the park as the most elaborately detailed park in the Disney system, featuring the best Disney has to offer in terms of restaurants, transportation, attractions, and shows that are so exceptional they truly make guests forget they are in Tokyo.[13]

Disney occasionally utilizes outside IP in its parks, but the twelve-acre 2017 addition of Pandora—The World of Avatar to Animal Kingdom park was a significant risk for the company. The expansion was a major investment, at over half a billion dollars, but Disney also secured long-term exclusive licensing agreements with Avatar creator James Cameron and his companies.[14] Disney and Imagineer Joe Rhode pushed the envelope on this endeavor, as designing a land with floating rock formations obviously presented unique challenges. The premier attraction in the new land, Avatar Flight of Passage, a video simulator that places guests on the back of a flying banshee from the original Avatar movie, is widely regarded as the best theme park ride in the world right now, and has driven Animal Kingdom to heightened popularity levels.

As expected, after building up the Star Wars franchise the years following Disney's 2012 purchase of Lucasfilm, Disney broke ground on new lands, Star Wars: Galaxy's Edge, in Hollywood Studios at Walt Disney World and Disneyland Park in California. Both lands are roughly fourteen acres each, and both are massive in vertical scale and loaded with intricate details. Disney has said that they are the largest single-land expansions in the history of their parks, featuring incredible detail and technology.[15] The estimated cost per land expansion is well over one billion dollars.

Adventures by Disney, an intimate, all-inclusive vacation experience program offered by Disney Parks, Experiences, and Consumer Products, was started in 2005 and is the company's number one guest-rated experience. Adventures by Disney, offering travel options to nearly forty global destinations, offers incredibly immersive trips for the whole family. Guests are treated to first-class service and care, two guides per small group of forty or less people, ethnically authentic experiences, and insider access to places not normally open to the public. The excursions range from four to twelve days and are physically, emotionally, and socially engaging.[16] Disney Cruise Line, started in 1996, is the second most highly rated Disney Parks, Experiences, and Consumer Products experience and one of the most respected cruise lines in the world. Adding cruise ships was a sizeable risk for the company, as the cruise line industry was focused on adults— not families—but Disney knew family entertainment and created cruise experiences that are immersive and kid- and family-friendly and feature unprecedented care and service. One Disney executive told us that the cruises are his family's favorite Disney vacation, as they provide a unique bow-to-stern experience offered nowhere else. Today's consumer craves engagement and experience,[17] so it is no surprise these experiences are rated so highly by guests.

The Hall of Presidents at Magic Kingdom is a great example of the attention to detail put into attractions and shows at Disney parks. The recently refurbished attraction uses animatronics of all past and current presidents to tell, in a stage show, the story of American leadership since its inception. The details in this attraction would have indeed made Walt proud. The presidents all breathe and have subtle movements (such as fingertip movement, slight head nodding, and eye blinking when others are speaking). Franklin Roosevelt even shifts in his wheelchair throughout the show. This allows guests to connect to the show and essentially lose track of time, and for even a brief moment they can envision former presidents of vastly different eras engaged in a modern-day conversation. Disney pays attention to details that others think don't matter. Guests need to be more than just satisfied. In a crowded marketplace, they need to be delighted and feel compelled to recommend you to other consumers and to realistically consider you the next time around.

DISNEY LESSON 29: CREATE DEEPLY IMMERSIVE EXPERIENCES FOR YOUR CUSTOMERS

By preserving the guest experience through storytelling details and immersion at all costs, Disney has not only maintained but dramatically strengthened its position as the runaway global leader of ultra-premium theme park, vacation, cruise, and resort experiences. Disney knows and is very comfortable with who and what it is, and premium pricing goes hand in hand with highly ornate detail and immersive experiences. Disney owns a unique position in the experience-based vacation market that caters to premium-seeking consumers. These consumers recognize that Disney transports them from everyday life and provides them with feelings and emotions that are uniquely Disney. No matter the industry, it is imperative that entrepreneurs find their niche in their space. Middle ground means no man's land, and low-price offerings are very susceptible to low barriers of entry. In a business that relies heavily on employee and guest engagement in a physical environment, details are everything. How can you create a premium experience that customers crave and for which they are willing to pay a premium? As an entrepreneur, what do you believe in? Do you believe in your offering enough to demonstrate that belief by properly investing in it?

Authenticity With a Heavy Dose of Fairytale

Disney Imagineers have the ability to create scenes that are better than reality without making them look corny or overdone. Main Street, U.S.A., depicted in Disney's flagship parks as a representative of turn of the century small town America, depicts a romanticized version of Marceline, Missouri. Walt wanted to depict the ideal Main Street, and that tradition is masterfully carried out across Disney parks and resorts today.

The Grizzly River Peak area in Disney California Adventure Park provides another example of authenticity with a heavy—yet classy—dose of romanticism. The area, which represents a western U.S. national park, features stunning details.

The signs—including road markers—in the area all have the look of U.S. national park signage in terms of colors, fonts, and materials used. There is a "park" map as you enter the area and a station wagon loaded down with family vacation gear and a canoe on top. The restrooms look like that of a national park, and a warning about not feeding the bears is painted on the outside wall. A billboard with the inscription "Grizzly River Peak Yours to Enjoy" marks the area and reminds guests that national parks are for everyone. One side of the area includes Grizzly Peak Airfield (featuring Disney's popular flight simulator, Soarin'), which is themed to fit the national park area. The centerpiece attraction, Grizzly River Run, is a rustic but extremely exhilarating five-minute water rapids ride that Disney built around an old mill and national park stream and waterfall area. Even the gift shop features pine floors, wood shelving, and large pine beam rafters. The area is lined with subtle yet classy landscaping and is nicely painted, but simple brown rails separate guests from the landscaping. Visitors would not see landscaping and well-maintained rails at a national park, but this is Disney's romanticized version of a national park.

Disney Imagineers do an unparalleled job of creating illusion through a trick called forced perspective. The objective is to make physical structures appear larger—and sometimes smaller—than they actually are. For instance, due to height restrictions that require flashing beacons to be placed on taller buildings for airplane safety, Cinderella Castle at Magic Kingdom park in Walt Disney World is under two hundred feet tall, yet to guests it appears several hundred feet tall. To overcome its relatively small stature, Imagineers employed innovative tricks to unveil this central "weenie" (visual magnet)[18] as guests enter the park. First, the view of the castle is blocked by the train station as guests enter the park. The train station serves as a curtain, as the stage (park) is unveiled on the other side. During the transition, posters from the various lands spark the imagination of guests and preview what they are about to experience in the various lands of the park. As guests enter the park, the theater on the right blocks the visual intrusion of the Contemporary Resort in the background. Disney Imagineers were careful to eliminate all distractions from the show, something Walt was not fully able to do at Disneyland because of the hotels built right up against his park's property. The buildings and road of Main Street, U.S.A., serve as a "red carpet" to the castle. While the buildings on Main Street are three stories, they are far from typical. They are made to appear bigger than they are, as windows are full scale on the first floor, seven-eighths scale on the second floor, and five-eighths scale on the third floor. Not only does this give the illusion that the buildings are larger but it also makes the castle in the distance appear larger and taller as well. Finally, the scaling trick is also used on windows and bricks on the castle, as they get progressively smaller as the structure rises in height. As previously mentioned, even Main Street, U.S.A., itself is heavily romanticized. While Main Street, U.S.A., is modeled after Marceline, Missouri (where Walt lived from the ages of five to nine),[19] it represents what an *ideal* version of the typical American small town would look, sound, feel, and smell like.

Guests don't visit Disney parks and resorts to see average and typical. Walt figured this out way before his time, and he capitalized on romanticizing the relatability of everyday places and things to drive guest engagement and experience. Entrepreneurs can employ similar tactics, whether physical or behavioral, to create a professional image and first-class experience. For example, using "we" and other language tricks can go a long way toward portraying the business as one that has been around a long time and is perhaps bigger than it really is. While entrepreneurs should not mislead customers about the capabilities of their companies, they can certainly work to eliminate any unnecessary mental blocks of doing business with them.

Additional Entrepreneurial Insights

Leveraging Intellectual Property (IP)

Disney Parks and Resorts also leverages the company's intellectual properties and host of franchises in the parks in an effort to better connect with guests. There are several strategies at play here, but this brand integration is becoming an increasingly effective strategy for the Walt Disney Company. First, it promotes newer franchises, such as Guardians of the Galaxy with the newly rethemed Guardians of the Galaxy—Mission: Breakout! from the former Twilight Zone Tower of Terror attraction at Disney California Adventure Park. Second, it allows guests to see and interact with familiar franchises from television and movies and to thus feel more at home upon entry to the parks. Third, it provides the company with an avenue to keep well-established brands alive. This was a key strategy in the Cars Land expansion at Disney California Adventure as well as Toy Story Land at Disney's Hollywood Studios and Shanghai Disneyland, Pixar Place at Disney California Adventure, and Star Wars: Galaxy's Edge at Disney's Hollywood Studios and Disneyland. Even the long-term strategy of Animal Kingdom's Pandora—World of Avatar started to make more sense to the general public in light of Disney's exclusive contracts with Avatar producer, James Cameron,[20] and its pending purchase of Twenty-First Century Fox,[21] given Fox will be producing at least two sequels of the highest grossing movie ever produced.[22]

A critical factor in Disney promoting its own intellectual properties is control. Disney can much more easily mitigate the risk of controversy or brand changes when it controls the IP. This is something to consider as you decide on using your own brands and IP or someone else's. Even if you have contractual checks and balances in place for the use of external IP, you could very well never recover from public relations nightmares you cannot entirely control.

Iger's acquisitions of Pixar, Lucasfilm, Marvel, and now possibly Twenty-First Century Fox, have positioned the company well to leverage a broad, diverse, and powerful IP portfolio across a wide variety of platforms,[23] and parks and resorts play a significant role in providing Disney fans with opportunities to touch and feel, i.e., experience, those properties. The parks make the franchises come to life for guests in ways traditional mediums just cannot. Entrepreneurs and leaders should be examining whether they are integrating and building their brands and properties into their customer experience to leverage those assets, build their popularity, uniquely engage them with customers, and increase their longevity.

Partnerships

Although Disney prefers to control as much of its own environment as tightly as it possibly can, Eisner and Iger were smart to recognize they needed to enhance their operations through sponsorships and partnerships with other best-in-class experts if they were going to realize the growth they needed to strengthen their position in the marketplace. This is perhaps most prevalent when it comes to merchandise and restaurants in the parks, though Disney is venturing into new territory in terms of technology. Walt started this practice with world's fair exhibit sponsorships from General Electric, Ford, Pepsi, and the state of Illinois,[24] and today Disney truly has partnerships down to a science.

Merchandise partners are easily identifiable by most Disney guests, but other parks and resorts collaborations are not as easily recognizable. Disney has co-branded merchandise with strong partners, such as Vera Bradley, Dooney & Bourke, Pandora, and Lego, among countless others. While Disney parks and resorts feature the best in dining, Disney recognizes it needs partners to run some of these locations. The experiences in these establishments are typically authentically Disney, and the guests are generally unaware that a given restaurant is not actually run by Disney or even employing Disney cast members. This is because Disney trains these employees as if they were its own, sets the same service and professionalism standards for its partners and their employees, and only collaborates with exceptional operators who have a proven track record. For example, Landry's and the Patina Group have a strong presence in Disney's domestic parks. Landry's, which operates over six hundred locations worldwide,[25] runs the famed Yak & Yeti restaurant in Animal Kingdom park. At Disney World and Disneyland, the Patina Group runs several locations, headlined by Via Napoli Ristorante e Pizzeria and Tutto Italia at Epcot and Naples Ristorante e Pizzeria and Tortilla Jo's in Downtown Disney at Disneyland Resort. Gibsons Steakhouse, an iconic restaurant chain out of Chicago that features its own grade of premium beef, locked arms with Disney to launch the Boathouse restaurant in 2015 as part of the Downtown Disney transformation into Disney Springs at Walt Disney World. Six months after opening, one manager described the training provided by Disney as extensive. He said they went as far as preparing them for the unusual sales volume typically realized by other Disney partners. He described the training as excellent but admitted that nothing could have totally prepared them for the traffic and revenue, which were several times higher than their very successful Chicago locations.

Disney Parks and Resorts also relies on entertainment partners, such as Cirque du Soleil. They have recently partnered with Pleasant Grove, California, technology company The VOID to offer Star Wars Virtual Reality (VR) experiences at Downtown Disney in California and Disney Springs in Florida. The company was founded in 2015 and features cutting edge VR offerings. There is strong speculation that Disney is partnering with The VOID to create one or more of the attractions in Star Wars: Galaxy's Edge lands at Disneyland and Hollywood Studios. Disney even partnered with Splitsville lanes in late 2012 to provide a unique bowling and dining experience at Disney Springs. The concept features more than fifty thousand square feet and over twenty lanes and has been so popular at Disney Springs that Disney partnered with the company to open a second location at Disneyland's Downtown Disney March 2018.

Finally, Disney has also partnered with international companies to make its global properties a reality. Its partnership with the publicly traded Japanese corporation Oriental Land Company (ORC) has made Tokyo Disney Resort a very profitable licensing venture. ORC owns the resort, Disney provides Imagineering support and standards, and ORC remits licensing fees and royalties to Disney. As previously mentioned, the result is what many in the industry regard as Disney's finest theme park resort. Disney even went so far as to partner with the Chinese government to create its newest resort, Shanghai Disneyland, in 2016, after more than a decade of negotiation and planning.

Disney understands the value of outside expertise and outside perspective. These partners not only provide Disney with space expertise but they also invite unique perspectives to Disney operations. Disney wants these partnerships to be win-win. They want their partners to learn and get better because of the relationship. Likewise, Disney wants to gain knowledge and improve as a result of collaborating with industry experts. While it is important to protect and maintain control of the integrity of your venture, as described above, do not overlook the benefits of leveraging partnerships with space experts to deliver an even better product. When compared with your competitors, these collaborations could very well be what put your offerings over the top.

Synergistic Innovations

Similar to the partnerships described above, Disney has never been afraid to merge different cultures and industries. Walt started this practice when he merged his concepts with the principles of the carnivals, amusemennt parks, and movies to create Disneyland. Mixing multiple industries with distinctly different cultures—particularly when one of those cultures is Disney and the other also holds its own very specific beliefs and values—is challenging, but the collision of very different worlds can result in incredible innovations. For some great examples, consider further examining the partnerships mentioned above. There is no question Disney's ability to merge its business model with the hotel, restaurant, retail, and merchandise industries has been a key factor in the company's success. Its humility in researching the leaders in those industries not only led to better Disney operations in those areas but also afforded Disney the luxury of reimagining what could be better about those functions—especially with an infusion of the Disney difference.

Remember how George Kalogridis brought the pin collecting hobby back to Walt Disney World from the Olympics? In order to successfully launch the pin business at Disney World, he and his team essentially had to blend the Olympic pin trading and Disney cultures together. A great deal of research went into what motivated different pin enthusiasts (Olympians, vendors, corporate sponsors, fans) in the Olympic Village and how what worked in that space could translate to the Disney cast member and fan culture.

The original idea for Adventures by Disney vacations came from European river cruises. The cruises included top-shelf accommodations but, more importantly, featured personalized service and unique vacation and touring experiences. Similarly, when Disney entered the cruise line industry in 1996, the company researched the industry with an eye toward how it could leverage what vacationers liked about cruises while also infusing Disney principles to create a unique market niche. The venture has been wildly successful because Disney has tested and stretched the boundaries of both ship makers and professionals in the industry. The other well-established cruise lines of the day had to think Disney was crazy for entering their space, but it did not take long for Disney to be a leader in the field. While the ship design and itinerary advances Disney activated in the industry are great, it should come as no surprise that cast members are the highest rated element of Disney cruises. Disney magic translates so well to other industries because Disney Imagineers and frontline cast members serve their guests better than any large company in the world.

Disney has even been extremely successful in blending the cultures of different countries. Consider the various countries represented in the World Showcase at Epcot. Disney recruits and hires the best and brightest of those countries to work for hourly wages via one-year visas. The hiring process is extremely competitive, but the international cast members view this as a great opportunity, and Disney does not disappoint. The training, enculturating, and onboarding are phenomenal, and thus the guest experience and atmosphere in the World Showcase are vibrant.

The greatest examples of Disney's ability to blend cultures are the Hawaiian Disney Vacation Club resort, Aulani, and Animal Kingdom park. Disney describes Aulani as uniquely Disney and authentically Hawaiian. The company put great care into absorbing Hawaiian values into Disney corporate values, and the local cast members and business partners have greatly appreciated it. Sure, the resort is impressive, but it is the care that was put into the business model, leader and supervisor training, and cast member training that has made Aulani such a great success. Similarly, Disney carefully consulted with animal and zoo experts when planning Animal Kingdom park. While zoo animals are assets on corporate balance sheets and expenses that go toward maintaining the health of those animals show up on income statements, Disney was very intentional about understanding and respecting the values of the zookeepers and other professionals who dedicate their lives to conservation and the care of animals. The dignity of the animals is to be respected at all times at Animal Kingdom. For example, a guest will never see an elephant wearing a tutu despite the fact that it would be a convenient and recognizable reference to Disney's Dumbo. Likewise, Disney had to bring along the animal caretaker culture in understanding the importance of appearance and guest service. Blending the two cultures was a significant challenge, but the end result was arguably the most unique and innovative theme park in the world, and a zoo atmosphere like no other.

Entrepreneurs and corporate innovators ought to overlook the challenges and consider the potential creative benefits of combining two distinctly different cultures when examining expansion, partnership, merger, or buyout opportunities. While everyone else is either not thinking of or quickly dismissing the concept of unlikely combinations, entrepreneurial companies can thrive by creating unforgettable experiences through successfully blending seemingly different business models, industries, cultures, and concepts.

Add-Ons and Premium Offerings

Success breeds opportunities for more success. No one has mastered the art of add-on and premium offerings like Disney, but the company has earned the right to present guests with these options because of the excellence of their operations over the years. They have figured out how to best cater to the wide variety of guests at their parks and resorts by offering everything from basic resorts and one-park-per-day admission tickets to extremely exquisite optional experience enhancements.

Walt Disney World offers literally hundreds of add-on and premium experiences. Enchanting carriage rides are offered at the Port Orleans and Fort Wilderness resort hotels. The property also has multiple miniature golf offerings, but the Fairways course is an incredibly unique experience that features holes with varying terrain, ranging from par three to five. Guests can treat their kids to a pirate costuming experience at the Pirates of the Caribbean attraction or a princess makeover at one of two locations at the beloved Bibbidi Bobbidi Boutique. Spouses or significant others can also take advantage of floral services to have gifts and floral arrangements sent to their hotel room during their stay.

Walt Disney World and Disneyland visitors can add various behind-the-scenes tours to their park admission. Disney World guests can add a photo service to their vacation package, while Disneyland visitors have the option of adding

MaxPass to their annual passes or daily admission tickets through their phone, which provides them with the opportunity to book electronic FastPasses for attractions and download photos from the resort. Similarly, after-hours parties offer access to the parks to a limited number of people, which provides easier access to attractions due to shorter lines. Some add-on experiences are quite expensive, such as dessert parties that provide access to premium fireworks viewing areas and VIP touring services that provide groups of up to ten with transportation and a guide and the ability to park hop and access unlimited FastPasses. Disney also offers special event tickets for concerts, festivals, and hugely popular holiday parties, such as Mickey's Not-So-ScaryHalloween Party and Mickey's Very Merry Christmas Party. The parks typically close early (seven o'clock) for these holiday parties, so Disney nearly doubles its ticket selling capacity on these days.

Like most premium hotels, Disney's deluxe resort hotels offer club level floors and rooms that provide dining options and concierge services. Wedding and event catering services are also available at deluxe resorts for family reunions, company events, and other gatherings.

Mathews Family Moment: Resort Experiences

Our kids love the campfires at Disney resorts. While marshmallows for roasting are provided for free, guests can also purchase s'mores kits. Further, Julie and I love the premium experience provided by booking a room at the Grand Californian Hotel & Spa at the Disneyland Resort in California. The classy resort features a resort guest exclusive entrance to Disney California Adventure Park that enters through the backside of the Grizzly River Peak area. As you can imagine from our description of the Grizzly Peak area at California Adventure, the craftsman-style resort is conveniently themed after national park lodges, though Disney romanticized it a great deal.

Have you perfected your offerings to the point that you have earned the right to sell add-on and premium services, products, and experiences to your customers? How could you leverage what you are already doing well to create and offer premium experiences? Entrepreneurs should examine where they can grow their offerings to further enhance the customer experience and maximize revenue and performance.

Attracting New Guests and Catering to a Variety of Demographics

You might have garnered the impression that Disney could just sit on its robust business model and rely on the extremely loyal customers it currently has. While the company caters to families with younger children, with its emphasis on princesses, it has historically had a reputation for catering to younger girls. Thus, the investments in Lucas and Marvel previously mentioned were extremely strategic, in that they provided Disney with avenues to engage males of all ages more than ever before. Because of this, Disney parks are quickly becoming complete family vacation destinations. This will be even more true as Marvel properties and Star Wars lands become a major piece of Disney theme parks and resorts (Disney recently confirmed a Star Wars themed hotel is also in the works for Walt Disney World)[26] moving forward.

There has also always been some level of cultural pressure on parents and grandparents to take their families to Disney resorts, and some people have been able to resist the urge to do so. Disney has strategies in place to draw new guests to the resorts to introduce them to the magic of their offerings. One of those penetration strategies has been to attract unsuspecting new guests through hosting conventions and Disney Institute[27] training sessions at convention centers at its resort hotels. Disney World hotels alone feature more than seven hundred thousand square feet of convention center space, and continue to expand.[28] These travelers are often required or heavily encouraged by their employers and industry trade associations to attend these conferences on Disney properties across the world. Once there, first-timers are treated to first-class amenities and catering and are immersed in the unique atmosphere and impeccable service of Disney resorts. Disney even works with the companies and trade organizations to provide unique character interactions and theme park experiences as a part of the conventions. We have taken groups from the university down to Walt Disney World each of the last ten years with great success, but a couple of years ago the service we experienced from our Boardwalk Inn group account manager, Matthew Harrelson, so impressed our group that many of them—including some previous Disney naysayers—were planning just a few days into the trip to bring their families back. These trips have always led to new Disney fans in our groups, and we have also witnessed participants from Disney Institute sessions we attended being converted as well. These events not only help Disney fill resort hotels during typically slower times but they also provide exposure to potential new customers.

Some people are drawn to Disney because it is viewed among families as a rite of passage for kids, but Disney is aware that theme parks are not going to appeal to everybody. Therefore, high-end Disney resorts feature complete spas, and guests can find high-end fine dining experiences like Victoria & Albert's in the Grand Floridian Resort & Spa at Walt Disney World. Disney World also offers four world-class golf courses, and a whole host of other activities, like carriage rides, miniature golf, and exclusive dessert parties, among countless others across Disney parks and resorts. Disney recognizes that some families will never be interested enough in theme parks to even consider visiting their traditional theme park-based resorts; thus, they also market the previously mentioned Disney Cruise Line and Adventures by Disney experiences to those demographics—as well as giving Disney enthusiasts new experiences to try.

The Disney college program at Walt Disney World is another great example of a potential connection with new customer groups. Because the program serves over nine thousand students at a time,[29] parents, and even friends and other family members that help students move to Florida, are exposed to first-class Disney service during their visit. This often leads to new "fans" of Disney.

Disney Vacation Club (DVC), the timeshare arm of the Walt Disney Company, has exploded onto the scene since its inception in 2001. DVC features fourteen domestic resorts. Ten of those destinations are at Walt Disney World and one is at the Disneyland Resort, with a new one scheduled to be added to Disneyland in 2019. Over two hundred thousand memberships have been sold. Three resorts are not associated with theme parks: Aulani in Hawaii, Vero Beach, Florida, and Hilton Head Island, South Carolina.[30] These resorts cater to a country club membership lifestyle demographic. As one Disney executive told us, as a leader, don't be too quick to dismiss something just because it doesn't personally appeal to you. Consider what new customer types you could cater to by expanding your offerings and providing unique experiences that match their lifestyle and needs.

Systems and Processes

We outlined Disney processes and systems at length in Chapter Six, but it is worth revisiting. All six of Disney's domestic theme parks welcome over nine million guests per year,[31] and their resort hotels are at or near capacity year-round. Some might argue that systems and processes surely must get in the way of Disney's high-class and service-oriented business model, but the opposite is actually true. Disney's model is threefold: deliver a quality cast member experience, deliver a high-quality guest experience, and build, implement, and continue to support, model, and innovate quality business processes that enhance high-level cast member and guest experiences. Disney *had* to build the systems in order to *manage* the high volume of guests in its parks and resorts. Only when process, people, and place come together can you have exceptional service and customer experiences.

In the corporate world, it is well known that Disney has the most sophisticated pricing models in business. This is not by chance, as the company employs hundreds of mathematicians to analyze the massive amount of data the company collects. As one Disney executive advised us, don't be afraid to hire experts—people that are smarter than you. Pricing is a delicate balance, especially at the premium experience level; thus, systems are critical. Even Disney's *The Lion King* uses the pricing models, and that led to becoming the first Broadway show to top one billion dollars in sales and the only Broadway play to out-gross *Phantom of the Opera*.[32]

Knowing your customer is a critical element of determining how and what systems you implement. As mentioned earlier in the chapter, Disneyland and

Walt Disney World cater to very different customer types; thus, the electronic customer engagement and self-management systems (web and phone applications) are very different. My Disney Experience and the FastPass+ system were built for the occasional Walt Disney World vacationer, while the MaxPass system was built for both locals who frequently visit the resort and vacationers. This is because Disneyland hosts significantly more locals than does Disney World. In fact, on any given day, local pass holders represent a minimum of 50 percent to a maximum of 90 percent of total park visitors.

DISNEY LESSON 30: PROCESSES AND SYSTEMS ARE CRITICAL TO MAKING YOUR ENTREPRENEURIAL DREAMS A REALITY

While systems and processes might—rightfully so in many cases—scare or even discourage entrepreneurs and corporate innovators, systems and processes that are created with employees, customers, and efficiency in mind are a critical element of realizing the entrepreneurial dream. Disney understands this and uses processes and systems to create and maintain seamless experiences. However, as we will discuss at the end of the chapter, it is critical to be humble when it comes to systems. Processes and systems need to always be up for discussion, improvement, and removal as the marketplace, employees, consumers, and technolgy evolve. Small and large companies alike should never be satisfied with their position. Innovation is a way of life for successful and sustainable organizations. In fact, Disney is as much a technology company as it is an entertainment company.

Attraction and Resort Innovations

We have provided details on countless innovations at Disney parks and resorts in this book. As one executive put it, Disney prides itself on ongoing, relentless innovation. As we have outlined in the last two chapters, that is why so many ideas come from all ranks in the company.

While Soarin' Around the World is a very popular attraction, the story of its creation is not well known. After the first design (modeled after a multitiered, moving dry-cleaning rack system) proved not to be feasible, Imagineer Mark Sumner developed a working prototype using his child's Erector set and string. The finished version of the ride holds eighty-seven guests on three tiers, all hoisted into the air using a cantilever system, where flight over California sights (the attraction now features global sights in its second version) is simulated using seat movement, sound, scents, and, of course, movement of IMAX video images on a very large screen.[33] An important final note on Soarin' is that it is not without flaws. First, riders seated in the lower two levels can see the dangling feet of riders above them. Second, the curve of the screen distorts the images for those sitting left and right of center. Fixing these hiccups in the ride system would have been cost prohibitive, both from financial and downtime standpoints. However, in true Disney fashion, Disney Imagineers addressed these issues when designing Avatar—Flight of Passage, a ride system that has many similarities to Soarin'.

In the late 1980s, Disney realized it was way behind the competition in terms of its water park offerings. Prior to 1989, Disney World had just one water park, River Country. The quaint park was situated on the shore of Bay Lake, right next to the Fort Wilderness Campground beach. River Country was a low-capacity water park, and with growing competition in the area, Disney realized it needed to make a strategic entrepreneurial move. The company did extensive research on the industry and once again sprinted past the competition, opening two highly themed water parks (Typhoon Lagoon in 1989 and Blizzard Beach in 1995). In addition, Disney included a "mini" water park with the 1990 opening of the Yacht and Beach Club resorts at Walt Disney World. The unique and impressive three acre facility,[34] Stormalong Bay, features a massive shipwreck slide, lazy river, sand bottom, and shallow beach area for younger children. River Country was a popular destination, but it was partially run on lake water, expensive to maintain, small, and lacking in modern attractions. The 2001 closing of River Country was a significant paradigm shift for Disney, but the company realized it was necessary to stay relevant in the water park industry. Entrepreneurs and leaders have to guard themselves against clinging too tightly to traditions or business models the market has sprinted past.

Seven Dwarfs Mine Train debuted in Magic Kingdom's New Fantasyland in 2014 and has consistently been one of the most sought after FastPasses, with one of the longest wait times in all of Disney World. The unique roller coaster features a brief ride in the mine, where media-enhanced animatronics come to life. The most innovative feature of the coaster is that the individual mine carts sway side to side as the ride twists and turns on the silky smooth track. The family-friendly coaster also has thrill elements, such as drops and tight turns. Imagineers brilliantly fit the ride into a relatively small space in the middle of New Fantasyland, and thus the only criticism of the attraction is the brevity of the ride itself. Disney opened Toy Story Land in Hollywood Studios in June 2018, premiering the Slinky Dog Dash roller coaster, which also uses the swaying engineering featured on Seven Dwarfs Mine Train. However, Slinky Dog Dash is about twice as long a ride as Seven Dwarfs Mine Train.

Many competitors and analysts have misjudged the innovation efforts of Disney Parks and Resorts. The company embraces relentless innovation at all levels, so why is this? Could it be that Disney's penchant for holding on to core values and traditions and key classic attractions blinds others from seeing

Disney's quest to constantly ask questions and reinvent itself through countless advancements?

There have been a plethora of Disney copycats over the last handful of decades, but almost all have failed miserably. Only Universal has had some notable success—just enough to hold Disney accountable to its continuous improvement standards—but even Universal has fought really hard only to see minimal attendance gains on Disney. Universal—despite some impressive attractions—has only been able to come close to the attendance levels of Disney's most lightly visited Orlando parks with its two signature theme parks in Orlando, Florida. Why is this? It is extremely unique for one company to completely dominate an industry for several decades in a row. It is because of the foundations laid by Walt and Roy (outlined in the first four chapters), the critical strategies employed by Eisner and Iger (outlined in Chapter Five), and the business principles covered in Chapters Six and Seven of this book. Disney has been able to consistently hold tightly to the values and principles of what has made the company so successful and admired while also always seeking feedback, listening to ideas, and reacting to changes in the marketplace. But Disney is not infallible. Organizations can fall into a rut (especially without the right leaders) and level off, just as the Disney Company did in the 1970s and early 1980s (discussed in Chapter Five). Given the current high levels of success of Disney parks and resorts, the company will have to guard against falling into the trap of complacency.

Patience and Humility

The general public has been fairly critical of Disney Parks and Resorts construction endeavors, considering them long-drawn-out projects, but the company has proven it is not afraid to take its time getting projects right. In fact, it is quite common for Disney to make design changes to new areas and lands along the entire process, from conception to construction to grand opening. Disney has made it very clear it is in it for the long haul time and time again. Take the Star Wars: Galaxy's Edge projects at Disneyland Park and Disney World's Hollywood Studios, for example. The largest land expansions in Disney parks history, both Galaxy's Edge additions are over-three-year projects. Finally, there is perhaps no greater example of Disney's patience than the transformation of Downtown Disney at Walt Disney World into Disney Springs. The massive project, featuring over 150 new tenants, tripled the number of restaurants and shops in the already expansive Downtown Disney district, but it also took more than three years to complete.[35]

Disney also understands the need to make changes and corrections. Just as we examined above, Disney recognizes when it is time to make advances by abandoning traditions or previous strategies or business models. In addition, sometimes projects take major turns. Such was the case with the Pop Century value resort expansion at Disney World, which was abruptly halted in 2008.

Disney decided it was not the right direction to go, as the parks were growing in popularity and more guests were willing to stay at moderate and deluxe level resort hotels. Disney redirected the resources originally dedicated to finishing the Pop Century expansion to the New Fantasyland project (another multiyear undertaking) at Magic Kingdom park. In addition to the fact that the highest volume park in the world desperately needed a capacity boost, Fantasyland was also in need of a facelift and modernization. The reimagined area not only features some of the most beloved attractions at Disney World, including Seven Dwarfs Mine Train, Enchanted Tales with Belle, Dumbo the Flying Elephant (with twice the capacity), Barnstormer, and Under the Sea—Journey with the Little Mermaid, it also includes the wildly popular, high-capacity Beauty and the Beast themed restaurant, Be Our Guest. The transformed area has truly become a favorite of guests. As for the abandoned Pop Century project, Disney recommenced construction in 2012 but rebranded the facility as its fifth value resort. However, the rebrand to Art of Animation took on an intriguing twist. A portion of the rooms were redeveloped into more premium, higher priced family suites themed after movie franchises, i.e., *Cars*, *Finding Nemo*, *The Little Mermaid*, and *The Lion King*. Disney's ability to pivot based on the most critical needs of the entire organization speaks to the willingness of leaders to swallow their pride and think innovation first. The lesson for entrepreneurs and corporate innovators? Never become too prideful about your ideas, or even your works in progress. Changing gears is often the difference between success and failure. If your data, customers, employees, and instincts are telling you to pivot, you owe it to yourself and your stakeholders to at least pause and consider your options.

As good as Disney is when it comes to creating magical vacations, the company makes plenty of mistakes. As one Disney executive told us years ago, the guests provide feedback through your financials. Sometimes humility means improving elements of your business model that are actually *good*, or even *very good*. Think back to our discussion of the Tower of Terror attraction. While the version at Disney California Adventure Park was good, Imagineers learned from cast member and guest feedback that there could be improvements to make it a better experience. They made changes in other versions across the country based on the feedback, and the result was dramatically improved guest experience ratings at those locations. As always, Disney evaluated California Adventure's version of Tower of Terror against Disney standards—not typical theme park benchmarks. As we outlined earlier in this chapter, they even went so far as to reimagine the California version into Guardians of the Galaxy—Mission: Breakout!

Other times, humility means admitting failure and making dramatic changes. Such was the case at Disneyland Paris and Disney California Adventure Park, two of the company's most famous reboots. Disneyland Paris—originally named Euro Disney—was a joint venture with Kingdom Holding Company, and opened in 1982. The resort was such a disappointment that one executive described the grand opening weekend as "miserable, lonely, and depressing." According to that leader, Disney employees were essentially the only guests of the resort's flagship hotel that weekend. Other challenges included Paris weather, French attitudes toward American culture, French work ideologies, and French personalities conflicting with the importance Disney placed on extroversion and service. The resort continued to be a huge financial drain on the company until several investments were made, including new attractions and a second gate, Walt Disney Studios, in 2002. Despite these significant investments, the resort showed only minimal profit that proved challenging to sustain. In 2017, Disney made a bold move to purchase the bulk of the outstanding stock in Disneyland Paris. With Disney officially running the show and planning and announcing multibillion-dollar investments in the resort, the company is expecting a financial turnaround there.[36]

Disney California Adventure Park at Disneyland Resort in Anaheim, California, fell far short of meeting company and guest expectations. Eisner opened the park in 2001 as the second gate to the iconic Disneyland Resort. The much-maligned park was not embraced by the local Disney enthusiasts to such an extent that—despite Disney's "released" annual attendance numbers ranging from one to five million—cast members who worked the park in that era say that most days total guests numbered in the *hundreds at best*. In fact, one cast member who had worked at Carthay Circle restaurant told us that it was not uncommon for whole days to go by without *any* guests dining there. The first-year guest experience satisfaction rates were only 20 percent at California Adventure. Disney spent about five to six years discounting ticket prices and adding attractions to bolster the modest park, which was described by Bob Iger in his 2007 announcement of a $1.1 billion expansion of the park as "mediocre" and a detriment to the Disney brand. All areas of the park were reimagined, several headliner attractions were added, a more family-friendly atmosphere was created, a unique nighttime show was added, and as outlined earlier in the chapter, the impressive and immersive addition of Cars Land was built to bring the park up to Disney standards. The park grand reopening was held in 2012 after the massive, multistage, five-year project.[37] The guests approved, as attendance skyrocketed to the point where Disney California Adventure ranked as the eleventh most attended park in the world in 2016, with just under 9.3 million visitors.[38]

These two ventures were in a fairly long list of bold and aggressive expansions by Eisner that did not hit the mark like his other projects. There is no doubt Eisner laid the valuable framework for what is making Disney parks and resorts thrive today, but Disney benefitted from Iger's bold decision to build out and perfect that infrastructure. Eisner's overconfidence in the Disney brand led to challenges with these two projects. Disneyland Paris and Disney California Adventure Park seem to be the result of a highly successful, yet spontaneous and creative artist entrepreneurial leader being able to sell most anything through his more than adequate evangelical talents. Have you ever had a setback shortly after a big success? Are you willing to allow customers, employees, and partners to hold you accountable? Have you gone into ventures relying on your name or current position in the market alone? Will you react to feedback by making bold moves to protect your offerings and your brand? These are critical self-examinations that entrepreneurs and corporate innovators and leaders must be willing to make on a perpetual basis.

Further, if your financials are speaking to you, that means your customers are sending you a message. These messages cannot be ignored or put on the backburner. Instead, be grateful for the feedback. This data reminds you that it is time to lean in, listen to the perspectives of customers, vendors, and employees—and innovate. Instead of looking at financial disappointments as a failure, reframe them as opportunities. What has made Disney such an enduring company is its ability to so intimately connect to its customers. Disney's model takes an incredible amount of diligence, intentionality, and discipline, but it can be replicated in part or in whole.

Conclusion

Disney parks and resorts connect with their guests better than anyone in the business world. It is rare to see employees elsewhere as genuinely engaged with the customer as Disney cast members are, especially in today's marketplace. Guests have such a fondness for their encounters with frontline cast members that the vast majority of their follow-up communication with the company is about service experiences while at the parks and resorts. Guests actually speak of the cast members more than the impressive physical environments and attractions in their feedback to Disney. That's not true of very many organizations, if any. Make no mistake, the concept of place is a key ingredient in Disney's success, but positive human interactions and relationships are what motivate people to return to a park.

What sets Disney parks and resorts apart cannot simply be passed off as magic—*it doesn't just magically happen!* Disney and its leaders are diligent about striving for excellence in hiring, onboarding, training, and ongoing coaching relationships with cast members. Further, they give cast members creative license and empower spontaneity to delight guests in the moment. Finally, they listen to their ideas and perspectives and act on their input, which encourages aspirational thinking and behavior. So, no, it doesn't just magically happen. Disney is a very disciplined company that intentionally and diligently prepares and empowers its cast members to build lasting relationships with guests.

Disney is also intentional about providing opportunities for cast members to engage with guests and provide magical moments. For instance, sometimes the backstage becomes onstage, as is the case with animal surgery viewing times at the Animal Kingdom Conservation Station and backstage tours. Other times, guests enter the show, which we see with *Festival of the Lion King*, Jedi Training, the Enchanted Tales with Belle attraction, and park rope drop ceremonies, among others. In addition, merchandise (such as pin trading) and premium experiences (such as dessert and holiday parties), among other tools, drive cast member engagement with guests. Disney understands the power of stirring emotions in consumers and has built a powerful formula for success in doing so.

If guests remember cast members over attractions and physical environment, then why does Disney emphasize place so much? The answer is simple— excellence in place accomplishes two key objectives for Disney: 1) it supports the mission of the company (best in entertainment), sending the message that the company is committed to that mission; and 2) the spectacular physical environments support cast members in creating happiness and making magic for guests. Physical environment and tools to do the job at a high level are never in question for Disney cast members. The two go hand in hand. You can't have one without the other. Consider big box retail stores. They build impressive physical places and systems, but they rarely have an emotional connection with the customer, which leaves them eternally vulnerable to the lower priced option or next best shop that opens down the street (or on the internet).

We outlined many of the ways in which Disney supports its mission and cast members in delivering on its mission. These include partnerships (like the ones with Landry and the Patina Group), synergistic innovations by pairing unlikely concepts or industries (such as theme park and zoo industries; Animal Kingdom), leveraging IP in the parks (like Marvel and *Star Wars*), technology (such as MyMagic+ and MaxPass), operational systems and processes (like sophisticated pricing models and detailed operation manuals), and meeting the demands of a broad set of demographics through ancillary offerings (such as golf, vacation club memberships, and conventions).

Finally, we covered how Disney achieves excellence with its physical environments in its parks and resorts. Tools used by Disney include immersion through storytelling and fairytale, sensory appeal (lighting, sound, and smell), illusion and forced perspective (i.e., Main Street, U.S.A., and the castles), and building strong first and last impressions (park entrances, greetings, and line queues). Disney also exhibits a great deal of patience during design and construction phases to get projects done right, and exhibits humility through research and in listening to diverse perspectives and correcting mistakes.

Perhaps what is most impressive is the Walt Disney Company of today is a culmination of Walt's enduring principles and legacy and what company leaders have learned through triumphs and failures since his death. Walt and Roy toiled for decades to build their animation business, Disneyland, and Walt Disney World

Resorts. Their successors worked hard to regain the magic and navigate a changing competitive environment with great success. What lies next for the Walt Disney Company? Only time will tell, but if the past is any indication of future success, the Walt Disney Company will be just fine.

Disney Principles

- Give your employees the creative license to make spontaneous decisions to delight your customers.
- Immerse your customers in an experience like no other in your industry. Build your physical place and environment with such amazing detail that your customers escape from the realities of their lives. Invite them into your "show" by pulling back the curtain or inviting them to be a part of what you're doing.
- First and last impressions carry a great deal of weight in what your customers say about you and whether they come back.
- Leverage your resources. Look for underutilized assets or opportunities you can leverage to enhance the customer experience. Always look for ways to offer premium and add-on experiences.
- Consider the value of partnerships and seemingly awkward pairings. Don't be afraid to find someone who can pull off a part of your dream better than you can.
- Use systems and processes to further your dream, but also be cognizant of the need to constantly check the value and effectiveness of those controls.
- Have patience to do things the right way. This is especially true of capital expenditures—like construction—that will have a long-term effect on your organization. Also, have the humility to change and adapt if something isn't working. Be flexible!

Work Like Disney: Exercises

1. Are your physical space and environment accurately portraying the image you want to achieve? In what ways could you transform your physical place and environment to operate more like Disney? How would you evaluate those ideas?
2. When you see a new customer, quiz them on their first and last impressions of your organization. Ask them for their honest feedback. Have your employees do the same. Compile the results and solicit ideas for improvement.
3. Are your physical space and environment immersive to the point that customers get a unique experience that emotionally connects them to your company? If not, what could you do to take steps toward greater immersion?
4. Are there functions your organization views as necessary evils and, thus, not performing at a very high level? If so, could you outsource any of those tasks

to better represent your organization? Could you engage a partner where there could be mutual benefit? What quality level would be acceptable to match your brand promise?

5. What functions in your organization could be better organized? Are your employees not providing the best possible customer experience because there is not a well-defined routine or system in place to manage the flow of customers, products, conversations, etc.?

Notes

1. Pine II, B.J., and Gilmore, J.H. (2011). *The Experience Economy*. Boston: Harvard Business Review Press.
2. Meyer, D. (2006). *Setting the Table*. New York: HarperBusiness.
3. Disney Wiki. (2018). *Sword in the Stone Attraction*. Retrieved from http://disney.wikia.com/wiki/Sword_in_the_Stone_(attraction).
4. McEwen, W.J., and Fleming, J.H. (2003, March 13). *Customer Satisfaction Doesn't Count*. Retrieved from http://news.gallup.com/businessjournal/1012/customer-satisfaction-doesnt-count.aspx.
5. Themed Entertainment Association. (2016). *Theme Index Museum Index 2016: Global Attractions Attendance Report*. Retrieved from www.teaconnect.org/images/files/TEA_235_103719_170601.pdf.
6. There is some debate as to what constitutes the actual "kiss goodnight." Others say the kiss goodnight is a final post-closing time show that consists of music, castle projections, and opportunities for guests to get pristine photos of the park while virtually empty.
7. Blank, S. (2013). *The Four Steps to the Epiphany: Successful Strategies for Products that Win*. Sussex, WI: Quad/ Graphics.
8. Hench, J. (2009). *Designing Disney: Imagineering and the Art of Show*. New York: Camphor Tree Book
9. Levine, A. (2016, June 1). *Disney Springs: The Story Behind Disney World's Former Downtown Disney*. Retrieved from https://usatoday.com/story/travel/experience/america/2016/06/01/disney-springs-downtown-disney-walt-disney-world/85208362/.
10. Prosperi, L. (2016). *The Imagineering Pyramid: Using Disney Theme Park Principles to Develop and Promote Your Creative Ideas*. Lexington: Theme Park Press.
11. Norman, D. (2008, August 21). *The Psychology of Waiting Lines*. Retrieved from www.jnd.org/ms/Norman%20The%20Psychology %20of%20 Waiting%20Lines.pdf.
12. Sim, N. (20109, October 31). *Preview: Cars Land at Disney California Adventure*. Retrieved from https://themeparktourist.com/features/20101031/ 2558/preview-cars-land-disney-california-adventure.
13. Bricker, T. (n.d.). *10 Reasons Tokyo DisneySea Is Disney's Best Park*. Retrieved from http://disneytouristblog.com/tokyo-disneysea-best-theme-park/.
14. Chmielewski, D.C., and Keegan, R. (2011, September 21). *Disney to License Rights to 'Avatar' for Theme Park Attractions*. Retrieved from http://articles.latimes.com/2011/sep/21/business/la-fi-ct-disney-avatar-20110921.
15. The Walt Disney Company. (2018). *Adventures By Disney*. Retrieved from www.adventuresbydisney.com/.

16. Ibid.
17. Pine II, B.J., and Gilmore, J.H. (2011). *The Experience Economy*. Boston: Harvard Business Review Press.
18. Prosperi, L. (2016). *The Imagineering Pyramid: Using Disney Theme Park Principles to Develop and Promote Your Creative Ideas*. Lexington: Theme Park Press.
19. Reynolds, C. (2015, July 10). *Disneyland: How Main Street, U.S.A. Is Rooted in Walt Disney's Missouri Childhood*. Retrieved from http://latimes.com/travel/la-tr-d-disneyland-marceline-20150712-story.html.
20. Chmielewski, D.C., and Keegan, R. (2011, September 21). *Disney to License Rights to 'Avatar' for Theme Park Attractions*. Retrieved from http://articles.latimes.com/2011/sep/21/business/la-fi-ct-disney-avatar-20110921.
21. Barnes, B. (2017, December 14). *Disney Makes $52.4 Billion Deal for 21st Century Fox in Big Bet on Streaming*. Retrieved from https://nytimes.com/2017/12/14/business/dealbook/disney-fox-deal.html
22. Box Office Mojo. (n.d.). *Avatar*. Retrieved from www.boxofficemojo.com/movies/?id=avatar.htm.
23. Miller, D. (2015, June 6). *How Robert Iger's 'Fearless' Deal-making Transformed Disney*. Retrieved from http://latimes.com/entertainment/envelope/cotown/la-et-ct-disney-iger-20150607-story.html.
24. Walt Disney Family Museum. (2012, June 26). *Look Closer: 1964 New York World's Fair*. Retrieved from www.waltdisney.org/blog/look-closer-1964-new-york-world%E2%80%99s-fair.
25. Landry's. (2018). *Who We Are*. Retrieved from http://landrysinc.com/aboutUs/default.asp.
26. Fickley-Baker, J. (2017, July 15). *Plans Unveiled for Star Wars-themed Resort at Walt Disney World*. Retrieved from https://disneyparks.disney.go.com/blog/2017/07/plans-unveiled-for-star-wars-inspired-themed-resort-at-walt-disney-world/?CMP=KNC-FY18_WDPR_DPK_INS_DOME_ParksPortfolio_DSA|NB|G|4181000.EPCOT.AM.01.01|NA_NA_NA_NA&keyword_id=aud-309850603842:dsa-140082375613|dc||256030976522|b|5053:3|&gclid=Cj0KCQjw8MvWBRC8ARIsAOFSVBXB9VhaiyQIC3sAVJqCu3q6hS4CCFhNCMK0AZFPCLpx6UyFULNKIB0aAr0yEALw_wcB&s_kwcid=AL!5053!3!256030976522!b!!g!!&ef_id=WtIA0AAAAMQQByvl:20180415180002:s&dclid=COWNiv_tvNoCFYopaQod9Y0IHg.
27. Disney Institute is Disney's external training subsidiary that hosts professional development sessions that share Disney best practices.
28. Walt Disney Company. (2018). *Disney Meetings*. Retrieved from https://disneymeetings.com/disneyworld/.
29. Disney Institute. (2017). *Disney's Approach to Employee Engagement*. Lake Buena Vista, FL: Disney Institute.
30. Walt Disney Company. (2018). *Disney Vacation Club*. Retrieved from https://disneyvacationclub.disney.go.com/destinations/dvc-resorts/?sourcecode=D-023244&CMP=KNC-FY18_WDPR_DVC_ACT_DOM_ClubNAT_RLSA-GOLD-EX|BR|G|4184700.MG.AM.01.04|-_-_SL_EOD&keyword_id=aud-258930846217:kwd-29202966|dc|dvc|241565878978|e|5058:3|&gclid=Cj0KCQjw_ODWBRCTARIsAE2_EvXcb5JEWZ3TAXl43uyVJfh_nE4Q0RImGa6lMb14ViAEJauxFY4iQMcaAiv1EALw_wcB&s_kwcid=AL!5058!3!241565878978!e!!g!!dvc&ef_id=WtIA0AAAAMQQByvl:20180419190626:s&dclid=CKPKpaWEx9oCFUnZwAodbVAK7A.

31. Themed Entertainment Association. (2016). *Theme Index Museum Index 2016: Global Attractions Attendance Report.* Retrieved from www.teaconnect.org/images/files/TEA_235_103719_170601.pdf.
32. Sun, R. (2013, October 16). *'Lion King' Is Broadway's First $1 Billion Show.* Retrieved from www.hollywoodreporter.com/news/lion-king-is-broadways-first-648455.
33. Mumpower, D. (2015, January 24). *Behind the Ride: 4 Mind-bending Tricks Employed By Disney's Soarin' Over California.* Retrieved from www.themeparktourist.com/features/20150122/29885/behind-ride-4-amazing-details-about-soarin-over-california.
34. Walt Disney World. (2018). *Pools at Disney's Beach Club Resort.* Retrieved from https://disneyworld.disney.go.com/recreation/beach-club-resort/pools-beach-club-resort/.
35. Fickley-Baker, J. (2016, January 26). *All in the Details: Putting the 'Springs' in Disney Springs.* Retrieved from https://disneyparks.disney.go.com/ blog/2016/01/all-in-the-details-putting-the-springs-into-disney-springs/?CMP=SOC-FBPAGE 20160202143000.
36. Hugo, M. (2017, February 10). *Disney to Invest Big Money in Struggling Euro Disney.* Retrieved from www.latimes.com/business/la-fi-euro-disney-20170210-story.html.
37. Krosnick, B. (2015, December 15). *How Disney Turned One of Its Biggest Failures Into a Massive Success in Just Five Years.* Retrieved from https://themeparktourist.com/features/20151212/31106/california-mis-adventure-how-disneylands-second-gate-crashed-burned-and-was?page=5.
38. Themed Entertainment Association. (2016). *Theme Index Museum Index 2016: Global Attractions Attendance Report.* Retrieved from www.teaconnect.org/images/files/TEA_235_103719_170601.pdf.

INDEX

Page numbers in *italic* indicate a figure on the corresponding page